PARTICIPATORY WATERSHED DEVELOPMENT
Challenges for the Twenty-First Century

The growing number of individuals committed to the reduction of rural poverty in India—both within and outside the public sector—have given much to this book. May it, in turn, help to renew and sustain their efforts.

Participatory Watershed Development

Challenges for the Twenty-First Century

Edited by

**John Farrington, Cathryn Turton
and A.J. James**

OXFORD
UNIVERSITY PRESS

OXFORD
UNIVERSITY PRESS

YMCA Library Building, Jai Singh Road, New Delhi 110001

Oxford University Press is a department of the University of Oxford. It furthers the
University's objective of excellence in research, scholarship, and education
by publishing worldwide in

Oxford   New York

Athens   Auckland   Bangkok   Bogota   Buenos Aires   Calcutta
Cape Town   Chennai   Dar es Salaam   Delhi   Florence   Hong Kong   Istanbul
Karachi   Kuala Lumpur   Madrid   Melbourne   Mexico City   Mumbai
Nairobi   Paris   Sao Paolo   Singapore   Taipei   Tokyo   Toronto   Warsaw

with associated companies in Berlin Ibadan

Oxford is a registered trade mark of Oxford University Press
in the UK and in certain other countries

Published in India
By Oxford University Press, New Delhi

ISBN 0 19 565135 9

Camera-ready-copy provided by editors
Technical editing by Paul Mundy, Bergisch Gladbach, Germany
Printed by Saurab Print-O-Pack, NOIDA
Published by Manzar Khan, Oxford University Press
YMCA Library Building, Jai Singh Road, New Delhi 110 001

Contents

Tables

Figures

Boxes

Foreword

More than two-thirds of India's population is dependent on land. It is significant that this percentage has remained unchanged in the last 80 years. The reason is not far to seek. Employment generation in the secondary and tertiary sectors of the economy is not able to absorb even the additional urban labour force, and, therefore, the scope of the rural workforce for finding meaningful employment in the urban sector is severely limited. With increasing capital output ratios, the income-elasticity of employment in the non-agricultural sector keeps on declining, making it more difficult for the cities to absorb the extra labour released from the land.

During the last three decades, three programmes have tried on a large scale to help alleviate rural poverty: land reforms, the Integrated Rural Development Programme (focusing on self-employment in the non-agricultural sector) and wage-employment programmes. These were not generally targeted to improve productivity of marginal lands in rainfed areas, and therefore have not resulted in sustained increases in rural incomes. On the other hand, due to soil erosion and water runoff, the health of two of the most important resources in the rural India—land and water—has been declining fast.

Land degradation and soil erosion, especially of village commons, roadsides, tank foreshores and other such open-access lands, was attributed in the 1970s to the 'tragedy of the commons' phenomenon, where exploitation is by all, but maintenance by none. The government followed a laissez-faire policy towards these lands. No funds were allocated, nor was any specific government department made responsible for their management. One of the first programmes in India for the rehabilitation of common lands was the social forestry programme started in the late 1970s. This brought these lands under the Forest Department's control, in the hope that the trees would later be handed over to the village communities for protection and management. Apart from the fact that local people were not involved during the design and plantation stages (leading to large numbers of trees dying), the programme suffered from several conceptual weaknesses.

The problem of degeneration of village lands was seen as arising from peoples' demands for fuelwood and fodder, resulting in over-exploitation. However, actually the loss of soil from such lands was due more to a lack of control of rainwater runoff. It was not so much a problem of demand as one of land management, especially of common lands. Without controlling runoff, it was not possible to stabilise water regimes even for croplands, and thus it was a mistake in rainfed areas to look at the degradation of common lands in isolation from the other issues of low cropland productivity. It is difficult to rehabilitate degraded lands without introducing moisture-conservation and water-harvesting measures. Such measures are, in fact, needed for all rainfed areas put to biomass production, and not just uncultivated lands.

One of the least understood, but most useful, concepts is the issue of complementarity between uncultivated and cultivated lands, especially in upland agriculture. Traditional agroforestry patterns are a reflection of farmers' own perceptions of the complementarity between trees and crops, but the issue of complementarity between uncultivated and cultivated lands is wider than that between trees and crops. If it is strengthened, the local community develops a stake in the maintenance of common lands and the preservation of forests, which can deter individual attempts at encroachment or degradation. To enrich this complementarity, the objective of land management should be to preserve soil and moisture in a demonstrative fashion. The main thrust of programmes in rainfed areas thus should be on activities relating to soil conservation, land shaping and development, pasture development, and water-resources conservation for the entire watershed—and not merely on afforestation. Soil- and water-conservation measures such as contour trenching, vegetative bunding, and small check-dams can enhance soil moisture and the accumulation of topsoil, accelerating the rehabilitation of the micro-environment. This by itself would help in regeneration and better survival of plants.

Realising the importance of rehabilitating micro-watersheds, from 1990 onwards the Government of India set aside substantial budgetary provisions for a programme called the 'National Watershed Development Programme for Rainfed Areas'. It focused mainly on the delivery of technical inputs through government machinery on agricultural lands, but without linking these with uncultivated lands and without sound peoples' participation. The overwhelming evidence from natural-resource-management projects is that without peoples' involvement, the benefits are not sustainable in the long term. After funds from the government or donors dry up, conservation structures disappear, committees are disbanded or abandoned, and the livelihood base of the people remains only marginally improved, if at all.

Equally important are institutional constraints in watershed-management programmes. Studies of other, similar programmes show that planning, organisation and management have been issues of major concern in all projects. In particular, the impact of watershed treatments has been impaired by poor co-ordination between line agencies, and there has been a marked absence of land-user participation in treatment planning and implementation.

Luckily, these shortcomings were taken care of with the acceptance of new guidelines on watershed development, based on the Hanumantha Rao Committee findings, which took effect on 1 April 1995. Several government programmes, such as the Drought Prone Area Programme, the Desert Development Programme, and the Integrated Wastelands Developments Project, now provide for the development of an entire compact micro-watershed, rather than pieces of wastelands or croplands scattered in different places. Their basic objective is integrated land development based on village or micro-watershed plans. These plans are prepared after taking into consideration the land capability, site condition and local needs of the people. The scheme also aims at rural employment besides enhancing the contents of people's participation in the land-development programmes at all stages, which is ensured by providing modalities for equitable and sustainable sharing of benefits and usufructs arising from such projects. In April 1999, the Government of India created a new Department of Land Resources. This has the mandate of enabling rural people to prevent, arrest and reverse degradation of life-support systems, particularly land and water, so as to produce biomass in a sustainable and equitable manner.

Participatory policies are highly relevant to India and are consistent with the India's overall development strategy of reducing poverty, protecting the environment, developing human resources, and fostering farm-sector growth. However, a period of only a few years is not sufficient to judge whether the stated physical, financial, institutional or policy-related goals have been met, or are likely to be met. Their successful implementation should draw strength from documentation and knowledge about grassroots experience. The experience so far shows that unless the process through which participation is to be secured is described in detail and monitored, it is likely to be ignored—both because of a lack of commitment among government staff, and a lack of knowledge about the road map to the destination.

The present book is a result of a long and abiding interest of its editors and authors in watershed-development programmes in India. It will help both practitioners and policy-makers in understanding the circumstances under which the programme does well, and what needs to be done in order to scale up the participatory and equitable approaches to watershed development to cover a larger number of villages. Experience from a diverse range of ecological and social contexts has been considered in the book, with a view to synthesising such experiments and identifying the key factors that must be evaluated in order to explain, predict or improve the sustainability of watershed-development projects. One of the first source books on this subject, it is going to be of immense value to state governments, field workers, policy-makers, donors and researchers. It offers a new vision that emphasises equitable access to natural resources, and shows us the way to achieve higher productivity and ecological sustainability in rainfed areas.

I wish the book a great success.

New Delhi   N. C. Saxena
12 July, 1999   Planning Commission
                                                    Government of India

Preface

This book marks the culmination of three years of work by staff of the London-based Overseas Development Institute, and colleagues from many other organisations in India and elsewhere, on participatory approaches to micro-watershed rehabilitation. The arguments for micro-watershed rehabilitation as a means of strengthening rural people's livelihoods through integrated, productive and sustainable use of natural resources are compelling. Equally compelling is the evidence from many small-scale projects, often run by NGOs, that a rehabilitated watershed will quickly degrade again unless local institutions capable of managing the resource are strengthened. Of particular importance is the evidence that the interests of the poorer sectors—often in common forest or grazing lands—will be overridden unless their voice in these institutions is strengthened.

Small-scale projects have demonstrated how, with much patience and skill, watershed development can be made both ecologically and institutionally sustainable, and the weaker sections can be empowered to exert their voice. However, until recently, much investment by the public sector in watershed development was concerned more with physical works than with longer-term sustainability. Can public-sector approaches be modified to incorporate some of the best practices, in respect of participation and institution-building, of small-scale NGO projects? What kinds of organisational and institutional changes are needed if this is to happen? What prospects for more participatory approaches do the government's own guidelines hold? What should be the respective roles of state and central government, of administrative and local-level political bodies? These are some of the questions that this book attempts to address. In some cases, the answers are clear; in others, we are still at the stage of identifying the right questions to ask.

This book draws primarily on the papers and discussions at the National Workshop on Watershed Approaches for Wastelands Development: Challenges for the 21st Century, held in Vigyan Bhawan, New Delhi, from 28 to 30 April 1998. The editors are indebted to the then

Secretary for Rural Development, Dr N. C. Saxena, and to officers of the Department of Wastelands Development for their personal and practical support in designing and implementing the workshop, and in producing a summary version of the proceedings. Further support for the workshop was provided by the UK Department for International Development, the Swiss Agency for Development and Cooperation, the Danish International Development Agency, and the Swedish International Development Cooperation Agency. Much of the background work on the theme of participatory approaches to watershed development was funded by a grant to ODI from the Department for International Development. The editors are indebted to all of the above, but must stress that the views and interpretations presented here are theirs alone and should not be taken to represent the positions of any of the above organisations.

London and Delhi, 1999   John Farrington
                                                         Cathryn Turton
                                                         A. J. James

1 Introduction

UNDERLYING CONCERNS: WATERSHEDS, LIVELIHOODS AND PARTICIPATION

This book is concerned with watershed management and rehabilitation as a means of rural development. In common usage, a watershed is understood to be a catchment area feeding an identifiable drainage system, such as a stream or river. Watersheds contain a number of biophysical resources: soil and water, along with vegetation in the form of trees, grasses and crops, and provide the sustenance for a number of further enterprises such as livestock production.

In India, watershed rehabilitation was not originally conceived as a vehicle for rural development. The original concept of watershed management or rehabilitation focused on the management of these resources in medium or large river valleys, in ways that would prevent rapid runoff of water (and concomitant soil erosion), and so would slow down the rates of siltation of reservoirs and limit the incidence of potentially damaging flash flooding in river courses (Paul 1997).

Managing watersheds for rural development in developing countries is a relatively new concept. In many ways it is also much more complex than the original concept. It is concerned not merely with stabilising soil, water and vegetation, but with enhancing the productivity of resources in ways that are ecologically and institutionally sustainable.

This has three immediate implications. First, the concern is not only with the individual resources, but with the interactions among them, especially those that have positive or negative implications for gains in productivity, and for the sustainability of those gains. A simple example is the increased livestock production made possible by the rising supply of fodder as grassland, shrubs and trees are rehabilitated.

Second, in some developing countries, including India, much of the land within watersheds is not under private control. Some may be under the State Department of Forests, some may be under the Revenue

Department, and some under communal, village-based ownership arrangements. Inevitably, some of this land—especially forest land—is on the upper slopes, so if it is excluded from treatment, substantial penalties in terms of reduced soil and water control may be incurred.

Approaches to watershed rehabilitation must therefore deal resource-control or ownership modes other than pure private ownership. In India, this may mean dealing with government departments in order to ensure that their resource-management strategies are compatible with watershed approaches. With both government- and village-controlled common resources, institutionally sustainable rehabilitation and management are possible only where rural people act jointly to manage the resource. They can do this either spontaneously or with outside support.

Third, in watersheds where some resources are not privately owned, the question arises of how best to manage interactions between common-pool resources[1] and those which are privately owned. For instance, constructing bunds, terraces or check-dams on the upper slopes (at times, on non-private land) can, under many geological conditions, recharge groundwater and increase the reliability or productivity of crops grown almost universally on private land. Another example is where privately owned livestock get some of their fodder from common-pool resources.

These three themes—management of the interface between different kinds of resource; management of resources which are not privately owned, and management of the interface between private and non-private—are central issues in watershed management for rural development, and are recurrent themes in the chapters that follow.

But there is a further theme: the poor—often landless and women—rely disproportionately on common-pool resources for fodder, fuel and other forest products. Watershed rehabilitation is essentially a resource-based approach to livelihood enhancement. Unless adequate safeguards

---

[1] 'Common-pool resources' are those which are not privately owned. By contrast, 'common property' refers to arrangements for managing such resources. Where they are not managed under some such arrangement, they are generally 'open access'. Arnold (1997) describes these arrangements much more fully in relation to India. Hardin's (1968) 'tragedy of the commons' is based on open-access arrangements, but has been widely misapplied to common property. Ostrom (1990) and Wade (1988) describe a number of common-property arrangements, and Hobley and Shah (1996) draw together the conditions for successful joint action. A more sophisticated definition would elaborate on the relationship between ownership and management arrangements. For instance, after harvest in some areas, farmers allow herders to graze stubble under open access or managed arrangements in return for the manure obtained.

can be built in, the danger is that, as the commons become more productive, better-off farmers are tempted to take over control of them, and the customary access rights of the poor are denied.

In India, national policy on watershed development has recently been characterised by a concern that decisions on rehabilitation and subsequent rights and responsibilities should be taken in ways which support the livelihood of poorer groups (and especially of poorer women), and are institutionally sustainable. The publication in 1994 of the Guidelines on Watershed Development ('Common Guidelines') by the Ministry of Rural Areas and Employment (Annex 1, GoI 1994) marked a significant step towards approaches that are participatory and involve a high degree of decentralised decision taking and allocation of funding.

Many of the ideas contained in the Guidelines were drawn from the earlier experience of non-government organisations (NGOs) in watershed development. During the last decade, the role of NGOs in India has intensified. In the Eighth Five-Year Plan, the Indian government explicitly stated that attempts would be made to involve NGOs as collaboration partners in various development programmes.

The NGO sector is, however, characterised by great disparity in terms of size, professional qualifications, geographical and sectoral areas of work, and by diversity in approaches, scales of financial support, networks and linkages. At the upper end of the scale there are NGOs such as the National Centre for Human Settlements and Environment, the Bharatiya Agro-Industries Foundation (BAIF), the Aga Khan Rural Support Programme, the Mysore Relief and Development Agency (MYRADA), and several others. These are involved in the rehabilitation of several watersheds; they generally have little difficulty in obtaining funds, and have a number of professionals on their staff. Their experience and connections with people in state and national governments facilitate excellent working relationships at different levels.

At the opposite end of the scale are many hundreds of opportunistic, 'fly-by-night' operations. In Bolangir district of Orissa, for instance, over 60 new NGOs registered themselves within a few months of hearing that the UK Department for International Development (DFID) might be starting a new watershed project there.

Participatory management has been defined as a process whereby 'those with legitimate interests in a project both influence decisions which affect them and receive a proportion of any benefits which may accrue' (ODA 1996). It is now widely accepted that to enhance and sustain the productivity of natural resources, those engaged in and affected by managing the resource—at the most basic level, its users—must participate in planning its rehabilitation and management. Their participation will generate a stake in the process and enhance the prospects of both institutional and ecological sustainability.

A participatory approach therefore implies a major, but not exclusive, role for local populations in allocating rights and responsibilities over resources. It may involve partnerships with other interest groups at micro and macro levels, such as district line-agencies, local political bodies, ministries of finance, and policy-makers. A key concern for micro-watershed development is to identify approaches which ensure that the interface between rural people, local organisations and the state is managed in a way which is most likely to enhance efficiency, effectiveness and accountability (Carney and Farrington 1998).

The substance of participation is however often ill defined, and clarification is needed regarding who is participating, how, and in what. Despite the 'feel-good' factor associated with participation, it must be recognised that it is not a neutral concept, and involves a set of political issues concerning who has decision-making power and who has access to resources. Pimbert and Pretty (1997) provide a useful summary of the main forms of participation (Table 1.1).

NGO approaches have traditionally focused at the mobilisation end of the spectrum, concentrating on strengthening rural people's capacity to articulate their requirements, form groups, plan for and undertake joint action, and so on. However, a route which insists on long-term, face-to-face, empowering approaches in individual villages may achieve institutional sustainability at the cost of very slow spread (Farrington and Boyd 1997). This approach contrasts with that of some government departments and donors, in which large amounts of funding are provided and area-wide adoption is an explicit programme objective. Participation has been limited to the provision of labour at worst, and information-giving or consultation at best. Consequently such projects have performed poorly with respect to long-term sustainability (Jain 1995).

The fundamental question addressed by this book is: can participatory, equitable approaches to watershed development be scaled up to cover larger numbers of villages, or are they by nature resource-intensive, and therefore only possible on a small scale?

Table 1.1   A Typology of Participation

Typology	*Components of each type*
Passive participation	People participate by being told what is going to happen or has already happened.
Participation in information giving	People participate by giving answers to questions posed by extractive researchers and project managers.
Participation by consultation	People participate by being consulted and external agencies listen to their views. External agencies define both problems and solutions.
Participation for material resources	People participate by providing resources, for example labour in return for cash or food.
Functional participation	People participate by forming groups to meet predetermined objectives relating to the project, which can involve the development or promotion of externally initiated social organisation.
Interactive participation	People participate in joint analysis, which leads to joint action-plans and formation of new groups or strengthening of old ones.
Self-mobilisation	People participate by taking initiatives independent of external change systems.

Source: adapted from Pimbert and Pretty (1997)

WATERSHEDS IN INDIA

Approximately 170 million hectares in India are classified as degraded land, roughly half of which falls in undulating semi-arid areas where rainfed farming is practised. Long-term experiments by a number of research organisations in India in the 1970s and 1980s confirmed that the introduction of appropriate physical barriers to soil and water flows, together with revegetation, could generate considerable increases in resource productivity. These, in turn, stimulated the formulation of a number of government projects, schemes and programmes in support of micro-watershed development.

In India, micro-watersheds are generally defined as falling in the range 500–1000ha. A mini-watershed comprises a number of micro-watersheds and covers around 5000ha. A macro-watershed is equivalent to a river basin and may encompass many thousands of hectares. The micro-watershed concept aims to 'establish an enabling environment for the integrated use, regulation and treatment of water and land resources of a watershed-based ecosystem to accomplish resource conservation and biomass production objectives' (Jensen et al. 1996).

Although a micro-watershed may be a sensible planning unit from a biophysical perspective, many would argue against the appropriateness of such a unit for rural development. Social institutions to promote cooperation—needed to protect and rehabilitate private and common-pool resources—are usually village-based. Often, however, biophysical and socio-political boundaries do not coincide. The majority of projects do not, therefore, strictly entail the development of 'a watershed'; rather they adopt an approach to rural development incorporating principles from the watershed approach.

Estimates of biophysical gains from these early experiments are presented in Chapter 2. The substantial gains reported appear largely attributable to the special attention given by scientists and extension workers to these 'model' sites. Such large gains have rarely been achieved on a wider scale. Shah (1998), drawing on three case studies (all benefiting from special management or funding conditions) doubts the efficacy of watershed-based approaches unless topography and climate are appropriate. Kerr et al. (1998, see Extract 1.1), reporting on a major survey of projects completed under a range of schemes and programmes in the 1980s and early 1990s, came to the conclusion that the benefits of watershed development have been negligible, except in a few cases in which participatory approaches have been pursued effectively. Chopra (1998, Extract 2.2) and Landell-Mills (1998, Extract 2.3) are concerned both with the economic returns attributable to watershed development and with the methodology of assessing returns.

A broad conclusion is that it is not difficult to generate positive returns under 'special projects' of various kinds, but there are two caveats:

• the sustainability of these special projects is neither guaranteed nor cost-free;
• there are major questions as to whether the necessary minimum set of conditions underpinning these gains can be replicated at acceptable cost on the much wider scale that is currently being pursued by government.

PUBLIC SECTOR INVESTMENT IN WATERSHED DEVELOPMENT IN INDIA

Over the last decade, the Government of India has set aside substantial budgetary provisions for micro-watershed rehabilitation and development. This initiative underpins a shift in agricultural policy, which acknowledges the neglect of rainfed and common areas during the period of the 'green revolution', and accepts a link between the degradation of rainfed areas and the poverty of large numbers of people. There has been strong growth in both governmental and non-governmental institutional capacity to implement wasteland- and watershed-development projects. Predominantly this capacity has been directed at micro-watersheds (500–1000 ha).

The number and scope of watershed development programmes continue to increase. Through a range of schemes and programmes the government is investing over US$ 500 million per year into the rehabilitation of micro-watersheds. Within semi-arid areas, one may often find co-existing (but rarely interacting) programmes under the auspices of several different agencies, including the Ministry of Agriculture and Cooperation, Ministry of Rural Areas and Employment, and the Ministry of Environment and Forests, as well as various bilateral and multilateral donors.

Under the first of these, the National Watershed Development Programme for Rainfed Areas was formulated in 1990. This programme has a budget of Rs 133,800 million under the Eighth Five-Year Plan, and by 1994, had covered 2,554 micro-watersheds. The Ministry of Rural Areas and Employment administers the Drought Prone Areas Programme, the Desert Development Programme, the Integrated Watershed Development Programme, and the Employment Assurance Scheme, a part of which is allocated to watershed development.

After 20 years of efforts in poverty alleviation and drought mitigation, the government constituted several committees, culminating in a technical committee headed by Dr C. Hanumantha Rao in 1993, to make specific recommendations on the implementation of the Drought Prone Areas and the Desert Development programmes with a watershed approach. The committee submitted its recommendations is 1994. Based on these recommendations, a new set of Guidelines for Watershed Development (GoI 1994) were formulated by the Ministry of Rural Areas and Employment. These came into effect on 1 April 1995, and now apply to all the ministry's watershed projects. Now generally known as the 'Common Guidelines', they mark the beginning of a new era in public-sector rural development programmes. They envisage a 'bottom-up planning' approach, working where possible though NGOs, and with community participation as a central principle. The guidelines set up a cost norm of Rs 4000[2] per hectare for each watershed of about 500 hectares. The main provisions of these Common Guidelines are summarised in Annex 1.

The Guidelines envisage new arrangements for channelling funds and managing projects (Figure 1.1). The District Rural Development Agency (DRDA) or *zilla parishad* (district-level local government) have overall responsibility for programme implementation in the district. They appoint a 'watershed development advisory committee' to advise on issues such as the selection of villages, training and monitoring. Project implementation agencies are selected by the DRDA or *zilla parishad*; they are responsible for appointing a 'watershed development team' of four members representing disciplines such as agriculture, engineering, life sciences and social work.

The watershed development team works with the communities in planning and implementing the watershed programme. Each team is expected to handle 10 micro-watersheds. The 'watershed association' represents all members of the community who are directly or indirectly dependent on the watershed area. The association appoints a 'watershed committee' consisting of representatives of user groups, self-help groups, the *gram panchayat* (elected village assembly) and the watershed development team. Each committee has a paid secretary who maintains the records and accounts.

Each of the schemes, projects and programmes listed above has a somewhat different focus. The National Watershed Development Programme for Rainfed Areas focuses mainly on the rehabilitation of agricultural land; the Integrated Watershed Development Programme on wastelands; the Employment Assurance Scheme on employment-creation opportunities; and the focus of Drought Prone Areas and the Desert Development programmes is determined by agroclimatic conditions. The National Watershed Development Programme has its own guidelines for project implementation, as do NGO projects.

[2] Rs 40=approximately US$ 1.00

Figure 1.1 Administrative Hierarchy for Projects under the New Guidelines

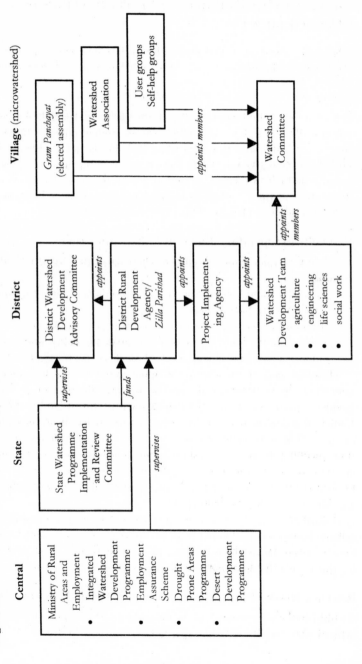

DIFFICULTIES IN PARTICIPATORY WATERSHED MANAGEMENT

Experience suggests several difficulties in designing and implementing participatory approaches to watershed rehabilitation and management.

Technology

It is clear that technologies are limited for successful watershed rehabilitation in the drier areas (i.e., under 400mm annual rainfall). Indeed, it may be over-ambitious to expect watershed approaches to enhance livelihoods to any marked degree in these areas, especially where population pressure is high in relation to the quality of the natural resources. In many areas adaptive research is required to tailor available technologies to local conditions (Turton et al. 1998).

Difficulty in Operating 'Ridge-to-Valley' Approaches

Lands in the upper slopes should be rehabilitated first for at least three reasons:

*   the landless and low-income farmers who depend most on the upper slopes can benefit first;
*   groundwater recharge commences as early as possible; and
*   by the time the lower catchment is treated, any debris and erosion running down from the upper catchment has been minimised.

However, part of the land in the upper slopes is typically under the control of the Department of Forests, and the only mechanism for introducing participation into the management of forest land is through Joint Forest Management (JFM) arrangements. It has been difficult to establish JFM some states where the forestry-service traditions of centrally planning the resource and protecting it against illicit use by villagers remain paramount. The strengths and weaknesses of current approaches to JFM are reviewed by Agarwal and Saigal (1996), Poffenberger and McGean (1996) and Raju (1997).

A further difficulty is that one government project, programme or scheme is generally prohibited from operating in the same watersheds as others. Given the size limit imposed by some guidelines of around 500 ha, this means that large parts of some watersheds go untreated.

Resource Needs of Deeply Empowering Participatory Approaches

As indicated above, most NGOs are committed to types of empowerment that may broadly be regarded as Freirian (Freire 1972), and comprise a sequence of diagnosis by a group or community of the problems it faces, the design and implementation of a response, (as far as possible from its own resources), and the articulation of demands on government or other service providers for those requirements which cannot be met from own resources. A number of cases have been reported in which NGOs have succeeded in establishing groups based on a village (or on part—usually the disadvantaged part—of its population) in order to rehabilitate and manage watersheds on these principles (Mascarenhas 1998, Fernandez 1993, Farrington and Lobo 1997, Hazare et al. 1996). However, with the exception of the Indo-German Watershed Development Programme (Farrington and Lobo 1997) the expansion pathway for these has been slow, relying on replication of the same approach in subsequent areas.

Difficulties in Achieving Even Modest Levels of Participation

Government projects, schemes and programmes generally aim to achieve a moderate 'functional' degree of participation (Farrington 1998), and yet have been characterised by a number of difficulties. For instance, projects under the National Watershed Development Programme for Rainfed Areas are designed largely on the basis of technical norms, with very little participation by local people. The 1994 Common Guidelines have done much to commit the public sector to a strategy of decentralised and participatory design and implementation of watershed development.

A recent review (Turton et al. 1998, Annex 2), however, suggests the public sector faces several challenges: pressure to spend substantial resources by a fixed deadline, the limited time permitted for preparatory (especially group-formation) activities, unclear criteria for selecting areas and villages to be rehabilitated, and limited human-resource capabilities to respond to novel and challenging requirements. A study of the performance of local government in Mahbubnagar District of Andhra Pradesh by Krishna (1997) drew attention to how numerous pressures—not least the pressure to spend allotted monies—were causing officials to shortcut participatory processes. The same study also noted that many Project Implementing Agencies constituted by government staff were, in fact, operating part-time, and had little prospect of meeting the standards of participation and consultation set out in the 1994 Guidelines.

TAKING STOCK: CHALLENGES FOR IMPLEMENTING PARTICIPATORY APPROACHES

Turton et al. (1998) argued that successful projects are, so far, few in number and have operated under special conditions which cannot easily be replicated. If success is to be sustained, and is to spread quickly to new areas, new partnerships will be needed between central and state governments, district administration, *Panchayati Raj* institutions, NGOs, line agencies and communities themselves. This implies a move away from 'enclave' projects by donors, and a stronger capacity and motivation towards learning, partnerships and flexibility by government.

The limited speed at which highly empowering NGO approaches can be implemented, and the shortcomings of public-sector efforts to institute participatory approaches, make it opportune to consider what challenges the next decade holds, and how the public sector, NGOs and international funding agencies might respond to them.

This book is shaped by forward perspectives of this type. The remaining chapters address the following themes:

Chapter 2   There has been substantial public support for watershed development over the last decade. What evidence was this support based on? Did this evidence come from atypical projects? Did it suffer methodological weaknesses?

Chapter 3   How can an appropriate balance between the interests of stakeholders at a local level be achieved? In particular, how can the interests of the poor be represented?

Chapter 4   Do poor women have particular requirements in the context of watershed development? What can be done to meet them?

Chapter 5   How can the roles of different organisations (NGO, government, community-based) be defined at the local level, both singly and in collaboration? Can a practical framework for collaboration be devised?

Chapter 6   How can administrative decentralisation (notably, in relation to watershed development) best interface with the vision and practice of political decentralisation through the *Panchayati Raj* local government reforms?

Chapter 7   How can the capacity of individuals and organisations at all levels be raised so as to enhance the quality of implementation of the types of participatory approach enshrined in the Common Guidelines?

Chapter 8   How can structures and procedures be established to ensure the organisational and institutional sustainability of rehabilitated watersheds?

The arguments in each chapter are illuminated by extracts from papers presented at the National Workshop on Watershed Approaches to Wastelands Development in India, organised by ODI and the Ministry of Rural Areas and Employment (Department of Wastelands Development)[3] and held in Delhi on 27–29 April 1998.[4] Details of the papers from which the extracts are drawn are provided at the foot of the first page of each.

EXTRACT 1.1
THE IMPACT OF WATERSHED DEVELOPMENT: RESULTS FROM A MAJOR FIELD SURVEY[5]

JOHN KERR,[6] GANESH PANGARE,[7] VASUDHA LOKUR-PANGARE,[7] P.J. GEORGE AND SHASHI KOLAVALLI[8]

This study is an attempt to evaluate India's experience with watershed projects to date. It seeks to answer the following questions:

- What has been the role of watershed projects in achieving the objectives of improving natural resource management, agricultural development and livelihoods of different groups of rural people?
- What approaches to watershed development have worked best to achieve these objectives?
- What other factors besides watershed projects help determine the achievement of these objectives?

Assessing the performance of watershed projects requires examining the determinants of agricultural and rural development from a broader perspective. Regardless of the efforts of any given development project, conditions in rural areas are determined by a variety of other factors, such as infrastructure, access to markets, social institutions in the villages, and agro-ecological conditions. Because watershed projects do not

[3] Support for the workshop was provided by the UK Department for International Development (DFID), the Swedish International Development Agency (SIDA), the Swiss Agency for Development and Cooperation (SDC), and the Danish International Development Agency (Danida).

[4] The full proceedings are available from the authors at ODI on CD-ROM only. A reduced version of the proceedings has been published by DoWD (1998).

[5] This Extract draws on Kerr et al. (1998).

[6] International Food Policy Research Institute, Washington DC, USA.

[7] Oikos, Flat 4 Saikrupa, 34/4 Prabhat Road, Pune 4, India.

[8] PO Box 429A, Basavanagudi, Bangalore 560004, India.

operate in isolation from other forces, analysing their performance without considering a wider set of influences would give misleading results.

Accordingly, this study takes a broad look at the determinants of changes in agriculture production, natural resource management and human welfare in rural areas. While the study is organised around watershed projects, it covers a variety of issues at the village, plot and household levels. The study is based on primary data from a field survey of two states, Andhra Pradesh and Maharashtra.

Limitations of the Study

An important limitation of this study—and one that would plague any similar study of watershed management projects in India—is the lack of baseline data from the study sites. A thorough analysis requires examining the pre-and post-project conditions in a watershed or village, but baseline and monitoring data are rarely available for any watershed project. Even in the exceptional cases where background information is available, it is not useful for comparison with other projects that lack such data. As a result, this study is limited to (a) some secondary data available for both the pre-project period and the present, primary data of current conditions based on interviews and visual assessments, and (b) primary data of past conditions based on the recall of local inhabitants. Inevitably there are weaknesses in the data that limit the study's analytical power.

This research was originally designed to examine only completed projects. However, despite the large literature on watershed development in India, the number of projects where work has actually been completed is quite small, so the intended approach was not feasible. Instead, the study covers mainly projects that are well established, with a few that have been completed.

This report represents an initial effort to examine some of the patterns found in the performance of watershed management projects in the study area. As a first step, it presents descriptive statistics in order to profile the project areas and demonstrate variations in performance associated with differences in watershed-project categories and other conditions such as agroclimatic and socio-economic factors. In several cases it is difficult to determine whether variation in performance results from differences in watershed projects or is because of other factors. In these cases, the study shows where subsequent analysis should be focused.[9]

[9] In the event, subsequent detailed statistical analysis largely confirmed the preliminary findings presented here. See Kerr et al. (1998).

Projects Covered

The projects covered under the study include all the kinds of well-established projects operating in Andhra Pradesh and Maharashtra. They include the following:

* Projects under the Ministry of Agriculture focusing primarily on technical aspects of developing rainfed agriculture (National Watershed Development Programme for Rainfed Areas (NWDPRA), World Bank, Indian Council of Agriculture Research (ICAR)).
* Engineering-oriented projects that focus on water harvesting through construction of percolation tanks, contour bunds and other structures. These fall under the Maharashtra Department of Soil and Water Conservation (Jal Sandharan) and the Ministry of Rural Development's Drought Prone Areas Programme (DPAP).
* Non-government organisations, which typically place greater emphasis on social organisation relative to the government programmes.
* Collaborative projects between government and non-government organisations (Indo-German Watershed Development Project (IGWDP), Adarsh Gaon Yojana (AGY)), which seek to combine the technical approach of government projects with the NGOs' orientation toward social organisation. These projects are found only in Maharashtra.
* Control villages with no projects.

Framework for Analysis and Performance Indicators

The study examined the performance of various indicators of agriculture productivity, natural resource management, and human welfare. Indicators were collected at the level of the village, the plot and the household. The village-level analysis was based on 70 villages in Maharashtra, while the plot and household analyses were based on about 350 plots and households from 29 villages in both Andhra Pradesh and Maharashtra. Where possible, performance indicators were collected for 1987, before the projects began, and 1997, where all the projects were either well established or completed. However, in some cases data were not available for the pre-project period.

Performance indicators Performance indicators for evaluating watershed projects reflect the diversity of objectives of different projects. These include, among others:

* higher rainfed-agricultural productivity;
* recharged groundwater for drinking and irrigation;
* higher productivity of non-arable lands;

- reduced soil erosion;
- benefits skewed toward poorer members of society;
- employment creation (directly and indirectly); and
- promotion of collective action.

Determinants of performance   Variables that help explain agricultural productivity, natural resource conditions and human welfare include
agroclimatic and socio-economic conditions at multiple levels, such as
the plot, the household, the village and the region. Most of these variables are obtained through household- and village-level surveys, while
some are based on secondary data.

Approach to analysis   Thorough analysis of the contribution of all the
different determinants of performance requires a multivariate regres-
sion analysis. This approach is complicated by the presence of selection
bias due to differences in the way that each project selects villages to be
covered by their work. In short, if each project category has different
criteria for selecting villages, then it is possible that differences in performance can result more from differences in initial, pre-project conditions than from the work undertaken by the watershed project. Statistical methods for controlling for selection bias are well-established for
analysis of only two categories (such as a single treatment and a control), but the current study covers six project categories, and this makes
the problem much more complex. The statistical approach is still being
developed, so this paper presents preliminary findings based on bivariate
analysis.

Findings of the Village-level Analysis

The village-level analysis revealed very little in the way of favourable
project performance. The results for each village-level performance indicator can be summarised as follows. It is important to note that unless
otherwise mentioned, the differences across project categories are not
statistically significant.

Drinking Water   All projects that promote water harvesting through
small tanks and dams directly or indirectly try to increase the level
of water in wells for drinking water. In Maharashtra, this includes
every project except the NWDPRA. Excluding villages with additional drinking water schemes, the AGY/IGWDP projects had the
largest increase in the percentage of villages with adequate drinking
water and, surprisingly, the NWDPRA had the second-highest increase. Control villages had higher improvements than either NGO
or Jal Sandharan villages.

Increase in village-level percent irrigated area   Since changes in irrigated area depend on numerous factors, many of which could not be measured in the current study, the findings here must be treated cautiously. With this in mind, control villages had by far the largest percent increase in irrigated area, followed by AGY and IGWDP villages. Villages from other categories only had very small increases. A possible explanation for the large increase by the control villages is that they began the study period with low percent-irrigated area, but favourable agroclimatic and infrastructure conditions could have helped stimulate investment. AGY and IGWDP villages also benefited from infrastructure improvements, including widespread introduction of agricultural electricity.

Changes in wages and employment   Changes in male and female daily wages over the study period showed virtually no difference across project categories. This is not surprising, since wages are likely to equalise across villages as workers move among neighbouring villages as employment opportunities change. However, a household-level survey of a subset of the study villages indicated that employment availability had the highest growth in AGY and IGWDP villages.

Changes in seasonal migration   Changes in migration can indicate changes in employment opportunities, agricultural productivity and overall quality of life. With the exception of the AGY and IGWDP villages, seasonal migration rose in every project category. The AGY and IGWDP villages had a net reduction in migration overall; improvements in infrastructure and access to services may help to explain this finding. However, the average figures mask the fact that more AGY and IGWDP villages experienced net out-migration than net in-migration.

Erosion and conservation on cultivated lands   Irrigated plots are almost uniformly well maintained, while rainfed plots have more problems. Rainfed plots under the NWDPRA scored better than those of other categories in terms of both erosion and conservation. Control villages performed slightly worse than other categories in terms of erosion but in the middle of the group in terms of conservation.

Erosion and conservation on uncultivated lands   The findings for uncultivated lands are almost opposite those of cultivated lands. Both in terms of erosion and conservation, uncultivated lands under the NWDPRA scored worse than all other categories, while plots in control villages performed the best. This finding is disappointing, given that all projects in Maharashtra focus on uncultivated lands and that the average duration of watershed activity in all project villages was 13 years. Given that the bivariate analysis by project type was not sufficient to show significant relationships, further multivariate analysis is needed to test the relationship between project category and village-performance indicators. More specifically, multivariate techniques will control the analysis for covariates that are also expected to affect project performance.

Condition of drainage lines   All watershed projects in Maharashtra also focus on treating the drainage line, and here they performed better than on uncultivated lands. AGY and IGWDP villages performed much better than others, while control villages performed the worst. The condition of the drainage lines improved with the duration of project activities and the percentage of the village covered. Differences associated with these factors—project category, duration and percent of area covered—were all statistically significant.

Changes in availability of products from common revenue lands   Grass fodder, tree fodder and fuel were the only products from common lands found in enough villages to warrant analysis. On average, the availability of these products declined in villages under all project categories. For grass fodder, performance was best in NGO villages, followed closely by AGY and IGWDP villages; the worst performance was in NWDPRA and control villages. For tree fodder, the findings were almost the opposite, with the NWDPRA and Jal Sandharan performing the best, and the NGOs and AGY and IGWDP performing the worst. For fuel, the situation was somewhere in between, with NGOs and NWDPRA performing slightly better than the others. It is important to stress that even for the best performers, no project category reported an overall net increase in availability of any of these products from the commons.

Changes in population of wild animals and migratory birds   Wild animals will concentrate in the village if the forest cover is increasing, and migratory birds will stop in the village if there are water bodies, such as percolation tanks, in the winter (dry) season. So the change in presence of birds and wild animals provides an indication of the success of the village's afforestation and water-harvesting efforts. Very little difference was reported across project categories in the change in wild animal populations during the study period. The AGY and IGWDP villages were the only ones to report a slight net increase, while the Jal Sandharan and NWDPRA villages reported a slight net decrease. For migratory birds, NGO villages reported a noticeable net increase, control villages reported no change on average, and the remaining categories reported declines.

Discussion of the village-level findings   It is difficult to state that the lack of significant relationship between the performance variables and the project categories reflects poor project performance. There are two reasons for this. First, the lack of significance more likely suggests that the relationship between project-type and performance is mediated by several different factors. Although the performance indicators that were developed for this analysis are sound in principle, it is likely that factors other than project category would also affect the outcomes. Thus, grouping the villages broadly by project type most likely provided only part of the explanation for the outcome variables of interest.

Another reason for the lack of significant relationships may be the unit of analysis chosen. The village was selected as the unit of analysis, since most projects aim to develop villages and micro-watersheds within villages. However, a project may affect areas within a village differently. In addition, no projects actually treat every hectare in a village. Hence, a project village will contain significant areas that have not received any project treatment. The village may thus have been too large and too heterogeneous as a unit of analysis to reveal significant changes with only bivariate analysis. The plot-level analysis, which differentiates between plots that were treated under a project and plots that were not, may be more effective in overcoming these problems.

Findings of the Plot-level Analysis

The analysis at the plot level shows more interesting results than that at the village level. This is not surprising, since the plot has the advantage of being a more homogeneous unit than the village.

For indicators that were defined in terms of the difference between the pre-and post-project period—change in irrigation intensity, change in the use of improved varieties, and change in yields—the plots in villages under the AGY and IGWDP performed better than all other project categories, including the control. For soil- and water-conservation investments on rainfed plots, these projects had the second-highest levels (after plots under NGO projects), but they received by far the highest investments financed by the farmers' own savings. Rainfed plots under the AGY and IGWDP also had the second-highest net returns to cultivation per hectare (after plots under NGOs). At face value, this consistently strong performance in the AGY and IGWDP project category suggests that these projects have quite an impact. However, villagers covered by these projects also had the greatest reason to believe that investing their own savings could also have contributed to the better performance. This is especially so since the IGWDP and AGY projects' primary focus was on water harvesting and pasture protection, not rainfed agriculture *per se*. Multivariate analysis is required to sort out these differences before strong conclusions can be drawn regarding the success of these projects in generating improvements in rainfed agriculture.

Those projects that did focus on rainfed agriculture, particularly the World Bank, ICAR and NWDPRA, did not appear to perform very well in encouraging adoption of improved varieties and raising yields, although they did slightly better than the control villages. One important comment to make regarding the World Bank and ICAR projects is that they were the only ones covered by the study in which the work had been completed and the staff had withdrawn. This means that the effects of their work had a much longer time to erode, thus it is not fair to compare them to the effects or projects that are still ongoing. The same is not true for the NWDPRA, however.

One area where all the Andhra Pradesh projects appear to have had an impact is in promoting cultivation across the slope. On the other hand, no farmers in the sample practised strict contour cultivation, which the NWDPRA, World Bank and ICAR projects all promote. Nevertheless, cultivation across the slope is nearly as effective as following the contour closely when cultivating, and it represents a superior, easily adoptable alternative to cultivation up and down the slope. Farmers who interacted with project staff were more likely to cultivate across the slope than those who did not, and all farmers in project villages were much more likely to cultivate across the slope than farmers in control villages. This suggests that information regarding cultivation across the slope has spread from farmer to farmer, and this is not surprising since it does not cost anything. Of course, the fact that it is costless also suggests that it could probably be promoted even without expensive watershed development projects.

Investment in land improvement on sloping rainfed lands is another area where projects appear to have made an impact. Farmers used their own investment funds on flat lands, but they appear to have neglected their sloping lands. Watershed projects, on the other hand, concentrated their investment funds on sloping lands, thus apparently playing a useful, complementary role. One problem is that maintenance levels of these land-improvement investments tend to fall as the portion of the investment cost paid for by the project increases. It appears from the maintenance levels of investments under NGO projects (some of which require a farmer's contribution) that higher maintenance levels could be achieved if all projects made a more serious commitment to requiring farmers to contribute substantially to the cost of investments on their own land.

Convincing farmers to contribute to the costs of investments financed by watershed projects would require at least two important steps. First, farmers will only be willing to contribute if they make the decision about what kinds of measures are introduced on their plots. Currently the NGO and collaborative NGO–government projects take this approach, but the government projects do not give farmers the same choice (despite language in their project guidelines saying that they are open to it). The second step is that a cost-sharing approach would probably require making credit more easily available; otherwise many farmers will be unable to pay their share. Banks do not offer loans for land improvement on rainfed plots, except sometimes when it is tied to specific measures in which farmers have no interest. Bank credit was not used for land-improvement investments on any of the rainfed plots out of the 238 surveyed, and this strongly suggests the need for a change in lending policy. As with the case of cost-sharing, it cannot work unless farmers are allowed to select their own technology. Of course professionals should work with farmers and help them develop improved approaches that are both effective as well as adoptable, but farmers should have the last word. Such a policy would force professionals to try to develop new approaches to conservation that are based on conditions prevailing in farmers' fields rather than those that confined to the idealised environment of the research station. The bottom line is that this can only happen if there is real commitment to working with farmers as equal partners. This is discussed further in Kolavalli (1998a).

Findings Related to Changes in Human Welfare

Most respondents said that they had benefited from the watershed projects, but the landless and nearly landless were the most likely to express dissatisfaction. The problem arises because watershed projects seal off access to common property lands so that plants can be protected while revegetation efforts are underway. Many landless people depend on these lands for their livelihood, particularly for grazing sheep and goats, so the loss of access harms their interests. All projects try to compensate landless people by offering employment within the project, and respondents generally expressed satisfaction with employment opportunities. In several cases, however, they complained that employment under the project did not adequately compensate for loss of access to common lands, or that employment opportunities had diminished after several years of the project while grazing bans were still in place.

Uneven distribution of costs and benefits of watershed development has critical implications for project success. If steps are not taken to ensure that everyone shares in the benefits, there are two possible outcomes. First, some people may benefit at the expense of others. Second, those whose interests are harmed may take steps to undermine the work of the project, so that no one benefits. This latter scenario is a serious problem, since protecting common lands requires collective action that is difficult to enforce.

While this tension between the interests of herders and others will always be an issue in watershed-development projects, lessons can be learned from some of the NGOs operating in Andhra Pradesh. In these projects, special efforts are made not just to compensate landless people for the loss of access to common property resources, but rather to build their interests into the design of the project. The way to achieve this is by granting landless people rights to some of the resource being developed by the project, such as access rights to water bodies for fishing, or access to the protected common lands for certain products such as timber. Some projects have shown that creative experimentation with institutional arrangements can go a long way toward ensuring that watershed development is in everyone's interest.

Preliminary Conclusions

There is little evidence to recommend further large-scale investment in watershed development, at least under the approach of existing projects.[10] This statement requires some explanation.

First, the large-scale projects covered by the study (the NWDPRA and DPAP) do not show much evidence of impact. These projects follow strict guidelines and are evaluated on the basis of physical targets achieved, which limits the scope for participation by inhabitants of the project area. The World Bank took a similarly inflexible approach. All of these projects scored poorly for most project indicators, failing to distinguish themselves from control villages on the whole. It would be difficult to justify large-scale investment in these approaches in the future.

Of course, the DPAP and World Bank have already changed their approaches, and the findings are not reflected in this paper. However, Kolavalli (1998b) examined the World Bank projects in Rajasthan and Orissa and identified continued problems with their performance. In particular, the approach to the choice of technology is still too inflexible, with little or no room for input by farmers, and there is insufficient

---

[10] It should be stressed that practically all the projects reviewed here pre-date or fall outside the 1994 Common Guidelines.

attention to developing and strengthening community institutions to support collective action.

The DPAP underwent a radical change in 1995, but the state- and district-level administrations have found it very difficult to implement the new guidelines (Kolavalli 1998b). In fact, few if any new DPAP projects had made any progress in Maharashtra by the time of this study, and the situation is not much better in most other states. Implementing the new guidelines requires a change in the way government agencies work, and this will take time. To the credit of the DPAP project authorities, they have been careful to withhold funds in places where the local authorities remain unprepared to carry out the new guidelines.

The AGY, IGWDP and some NGOs covered by this study presented quite a different picture from the NWDPRA, old DPAP and World Bank projects. They have demonstrated that watershed development can in fact contribute to improved natural resource management and agricultural productivity in rainfed areas, but their success continues to be limited to a small scale. The AGY and IGWDP appear to have successfully blended the advantages of NGOs and government agencies, and scaled them up to beyond what individual NGOs can achieve, but it is important to keep this success in perspective. In particular, their experience so far is limited to only a few hundred villages that met strict selection criteria that would be difficult for most villages to meet. Participating villages have also benefited from special treatment apart from investment in watershed development, mainly in the form of much-improved infrastructure, which may be as important as watershed investments in stimulating higher agricultural productivity and improved natural resource management. Also, both programmes have operated on a pilot scale so far, working with relatively experienced NGO partners and with relatively high administrative input that would be difficult to maintain should the programme expand. Thus, while the AGY and IGWDP have performed very well, it would be a mistake to assume that their approach can be replicated on a large scale.

Instead, the experience of the AGY and IGWDP can best be replicated by initiating similar projects that take a flexible approach and operate on a similar scale. These projects represent experimental approaches to government–NGO collaboration, and there is much more room for further experimentation. Future investments in watershed development can only benefit from additional lessons from similar experiments.

2 Biophysical and Economic Gains from Special Watershed Projects

The analysis by Kerr et al. (1998), reported in Extract 1.1, examines the impact of a wide range of watershed projects implemented before the 1994 Guidelines were introduced. Essentially, Kerr et al. found that, with a few exceptions (mainly in the form of highly participatory and well-implemented projects), efforts by government and some international agencies such as the World Bank to introduce watershed rehabilitation on a large scale have left little lasting impact on the ground. The 1994 Guidelines have been in force for long enough to begin only now to have an impact on implementation. If implementation problems of the kind documented by Turton et al. (1998) (see also Annex 2) can be overcome then, clearly, improved performance can be expected in the future.

The purpose of this chapter is to take a step back and examine the kinds of evidence that helped to support such substantial public sector financing of watershed development over the last decade. This level of investment would have been unlikely if the only evidence available were of the kind presented by Kerr et al. That no such evidence was being unearthed on a continuing basis over the years reveals starkly the shortcomings of monitoring and evaluation procedures. What, therefore, was the evidence on which such investment plans were made? Was it generated from projects in some way atypical of the norm? Did it suffer methodological weaknesses of other kinds?

After this introductory section, this chapter examines the biophysical characteristics and performance of one of the most widely cited watersheds rehabilitated in the 1980s in semi-arid areas (Kharaiya Nala) (Extract 2.1). It then presents two assessments of the rates of economic return generated by pilot projects under a wide range of conditions, drawing out methodological questions where necessary (Extract 2.2 by Chopra and Extract 2.3 by Landell-Mills).

PERFORMANCE OF KHARAIYA NALA WATERSHED

Hazra (1998) gives details of the climate, soils, vegetation and topography of Kharaiya Nala watershed. They are typical of the semi-arid Bhundelkand area of southern Uttar Pradesh, with annual rainfall of some 900–1000 mm, substantially lower than for another watershed widely noted as successful—Sukhomajri, located in the higher rainfall area of Haryana.

Watershed treatments closely involved the communities concerned, and benefited from close support from the Department of Agriculture and from the Indian Grassland and Fodder Research Institute based nearby at Jhansi. The treatments followed a typical ridge-to-valley approach, involving contour trenches on the slopes, fencing of the common land, and regeneration of existing species, together with supplementary planting of new species. Check-dams were constructed on the main watercourses, and gullies were plugged as necessary. Soil- and water-conservation measures were undertaken on the agricultural land, and cropping intensity increased markedly as a result of improved soil-moisture content and increased possibilities of irrigation. The main results are summarised in Extract 2.1.

ASSESSING ECONOMIC RETURNS

Chopra (1998) (Extract 2.2) reviews several economic evaluations of what are essentially special projects of one kind or another in India. Most use versions of social cost–benefit analysis. She then proceeds to critique this methodology. She develops multi-criteria analysis, principally on the grounds that this better allows for the multiple objectives of watershed projects (such as reduced soil loss, increased soil-moisture conservation, and increased biomass for fuel, fodder, etc), and allows separate weights to be attached to each of these according to their perceived importance. It also allows qualitative information to be taken into account more adequately than does cost–benefit analysis. It allows options to be ranked on the basis of perceptions of likely effect, and unlike cost–benefit analysis, does not generate a net present value, or rate of return, on the basis of some presumed initial level of investment.

Landell-Mills (1998) (Extract 2.3) adds to the critique developed by Chopra of cost–benefit analysis, comments on the strengths and weaknesses of multi-criteria analysis, and proposes a modification of cost–benefit analysis.

SPECIAL CONDITIONS FOR SUCCESS?

Overall, whilst some flaws in early economics methodology can be detected from these reviews and analyses, the generally high rates of return which were obtained appear attributable less to this than to the 'special' nature of many of the projects reviewed. The Sukhomajri and Ralegaon Siddhi projects (Extract 2.2) have benefited from charismatic leadership. Similarly, the Kharaiya Nala projects reviewed by Hazra (1998) have been the subject of special attention by the Uttar Pradesh Department of Agriculture and the Indian Grassland and Fodder Research Institute for many years. Other projects have received exceptionally strong support for people's participation from experienced NGOs such as MYRADA. Given this evidence, it does not appear unreasonable to conclude that policy towards large-scale support for micro-watershed rehabilitation was conceived without adequate consideration of whether these special preconditions for success could be introduced on a wide scale.

EXTRACT 2.1
BIOPHYSICAL RESULTS OF WATERSHED
REHABILITATION IN KHARAIYA NALA[1]

C.R. HAZRA[2]

Following major rehabilitation of five watersheds in this area (Hazra 1998) the project impact was measured in terms of: (a) reduction in runoff water and sediment yield from hills or hillocks and wastelands; (b) rise in groundwater table; (c) increase in crop productivity and cropping intensity; (d) increase in forage and firewood production from field bunds and common lands; (e) change in livestock composition; and (f) increase in use of cow dung as manure.

Reduction in Rainwater Loss and Sediment Yield

The effect of regeneration of vegetation, along with soil and water conservation measures on hillslopes and wastelands was substantial. Runoff water loss on barren hills was reduced from 70 per cent pre-treatment to 22 per cent by the third year after treatment, and soil losses fell from 41 t/ha to 1.9 t/ha per year.

[1] For further details, see Hazra (1998).
[2] Commissioner, Department of Agriculture and Cooperation, Ministry of Agriculture, New Delhi.

The progressive reduction in soil and water loss and sediment yield as a result of quick recovery of vegetation on hillslopes and lands adjoining the foothills has resulted in a greatly improving surface and groundwater regime of the micro-watershed.

Augmentation of Ground- and Surface-Water Resources

The water table rose from 12m depth to 6m within three years of project completion. As a consequence, the number of dug wells went up from 12 to 483 in the micro-watersheds: a 40-fold increase, giving one well now for every 7.6 ha. Interestingly enough, these wells were dug by villagers without any loan from the government. In addition, 17 checkdams impounded 60 ha m of runoff water, which is used for watering animals, washing and irrigation. As a result of the increased water potential in the micro-watersheds, the area under irrigated cropping increased from 9.6 per cent to 69 per cent.

Change in Cropping Pattern, Cropping Intensity and Crop Productivity

As a result of the improved soil-moisture regime during the *kharif*, the increase in supplementary irrigation resources and increased use of fertiliser (including cow dung), the area under *kharif* and *rabi* increased by 85 per cent and 233 per cent respectively. The area under *zaid* rose from nil to 146 ha, i.e. 4 per cent of the cultivated area. Among the main *kharif* crops, groundnut and soya bean, which are new introductions in the area, covered 49 per cent and 6 per cent of the total cultivated area respectively. Of the total *kharif* cropped area, the area under sorghum slightly (29 per cent) decreased whereas there was steep decline (from 29 per cent to 4 per cent) in the area under sorghum + pigeonpea mixtures. In the case of *rabi* crops, the area under wheat (260 per cent), gram (204 per cent) and vegetables, especially tomato (2383 per cent), exhibited a phenomenal increase. Among the summer crops, vegetables, namely, onion, colocasia, bottle gourd, bitter gourd and ladies' finger were grown over 112 ha. This resulted in an increase in the cropping intensity from 81 per cent to 172 per cent. The productivity of *kharif*, *rabi* and *zaid* crops increased by 667, 369 and 80 per cent respectively over the yield recorded during the pre-project phase.

Increase in Firewood Availability

Based on pre-project surveys, the total annual fuel needs of the 1980 households in the seven micro-watersheds was 4364 tonnes per year.

According to the villagers' felt need, 65 per cent of the total fuel should have been met through fuelwood, giving a total annual firewood requirement of 2837 tonnes. The data on firewood availability from different sources during the pre- and post-project phases reveal that rehabilitation of hillslopes (community land) and tree planting on field bunds, gully plugs, homestead and in groves increased the availability of firewood seven-fold over the pre-project phase. This has helped in reducing the initial firewood gap from 89 to 15 per cent.

Livestock composition changed substantially from before the project to the third year after completion: the number of buffaloes increased, but other livestock fell in number. The decline in the sheep population was particularly steep, which was due to the fact that mostly landless and marginal farmers were keeping sheep and goats, which had free access to common grazing lands and wastelands. As a result of the project intervention, lands which were hitherto lying waste were reclaimed and brought under cultivation. Grazing was stopped in common lands under regeneration, reducing the grazing area and depleting the forage potential. This made it difficult for sheep and goat owners to maintain large numbers of animals, so they disposed of part of their stock. However, many of these people also got alternative employment as daily paid labourers in agricultural fields, and also through self-employment making baskets and leaf-plates, almost on a year-round basis. The assured availability of fodder as a result of reseeding of common lands and field bunds with high-yielding grass and legume species paved the way for the farmers to go in for increased number of buffaloes, whose high milk yield, with its high fat content, fetches good market prices. Bullock power is still the main source of farm energy. The increase in the number of bullocks is due to the high cropping intensity and the larger area under cultivation as a result of reclamation of arable wasteland and the adoption of soil- and moisture-conservation practices.

Grass and Fodder Production

As a result of the project, the area available for free grazing for village livestock fell to almost nil. There was also a substantial reduction in non-arable land (mainly community grazing-land and land used for miscellaneous purposes). The entire 317 ha of arable wasteland was reclaimed and brought under crop production. There was, however, an addition of 132 ha of field bunds and 12 ha of gully-plugs, which were assigned to grass production.

In spite of a 23 per cent reduction in the total area available for grazing, dry forage production increased by 235 per cent compared to the pre-project phase. The increase in dry forage production is mainly due to reseeding of field bunds and hillslopes with grasses and legumes, and regenerating old rootstocks on hill slopes. The average dry forage productivity went up from 0.70 to 5.30 tonnes/ha/year during the post-project phase. *Bhusa* (wheat straw) production increased by 213 per cent due to the increase in total cropped area and cropping intensity.

A comparison of the data on the total forage requirement and total forage deficit during the pre- and post-project phases suggests that there was initially a forage deficit of 5899 tonnes/year. This deficit, as a result of project intervention, was not merely wiped out; the area produced a surplus of 1611 tonnes per year. The surplus was mainly due to *bhusa*, which the villagers sold, thereby adding to their income.

Fuel Production

During the pre-project phase, 87 per cent of the total energy needs of the households were met by cow-dung cakes, whereas firewood and crop residues contributed only 7 and 6 per cent respectively. Fuel consumption pattern changed dramatically during the post-project phase, when consumption of firewood and crop residues went up to 55 and 20 per cent, respectively. The use of cow dung as fuel fell by 62 per cent, thus enabling the farmers to divert substantial quantities of the much-needed cow dung to crop lands as manure. This change in the fuel consumption pattern was brought about by the increased availability of firewood as a result of tree planting on field bunds and aiding the natural regeneration of old rootstocks of different species on the hillslopes of the common lands. The use of cow dung as organic manure has resulted in the availability of 120 t of nitrogen fertiliser, 35 t of phosphorus and 170 t of potassium per year in the village, which otherwise were being lost due to burning. This has manifested itself in increased crop productivity. There is however, still a deficit of 444 tonnes of firewood each year. In order to narrow this gap, it would be necessary to introduce fuel-efficient *chulhas*, and biogas plants preferably for a cluster of families.

Improvement of Soil Fertility

In order to assess the effect of vegetation regeneration and soil- and water-conservation measures on soil fertility, studies were carried out in Gaharawa micro-watershed three years after the treatment. The data on soil pH, electric conductivity, organic carbon and available nutrients under the four types of land use are summarised in Hazra (1998).

In the case of natural grasslands, protection allowed the recovery of natural grasses, improving the organic carbon content of the soil and also the available nutrient (NPK) status. Similarly degraded lands, when brought under the silvipasture system of land management, along with soil- and water-conservation measures, showed a marked increase in organic matter and available nutrients as compared to the untreated degraded lands. This increase was also more than the one obtained under the protected natural grasslands, which may be due to the development of better grass and tree cover as a result of improved soil and moisture conditions. Amongst all the land types, the greatest improvement in soil fertility status was observed in the case of treated hills, which became covered with dense grass and trees.

Usufruct Sharing

In the Tejpura micro-watershed, which is the oldest of the seven treated micro-watersheds, grass from common lands is auctioned among the villagers of Tejpura only, and the sale proceeds go to the *panchayat* fund. Between 1992 and 1993, Rs 35,000 were realised from such auctions. Rs 1 per head-load of firewood is charged to the villagers, which they often sell in market for Rs 7–10 per head-load. In the case of fish, the auction is limited to only fishermen of the micro-watershed concerned. Like grass and firewood, the sale proceeds also go to the *panchayat* fund. Villagers are able to loan money at the nominal interest of 1–2 per cent per year from the *panchayat* fund. This provides much-needed relief to local people in meeting contingencies, and frees them from the tyranny of local moneylenders, who lend at a very high rate of interest.

EXTRACT 2.2
EVALUATIONS OF WATERSHED PROGRAMMES IN INDIA—A REVIEW[3]

KANCHAN CHOPRA[4]

Diverse approaches have been adopted in the evaluation of watershed programmes in India. A large number of studies identify technological components of the watershed programme and then list the impact of each component. Others use financial or social cost-benefit analysis to

---

[3] Source: Chopra (1998).
[4] Institute of Economic Growth, University Enclave, Delhi 110007, India.

arrive at rates of return to individual components of projects. A brief review of these studies (summarised in Table 2.1) is attempted in this section. It is important to keep in mind that unit costs of watershed-management projects may also vary considerably. The cost per hectare of area varies from Rs 1000 to Rs 9500 (Vaidyanathan 1991).

Studies by Saksena et al. (1989) in the plateau and hill region of western Maharashtra found that a benefit–cost ratio of 1.28 and an internal rate of return of 12.33 per cent could be obtained from a project which included water harvesting. In the same region, Nawadhakar and Shaikh (1989) reported increases in net sown area of about 14 per cent with land shaping, contour bunding and moisture conservation as the major project components.

ASCI (1990) found that in Maheswaram Watershed in Andhra Pradesh, watershed technologies raised yields of sorghum and castor substantially: from 5.5 to 10.3 quintals for sorghum, and from 4.8 to 9.6 quintals for castor. However, about 75 per cent of the *Leucaena leucocephala* plants, part of the project's plantation component, did not survive. Even where the plants survived, their growth rate was poor.

Chopra et al. (1990) reported that in the lower Siwalik region of northern India, the use of participatory approaches resulted in moderate-to-high rates of return to watershed management, greater than 12 per cent, the cut-off social rate of discount usually adopted by the Indian Planning Commission. Further, the incremental income accrued to different sets of beneficiaries. Between households and village society, about 71–82 per cent of net benefits were shared by the project region. Externalities accruing to the government comprised 18–29 per cent of net benefits. This estimation of benefits to the project region has allowed for the direct and indirect impacts of participatory institutions on incomes of the people as well as of government agencies.

Singh (1989) reviewed the experience of four watershed projects: Mittermari and PIDOW in Karnataka, Ralegaon-Siddhi in Maharashtra, and Sukhomajri in Haryana. The review reiterates that programme interventions seeking to enhance the expected benefits to people, or reduce the expected costs, are likely to elicit stronger people's participation. Other determinants are organisation of people into small groups (as in PIDOW) and leadership (as in Maharashtra), equitable sharing of benefits from collective action (as in Sukhomajri), and availability of complementary investment from government.

Singh et al. (1991) studied the Kandi watershed, an economically backward tract of Punjab. The different components of this project and

Table 2.1 Impact of Soil and Water Conservation Technologies in India

Project location, agro-climatic zone	Source	Nature of project	Increase in cropping intensity (%)	Incremental yield (% or quintals/ha)[c]	Gross return (Rs/ha)	Rate of return[b]
Maharashtra: W plateau & hills	Saksena et al. (1989)	Water reservoir			3900-5000 Rs/ha	B/C = 1.28 IRR = 12.33
Maharashtra: W plateau & hills	Nawadhakar and Shaikh (1989)	Land shaping, contour bunding, moisture conserv.			2455 Rs/ha (103% increase)	Increase in net sown area = 14%
Karnataka: S plateau & hills	Kulkarni et al. (1989)	Soil & runoff conservation	7.45%	*Kharif:* sorghum +3.62, groundnut +3.26, chilli +12.44, cotton +16.14, *Rabi:* sorghum +1.44		Net return increase in *kharif* sorghum
Karnataka: S plateau & hills	Singh, Katar (1989)	Bunds, graded contours, farm ponds		Groundnut +1.68 q, local gdnut +1.19, finger millet +0.88, fgr millet +2.40, HYV gdnut +2.68, local pigeon-pea+fgr millet +5.23, HYV fgr millet +4.42	Incremental net benefit: Rs 9170/ha	

Table 2.1 (continued)

Project location, agro-climatic zone	Source	Nature of project	Increase in cropping intensity (%)	Incremental yield (% or quintals/ha)[a]	Gross return (Rs/ha)	Rate of return[b]
Punjab: Himalayan foothills	Singh et al. (1991)	Livestock development, soil conservation				Rate of return = 12.5%, on forestry 15.3%
Haryana: Himalayan foothills	Chopra et al. (1990)	Water reservoir afforestation, new institutions				Rate of return = 19%
Maheswaram: semi-arid agro-climatic zone, Andhra Pradesh	Rao (1993)	Integrated project, soil & water conserv., horticulture, pastures, forestry		Engineering measures: sorghum +1.49, castor +0.53 Veg measures: sorghum +2.47, castor +0.98	Eng: sorghum 1599, castor 1487; Veg: sorghum 1763, castor 1578	
Matatila, Andhra Pradesh	AFC (1988)	River valley, soil conservation, mini storage, afforestation	85.6-115.4%	10-76.2%		B/C = 3.8 IRR = 41%
Nizamsagar, Andhra Pradesh			89.6-114.5%	27-11.3%	39%	B/C = 1.25

Table 2.1 (continued)

Project location, agro-climatic zone	Source	Nature of project	Increase in cropping intensity (%)	Incremental yield (% or quintals/ha)[a]	Gross return (Rs/ha)	Rate of return[b]
Ukai, Andhra Pradesh			89-100%	40.3-74.8%	43.7%	B/C = 1.36
Punjab (Kandi)	Singh et al. (1991)	Watershed & area dev for rehabil & flood protection	Under orchards: 28.1-32.1%			IRR: *kinnow* (citrus) 38%, mangoes 26%, guava 44%
Maharashtra (2 agro-climatic zones)	Deshpan-de (1997)	Land dev+bunds, tree plantation on farms, pasture dev, water & soil conserv.	Scarcity zone 111-113%, Transition zone 126-130%		Increase in income/ha: Scarcity zone 45%, Transition zone 30%	Not reported
Gujarat (2 regions)	Shah (1997)	Land dev, levelling, bunds, check-dams, conserv measures		Veg barriers 5-6%, land levelling 18-27%, earth bunding 21-22%		

[a]1 quintal = 100 kg; + = net addition
[b]IRR = internal rate of return; B/C = benefit-cost ratio; HYV = high-yielding variety

their associated rates of return were forestry (12 per cent), animal husbandry (9 per cent), soil conservation (10 per cent), horticulture (22 per
cent), and irrigation (2 per cent). The overall project internal rate of
return of 8 per cent represents a substantial shortfall from the earlier
expectations of 12–20 per cent according to the feasibility studies. However, the internal rate of return and benefit–cost ratios are 38 per cent
and 2.23 for *kinnow* (a type of citrus fruit), 26 per cent (2.48) for mango,
and 44 per cent (2.30) for guava. An increase in cultivated area is reported from 80.3 to 99.3 per cent, while the irrigated area increases from
11.4 to 48.9 per cent.

The forestry component could have performed better had adequate
provision been made for maintenance, so that the high tree-mortality
rate could have been reduced. The indifferent performance of the ani-
mal-husbandry component is mainly due to a sharp drop in the milk
yields of high quality cattle provided. This performance could be attributed to inadequate provision of fodder and feed, weak extension services and lack of milk-marketing infrastructure. The poor performance
of soil-conservation components was largely due to the failure of the
irrigation component, as the attainment of full benefits of this component was contingent upon the availability of timely irrigation. The main
reason for the poor performance of the irrigation component was the
inordinate delay in implementation and the limited area actually brought
under irrigation.

In a more recent study, Shah (1997) has examined watershed programmes in western Gujarat. A yield gain of 20–30 per cent is expected
with an average investment of about Rs 6000 per hectare. In terms of
the acceptability of different components of watershed technology, she
reports that in a dynamic rainfed region, returns from capital-intensive
measures such as land levelling, water harvesting and commercial plantation are likely to be higher and are also likely to evoke more interest
and participation. *In situ* conservation measures by themselves (including vegetative barriers) may not succeed unless accompanied by measures that are perceived to be income-enhancing. She also maintains that
farmers need appropriate technology, even if it is not low cost.

Economic Analysis of Three Watersheds, and Methodological Questions

The Three Watersheds   This Extract analyses the economic performance
of activities in three watersheds: Tatarpur (Alwar district, Rajasthan),
Pithalpur (Sikar district, Rajasthan), and Ralegaon Siddhi (Maharashtra).

The first two are part of the Sahibi project, undertaken in 1978–79 in Alwar, Sikar and Jaipur districts under the centrally sponsored scheme for integrated watershed management. These districts are in a semi-arid part of Rajasthan, with an average annual rainfall of 450mm. At about the same time, work was initiated under a non-government initiative in Ralegaon Siddhi in Ahmednagar district, Maharashtra, a region with an average rainfall of about 570mm. In both cases, agricultural land constituted a major part of the project area, and an increase in agricultural productivity constituted an important objective of the project. Major problems were land degradation, unspecified property rights, and rising cattle and human populations—elements common to most rainfed regions of the country.

The Sahibi and Ralegaon Siddhi projects differed in terms of their institutional set-up. While Ralegaon Siddhi was among the first non-governmental initiatives in the country, the Sahibi project was executed by the Forest Department of Rajasthan. However, the notion of making people's participation a part of development planning had permeated into the planning process by the time that work on the second selected watershed (Pithalpur) began. Together, therefore, the three watersheds reflect three institutional patterns:

- a non-government initiative (Ralegaon Siddhi);
- a project executed by a government department; (Tatarpur) and
- a project executed by a government agency with peoples' participation (Pithalpur).

The two Sahibi project sub-watersheds, Tatarpur and Pithalpur, were selected as they represent the spectrum of conditions prevailing in the Sahibi area. The former is 'saturated', in that all the work planned has been completed. It was completed more than a decade ago. The latter was completed five years ago. These two sub-watersheds are located in separate districts, with widely different soils and groundwater availability. They thus represent the conditions in the Sahibi watershed project as a whole. Whereas Tatarpur is a 'very high priority' area, Pithalpur is in the next category, merely 'high priority'. The level of participation by local communities was far higher in Pithalpur, although soil and other natural conditions seem far more inhospitable there. Both secondary information and field visits confirmed this.

These two watersheds also represent different technological mixes, encompassing both water harvesting and engineering. The choice of technology was in accordance with guidelines issued by the Indian government in 1978. The project is now being implemented as per the re-

vised Guidelines of 1994. This has imposed some restrictions on the
choice of technology. The technology selected under the Ralegaon Siddhi
project did not operate within any such constraints.

The Sahibi project and the Ralegaon Siddhi initiative are located in
Rajasthan and Maharashtra respectively, which together comprise a large
part of the semi-arid region of the country. A comparison of the performance of these two projects is therefore an appropriate starting-point
for developing watershed-management policies in the semi-arid tropics.

Methodologies for Project Evaluation

The evolution of techniques to evaluate alternative investments has been
one of the central concerns of investment-planning literature since the
late 1960s. This was the outcome partly of the accent on centralised
planning and its need to choose between large, centrally planned, investments. Cost–benefit analysis emerged as the most widely used technique
at that time. In the initial stages it was used mainly in the analysis of
public-sector industrial projects[5] which had well-specified streams of
benefits and costs. Over time, however, the range of application of the
technique was extended to include projects in the private sector and in
the areas of agriculture, infrastructure and even social services such as
education and health. Each application witnessed innovations in the technique itself to cope with the new range of questions being asked. In the
application to investments in the private sector, for instance, streams of
benefits and costs were valued at market prices only. Alternatively, an
evaluation of public sector projects necessitated the valuing of these
time streams at 'social' or 'shadow' prices.

The emergence of environmental impacts as an important dimension in the analysis of projects gave rise to a new set of issues. How
were these impacts to be assessed, measured and taken account of within
the dimensions of the technique? In view of the longer time horizon in
which environmental effects manifest themselves, was it correct to use
similar discount rates and discounting techniques as for economic costs
and benefits? While the latter question stimulated a growing theoretical
literature (Pearce et al. 1989), the former was tackled by looking at benefits and costs as they accrued in the context of specific projects.

Additionally, externalities are crucial in estimating environmental effects, and the physical unit over which the effect of the investment is
spread becomes important. This is in particular true of soil- and water-

---

[5] See UNIDO (1972) for a detailed exposition of the theoretical basis and the earliest
applications in developing countries.

conservation projects undertaken within watersheds. When it is possible to identify groups to whom principal or externality benefits (or costs) accrue, the effects on them measure the externality benefits (or costs).[6] Some other exercises distinguish between on- site and off-site effects of investment: the former being measured by direct evaluation of increased productivity, and the latter by benefit from silt retention as approximated by saving on alternative investments (such as mechanical dredging of downstream water bodies).

It can be concluded that most analysis of environmental effects within the framework of cost–benefit analysis approximates the effects in indirect ways. This is fine as long as these effects are treated as externalities arising out of the operation of the project. One recent approach to environmental problems maintains that they impose a constraint on the scale of economic activity, due to the crossing of acceptable threshold levels of intervention in the environment (Hueting 1991). Such a view implies that cost–benefit analysis becomes somewhat irrelevant, as it views only marginal impacts without examining the scale problem.

These and other shortcomings—including questions of how cost–benefit analysis should be modified for ex-post applications (when it had initially been conceived in ex-ante settings)—led to the use of other methodologies for evaluation. One of these is multi-criteria analysis.

Multi-criteria analysis has been used for evaluation of alternative projects in the work reported here. It has been selected in preference to cost–benefit analysis on a number of counts. Cost–benefit analysis arrives at rates of return or net present values of projects, envisaging a certain amount of initial investment. The outcome is a kind of judgement on the desirability or otherwise of investment in alternative projects. In this exercise, the objective is different. It is to rank projects embodying different technologies and institutional frameworks in terms of the total impact they have had on a selected set of effects. Multi-objective decision models (of which multi-criteria analysis is one), allow for more accurate representation of such decision problems, in the sense that several objectives can be accounted for. Objectives of watershed projects, for instance, may be reduction of soil loss, increase in *in situ* moisture conservation which increases productivity, reduction of non-point pollution of surface and groundwater, general improvement in the environment, etc. Each of these effects may be given different weights, the

---

[6] See the analysis of investments undertaken in the Sukhomajri watershed in Chopra et al. (1990).

weights to be assigned being determined by user group valuation, rapid appraisal methods, etc.

Further, accounting for qualitative as well as quantitative variables became a critical factor in the evaluation of the selected projects. Each project impacted on environmental and economic variables. Some environmental effects, such as reduced sediment yield, could be measured with precision only in situations where silt monitoring had been undertaken. Other variables in this category had simply not been measured with quantitative precision. There existed, however qualitative judgements or estimates of them. Economic effects were more amenable to quantitative measurement. Multi-criteria analysis enables us to take account of both these sets of variables in the evaluation of the projects. Scores are estimated for each project or technology, and then a ranking is obtained making use of all kinds of effects that the project may have had. Both positive effects of the projects (which can be conceived of as benefits) and negative effects (to be thought of as costs) can be used in the analysis.

This methodology also allows for different weights to be given to sets of variables, and for a sensitivity analysis of results based on either weights-uncertainty or effects-uncertainty. All these characteristics of the technique make it suitable for analysing effects of alternative technologies or projects with a fair degree of certainty with respect to the ranges within which the effects lie.

Methodology as Applied: Kinds of Impact Studied

The methodology of multi-criteria analysis consists of two steps: (a) drawing up of an effects table, and (b) determining ranks and scores for projects on the basis of this.

The effects table is a fairly detailed description of the economic and environmental impact of each project alternative. The effects of each project are identified on the basis of four sets of variables: economic, environmental, costs of alternatives, and institutional. Further, all effects are defined as incremental changes in the variable. This is found by subtracting the value of the benefit in a non-treated area (used as a benchmark) from that accruing in the treated area. The approach adopted is similar to the 'with' and 'without' project formulation used in standard project-evaluation literature.[7]

---

[7] This is the approach that has been preferred to the 'before' and 'after' approach for the identification of benefits. See the literature on project appraisal, for instance, UNIDO (1972).

For this study, data were collected on two sets of variables (economic and environmental) in the 'with' and 'without' situations. The economic variables included:

- crop yields, defined to include the weighted yields of major crops grown in the region;
- increase in area under cultivation (this accounts for the impact on expansion of agricultural activity);
- increase or decrease in livestock numbers, measured in standard cattle units, using conversion factors from the National Commission on Agriculture;
- increase in milk production;
- employment benefit from project construction and from agricultural intensification effects;
- increases in area under horticulture and private plantations, and in fodder and fuelwood availability.

The environmental variables taken are:

- reduction in sediment yield from silt-monitoring data;
- reduction in runoff (here again, ordinal values based on secondary information are given);
- water table (some quantitative information on increase in number of wells in the area around Pithalpur is available; however, a qualitative index is used);
- flood control is also taken into account by assuming uniform success in both watersheds of the Sahibi project; but this was not relevant elsewhere.

Costs of all three kinds of investment activity, engineering structures, water harvesting structures and afforestation activity are taken from the project authorities, adjusted for inflation and accounted for at 1995–96 prices.

As evidenced from field visits, supported by indirect evidence from available documents, it is assumed that the level of people's participation is higher in Pithalpur than in Tatarpur. Since Ralegaon Siddhi is the NGO initiative, it is taken as being highest there.

Sources of data include secondary (provided by the project authorities and independent studies) and primary (based on surveys). Primary data were used in areas where information from the project authorities was not exhaustive.

Benefits from treatment with soil- and water-conservation measures were found on the basis of a random sample of households in villages where a maximum number of people are known to have benefited from the project. In Tatarpur, the sample of 21 households came from two villages, namely Tatarpur and Raipur. A sample of households was selected in Tatarpur village (Badli and Rundh hamlets), which benefited from engineering structures such as bunds and check-dams. In Raipur, five households were selected from among those who had benefited from water-harvesting structures. In the non-beneficiary category, households were sampled in Bahram Ka Bas village, 25 km away from the watershed area. In Pithalpur sub-watershed area, a group of 20 beneficiaries was interviewed in two villages, Pithalpur and Hamirsing Ki Dhani, to capture the benefits from the adoption of engineering and water harvesting structures respectively. To represent the non-beneficiary category, a sample of 10 households were selected in Triveni Nursery area, 20 km away from the Pithalpur watershed.

Table 2.2 and Table 2.3 provide data on incremental benefits and costs for Tatarpur and Pithalpur sub-watersheds with respect to engineering and water-harvesting technologies. Three levels are identified for each project: the level in the project area, outside the project area, and the net difference.

To calculate the incremental benefits, the figures for the non-watershed area (i.e., the control) are deducted from the those in the project area. The difference (final two columns in Tables 2.2 and 2.3) are regarded as being due to the project, and are used to judge the ranking of projects and technologies.

A similar estimate of net change in the selected variables for Ralegaon Siddhi enables us to set up the effects table for all five alternatives (Table 2.4). This shows that increases of *bajra* and wheat yields are highest for the water-harvesting option in Pithalpur. *Jowar* and onion are relevant only for Ralegaon Siddhi, as are the areas under horticulture and plant protection. In the Sahibi watersheds (for both the engineering and water-harvesting technologies), the incremental fuel and fodder benefits can be identified on a seasonal basis and are duly accounted for as an effect. Wherever fuel or fodder availability has decreased in a particular season, it is recorded as a cost.

Ranking of Projects

When interpreted on the basis of the expected-value method, Table 2.4 generates scores and ranks for the five alternative approaches. The results are arrived at on the basis of: (a) different weights given to alternative effects, and (b) different levels of uncertainty assigned to sets of effects.

Table 2.2 Economic Impact of Investment in Tatarpur Sub-watershed

Effect	Unit	Within project		Non-project (control)	Net difference	
		Engin-eering	Water harvesting		Engin-eering	Water harvesting
Crops						
Bajra	kg/*bigha*	355	329	294	61	35
Wheat	kg/*bigha*	1099	1058	870	229	188
Mustard	kg/*bigha*	383	306	278	105	28
Gram	kg/*bigha*	391	340	280	111	60
Crop area (increase)	*bigha*/family	1.38	0	0	1.38	0
Livestock	std cattle units	0.77	1.00	0.33	0.44	0.67
Milk	ltr/buf-falo/year	1580	1722	644	936	1078
Fodder						
Summer	tonnes	23.3	6.1	11.3	11.9	-5.3
Winter	tonnes	19.1	2.2	20.9	-1.8	-18.7
Rainy	tonnes	15.4	9.4	79.0	-63.7	-69.6
Fuel						
Summer	tonnes	5.8	4.6	27.0	-21.2	-22.4
Winter	tonnes	23.8	7.0	13.2	10.6	-6.2
Rainy	tonnes	4.0	0	27.2	-23.3	-27.2
New employment	days/year /family	75	142	0	75	142
Investment costs (1995-96 prices)						
Engineering	Rs/ha	2073			2073	
Water harvesting	Rs/unit		120,000			120,000
Afforestation	Rs/ha	812	818		812	818

Three sets of results are obtained with variables measuring environmental effects being given greater weight than, the same as, and less than those measuring economic effects. These are given in Tables 2.5, 2.6 and 2.7.

With environmental effects weighted more than economic effects, Ralegaon Siddhi, with a score of 0.68, is ranked first (Table 2.5). Water

Table 2.3 Economic Impact of Investment in Pithalpur Sub-watershed

Effect	Unit	Within project		Non-project (control)	Net difference	
		Engineering	Water harvesting		Engineering	Water harvesting
Crops				•		
Bajra	kg/*bigha*	216	440	175	41	264
Wheat	kg/*bigha*	465	800	444	21	356
Crop area (increase)	*bigha*/family	0	0.75	0	0	0.75
Livestock	std cattle units	0.60	-0.48	0.48	0.12	-0.96
Milk	ltr/buffalo/year	523	720	564	-41	156
Fodder						
Summer	tonnes	0	0	96.0	-96.0	-96.0
Winter	tonnes	24.0	60.0	33.2	-9.2	26.8
Rainy	tonnes	0	0	96.0	-96.0	-96.0
Fuel						
Summer	tonnes	12.8	24.8	4.5	8.3	20.3
Winter	tonnes	24.0	24.0	14.1	9.9	9.9
Rainy	tonnes	0	0	4.5	-4.5	-4.5
New employment	days/year /family	41	41	0	41	41
Investment costs (1995-96 prices)						
Engineering	Rs/ha	3838			3838	
Water harvesting	Rs/unit		69,500			69,500
Afforestation	Rs/ha	894	894		894	894

harvesting in Pithalpur is a close second, with a score of 0.67. Tatarpur engineering is third, Pithalpur engineering fourth, and water harvesting in Tatarpur is fifth. These results assume perfect certainty in the different effects.

When uncertainty at two levels, low and high, is introduced, Pithalpur water harvesting and Ralegaon Siddhi tie for first place, and the rest of the ordering remains unchanged. It is interesting to note that the cases

Table 2.4   Effects of Alternative Technological and Institutional Scenarios: Tatarpur, Pithalpur and Ralegaon Siddhi Watersheds

Effects	Unit	Tatarpur		Pithalpur		Ralegaon Siddhi
		Engineering	*Water harvesting*	*Engineering*	*Water harvesting*	
Economic variables						
Crops						
Bajra	kg/*bigha*	61	35	41	264	65
Wheat	kg/*bigha*	229	188	21	356	
Mustard	kg/*bigha*	105	28			
Gram	kg/*bigha*	111	60			
Jowar	kg/*bigha*					163.9
Onion	t/ha					4.10
Crop area increase	*bigha*/family	1.38	0	0	0.75	1.51
Hort area	ha					26
Plant protect'n area	ha					220
Livestock	std cattle units	0.44	0.67	0.60	-0.96	2.60
Milk	litres/buffalo/year	936	1078	-41	156	1050
Fodder						
Summer	tonnes	11.9	-5.3	-96.0	-96.0	
Winter	tonnes	-1.8	-18.7	-9.20	26.80	
Rainy	tonnes	-63.7	-69.6	-96.0	-96.0	
Fuel						
Summer	tonnes	-21.2	-22.4	8.30	20.3	
Winter	tonnes	10.6	-6.2	9.9	9.9	
Rainy	tonnes	-23.3	-27.2	-4.5	-4.5	
Employment	days/yr/family	75	142	41	41	105
Environmental variables						
Water table		+	++	+	++	+++
Sediment yld reduction		++	+	++	+	++
Runoff reduction		+	++	+	++	+++
Flood control		+	+	+	+	
Investment costs						
Engnring	Rs/ha/yr	2073		3838		-1921
Wtr harv	Rs/unit		120,000		69,500	2,600,000
Afforest	Rs/ha/yr	812	818	-894	-894	-394
People's participation		+	+	+++	+++	+++

Table 2.5 Ranks and Scores with Greater Weight to Environmental than Economic Variables: Tatarpur, Pithalpur and Ralegaon Siddhi Watersheds

	Tatarpur		Pithalpur		Ralegaon Siddhi
	Engineering	*Water harvesting*	*Engineering*	*Water harvesting*	
No uncertainty					
Score	0.65	0.53	0.59	0.67	0.68
Rank	3	5	4	2	1
Low uncertainty	3	5	4	1	1
High uncertainty	3	5	4	1	1

Table 2.6 Ranks and Scores: Equal Weighting to All Variables

	Tatarpur		Pithalpur		Ralegaon Siddhi
	Engineering	*Water harvesting*	*Engineering*	*Water harvesting*	
No uncertainty					
Score	0.56	0.37	0.46	0.59	0.65
Rank	3	5	4	2	1
Low uncertainty	3	5	4	1	1
High uncertainty	3	5	4	2	1

Table 2.7 Ranks and Scores with Higher Weight for Economic Variables

	Tatarpur		Pithalpur		Ralegaon Siddhi
	Engineering	*Water harvesting*	*Engineering*	*Water harvesting*	
No uncertainty					
Score	0.53	0.27	0.37	0.53	0.63
Rank	3	5	4	2	1
Low uncertainty	3	5	4	2	1
High uncertainty	3	5	4	2	1

of low and high uncertainty[8] yield precisely the same ordering. With uncertainty included, the performance of Pithalpur, a project planned and executed by government departments, improves *vis-à-vis* that of Ralegaon Siddhi. Although the difference in scores is very small, this can be interpreted as implying that the technology there is perhaps more robust and can withstand some degree of variation in levels of accrual of benefits. Even where Pithalpur water harvesting is ranked second, its score is very close to that of Ralegaon Siddhi.

With economic variables being accorded the same weighting as environmental ones (Table 2.6), the score of Pithalpur water harvesting is 0.59, considerably lower than Ralegaon Siddhi (0.65), though it is still ranked second. The ranks of the other alternatives are also unaltered. The introduction of low uncertainty improves the rank of Pithalpur water harvesting, bringing it to joint first place.

This has two implications. With equal weight given to economic variables, the score of Ralegaon Siddhi improves relative to Pithalpur. This may have its origin in the more people-centred development process in Ralegaon Siddhi. Economic variables received a larger emphasis in this project. Secondly, Pithalpur has an in-built capacity to cater to uncertainty. This aspect seems to be a characteristic of the design of water harvesting in Pithalpur.

Table 2.7 shows the results when greater weights are given to the economic variables. The findings in this case corroborate the directional change shown in the previous table. Greater emphasis on the economic aspects of watershed management only reiterates the relative superiority of Ralegaon Siddhi. This happens at all the uncertainty levels tested.

Conclusions and Policy Implications

The main feature of developments in the last few decades in the area of watershed management has been the coexistence of government-run programmes based on technology emerging from pilot projects, and experiments carried out by NGOs. While the former have focused on the different possible components of the technology of watershed management, the latter have dealt with the social and property-rights aspects. In an attempt to formulate a strategy for watershed management, the present study examines both these initiatives. Large variations in soil and water conservation and in its effects on productivity in different

---

[8] Low and high uncertainty are taken to stand for a combination of different levels of uncertainty in the environmental, economic, cost related and participation related variables.

agro-climatic regions mean that such an examination must rely on experiments in different parts of the country. We first describe projects in the light of their effect on productivity and environmental preservation, and then provide the building blocks for arriving at a comprehensive approach to problems encountered in watershed management.

The key elements of a soil- and water-conservation strategy are technology and institutional structure. The first addresses the issue of the best possible method of capturing runoff and decreasing sediment yields. The second examines how best to provide for sustainability through an appropriate property-rights structure on private, government and common land. Without sustainability, productivity increases achieved through appropriate technology are often frittered away with time.

Agricultural productivity increases in a watershed primarily when more moisture and topsoil are retained within its boundaries. Capturing runoff and increased agricultural productivity in the short run set off a series of ecological and economic effects that need to be studied to arrive at an overall evaluation of the project. The long-run stability of the initial productivity increases depends on the nature of these diverse effects. We used multi-criteria analysis to evaluate the watershed management programmes in Sahibi and Ralegaon Siddhi on the basis of economic, environmental, cost and participatory variables.

The analysis covers four alternatives representing different technologies (engineering and water harvesting) and locations (Tatarpur and Pithalpur) in the Sahibi project, as well as alternative institutional structures (based on the Ralegaon Siddhi project). Assumptions included different levels of project uncertainty, and different weights to economic (crop productivity, employment generation, availability of direct consumer goods) and environment effects (runoff capture, sediment yield capture and flood control). The analysis produced the following results.

Technology options   Comparing Tatarpur and Pithalpur, the engineering option at Tatarpur is considered the best, if policy-makers consider economic effects to be of greater significance than environmental effects. Pithalpur water harvesting follows this. When a high degree of uncertainty is introduced, the two alternatives of water harvesting in Pithalpur and engineering in Tatarpur are equally attractive.

When environmental effects are given higher weights, and if there is no uncertainty in the project's effects, the alternative of water harvesting at Pithalpur gets the first rank. It is followed closely by Tatarpur engineering. The other two options receive low scores. The introduction of a low level of uncertainty does not change the ranking. However, if a high level of uncertainty is introduced, Tatarpur engineering emerges as the best alternative.

Locational options   A comparison between different locations is also useful. It appears that at Tatarpur, the engineering technology has been more successful than the water-harvesting technology. At Pithalpur, it is the other way round. This may be due to the locational characteristics of the two places.

In an overall comparison among the four alternatives, the relative weighing given to economic and environmental variables acquires significance. The option that succeeds in building a closer integration between economic and environmental variables is preferred.

Institutional options   The results with respect to this are obtained by comparing five options: the earlier four, together with that of Ralegaon Siddhi—a project which used broadly similar technology of watershed management but operated under a different institutional regime, that of a non-governmental initiative. This set of results is significant in that it compares a much-cited NGO project with one carried out within the government sector with people's participation introduced as an important component. They show that whereas the non-governmental framework performs better than run-of-the-mill government projects, it is possible for the latter to approximate the performance of NGOs.

The watershed comprises the appropriate unit for planning projects on degraded land, primarily because externality effects of soil and water movements between watersheds are limited in comparison with those within watersheds. This may imply some initial work to arriving at correspondences between administrative units, such as villages and *talukas*, and the relevant watersheds. However, this effort should ensure sustainability of the environmental and consequently the economic benefits.

The comparison across projects presented here suggests that the technology components are location-specific. While engineering methods (such as check-dams, etc.) may comprise the better option in some cases, water harvesting in larger tanks may be preferable in others. It can be concluded that the policy needs to be implemented in a decentralised fashion with considerable local inputs.

Vegetative measures (afforestation and grass planting on field boundaries to control erosion) must be an integral part of all technology. They are cost-effective, increase the seasonal availability of fuel and fodder, and comprise an important economic benefit from the people's viewpoint. These can easily be treated as complementary with the other two components, engineering and water harvesting.

The level of certainty expected for project effects is significant in determining the ranking of the project in terms of its performance. Here, the range of technology available with government organisations as a consequence of experience in diverse environments puts them at an advantage as compared to NGOs. This advantage needs to be capitalised on.

Policy also needs to take cognisance of the wealth of experience now available in the non-governmental sector. In some sense this is already done in that government projects now stress people's participation. Except in some projects, however, this happens in a somewhat superficial manner. A method has to be found which ensures that the best of the two sectors is brought together in project execution. As stated above, government projects can, with some ingenuity, approximate the performance of NGO projects. Alternatively, the government can also take on the role of an enabler in the dissemination of technology to the nongovernmental sector. This is significant in the context of the tremendous input of organisation needed to implement a large-scale watershed-management programme—for only large-scale programmes can have perceptible economic and environmental effects.

EXTRACT 2.3
ECONOMIC EVALUATION OF WATERSHEDS: METHODOLOGICAL ISSUES[9]

N. LANDELL-MILLS[10]

Introduction

Economic appraisals of spending options are made to help ensure that the government allocates resources to projects that yield the greatest improvement in national welfare. Traditionally, economic appraisals of watershed development have focused on comparing the expected costs and benefits of a project over its life using cost–benefit analysis. An economic appraisal of a watershed project is complicated by the fact

---

[9] Source: Landell-Mills (1998).
[10] Formerly Research Associate, ODI; currently with the International Institute for Environment and Development, 3 Endsleigh St., London, UK.

that it involves environmental impacts that are not easily valued, and off-site impacts that are imperfectly understood.

In addition to estimation problems, institutional economics point to a more fundamental flaw with cost–benefit analysis. Namely, it ignores the institutional arrangements which underlie the management of watershed resources and which determine whether a project will be sustained once external support is removed. Even when a project's aggregate social benefits are greater than aggregate social costs, it does not necessarily follow that everyone gains. Losers may threaten the success of a project by refusing to comply with rules of resource use.

Growing evidence that watershed projects undertaken by the government are not sustained, despite estimates of high returns using cost–benefit analysis, lends support to such arguments. Planners are increasingly looking to the achievements of NGOs which have adopted an institutional approach to watershed development. Central to the NGO approach is the involvement of local communities at all stages of project development to ensure cooperation. The government's adoption of the principle of participation is reflected in the 1994 Guidelines.

The adoption of an institutional approach to watershed development has brought with it new costs. Increased involvement of local people in planning requires training and long-term, face-to-face contact between community members and government officials while trust is established and village societies strengthened. So far, attention has been focused on the benefits of participation, and few attempts have been made to calculate the costs of local involvement. To justify the increased spending on institutional approaches to watershed development, it is essential that the benefits to society are shown to be greater than the costs.

This Extract starts by reviewing conventional cost–benefit analysis methodology and the challenges it faces when applied to watershed development. Examples of cost–benefit analysis undertaken in India are given, followed by an explanation of why this approach fails to predict project sustainability. I go on to outline an institutional approach to watershed development and emphasise the need to incorporate institutional arrangements as a component of project proposals. I suggest modifications to cost–benefit analysis to take on board lessons from the 'institutionalists', and give two examples at attempts to do this. Before concluding, I consider whether multi-criteria analysis (as applied by Chopra in Extract 2.2) offers a more useful evaluation technique for assessing watershed development projects.

Cost–Benefit Analysis and Watershed Development

Before cost–benefit analysis is undertaken, the perspective from which costs and benefits are measured must be chosen. A project carried out by the government is likely to be concerned with the project's impact on national welfare. In this case, all social costs and benefits must be calculated, including 'off-site' effects (e.g., downstream impacts), and these must be valued using economic prices. If, on the other hand, an appraisal is undertaken from an individual's perspective (e.g., a farmer involved in watershed development), then the 'private' cost–benefit analysis would focus on the financial costs and benefits experienced by the individual concerned. Unless downstream impacts result in the payment or receipt of resources, these would not be considered in a farmer's evaluation. This paper is concerned with cost–benefit analysis as a tool for evaluating watershed projects from the government viewpoint, so references to cost–benefit analysis mean its social form.

Once a project has been defined and the perspective for analysis identified, four steps must be followed to complete a cost–benefit analysis: (a) calculate project inputs and their costs; (b) identify the physical impacts of the project as compared to the 'without project' scenario; (c) convert the estimates of physical impacts into economic impacts, i.e. expressed in a form that can be valued in money terms (such as higher crop yields); (d) discount the economic impacts and the project costs to present-value terms, and calculate the net present value, benefit–cost ratio or the internal rate of return. Economic prices, or shadow prices, refer to the opportunity cost of using resources; they may differ from market prices due to distortions such as government intervention.

Watershed development impacts on human welfare partly via its effects on water and soil resources. The construction of terraces or reforestation of bare slopes, for example, would tend to stabilise the soil, reduce soil erosion and water runoff, and lead to increased water infiltration and a higher groundwater table. These impacts on environmental factors affect output, drinking-water supply, hydroelectric power, etc. Attempts to capture the impacts of watershed development on humans using cost–benefit analysis is difficult due to imperfect information concerning technical linkages and the existence of non-marketed items.

Despite extensive research to develop valuation techniques such as the replacement-cost method, contingent valuation, or the travel-cost method, in relation to such non-marketed items as enhanced biodiversity, data limitations diminish their applicability in developing countries. Nevertheless leaving out benefits or costs from the analysis would lead to inefficient decision-making, and every attempt should be made to include these effects, either through valuation or by listing them in a project appraisal.

It should be stressed that the valuation of environmental goods and services referred to above should only be used for those items not already valued in terms of their impacts on economic variables. If the impact of watershed development on soil erosion is already captured in terms of improved crop yields, for example, to value this effect again may result in double counting. This does not mean that all the benefits arising from reduced soil erosion are captured in measures of increased crop yields, but additional benefits (e.g., increased vegetation cover on non-agricultural land), need to be identified and valued separately.

Case Studies in India

Faced with the challenges of conducting cost–benefit analysis for watershed development, as well as time and budgetary constraints, few comprehensive economic appraisals have been completed in India. Perhaps the most complete study is Chopra et al.'s (1990) evaluation of the Sukhomajri project in Haryana. Although this study does not include environmental impacts, it includes on-site, off-site, private and public benefits and costs. Using shadow prices and a 12% discount rate, the benefit–cost ratio comes to 1.33. When distributional weights are used to increase the relative importance of gains to the poorer members of the community, the benefit–cost ratio rises to 1.78. Both ratios are greater than one, indicating a gain to society following the project.

Most other social cost–benefit analyses tend to exclude off-site impacts and non-marketed impacts. A useful compilation of studies is found in the 1991 issues of the *Indian Journal of Agricultural Economics* (IJAE). The general results from these studies are summarised by Kerr (1996); his main points are reproduced below.

First, Kerr finds that estimated returns to investments in watersheds are generally high, with benefit–cost ratios ranging from one to greater than two. While they leave out crucial off-site and non-marketed impacts which would be likely to raise projects' net benefits, the IJAE studies fail to consider two important problems. First, they have a tendency to attribute the causation of improved crop and livestock productivity to soil- and water-conservation inputs, even though the improvements may have been caused by other factors such as good weather. Second, they measure improvements achieved while government support continues, or just after support is ended, and assume these gains are sustained into the future. Kerr stresses that there is little or no evidence that the projects are sustained.

In 1997, the Central Soil and Water Conservation Research and Training Institute published a summary of economic evaluations undertaken by research institutes, state departments and other central or state organisations (Babu et al. 1997). Of the 29 watershed projects listed, all have benefit–cost ratios greater than 1.07, and one (Sutle, in the western Himalayas) has a ratio as high as 7.06. For those cases which calculated an internal rate of return, results varied between 17 and 67 per cent.

These results suggest that watershed development projects lead to higher returns than reported in the IJAE. Like the IJAE studies, however, the majority of these analyses leave out non-marketed and off-site impacts. Three cases include protective benefits such as reduced runoff and erosion, but it is not clear how these benefits are valued. In addition, the details of calculating the marketed benefits are not always clear, and a wide variety of techniques and assumptions are used in individual studies which prevents simple comparisons. Not only are different discount rates and time horizons used, but the studies appear to differ in the types of impacts they include.

Despite the measurement difficulties mentioned, the general picture given by existing studies is that watershed investments yield high returns. If off-site and non-marketed effects were added, the returns are likely to be even more impressive. These results are, however, at odds with growing evidence of project failure once the government or supporting agency withdraws. Either cost–benefit analysis needs to be revised to ensure it gives correct estimates, or an alternative technique needs to be developed. In what follows, we consider the reasons behind the failure of cost–benefit analysis to predict project sustainability as a first step in solving the problem.

Why Cost–Benefit Analysis does not Predict Project Sustainability

To understand why cost–benefit analysis fails to predict project sustainability, we need to look at the assumptions underlying the technique. Cost–benefit analysis is based on orthodox assumptions of perfect information, well-defined property rights, and complete markets. The orthodox model allows for isolated cases of market failure, e.g., externalities, which are dealt with through government intervention. Cost–benefit analysis serves as a tool for policy-makers to identify whether the benefits of intervention exceed the costs and, hence, whether a proposed intervention is efficient.

A central feature of conventional cost–benefit analysis is that it is not concerned with the efficiency implications of the distribution of costs and benefits arising from projects. In an orthodox world, the market would find a way to ensure all participants gain from a project which results in an aggregate net gain.

Orthodox assumptions are, however, not a true reflection of reality, and watershed projects are undertaken in an environment of imperfect information, poorly defined property rights, and incomplete markets. The lack of knowledge concerning physical linkages between soil- and water-conservation techniques and economic factors, and the existence of externalities, have already been emphasised. Missing credit markets is another market failure that is frequently highlighted. In addition, watersheds include common-pool resources and public goods that have poorly defined property rights. For these reasons, bargaining between gainers and losers involves risks, and may not happen. An increase in aggregate welfare does not necessarily lead to project sustainability. The failure of orthodox economics to deal with real-world problems lies at the heart of developments in 'new institutional economics', covered in the next section.

The failure of cost–benefit analysis to incorporate the problems posed by non-cooperation in projects has not gone unnoticed by planners. Stakeholder analysis is increasingly used to complement economic evaluations. Although the details of stakeholder may vary among applications, they all attempt to identify individuals with an interest in a project, the impact of a project on these stakeholders, the incentives facing stakeholders, and their capacity to block a project. Stakeholder analysis is implicitly assessing the private cost–benefit analysis of stakeholders and the potential for losers to disrupt implementation.

Although stakeholder analysis helps offset the failure of cost–benefit analysis to predict conflicts between stakeholders, it does not mean we should not improve cost–benefit analysis. The ability of cost–benefit analysis to give reliable results depends on the quality of the data it is based on. To the extent that cost–benefit analysis has been based on false assumptions of project sustainability, it will give misleading results. The next section gives an overview of the institutional approach to watershed development and argues that only when institutional aspects of projects are incorporated into cost–benefit analysis will its usefulness be reinstated.

An Institutional Approach to Watershed Development

New institutional economics Institutional economics emphasises that, in the real world, people are not fully informed and have to make decisions based on a limited set of data. They act with what 'new institutional economics' calls 'bounded rationality'. Moreover, gathering information is costly and uses scarce resources that may be used more productively elsewhere. Incomplete information opens up possibilities for individuals to act opportunistically and introduces risks in people's dealings with one another. In an uncertain world, markets will not always evolve to allocate resources, and non-market institutions become critical to economic activity.

The working rules that are part of an institutional framework may be informal social norms or enforceable laws. Modern institutional economics focuses on the role of property rights in influencing the allocation and utilisation of economic goods. Property rights are commonly defined as access rights which give the holder the right to use, appropriate returns from, and transfer the asset in question. Three types of property rights may be identified: (a) private property, where resources (or goods) are owned by individuals; (b) state property, where resources are owned by the government; and (c) common property, where resources are owned by a defined group. When none of these arrangements holds, a situation of open access may arise, where anyone can use the resource. Whereas the orthodox model only concerned itself with private property rights and the market system, new institutional economics investigates which property-rights system will maximise welfare under a specific set of constraints.

Closely linked to identifying the optimal property-rights system is the estimation of the costs of implementing and operating the system. Transaction-cost economics (Coase 1960) sees these costs as the main factor determining which institutional arrangement prevails. In a market system, transaction costs include the costs of establishing private property rights, costs of individuals searching for people to bargain with, costs of gathering information, costs of drawing up a contract, and costs of monitoring and enforcing that contract. If the transaction costs are greater than the expected benefit from a contract, then the bargain will not take place. Transaction-cost economists argue that society will seek to develop institutional structures that minimise the combination of production costs and transaction costs. Where market arrangements fail due to high transaction costs, for example, an alternative system, such as government administration or a cooperative arrangement, may be preferable. Whereas orthodox economists assume government intervention is necessary to overcome market failure, new institutional economics compare the transaction costs of alternative arrangements before making a decision.

Implications for watershed projects   New institutional economics may be applied in the design of watershed-development projects. As emphasised above, government intervention to solve watershed problems has not always resulted in lasting welfare improvements. Analysing the problem from an institutional perspective offers insights into improving project design.

Watersheds pose a challenge to the establishment of institutions as they are characterised by common-pool resources and public goods. Unlike private goods, common-pool resources and public goods are 'non-excludable': i.e., people cannot be excluded from using them. Public goods are also 'non-subtractable': if one person uses the resource, it does not reduce the amount available to others. Even though consumption of public goods cannot be limited, this will not affect the amount supplied. An example of a public good is national defence. One citizen's consumption of defence does not reduce anyone else's consumption. In fact, it is impossible for a nation's citizens not to consume the service. Common-pool resources pose a more immediate worry than public goods, as they may be depleted if overused. Examples of common-pool resources in India include common pastures, protected or unclassed forest, wastelands, and ponds.

Where the users of a resource such as grazing land do not cooperate, free-rider problems occur, and total production is lower than if everyone were to cooperate. Solving the free-rider problem requires the creation of institutions to ensure that the herders' dominant strategy is one of cooperation. Privatisation of the resource—generally proposed by economic orthodoxy—is not necessarily an optimal solution if the costs to a private owner of monitoring and enforcing rules for resource use (including payment) are high.

High-to-infinite transaction costs associated with private and state management of common-pool resources have led to a consensus that cooperation may offer the most efficient arrangement. A growing body of evidence from NGOs implementing participatory approaches to watershed development supports this theory. Chopra and Rao (1996) show that in five projects in Madhya Pradesh, Rajasthan and Maharashtra, a highly significant relationship between environmental improvement (e.g., a rise in the groundwater table or increased survival of planted trees) and increased participation exists.

Defining an optimal cooperative institution Which cooperative arrangement will be optimal? In the orthodox model, optimality is achieved when it is impossible to make anyone better off without making at least one other person worse off. This is called the 'Pareto-efficient outcome'. Defining an optimal outcome in an imperfect world that is constantly changing is, however, extremely complicated. As constraints alter, the transaction costs associated with alternative institutional arrangements change, and hence the optimal system also changes.

The difficulties associated with defining an optimum do not prevent the identification of institutions that are relatively efficient. In an imperfect world (such as the real world), an optimal institution can be defined as that which, selected from a group of alternatives, achieves its objective of organising economic activity efficiently, is sustainable (i.e., is supported by all those who participate), and does this at minimum cost. Little research comparing alternative cooperative institutional arrangements in different watershed situations has been done in India. Moreover few studies, inside or outside India, exist which try to calculate the transaction costs of cooperative institutions. Until more information is available, lessons from experiences gained by NGOs may guide policymakers as to which arrangements are relatively successful. Ostrom (1990) has conducted research into empirical results around the world and identified favourable conditions for the formation of self-governing and self-organised institutions (Box 2.1).

When a common-pool resource is managed through the cooperation of its users, having a clearly defined resource and group of users will make it easier and cheaper to negotiate rules, monitor the resource use, prevent unauthorised use, and ensure that all the stakeholders are in-

---

Box 2.1 Favourable Conditions for the Development of Self-Governing and Self-Organised Institutions

1. Clearly defined common-pool resources and users
2. Congruence between appropriation and provision rules and local conditions
3. High levels of participation by stakeholders
4. Accountable monitors
5. Graduated sanctions
6. Cheap and accessible conflict-resolution mechanisms
7. Recognition of local authority by the central authority
8. Nested enterprises for common-pool resources that are part of larger systems

Source: Ostrom (1990).

volved. Full participation is itself crucial for lowering the monitoring costs by reducing the risk of free-riding by non-participants. The second condition in Box 2.1 emphasises that the rules about who bears the costs of resource management (e.g., labour for forest and grazing areas) should be linked to the rules setting out how the benefits of improved resource productivity are distributed. This is necessary for the arrangement to be deemed fair.

Conditions four to seven relate to increasing the credibility of rules by ensuring that cheats will be caught and penalised. Recognition of local rules by the central authority is critical in increasing the power of local groups to enforce rules.

The last condition highlighted in Box 2.1 is the role played by nested enterprises in managing common-pool resources which are part of larger systems. Watershed development, for example, may be most efficiently organised by establishing several layers of management from the village level through to district and state levels, as is done in the IGWDP (see Extract 8.4). This approach helps to ensure management is done in a holistic way.

In addition to the factors identified in Box 2.1, Ostrom notes that smaller groups of well-informed individuals with common interests will face lower transaction costs than large diverse groups, and will be more likely to develop sustainable institutions. In addition, she stresses the potentially critical role played by a strong, charismatic leader in initiating cooperation.

Ostrom's conditions are useful in illustrating situations in which government planners may wish to develop self-organised, self-governing institutions to manage watershed development. What is needed, however, is data on alternative cooperative institutional structures, particularly complex ones such as those used in the IGWDP, that have been implemented and shown to work under less favourable conditions. With this information and estimates of the transaction costs, planners can build up a set of workable options.

Modifying Cost–Benefit Analysis

Incorporating transaction costs   Although there do not seem to be any studies that deal with transaction costs in a thorough way, the two examples outlined below incorporate some institution-building costs and give an insight into the potential importance of these costs.

Chopra et al.'s (1990) ex-post evaluation of the Sukhomajri project, extends cost–benefit analysis to incorporate institution-building costs.

In addition to the costs of building the engineering structures, establishing plantations, purchasing new cattle and equipment, etc., and the costs of maintaining the structures, Chopra et al. add the costs of training the villagers in conservation techniques, organisational leadership, and motivational inputs. The training costs were based on labour inputs by the government, the Ford Foundation and the CSWCRTI. Together, the training and motivational inputs may be classified as costs of institution building.

Given a 12 per cent discount rate and using shadow prices for labour and capital inputs, the benefit–cost ratio falls from 1.33, when these transaction costs are excluded, to 0.73 when they are included. This result is worrying, as it suggests that given the high costs of institution-building, the project may not have been an efficient investment from the government's perspective. Moreover, the full set of transaction costs has not been added. If costs of continued negotiation, monitoring, enforcing rules, etc., are added, it would lower the benefit–cost ratio further.

This conclusion needs to be qualified for several reasons First, the creation of enduring institutions is likely to contribute to more than one project, and the costs of establishing them should be spread between all the beneficiaries. Secondly, the benefit–cost ratio is calculated using a 12 per cent discount rate, which may be higher than the true opportunity cost of capital, or the true social-time preference. A third factor is that environmental benefits, such as improved water quality, are not included. Without more data it is difficult to judge the desirability of the Sukhomajri project. What is clear, however, is that transaction costs make a significant difference to the final evaluation and need to be included.

An economic evaluation of the Karnataka Watershed Development Project undertaken for DFID in 1995, represents another attempt to include institutional factors in cost–benefit analysis. Investments in training and community human-resource development, NGO training, and community savings-and-credit schemes are examples of institution-building costs included. Together they account for 34 per cent of the total project costs. In addition, the project proposal includes investment in non-land-based activities such as bakeries, bamboo-mat making and brickmaking as essential measures to ensure a spread of benefits to landless villagers. Expanding these activities would guarantee the landless, who are prevented from using the common-pool resource, an alternative source of livelihood and reduce their incentive to undermine the project. The development of non-land-based activities, amounting to

14 per cent of project costs, is essentially a payoff to the losers to alter their incentive structure and ensure cooperation is their dominant strategy. The risk with this approach, is that once eternal assistance is ended, the non-land activities may disappear, and conflicts between the losers and gainers may re-emerge. At that point, gainers may decide to compensate the losers themselves.

The results of the Karnataka evaluation are impressive. The internal rate of return comes to almost 50 per cent, well above the 12 per cent minimum favoured by the India Planning Commission. The largest net benefits were generated by tree output (fruits and leaves, timber, firewood and fodder), followed by benefits from non-land activities. Non-land estimates are based on investigations of businesses in neighbouring areas, as well as interviews with individuals. The net benefits from improved crop output were the third-largest contributor. Although the author stresses caution in interpreting the results, sensitivity analysis shows that the conclusions are robust when the values of benefits from the common-pool resources and non-land activities are reduced by 10 per cent.

Although the Karnataka project analysis includes several institution-building costs, as does the Sukhomajri cost–benefit analysis, it does not include longer-term costs associated with the operation of these new structures. To do this, however, it would be necessary to develop a detailed plan of the proposed institutional arrangement. Although devising a workable institutional structure is complicated, leaving out transaction costs may generate misleading results and a misallocation of resources

Multi-Criteria Analysis: An Alternative

The failure of conventional cost–benefit analysis to incorporate institutional factors, and the difficulties of including non-marketed environmental impacts into project evaluations, lie behind Chopra and Rao's (1996) adoption of multi-criteria analysis. This approach allows planners to rank projects according to a number of criteria, and impacts do not have to be quantified in money terms. Chopra and Rao identify economic, cost, environmental and institutional criteria to evaluate projects. Economic impacts are expressed in terms of volume changes (e.g., increased crop yields); costs are measured in money terms; environmental effects are given ordinal scores (e.g., the level of runoff may be scored –3 to +3); and institutional factors are given ordinal scores (the level of participation is scored –3 to +3). All the identified effects of a project are then summarised in an 'effects table' and combined, based on pre-determined weights, to arrive at a final score for the project. The final score is used to rank alternatives. As in cost–benefit analysis, each effect's score captures the impact of the project as compared to the 'without project' scenario. Positive scores are given to beneficial impacts, negative scores to damaging impacts.

Chopra and Rao compare five projects that differ in the technology used, location, and the level of participation of local groups. In addition, they experiment with different weighting schemes and levels of uncertainty to see how the results alter. Of the findings highlighted by the authors, the one relevant here is that participatory projects score higher than government-run projects in all cases. The discrepancy decreases when uncertainty rises, provided that the government projects incorporate people's views in their designs. Chopra and Rao's results support the argument that the success of watershed development requires local participation.

Chopra and Rao's multi-criteria analysis has not been widely reviewed, and difficulties may yet be uncovered. One error may arise from double-counting when Chopra and Rao sum economic effects (e.g., changes in crop yields, livestock output, fodder and fuelwood production) and environmental effects (e.g., changes in the sediment yield, runoff levels and the water-table height). Gregerson et al. (1987) have stressed that environmental effects of watershed development may be valued in terms of their impacts on economic variables. The impacts of contour bunding, for example, are valued according to improved crop yields and livestock production, rather than according to the implications for runoff and erosion rates. To include both sets of impacts may result in double-counting, unless people are found to value reduced runoff or erosion for their own sakes. Environmental effects that are not captured by economic variables, such as water quality, should be valued separately, but these are not included in Chopra and Rao's study.

A further observation on Chopra and Rao's analysis is that their inclusion of institutional aspects of watershed development is one-sided. In their analysis, participation is included as a beneficial effect, but no attention is given to the costs of involving people. This approach is misleading because high levels of participation achieved by NGOs are not necessarily replicable.

In addition to the data problems mentioned above, two criticisms of multi-criteria analysis as a technique for project appraisal should be emphasised. Firstly, despite claims by the proponents of multi-criteria analysis that the approach avoids problems associated with valuing non-marketed items, the weighting system it uses is simply another method of valuation. Weights reflect the relative importance of items, which is precisely what prices do. Moreover, the introduction of weights chosen by the researcher may mean that multi-criteria analysis is more subjective than cost–benefit analysis.

A second criticism of multi-criteria analysis is that it provides a ranking of selected projects and does not give projects absolute values, e.g., net present value, which can be used to compare projects to alternatives not included in the initial analysis. Moreover, although multi-criteria analysis will identify which project is the most desirable in a group, it does not say whether it should be undertaken at all. Just because a project is ranked first, this does not mean that its benefits are greater than its costs.

Taken together, the theoretical and data problems with Chopra and Rao's analysis may be significant. Although data problems may be more easily rectified, the theoretical critique is harder to overcome. Unless a new weighting system can be convincingly shown to offer improved valuation method than the price system, there seems to be little reason to prefer multi-criteria analysis over cost–benefit analysis.

Conclusion

This Extract proposes that cost–benefit analysis has given over-optimistic results for watershed projects in India, largely because it has been based on false assumptions of project sustainability. These assumptions have their roots in orthodox economics, which overlooks problems caused by the unequal distribution of benefits from projects, and neglects the need for institutions to guide the management of common-pool resources. Developments in new institutional economics, supported by field experience, have highlighted the need to incorporate institutions as a critical component of watershed projects. By modifying cost–benefit analysis to incorporate the transaction costs associated with the building and operation of institutions, its usefulness may be restored.

Before institutional aspects of watershed development can be included in cost–benefit analysis, however, the details of the desired institutional arrangement and its transaction costs need to be set out. The dynamics of specific contexts, however, make it near impossible to identify an optimal institution. A more useful approach would be to identify workable institutional structures and the costs associated with these, and select the one that maximises welfare. To do this, a database on empirical experiences with alternative institutional arrangements needs to be built up.

The failure of conventional cost–benefit analysis to include institutional aspects of watershed development as well as the difficulty of incorporating important non-marketed environmental effects spurred Chopra and Rao to adopt multi-criteria analysis as an alternative evaluation technique. Significant theoretical and data problems, however, argue against replacing cost–benefit analysis with multi-criteria analysis.

This Extract has not yet considered the question of what role the government should have in promoting watershed projects. This question is fundamental, since the form of intervention (i.e., whether the government acts as implementer or facilitator, how much it spends, and where the money is spent) is likely to impact on stakeholders incentives and, hence, project outcomes. It is crucial that alternative forms of government intervention in watershed development are analysed as part of research into alternative institutional arrangements.

As long as the government continues to initiate or implement watershed projects, it will need tools to help it allocate its resources. Despite its limitations, cost–benefit analysis offers a useful method to draw together numerous project impacts in a systematic way and provide planners with important information to make decisions. As with any tool, however, cost–benefit analysis is only as good as the data it is based on. The priority of current data collection should be to improve our understanding of institutional arrangements that work to support lasting watershed development.

3   Strengthening Participatory Processes with Emphasis on Increasing the Stake of the Poor

CONCEPTS AND CONCERNS

The search for equitable approaches to watershed development is driven by two central concerns. First, that the poor own only limited private resources, but generally have rights of access and usufruct to the commons on which their livelihoods heavily rely. The commons constitute a high proportion of individual watersheds in many semi-arid areas and, under current government policy, most are likely to remain as common-pool resources for the foreseeable future. Drawing on data from Andhra Pradesh, Jodha (1986) has argued that poor households depend more on the commons than richer ones do. They receive the bulk of their fuel supplies and fodder from these areas. Collecting products from the commons is an important source of employment and income, especially during times when other opportunities are almost non-existent. The livelihoods of poorer people may be disrupted by rehabilitation if access to the commons is restricted in order to promote, for instance, the regeneration of grazing or forest. In the longer term, as the commons become visibly more productive, they are likely to become the target for takeover by more powerful groups. In both short and long term, therefore, there is a need for thorough and consistent efforts to defend the rights of the poor to existing resources, and ensure that they obtain appropriate levels of access to new benefit streams.

The second concern is that there are important linkages between equity and sustainability, both institutional and environmental. For instance, if the poor are unable to maintain or enhance their livelihoods through access to existing or new benefit streams, then the tendency will increase for common-property-resource management arrangements—either within or outside the watershed—to break down into an open-access 'free-for-all'. Similarly, if common-pool resources are taken over by the more wealthy and so effectively privatised, then public funds—far from creating (as intended) a resource to benefit those with few assets—effectively subsidise the creation of a private resource by the more wealthy.

These considerations need to be located in the wider context of population growth and environmental degradation. Although the proportion of poverty has decreased by 20% since India's independence, the absolute numbers of poor people have doubled. India's food needs will double over the next 30 years, some 600m tonnes of topsoil are being lost each year, and deforestation and groundwater depletion are severe in many areas. In Box 3.1, biases against the poor in the watershed-development context are grouped into the three main categories of investment, technological and capital-formation biases.

Increases in population pressure have in some cases led to the breakdown of traditional common-property management arrangements, leading to a vicious spiral of free-for-all open access and inability of the poor to engage in long-term environmental restoration. The key step to a win–win dynamic is the creation of equitable and transparent institutions to manage the commons. Once these generate additional benefits, a number of positive economic and social effects follow. For instance, they allow seasonal migration to be reduced, so enhancing family stability. They may also allow the work done by children to be reduced, so increasing the prospects that they will be sent to school, and that parents will press for adequate educational services. In the long term, rates of economic growth in urban areas may continue to outstrip those in rural areas, stimulating continued rural–urban migration. However, for the medium term the priorities are to identify ways in which the poor can be supported in identifying their needs and asserting their rights in relation to watershed development, with the objective of creating robust institutions capable of managing the environment in a sustainable fashion.

A number of NGO- and donor-funded projects have attempted to address the challenges outlined in Table 3.1. In the remainder of this chapter, we first draw out the generic characteristics of these approaches, then examine how adequately public-sector projects and programmes have taken up the lessons deriving from NGO approaches. Finally we present a number of case studies of how equity issues have been addressed.

Table 3.1 Classification of Biases against the Poor in Watershed Development

Investment biases	Disproportionate amounts are spent on private lands, usually located in the more productive lower lands within a watershed, and usually owned by the relatively wealthy
Technological biases	Over-emphasis on water harvesting structures likely to be useful to better-off farmers in the lower slopes
	Under-emphasis on soil and moisture harvesting measures in the upper reaches
	General disregard of indigenous approaches to soil and water conservation
Capital-formation biases	Opportunities for savings and credit, the creation of assets and infrastructure, the creation of human capital (leadership skills), and institutional and social capital are all biased towards the wealthier areas and individuals within a watershed
	Skills in, for instance, assertiveness, leadership and conflict resolution are rarely found among the weaker sectors

Source: Mascarenhas, 1998

GENERIC FEATURES OF NGO AND DONOR-FUNDED APPROACHES

The following is a composite of 'best practices' drawn from a number of NGO and donor experiences. There is no suggestion that all agencies follow all aspects of this, but where possible, examples of organisations are given which pursue one or other aspect.

Village identification   One criterion widely used is that—following exploratory contacts—the project agency should not become involved until requested to do so by a substantial portion of the village population. Usually, the agency will have made clear what it is or is not able to offer, and on what terms. The detailed 'guidelines on participation' of the Indo-German Watershed Development Programme (IGWDP 1996) make village-selection procedures clear (see Extract 3.3). One criterion is that the villagers may be required to demonstrate a capacity for working together on some communal project such as the construction of a road or well. Often, agencies select villages having a high proportion of scheduled tribes or scheduled castes, which may be less socially stratified than mixed-caste villages. Specifically in terms of watershed rehabilitation, there may be a tendency to select villages whose administrative boundaries coincide with the topographical limits of a micro-watershed. The Rural Development Trust in Anantapur has argued for more rigorous criteria for selection of villages if poverty-alleviation objectives are to be achieved (Reddy 1998; see Extract 3.1).

Mobilisation NGOs place considerable emphasis on developing skills in rural people's leadership, conflict-resolution abilities, and capacity to identify the full economic, social and political contexts of the disadvantages they suffer, and eventually to plan joint action to address these problems, or to make demands on, for instance, public-sector services which are nominally available to them. Many will take sufficient time to allow leaders to emerge from initial meetings, and will provide a supportive role in responding to requests to help in the above, or in providing training in the necessary interpersonal or leadership spheres. Mascarenhas (1998) describes the experiences of the NGO OUTREACH in pursuing development as a learning approach (see Extract 7.1).

Entry point/focus group activities Almost universally, early in the process NGOs aim to identify any existing, moderately homogeneous, groups which are undertaking economic activities (such as small-scale artisanal production, marketing, or savings-and-credit), or other activities such as women-and-children's health care. The NGO will support these by helping to expand their activities within or beyond the existing area, as appropriate. The formation of rotating credit funds with an external loan, or the creation of savings-and-credit schemes, are often a means of achieving this. NGOs often also see these focus-group activities as a practical context in which rural people can develop leadership, negotiation and assertiveness skills in a relatively secure peer group before they enter the potentially much more conflictive arena of defending their rights and making decisions on watersheds. Such skills are seen as essential if the poorer sectors are successfully to resist exploitation by the better-off of the benefits from rehabilitated watersheds.

Resolution of outstanding disputes Some NGOs make a particular point of helping to resolve any disputes over land and other assets, in the belief that watershed rehabilitation will be threatened by such disputes becoming more acute as resource productivity rises. Support for resolving such disputes is likely to be needed over several years in the more intractable cases, yet it constitutes a fundamental dimension of the work of such NGOs as Seva Mandir (Extract 3.4) and PEDO (Vyas, pers. comm.).

Participatory planning Once the above actions have been taken, consultations can begin with the various interest groups in the village. These aim to establish what rights exists for access to resources; what responsibilities there are for maintaining them; how livelihoods would be affected by different rehabilitation options; and what safeguards need to be put in place. This assessment can be accompanied by an exploration of the current status and production potential of the biophysical resource, using such well-known participatory rural appraisal techniques as transects and participatory mapping. These maps will then generally form the basis for the development of a watershed-rehabilitation plan. The approach of Danida in promoting participatory planning is outlined in Extract 3.2 from the account by Seth and Damgaard-Larsen (1998).

Resource-management agreements Before rehabilitation starts, NGOs will generally encourage village groups to come to agreement on how resources—especially common-pool resources—are to be managed. This may involve the 'social fencing' of pastures and forest areas: access may be prevented altogether for a period until the resource is rehabilitated, and then permitted on a rotational basis. Production systems may also be modified: open grazing may be restricted to certain seasons, or may be abandoned altogether in favour of cut-and-carry feeding. Clearly, where this is the case, consideration has to be given to changes in the demands on labour time of women and children, for example, who generally have the main responsibility for tending livestock. Agreement will also have to be reached on rights of access to additional groundwater in farming areas, generated as a result of the project. For instance, it may be appropriate to ban the sinking of deep tubewells or the cultivation of certain water-demanding crops such as rice and sugarcane, since both of these practices will give undue advantage to the (usually better-off) farmers already owning substantial arable land and having access to groundwater. The IGWDP has encouraged communities to ban both open grazing and the sinking of deep tubewells (Farrington and Lobo 1997; see also Extract 8.4). Where additional groundwater or surface-stored water becomes available as a result of rehabilitation, NGOs will generally encourage decisions by the community on who should benefit from these, and what form their exploitation should take.

Implementing rehabilitation Many NGO approaches follow 'ridge-to-valley' rehabilitation, partly because the poor rely more heavily on resources in the upper slopes. Such approaches also permit the siting and construction of control structures on the lower slopes to be planned more rationally. This is because the degree of percolation achieved through revegetation will by then be known, and structures can be designed which are no larger than necessary to cope with the residual surface flows. NGOs' support for rehabilitation is generally premised on the regeneration of indigenous vegetation, the use of traditional methods of construction for check-dams, etc. (as far as possible), and the employment of local labour. On the latter point, particular emphasis may be given to creating employment opportunities of a kind (and at timings) that suit the most disadvantaged, and to ensuring that work rates and wages are fixed equitably between men and women. Additional income-earning opportunities may be channelled to these in the form of, for instance, management of nurseries for tree seedlings. Where land under the control of the Forest Department falls within a watershed, NGOs may attempt to negotiate JFM agreements in order to bring it into rehabilitation. In reality, the history of JFM in India is uneven, with many Forest Department staff reluctant to abandon entirely their former 'forest protection' philosophy. Examples do, however, exist in which the larger NGOs have succeeded in implementing JFM agreements successfully in the context of watershed rehabilitation (Extract 8.4).

Creation of a watershed fund By the time watershed rehabilitation is implemented, many villagers will already have gained substantial experience in generating savings and credit funds in relation to focus-group activities. There are substantial arguments in favour of building on this experience by creating a watershed fund, which can be drawn upon by common agreement in order to implement maintenance activities. Such funds are provided for in many NGO programmes and in the 1994 Common Guidelines. They can be created by a range of methods. For instance, the project authorities can calculate the monetary value equivalent of the time donated by village people to certain activities, and deposit this into the fund. This is the method favoured by the Indo-German Watershed Development Programme (Extract 3.3). Others argue strongly for insisting that villagers make a contribution of their own, since this ensures a substantial stake by the villagers in the project's continuing maintenance (Extract 3.1 by Malla Reddy and Extract 8.2 by Shah). Sharma and Virgo (Extract 8.6) provide a comprehensive account of village savings and investment in the European Union-supported Doon Valley Project.

Establishing wider linkages Cross-visits by villagers who are developing their own ideas about watershed rehabilitation to similar localities which are further along in the process often provide more powerful insights than any amount of discussion. Many NGOs attach considerable weight to cross-learning. In addition, some organise themselves as demonstration sites which other NGOs, government organisations and donors can visit (see the example of Ralegaon Sidhi described by Hazare et al. 1996).

Follow-through and exit strategies   NGOs generally find it difficult to design exit strategies well in advance, though there are exceptions (Farrington and Lobo 1997, Extract 8.4). There is a view among many that village groups will rarely be able to defend their interests successfully. Writing about the somewhat different context of groundwater exploitation, Sinha and Sinha (1996: 139) note that, despite periods of NGO support to the communities ranging from 7 to 12 years 'the social organisations or community groups involved do not appear to have reached a stage yet where external support...is no longer required'.

Notwithstanding the dangers of creating dependency that continuing NGO presence may bring, there will no doubt be instances in which only the NGO initially involved will be able to meet continuing needs, for instance, in an advisory or arbitration mode. Where the funds for rehabilitation are provided by the NGO itself, there may be little difficulty in achieving a continuing presence. However, where resources are time-bound and provided, for instance, under Common Guidelines projects, then this may be more difficult unless some clustering of watershed sites is achieved so that the NGO can remain present in the vicinity. Where resources are channelled through the *panchayati raj* system, as happens in some states (e.g., Madhya Pradesh) under the Common Guidelines, and will increasingly occur as more states implement the provisions of the 73rd Constitutional Amendment (see Chapter 6), NGOs may find it difficult to argue against the decisions of a democratically elected body, even if they perceive that the poor are disadvantaged by those decisions. This is one part of a wider set of tensions between democratically elected bodies and NGOs, whose office-bearers are not elected, and whose channels of accountability at times remain unclear.

The case study of Seva Mandir's experience presented below (Extract 3.4) illustrates many facets of the above approaches, including the long period of support needed by an NGO in order for the rural poor to assert themselves against the vested interests of local elites, the difficulties of dealing with land-dispute problems, and the emergence of group leaders as a local political force.

In the experience of Seva Mandir, land encroachments by the better-

off significantly disempower the poor, not only by decreasing the availability of common property, but also by creating an atmosphere in which
their access to the commons is viewed as a favour rather than as a right.
This phenomenon may also limit the pressure the poor can bring for
accountability by state agencies, and may undermine their capability to
press for new management practices that could help to rejuvenate the
commons.

Later in this book (Extract 8.5) we draw on a paper by Kolavalli (1998)
reviewing the effectiveness of a number of watershed projects implemented under different guidelines. He draws conclusions on approaches
to social organisation and programme design that have worked, and suggests what preconditions need to be in place for successful scaling up.

Government Guidelines on Equity

There are two main sets of Guidelines for watershed development at
the central government level: those of the National Watershed Development Programme for Rainfed Areas (NWDPRA) under the Ministry
of Agriculture and Cooperation, and those (i.e., the 1994 Common
Guidelines) under the Ministry of Rural Areas and Employment. The
NWDPRA guidelines contain no specific provisions concerning poverty and equity.

The 1994 Common Guidelines governing projects, programmes and
schemes under the Ministry of Rural Areas and Employment are based
strongly on NGO experience, and they are in many respects similar to
the guidelines governing the projects implemented by NGOs and funded
by the Council for Advancement of People's Action and Rural Technology. Some of their positions and provisions are as follows:

- They suggest that substantial lessons are to be learned from NGOs'
  efforts in participatory watershed development, arguing that 'success is achieved through the government's participation in people's
  programmes rather than the other way round' (section 7).
- The Guidelines urge 'special emphasis to improve the economic
  and social condition of the resource-poor and the disadvantaged...
  through... more equitable distribution of the benefits of land and
  water resources development and the consequent biomass production... greater access to income generating opportunities and focus
  on their human resource development' (section 14).
- They stress participation of all groups in decisions on rehabilitation, and their willingness to undertake maintenance of the assets
  created. Towards this end, the Guidelines envisage the creation of

'focus-', or 'self-help groups' embracing some 50 per cent of those directly or indirectly dependent on the watershed, with separate self-help groups for the scheduled castes and tribes. They also envisage that 'user' groups will be established from those relying on one or other resource within the watershed.

- It is expected that under the Guidelines, villages will be selected for rehabilitation which have a large proportion of scheduled castes and tribes. One of the three watershed volunteers designated to work in collaboration with the Watershed Secretary will be from a scheduled caste or tribe. 'A resolution from the *gram panchayat* [shall be obtained] to the effect that [it] shall be willing to share the benefits from [common] assets with the weaker sections of society such as scheduled castes, scheduled tribes, women and other persons below the poverty line in an equitable manner' (section 25).

- Priorities for watershed rehabilitation are to be consistent with the needs of the poor (section 72). The Guidelines urge cooperation to reach decisions on how new resources should be allocated, but there should be an intention that 'the benefits are shared equitably with a tilt in favour of the poor and the weak, particularly when public investments are being made for the creation of common assets' (section 75).

- At village level, the watershed committee should have 'adequate representation' (generally interpreted as 30 per cent) of women, of scheduled castes and tribes, and any other weaker section (section 37).

- In states where the 73rd Constitutional Amendment has been implemented, *panchayati raj* institutions at district and village levels are taking over the allocation of watershed development funds. Here, the prospects of influence by the poor on decisions is enhanced by the provision that at least 30 per cent of places on the *gram panchayats* must be reserved for scheduled castes and tribes, and women.

Performance of Resource-Based Programmes

Viewed in the context of the predominantly top-down planning and service delivery that characterises the Indian public sector, these initiatives are little short of revolutionary. It would be surprising if the capacity existed, especially in public-sector implementing agencies, to implement them smoothly. A major review of the quality of implementation of the Common Guidelines was instigated by the Ministry of Rural Areas and Employment in late 1997. This review (Turton et al. 1998:

iv) generally found that the response to the Common Guidelines at all levels had been strongly positive; however, it noted a number of implementation shortcomings, many of them in respect of poverty and equity provisions.

Overall, the review noted that 'to provide the poor and women with an equitable share of benefits requires more effort and vigilance than most implementing agencies can currently provide'. The review recognised that to remedy this would be a long-term process, involving capacity building and sensitisation at several levels. Specifically, the review found that inadequate time and resources were set aside for entry-point and group-formation activities, and that the scope for links with existing groups of the weaker sectors was not being fully exploited. There was also seen to be inadequate specification in watershed action-plans of how the benefits accruing from common land—of particular importance to the livelihoods of the poor—were to be shared.

In relation to the poverty-alleviation aspects of the Guidelines, the review recommended that there should be stronger roles for social scientists in the watershed development teams and elsewhere, that there should be clear criteria for the selection and (where necessary) de-selection of project implementation agencies.

The review recommended the establishment of systems of training to ensure adequate sensitisation to equity issues, and of monitoring and evaluation so that any need for course corrections could be identified at an early stage.

All the evidence suggests that it is extremely difficult to ensure that the rights of the poor are safeguarded in watershed rehabilitation, as in any other developmental activity. Nevertheless, what is certain is that if only weak efforts are made to do so, then the lion's share of the resource will be taken over by the wealthier.

Box 3.1 outlines some of the exploitative social relations noted by Baumann (1998) in Western Orissa. Clearly, the stronger these are, the less likely are the poor to benefit from watershed development. A further review by Adolph and Turton (1998) examined some earlier projects under the 1994 Guidelines, plus several projects under earlier guidelines in two districts of Andhra Pradesh. There has been some success in forming and sustaining women's self-help groups, especially for thrift and credit purposes, and especially where these were supported by an established NGO. However, groups of resource-users were generally weaker and more difficult to sustain. Government project implementation agencies generally paid much less attention to group formation.

In respect of group formation, the 1994 Guidelines are largely premised on the notion that the poor will best develop those skills necessary for negotiating watershed development (leadership, self-confidence, conflict-resolution and so on) if they are encouraged to do so first in homogeneous self-help groups. These findings show clearly that much more effort will have to be put into the group formation if such prior strengthening of the negotiating capacity of the disadvantaged is to succeed. If it does not succeed, then the prospects for equitable sharing of the benefits of watershed development are much reduced.

Resource-based Programmes in a Sustainable Rural Livelihood Perspective

Growing awareness that the poor derive their livelihoods from multiple sources, and that development efforts must build on the assets they possess, has led to a number of conceptual advances concerning poverty alleviation. In pragmatic terms, these have been brought together in what have come to be known as 'sustainable rural livelihood' approaches. The conceptual background to sustainable rural livelihood approaches, together with practical indications of how they might be implemented, are reviewed by Carney (1998).

Briefly, underpinning sustainable rural livelihood approaches is the notion that people rely on five main kinds of capital assets:

Box 3.1 Unequal Social Relations in Western Orissa

In a field study in mid-1998 in Bolangir and Nuapara Districts, Baumann (1998) found the following:

- high rates of interest chronic indebtedness and the 'bonding' of both land and labour by moneylenders;
- control by a powerful few over seasonal migration to urban areas, so that little remains once accommodation and travel costs, and advances (and related interest charges) have been deducted;
- the all-pervasive strength of the caste-reinforcing Jat Samaj, which enforces (often at the expense of lower castes and women) decisions on disputes over land and domestic matters;
- a long history of dependency by people on relief interventions from government;
- often a wide gap between what is allocated to the poor and what is actually delivered. For instance, only 10 days of the promised 100 days of labour per adult allocated to those districts under the Employment Assurance Scheme are actually delivered, funds for this remainder being lost in the 'system';
- little accountability by the *gram panchayats* to the *gram sabha*, and unremitting pressure to deliver block votes to members of state legislative assembly and others.

- *natural capital:* resources such as land, water, forests and biodiversity, and environmental cycles (water, nutrients etc);
- *social capital:* social resources such as trust, networks, groups, social relations, and associations;
- *human capital:* skills, knowledge, good health and ability to work;
- *physical capital:* basic infrastructure such as transport, shelter, communications and energy;
- *financial capital:* financial resources and services such as savings, access to credit, bank loans, remittances, and pensions.

The extent to which the poor can derive benefit streams from these assets depends primarily on arrangements governing ownership of, or access to, the assets. It also depends on the extent of vulnerability faced by rural people, and their options for responding to vulnerability as it arises. The way capital assets impact on livelihood outcomes is determined by the types of structures (government, private commercial, and NGO) and processes (laws, policies, markets, and other institutions) relevant to low-income people. There are two main ways in which these structures and processes impact on livelihoods:

- they are critical in determining who gains access to which type of asset, and the effective value of that asset;
- in conjunction with individuals' asset status, they help to define which livelihood strategies or activities—natural resource-based or otherwise —are open and attractive.

Three broad clusters of livelihood strategy are open to rural people. These are: (a) the intensification or extensification of natural resource-based activities; (b) the pursuit of options not primarily dependent on natural resources within the immediate locality; and (c) short- or longer-term migration in order to take advantage of opportunities available elsewhere. These are not mutually exclusive: in reality, people will switch among opportunities within each of these areas, according to changes in their own requirements, and in structures, institutions, the vulnerability context and the values of benefit flows obtainable from each in relation to the amount of effort required.

Benefit streams, in turn, impact on livelihood outcomes in a number of possible ways: increased income, increased wellbeing, reduced vulnerability, improved food security, and a more sustainable use of the natural resource base.

Sustainable rural livelihood approaches are being pursued by at least one agency (DFID) in relation to poverty in the context of watershed development. Early experiences suggest four important implications.

First, to concentrate only on developing natural capital (as watershed development primarily does) is to limit the range of options open to the poor for livelihood enhancement. The development of other assets (human, financial, physical, social) is important. The approach provides a framework that explicitly links these with natural capital, and with desired outcomes including reduced vulnerability;

Second, natural resource-based intensification (or extensification) has to be seen in the context of other livelihood options. Both currently and particularly for the long term, migration may be a desirable option, and expectations regarding labour inputs by the poor into watershed development need to be based on realistic assessments of likely levels of migration and of uptake of local options which are not based on natural resources.

Third, careful interpretation of sustainable rural livelihood perspectives make clear the specific sequences of effort are necessary to build up or draw upon different types of asset in order to achieve desirable outcomes. This is already implicit in, for instance, the build-up of human and social capital prior to watershed rehabilitation, for which resources are made available under the Common Guidelines, and which tends to form a strong component of NGO-led projects. DFID experience in preparation of the Western Orissa Rural Livelihoods Project in late 1998 (authors' observation) suggested that indebtedness and low health status constrained the livelihoods of the poor more than the quality of natural resources in themselves. As in many other settings, it was also clear that access to natural resources was likely to be an arena contested between poor and better-off. The decision was therefore taken to introduce a two-year preparatory period. During this time, the emphasis would be on interventions likely to be uncontested by the better-off, but which would break the cycle of indebtedness trapping the poor, and strengthen their human and social capital in ways that would equip them for negotiating access to natural resources under subsequent watershed rehabilitation. These included the creation of sustainable local capability for rehabilitating existing drinking-water supplies; the creation of small-scale credit schemes, and the establishment of backyard activities such as vegetable production.

Fourth, the role of processes and institutions in determining the type and level of livelihood outcomes resulting from different types of intervention is crucial. Sustainable rural livelihood approaches suggest that the types and combinations of process and institutions that are desirable will vary according to local circumstances, and so cannot be generalised. This point is revisited when a number of strands of argument are drawn together in Chapter 8.

Conclusions

The livelihoods of the poor in semi-arid areas are made up of a number of elements. Some may farm small plots of land; many others will rely to a high degree on small herds of their own livestock, on herding for others, selling fuel and fodder, petty trading and artisanal work. Perhaps most important is casual, unskilled employment within the village, in neighbouring areas or, on a seasonally migrant basis, in distant urban areas.

Watershed development, in the most favourable cases, may make a substantial contribution to enhancing the livelihoods of the poor. However such impact is generally dependent on a degree of empowerment generated through long-term support by NGOs, and there remain questions over how far it can be sustained once support organisations begin to withdraw.

Major new efforts towards poverty alleviation being pursued by the Indian government under the 1994 Common Guidelines are appropriately focused in broad terms on poverty and equity, but need to provide a longer period for capacity building and focus-group activities prior to the planning of rehabilitation. They also face substantial challenges at the implementation level, especially where government organisations serve as project-implementing agencies. As we argue in Chapter 7, capacity building is undoubtedly one appropriate response to these difficulties. However, it can only become fully effective where longer-term constraints on the performance of the public sector are alleviated, including restrictions on excessively frequent transfer of staff and the introduction of appropriate performance criteria and reward systems.

In the final analysis, the extent to which resource-based programmes such as watershed development can help to alleviate the poverty of those who have little land of their own and rely on customary or usufruct rights to the commons will be highly dependent on local social and economic conditions. Watershed programmes can, if designed and implemented with great care, benefit the poor substantially where the traditions of respecting such rights are strong. However, some areas are characterised by highly exploitative social relations. There must be doubts over the extent to which resource-based programmes can overcome severe problems of social structure, in which the poor are systematically exploited and excluded not only from their rights, but also from information about their rights (see Box 3.1).

A sustainable rural livelihoods approach offers a framework for considering how resource-based livelihood options interface with others. It helps identify the most appropriate options for drawing on or building up capital assets according to local circumstances, or for addressing necessary changes in structures and processes. With careful interpretation, it also allows identification of appropriate sequences of intervention.

EXTRACT 3.1
SELECTION CRITERIA AND CONDITIONS FOR SUCCESS IN RURAL DEVELOPMENT TRUST, ANANTAPUR[1]

MALLA REDDY[2]

Cost Sharing by Farmers and User Groups

Watershed development aims to benefit people by stabilising ecological carrying capacity. Relevant activities include soil and moisture conservation (contour bunding), rainwater harvesting (check-dams) and afforestation. These activities have been carried out in Indian villages for the past 50 years in a non-integrated manner. But until now farmers have never been asked to share costs, nor even make token contributions. Even now various agencies implement these activities in neighbouring villages without any local contribution. When farmers or user groups in villages are asked to contribute 10 per cent of the cost, they are surprised, since similar work has been done in the next village without any contribution. These attitudes are symptomatic of a 'dependency syndrome'.

On the other hand, the costs of other types of activities, such as horticulture, irrigation bore-wells, crop investments, and the mechanisation of wells, which are undertaken on private lands by farmers, are almost entirely borne by farmers. This is because they are direct investments, with direct and immediate benefit to the farmers. For these kinds of activities, only small and marginal farmers are given some subsidies and incentives by the government.

---

[1] Source: Reddy (1998).

[2] Director (Ecology), Rural Development Trust, Bangalore Highway, Anantapur 515001, Andhra Pradesh.

Despite these attitudes, and despite the risk of crop loss attributable to drought, it remains necessary to incorporate an element of cost sharing to whatever degree is possible. The barriers for cost sharing have to be broken down steadily. It may be hard to obtain a 10 per cent contribution from farmers at first. If so, it may be worth starting with a smaller percentage. A particular advantage lies in the creation of a 'watershed development fund' consisting of people's contributions, which can subsequently be used for the maintenance of common assets. The concept of cost sharing will succeed only after building people's participation.

Criteria and Process in Selection of a Watershed Village

The criteria followed for selecting villages for watershed rehabilitation under the Rural Development Trust, Anantapur, included biophysical indicators, matched with some social indicators such as literacy, landlessness, and problems of drinking water. The guiding principle is the urgency with which watershed development is needed in a given village. The biophysical indicators (rainfall, sediment yield, vegetation, groundwater level, etc.) are taken from the Andhra Pradesh Remote Sensing Agency's data.

At this stage of implementing a participatory watershed development programme, the 'success factors' in the village are also critically important. The choice of a village has to be based on the 'success criteria' matched with the biophysical need in the village. Experience in 'successful watersheds' suggests that unity and collective leadership in a village are critical for effective watershed development.

In this respect, it is important to be choosy. In addition to a village's need for watershed development, an important criterion should be whether the people in the village are willing to take initiative and leadership in a participatory approach.

In the first-generation phase of a participatory watershed development programme, villages need to be selected where a participatory approach can be successfully demonstrated. This would have a motivating effect on neighbouring villages and create demand for replication in neighbouring villages. This has a potential to promote social equity and harmony in place of faction and bloodshed in conflict-ridden villages. It may transform them from 'bloodshed' to 'watershed' development. Thus watershed development can be turned into a social movement. Such should be the strategy for replication. The operationalisation of a fully participatory approach in 'socially feasible' villages in watershed development will slowly reverse the 'top-down', conventional approach of government, even in other government development programmes.

Pre-conditions for Selecting a Village

People in a village must fulfil certain pre-conditions if that village is to be considered for watershed development. Typically, selection depends on the following. First, from remote-sensing data, macro-watersheds are prioritised based on their physical parameters of soil, water, vegetation, etc. This allows the generation of a list of priority villages for each district. A *gram sabha* convened by the *gram panchayat* or by informal leaders, with at least two-thirds of the voters present, should unanimously resolve:

- that the Rural Development Trust be requested to select their village for integrated watershed development;
- that the leaders, the *gram panchayat* and the people are willing to work actively and in unity, beyond the interests of political parties, caste groups and factions, for the overall development of the village;
- that the village community is prepared to follow the watershed guidelines and form a watershed association, watershed committee, user groups and self-help groups, on a consensus basis, and to follow the guidelines;
- that the families concerned are prepared to contribute each 10 per cent (or 5 per cent, as specified in the watershed guidelines), for watershed activities;
- that the village is prepared to take and enforce social decisions such as controlled grazing and social fencing for the development and conservation of the natural resources in the village.

Provisions for De-selection and Punitive Action

Villages can be 'de-selected' under the following conditions:

- if the village community is not willing to work together actively and collectively;
- if the village community fails to follow the guidelines in their planning, execution and functioning;
- if the village community is not able to collect contributions as per the guidelines;
- if the village community is not able to enforce the social decisions taken in the *gram sabha* or watershed committee;
- if any misappropriation of finances is evident.

Where any misappropriation of finances is noticed, appropriate criminal prosecution proceedings will be initiated and recoveries will be effected.

The process of selecting a village for watershed development is essentially a community organisation process of facilitating, organising, enabling and empowering the whole village. Many villages are still not in a position to self-facilitate and participate actively, but this will begin to occur gradually, especially if they can visit useful models in neighbouring villages.

EXTRACT 3.2
DANIDA-SUPPORTED PARTICIPATORY
WATERSHED DEVELOPMENT[3]

S.L. SETH[4] AND S. DAMGAARD-LARSEN[5]

The Danish Development Assistance policy document of 1990 states that 'the reduction of poverty constitutes a fundamental principle of the Danish Development Cooperation. This principle is emphasised in the new development strategy. Efforts designed to concretise poverty reduction will continue at all levels'. In consonance with this policy, attempts are made to follow participatory approaches in watershed development, characterised by the following.

Socially Balanced Economic Growth

The rural poor—landless, marginal farmers, village artisans and women—should participate in a fruitful manner. Watershed development used to be a land-based activity with benefits shared in proportion to the size of landholdings of different families. The rural poor were marginalised so far as benefits were concerned.

Danida projects follow 'biomass-based' watershed-development principles, so that the livelihood-support systems of the weaker sections, which depend on biomass processing, cottage industries, rearing of small ruminants, backyard poultry, kitchen gardening, bee-keeping, etc., are enhanced, and the rural poor also participate in a meaningful manner. *Sustainability through mainstreaming* To sustain participatory organisations, processes and mechanisms after the project ends, attempts are made to

[3] Source: Seth and Damgaard-Larsen (1998).
[4] Senior Technical Advisor, Danida, Watershed Development Coordination Unit, New Delhi.
[5] Programme Coordinator, Danida, New Delhi.

mainstream the systems created by the project by involving general development systems—line departments, credit institutions, etc.—so that the project areas do not stand in isolation.

Participatory approach: A dynamic and evolving process   As experience is accumulating and strengths and weakness are known, the processes and systems are being appropriately modified, restructured and evolved to support the basic purpose of participation by all sections of the watershed community.

Approach rooted in the socio-economic setting   Different variants of participatory approaches are followed in view of the diversity in village power-structures, the social composition of local populations, literacy levels, levels of technology absorption, etc. Financial assistance is given in a phased manner, so that more powerful villagers do not see large amounts of money available for expropriation. Also, executive-committee members are changed after an agreed period (two years in some projects) so that participatory institutions are not monopolised by a few people.

Participatory Approach in Different DANWADEP Projects: Karnataka Watershed Development Project

Phase I   This project was formulated in the late 1980s and launched in 1990. The first phase lasted from 1990 to 1996. Initially, people's participation was more consultative in nature. However, in 1993, the participatory approach was intensified and accelerated. The basic strategy has been to develop the capacity of the implementing agency—the State Agricultural Department—to promote the participatory approach within the department, rather than assigning social aspects to NGOs. Junior project officers were recruited, trained in social methodologies (extension techniques, participatory rural appraisal, rapid rural appraisal), accounting, book-keeping, group dynamics, organising people, etc., and deployed full-time to encourage participation.

The junior project officers organised village meetings and selected two volunteer 'link workers' (one man and one woman) to serve as a kind of spearhead group. Watershed development committees were constituted in each village. The project technical staff, junior project officers and the watershed development committees jointly planned, implemented and monitored activities. At the watershed level, a watershed-operation group provided a forum for representatives of village watershed-development committees, elected members of *panchayati raj* institutions, and selected heads of the line departments (forestry, horticulture, etc.) to discuss and recommend plans for ap-

proval by the district co-ordination committee under the chairman-
ship of the chief of the *zilla parishad.*

Phase II Based on the experiences gained in Phase I, the participatory
process was refined, fine-tuned and re-structured.

Broad-based, representative participatory organisations Instead of the village
watershed development committee being elected by the entire village,
self-help groups, user groups or groups around common interests (gender, occupation, landholdings, social classes) are first constituted. One
representative of each group constitutes the village development committee (VDC). Elected village *panchayat* members are also members of
the VDC. These members elect their executive committee.

Rotational leadership Executive committees of the VDC are rotated once
every two years.

Intensive and structured training An elaborate training schedule, indicating
various stages and steps for participatory learning, planning, implementation, monitoring and evaluation, has been adopted. This enhances the
capabilities of all the stakeholders (project staff, members of the self-
help groups, and watershed development committees) in technical, social and financial aspects of the project and in record-keeping.

Operational VDC VDCs with 20–25 members are operational and more
effective. If necessary, two or more VDCs may be constituted according
to the size and diversity of the village.

Clarity of roles, responsibilities and accountability Clear roles, functions and
accountability modes have been jointly worked out for the different
stakeholders.

Village general body A village general body comprising one representative from each household is organised. Once every six months, VDCs
and project staff present their action plan to the general body, and will
be accountable to it. This process aims to bring about transparency.

Preparation for participatory approach The first project year is devoted to
the creation of awareness, joint learning, building trust and confidence,
organising self-help groups and VDCs, participatory training, conducting participatory rural appraisals, and developing plans. No biophysical
works are done.

Finances and roles VDCs are given funds to implement all works on common lands, and will keep records. Individual landholders will be given
funds for implementing works on their own lands in instalments.

Participatory monitoring and modifications Self-help groups, VDCs and
project staff undertake periodical self-evaluation exercises and make
modifications, remove bottlenecks and resolve conflicts, if any arise.

Comprehensive Watershed Development Project, Tirunelveli and Ramanathapuram (Tamil Nadu)

These projects in the southern part of Tamil Nadu state were launched in 1991 (in Tirunelveli) and 1994 (in Ramanathapuram) to rehabilitate degraded lands prone to wind- and water erosion. Initially, shelter-belts were the main activity, and participation was limited to 'informing' or 'consulting' the beneficiaries about the project—which was like a public work fully funded by the project. But later, a participatory approach was adopted.

The strategy is to involve NGOs and government field functionaries, so that necessary attitudinal changes may be brought about. NGOs deputed their experienced staff as community organisers. Then government and non-government organisations start interacting together with rural households. The process starts with the selection of villages and pursues the following route.

- Discussions between government, NGO staff and beneficiaries
- Rapport and confidence building
- Further visits and discussions
- Formation of association and election of office-bearers
- Drafting and approval of by-laws
- Training of village development association/executive committee members
- Socio-economic surveys
- Situation analysis and dialogue
- Participatory watershed-plan formulation
- Implementation responsibilities
- Time schedule and budget
- Joint evaluation and reporting.

Salient features of the participatory process are given below:

Membership   All families are members of the Village Development Association

Savings-linked financial assistance   If the Farmers' Association opens an account in a bank or post office and saves for three months, a matching grant up to Rs 3000 is given to meet expenses for stationery related to conducting meetings, office expenses, etc. If the association makes savings and earns interest, up to Rs 5000 is also provided as 'seed money' for lending to their members, and to purchase implements for hiring out to members. This money is also used for establishing nurseries, watering, guarding and other works. The project helps members to take advantage of the National Bank for Agricultural and Rural Development's short-term loans to buy seeds, fertilisers and pesticides. Thus associations are financially integrated with mainstream rural credit, and are envisaged to become self-sustaining, so that, at the end of the project they will continue to function.

Functions of Village Development Associations beyond project activities Village Development Associations take up all aspects of village development, such as health care, education, economic activities, and common interest and welfare activities. The project does not provide any funding beyond project activities, but helps them as facilitators and informs and encourages them to take full advantage of various government and NGO schemes operating in the area.

Comprehensive Watershed Development Project–Koraput (Orissa)

This seven-year project in the drought-prone Koraput and Malkanagire districts of Orissa was formulated in the late 1980s and formally launched in 1992. The landscape is undulating, and heavy rains generate tremendous runoff and soil erosion. The population consists of a high proportion of tribal people, who have their own traditions but very low levels of literacy. The participatory approach attempts to combine tribal customs and *panchayati raj* institutions, as indicated below.

Village committees headed by traditional tribal head A village-level committee under the traditional village headman and one representative each of the landless, women's groups and small and marginal farmers is constituted in all village meetings.

Youth facilitators In the village meetings, two youth facilitators (one male and one female) are selected to facilitate participatory development. Youth facilitators are paid a small honorarium, as the population is very poor, and are provided with a bicycle.

Involvement of NGOs For each watershed, NGOs working in the area provide one male and one female field-organiser. They are paid by the project and provided with a motor cycle or a moped.

Watershed development committee Four representatives of village committees (one traditional headman, one woman, one landless person, and one small or marginal farmer) from each village constitute the watershed development committee. The chairman of this committee is the elected *panchayati raj sarapanch*, whose *panchayat* covers several villages.

Self-help groups Self-help groups are constituted according to their members' occupation and gender.

Intensive training Project staff, NGO staff, members of village and watershed development committees, youth facilitators, and self-help group members are given orientation training and told about their roles and responsibilities. Continuous training in technical, procedural and financial management is provided to project staff and NGO youth facilitators throughout the project.

Joint survey and planning   Technical surveys are done by the project staff, and socio-economic surveys by NGOs. Youth facilitators and members of village/watershed development committees take an active part. Joint planning is done by visits to individual holdings, where the landholder is the key person in choosing the treatments. For common lands, government and NGO staff, facilitators and committee members visit the site and develop a plan, which is discussed and finalised in the village meeting. Village plans are combined to make a watershed development plan, which is finally approved by the watershed development committee.

Joint implementation and monitoring   Contractors have been totally eliminated. Village committee members ensure that labourers from the same village (or adjoining villages) are employed; they are paid full minimum wages. So far, technical monitoring by tribal people has been weak. But with the use of indigenous technologies, which locals understand better, they are involving themselves with confidence. For example, in choosing the location of *chua* (water holes) to store water for crops during the dry period, tribal people show tremendous skill and wisdom.

Saving-linked gradual financial assistance   Self-help groups engaged in household production (such as basket making and poultry) and *mahila kisan* (women farmers') nurseries must initially open a bank or post-office account and save money regularly for three months. Thereafter, the project provides Rs 1000 in instalments as the group's performance improves and their capacity for financial management, bookkeeping, etc., is enhanced. Initially the financial assistance was Rs 1000; this has since been raised to Rs 3000 per family, provided in three instalments and linked to their performance.

Constraints and Considerations in Participatory Approaches

Harmonising village and watershed boundaries   Villages are administrative or revenue units, and their boundaries are man-made. But watersheds are geo-hydrological units, made by nature. Often the two sets of boundaries do not coincide. Whereas biophysical activities are based on natural boundaries, participation is based on villages (village development committees, etc.). Quite often, people reside in one village in the watershed but their landholdings are fully or partially in another village outside it.

Conversely, some farmers live in villages outside the watershed, but own land inside. Natural watersheds may also cover parts of many villages. In view of these realities, the harmonisation of natural units with social units becomes problematic.

Harmonising short-term socio-economic needs and long-term regeneration Watershed development in degraded areas aims primarily to regenerate the natural resource of land and water and to restore the ecological balance. Benefits accrué over the medium- to long term. But people in such areas are resource-poor and want immediate solutions to their immediate problems of drinking water, food, fuel, fodder and cash flow. Special efforts have to be made to combine short-term benefits with long-term impacts.

Equity considerations Patterns of landholdings and village power-structures are set in favour of a few rich and influential families, which manage to control most of the investment. The majority of the rural poor do not get an equitable share. Household and self-help groups have to be made the primary units of planning. Disturbing the village power equation and managing social tensions often creates problems, and innovative measures and special skills need to be instilled into field functionaries to handle behaviour patterns and resolve conflicting interests.

Harmonising technical requirements with local preferences A system exists where plans proposed by field functionaries are examined and technically approved at higher levels. The participatory approach is bottom-up 'planning'. Sometimes the site, design and dimensions of structures proposed by village organisations are not technically sound, raising the question of how to harmonise social choice with technical considerations. In practice, such situations often create conflicts.

Local people's priorities and scope of activities When participatory process are initiated, and villagers are requested to indicate their preferences, often drinking-water supply, a link road to the village, a bridge over a local river, a primary school, a village hospital and heath care are the top priorities. Canal irrigation or government tube wells are high local farming priorities. The regeneration of the natural resource base, and the slow but steady benefits which watershed development generates, do not catch the attention of opinion leaders, who want quick results for populist reasons. How can the scope of watershed development be enlarged to match the ambitions and priorities of local people, while retaining its natural resource management focus? This question merits special consideration.

Subsidy culture and dependency syndrome Local people perceive soil conser-

vation works to be government- or donor programmes, to be undertaken at the sponsor's expense. They are rather hesitant to 'own' the
programme, and perceive outside help only as an enabling input. Subsidies available at different rates in different schemes aggravate the problem.

Lack of enlightened local leadership   Many successful watershed development projects are inspired by committed local leaders—like Anna Saheb
Hazare, who promoted self-help culture and a participatory approach.
There are few local leaders who are committed to natural resource management, and who have the necessary in-depth knowledge, dedication
and patience.

In conclusion, there is an encouraging policy environment in favour
of participatory watershed development. There are many successful examples in various part of the country, but there is still a long way to go
to reach real, fruitful and sustainable participatory approaches.

EXTRACT 3.3
CRITERIA FOR SELECTION OF WATERSHEDS AND
NGO IMPLEMENTING AGENCIES[6]

Watersheds covering villages with the following physical and socio-economic characteristics are preferred for inclusion in the IGWDP programme.

Physical Characteristics

*   Dry and drought-prone, with the irrigated area not exceeding the
    average proportion for Maharashtra. That means not more than 20
    per cent of the cultivated area is irrigated; the rest is rain-fed.
*   Noticeable erosion, land-degradation, resource-depletion or water-
    scarcity problems.
*   Location in the upper part of drainage systems.
*   A project area of around 1000 ha (but not less than 500 ha).
*   Average rainfall around 1000 mm per annum.
*   Well defined watersheds, with the village boundaries coinciding to
    the greatest extent possible with the watershed boundary.
*   The general cropping sequence does not include high water-demand-
    ing and long-duration crops like sugarcane or banana. If such crops
    are grown in small pockets in the watershed, the villagers should

[6] Source: IGWDP (1996).

ensure that the area under such crops will not be extended during implementation or after completion of the watershed development project.

Socio-economic Characteristics

- Predominantly poor villages.
- A high proportion of scheduled castes and tribes in the population.
- Relatively small differences in the size of landholdings.
- A known history of coming together for common causes.
- A demonstrated concern for resource conservation.

Villages must be willing to commit themselves to the following:

- Ban felling of trees.
- Ban free grazing and undertake 'social fencing' to protect vegetation.
- Reduce the livestock population if it is in excess, and maintain livestock at the carrying capacity of the watershed (i.e., the number which can be supported by the watershed).
- Ban cultivation of water-intensive crops, like sugarcane and banana, or at least not to increase the area under such crops from the present situation.
- Contribute by way of *shramdaan* or otherwise, 10 per cent of the unskilled labour costs of the project, and also to collect such contributions equitably (impartially and in a just manner) from the village community. The landless and poor, single-parent households are excluded from such a contribution.
- Start and contribute to a maintenance fund for watershed development.
- Take all such steps as are necessary for achieving and maintaining a sustainable production system.
- Constitute, at the village level, a village watershed committee which will have to be registered during the implementation phase, so that it can undertake responsibility for maintenance of all the valuable property (assets) created and generated by the project.

Criteria for Selecting NGOs

Careful choice is also exercised regarding the selection of NGOs. They are selected for participation in the programme on the basis of the following factors (amongst others):

- Reputation and financial history.

- Method of operation, and rapport with people and local government agencies.
- Perspective on watershed development.
- Nature of projects handled in the past.
- Technical and managerial capability.

The NGO should have been active in the area for a significant period before proposing a watershed project for the area.

If the NGO and the village community do not have enough previous experience of watershed development or its component disciplines, they should be willing to demonstrate their commitment and ability by:

- visits to other watershed projects (exposure visits);
- appointing selected village youth and key persons, and sending them to specific training programmes;
- first preparing and implementing a demonstration project for a small area (of at least 100–150 ha).

NGOs and watershed communities with potential and willingness to implement a watershed project but having no previous experience would, if selected, have to go through a capacity-building programme and meet the qualifying criteria before undertaking a large-scale project.

EXTRACT 3.4
EXPERIENCE OF SEVA MANDIR IN SUPPORTING LOCAL ACTION FOR WATERSHED DEVELOPMENT[7]

AJAY MEHTA[8]

Seva Mandir, a grassroots NGO based in Udaipur (Rajasthan), has been working with poor peasants and forest dwellers in the South Aravallis for the last 25 years. In 1985, when the National Wastelands Development Board announced its policy to support NGOs to help create a people's movement to meet the environmental crisis facing the country, we felt well positioned to accept the challenge. The Seva Mandir board allowed us to formulate our own scheme to enable the rural poor to afforest vast tracts of degraded lands in the area. After consulting villagers and our field staff, we prepared an ambitious scheme which, contrary to all expectations, was fully endorsed by the board. Over a period of two years, the board sanc-

---

[7] Source: Mehta (1998).

[8] Formerly Director, Seva Mandir, Udaipur, Rajasthan.

tioned more than Rs 10m to operationalise our plans to afforest degraded lands through people's participation. Subsequently we were able to collect from other sources all the funds required to finance our wasteland development programme.

What appeared to be a simple problem from the outside—creating a people's movement for wasteland development—has turned out to be an extremely complex undertaking. Since we received the support of the board from 1986/87, we have not lacked funds for our forestry programmes. Over this period we have developed a substantial organisational and technical capability to undertake wasteland development. However, despite 10 years of systematic effort at creating a people's movement for wasteland development and forest protection, we cannot claim to have succeeded. This note attempts to describe these efforts and the lessons learned.

In the first two years of the programme (starting in the 1986 planting season), we provided a modest incentive to poor farmers, most of whom were tribal people, to plant trees on private holdings. We assumed that since they owned the land, they would have a strong stake in taking care of the trees being planted. Over a period of two years, more than a million saplings were raised in village nurseries and planted on private wastelands by around 5,000 farmers. The incentive we provided, though modest, motivated a large number of farmers to join the campaign. After the initial enthusiasm to plant, we found that the farmers' interest in nurturing the saplings tended to wane, and despite the incentives that rewarded them on the basis of actual survivals, the number of trees that survived was modest. As far as we could make out, this was due to adverse climatic conditions: the monsoons in 1986 and 1987 failed. But another reason was that the peasants did not have the wherewithal to protect the saplings from biotic interference.

In order to overcome this deficiency, we created options for farmers that addressed the latter problem. The incentive structure was improved, and greater technical support was provided. Farmers were asked to pool privately owned lands that were contiguous, and support was provided to the group to develop this pooled land. Under this scheme, we paid the full costs of land-development activities, and farmers were later expected to return 20 per cent of the costs to a village fund as a contribution, in small instalments. The scheme resulted in much better survival rates.

However what did not materialise was a strong demand for this scheme. We found that it was not easy for farmers to cooperate to develop their private holdings. It is difficult for people to come together, notwithstanding the benefits inherent in improving the productivity of their degraded lands. We experienced pockets of excellent work, but the spread effect was muted.

Besides working on private land, we also developed schemes for people to rehabilitate their degraded pasturelands, watersheds and, more recently, Joint Forest Management (JFM) sites. Despite attractive support for developing these lands, the demand for these schemes was also slow in crystallising.

The situation presents a puzzle. In an area of traditional forest dwellers, with great poverty and need for wage employment, people are not able to come together to develop the vast areas of degraded lands. The explanation for this apparent paradox has perhaps to do with the distorted nature of land ownership and land-rights management in the region. It is also to do with the fact that, contrary to what is often assumed about rural communities, the ties of social solidarity are no longer strong, and no longer underpin community action for forest protection, wasteland development and sustainable land use.

In the specific case of forest land, legal access to Forest Department lands is difficult due to the continuation of the colonial traditions of forest management (notwithstanding the recent JFM policy guidelines). Village people no longer have a well-defined collective stake in managing these lands because of the option of encroaching on them. The privatisation of forest lands on an ad-hoc and insecure-tenure basis does not lend itself to long-term productive investment in these lands.

The weak demand by people for developing private and village pasturelands seems to be due to the fact that the sense of community has been vitiated. Ties with powerful patrons holding political or bureaucratic authority have come to replace, in substantial measure, the stake in social solidarity that was characteristic of communities in an area where development patronage from outside was scarce.

Another factor responsible for poor community action on both private and public lands is the disempowerment of village people, because of the arbitrary management of all categories of land and the selective targeting of beneficiaries through a plethora of development schemes. Even in cases where people benefit substantially through development schemes or land grants, the social and political costs paid in terms of relinquishing power to patrons is tremendous. An individual or group of farmers not only run the risk of being alienated from their community by entering into an illicit or informal pact with local officials for private gain; they are also compromised into silence against wrongdoing by such officials. These processes of disempowerment have reduced the ability of people to demand accountability from state agencies in the better management of public lands, and have undermined local knowledge systems, cultural values and institutions necessary to enforce sustainable land use and forest protection.

The constraints to regenerating the environment lie in restructuring land- and social- and power relations. Unless these parameters are addressed, no amount of people's participation or reviving indigenous forest-management systems can enable the regeneration of degraded lands and cooperation among villagers to ensure sustainable land use.

What is lacking, and lacking systematically in policy and NGO action, is attention to issues of tenure, social cohesion and the capacity of people to articulate their rational self-interest. An approach to forest conservation and sustainable land use is required that is informed by a perspective to try to help village people align their land and social relations in favour of sustainable land use and socio-economic development.

The opportunities facing state authorities which deal with issues such as forestry in India are vast. Being the largest land owner, the authorities are in a position to help restructure social and land relations in a way that a stake is created for people to manage better their resource base. It is only when a strong sense of shared interest is created that people will be able to regenerate the environment and also experience the benefits of sustainable development. Merely improving people's stake in better land management may not be sufficient to empower communities and fulfil their livelihood needs. For this it is necessary that systematic efforts are made to enhance people's capabilities in terms of promoting greater gender equality, better health and literacy, while also exploring other sources of income generation for the rural poor.

The following section describes the experience of two villages in Seva Mandir's area of engagement. The two cases, while undoubtedly exceptional in terms of the degree to which people have made the transition to being socially cohesive and politically significant, appear to offer principles which are more generic.

Nayakheda

Nayakheda is a hamlet (comprising of about 30 households) located in the revenue village of Usan, some 30km north of Udaipur. It is part of a multi-caste village, consisting mostly of poor peasants and a small minority of landlords.

Seva Mandir had been working in this area for over two decades. In the 1970s Seva Mandir had done work to promote adult education. It had also done agricultural extension work, and towards the end of the decade it had tried to get villagers to form groups to enable them to better negotiate their entitlements *vis-à-vis* the state. However, the expectations from group formation and awareness-raising work were not to be realised. The failure of the groups to impact on government systems and officials led Seva Mandir in the mid-80s to create capacity at the level of the local people, and within Seva Mandir to service some of the development needs of the people. The choice of programmes to be supported was weighed in favour of cooperative efforts. Despite having created this capacity, no headway on development could be made in Nayakheda due to the nature of local politics. The nexus between the local landlord, officials and elected village council representatives was so powerful and self-serving that they refused space to the poor to undertake development activities with the help of Seva Mandir.

By contrast, in the neighbouring village of Barawa, excellent progress had been achieved as a consequence of village cohesion and committed leadership. There, the leaders had been offered a substantial bribe from a grant meant to develop their village pastureland to prevent Seva Mandir from helping people develop this land. A proposal to develop the pastureland had been made by the village people to the district development agency, but no action had been taken.

It was only when news reached the agency that the people had approached Seva Mandir, and that Seva Mandir had approved the proposal, that the agency reacted and approved money. Their idea was that out of the sanctioned grant for pasture development, 60 per cent would actually be made available for work, while the rest of the money would be shared as kick-backs between the elected village-council leaders and the officials responsible for administering the grant. The village elders rejected the offer, knowing that even if the entire amount of the grant were utilised for the rehabilitation of the land, it would not be sufficient. The people were reluctant to take government funds, thinking that it might curtail their rights and freedom of usufruct on the land. The project went through with the assistance of Seva Mandir. The land was enclosed, treated with soil- and water-conservation methods, and trees and shrubs were planted. Within a couple of years, a degraded resource had become productive for the village as a whole.

The success of this project was known to the people of Nayakheda, but they were unable to take advantage of the support available from

Seva Mandir. Not only was the local landlord resistant to the idea of people's land being improved; he had (along with the police and a revenue official) occupied a substantial part of the village pasturelands for mining purposes. Another segment of the village commons had been monopolised by other powerful people in the village, leaving no stake for ordinary villagers to invest in the improvement of these lands. This stand-off in terms of development was to end with a bizarre incident in 1990—the landlord and his two sons were sent to jail for the suspected murder of eleven people belonging to the family of a political and economic competitor. He remained in jail for three years before being released.

It was during his absence that people were able to organise themselves and take advantage of the support that was being offered by Seva Mandir. They were familiar with the ideas of working as a group and the advantages of transparency in their dealings. From a situation of little development work in the area, a large amount of work got initiated. The people were able to recover the usurped common lands, though it meant spending a lot of money in courts to disprove of the claim made by the landlord's family that the land was legally theirs. There was palpable enthusiasm on the part of the villagers for these works, because they felt that they were fully involved in the planning, execution and final benefit-sharing of the development programmes.

Even though the remuneration for land development works supported by Seva Mandir was lower than that offered by the government from a World Bank funded project, people were drawn to Seva Mandir because they felt they had control over the process of development, and that Seva Mandir was accountable and accessible to them on an on-going basis. This mobilisation for comprehensive land development involved the entire multi-caste population of seven hamlets, consisting of 150 households, including that of Nayakheda.

By the recovery of the village commons and the successful challenge to the unfair use of common property resources by powerful people, a stake had been created among the people to collectively improve the productivity of their resource base. Initially, people were brought together through the development works supported by Seva Mandir, but subsequently this solidarity developed a life of its own. This was to become manifest at the time of village council elections, and then continuously in their daily struggles against the landlord's desperate efforts to regain control after his return from jail in 1994. Their social solidarity expressed itself politically and began a significant political and attitudinal change in the area.

In the early part of 1995, village council elections were announced in Rajasthan after the passing of a new constitutional amendment regarding *panchayati raj* institutions. Under the new *panchayati raj* system, the seat of the village council head for this area was reserved for a tribal person. Knowing that Shivlal, a tribal person and an active member of the Nayakheda Seva Mandir group and a forestry extension worker with Seva Mandir, was immensely respected and popular, the Congress Party offered him a ticket to stand for office at the district level. Sensing this was a ploy to co-opt him by taking him away from his community, Shivlal decided to reject the offer on the advice of his village peers. Instead, the village group asked him to stand for the office of the village council head as an independent candidate. When he declared his intentions to stand against the nominee of the landlord (also the Congress candidate), the landlord threatened to have him and his close associate killed.

At the stage of filing nominations, the officer in charge tried to prevent Shivlal on procedural grounds. To be allowed to run in the election, Shivlal had to prove that he was a resident of the area; that he was not a government employee; and that he did not have debts to pay to the government. Initially officials tried to disqualify him on grounds of his being associated with Seva Mandir, and the last resort was to prevent him from obtaining the no-debt certificate. The village council secretary, a salaried government official responsible for giving this certificate, stopped coming to the office, having promised to provide the certificate on a number of occasions. Finally on the eve of the last day of filing the nominations, Shivlal and a few of his supporters decided to hire some transport at night and trace the official to his house in Udaipur. They refused to leave until he had given him the certificate. The village group of Nayakheda had realised that for development to occur, they had to fight the landlord lobby and be politically visible.

Shivlal had no funds for the campaign. The task of matching the Congress Party/landlord candidate appeared to be daunting. It is alleged that the Congress party candidate spent close to Rs 40,000 plying voters with gifts and liquor. Among the Congress party candidate's active campaigners was the government agricultural extension worker: while such partisan behaviour by officials is forbidden by the service conduct rules, it is not uncommon. The group members assured Shivlal that they needed no funds to persuade people about who to vote for. They did spend Rs 2000 on hiring transport and buying apples to popularise their election symbol. This money came from voluntary contributions.

After the polling, it was clear to the election agents of Shivlal that he

had won by a very large margin. Having experienced the partisan conduct of the election officials, Shivlal's supporters feared that the return-
ing officers might declare the Congress candidate as the winner. To prevent this, Shivlal's election agents took the shrewd step warning election
officials that the people waiting outside for the verdict would turn hostile if the result were manipulated. Shivlal was declared the winner, but
with a slender margin of 41 votes. Shivlal's election agents present at the
counting felt he had won by at least 500 votes.

Gaining political office has made life difficult for the leaders of the
movement and also for Seva Mandir field workers. They are continuously threatened and harassed. At another level, there has been a marked
change in the power relations in the area. Some of the close allies of the
landlord switched allegiance to Shivlal and prevented the landlord from
becoming vice-head of the village council; even the local revenue in-
spector has become more cooperative. The partisan agricultural extension worker was moved out of the area for his behaviour during the
elections. The legislator from the area has also showed occasional support to the Nayakheda group. He intervened in their favour in determining the location of a sanctioned water-supply tank—the landlord
was keen for it to be located in his hamlet. There is also growing faith in
the efficacy of a people-based approach to development on the part of
the neighbouring village people.

Villagers travel long distances regularly to attend Nayakheda Seva
Mandir meetings. Whether the politics of cooperation will survive and
grow in to a widespread movement is difficult to predict, and the odds
are stacked against it. What is clear is that by gaining control of the
panchayat, the villagers have entered a new phase in terms of their political standing and power base. They have become a strong local force, and
could increase their political power by increasing the development work
that benefits people in various ways. For this to happen, NGOs like Seva
Mandir will be critical in the short run. In the long run, political power
can change government functioning, but in the short run, such islands
of people's power can easily be isolated and marginalised by mainstream
state structures.

Shyampura

The experience of another village, called Shyampura, consisting of 100
households and located 70 km away to the southwest of Udaipur city,
underscores the Nayakheda experience of the power of people coming
together. It also shows how the constraints to development lie not so

much in dealing with powerful vested interests, as in the case of Nayakheda, but have to do with overcoming constraints internal to the community. These are issues to do with insecure land tenure, lack of cohesion and a leadership empowered enough to build consensus among people to promote their common interest.

The essence of the story of Shyampura is about leveraging support to change social and land relations, enabling people to become politically significant and autonomous of the politics of control. Seva Mandir started working in Shyampura in 1982 with a programme to promote adult literacy among poor peasants. Later, Seva Mandir also encouraged villagers to form groups as a means of better accessing their entitlements from the state. A component of the group-building programme was to encourage people to take more responsibility for trying to solve their internal problems. In the mid-1980s, Seva Mandir expanded its role to help villagers service their individual and collective development needs.

Again, the lack of adequate response from the state, despite repeated efforts by groups to claim its attention, made us realise that people would lose faith in themselves and the value of coming together if they did not experience some positive outcomes. Seva Mandir then developed a major programme to enable villagers to afforest their degraded private and common lands, and also developed capacity to build dams—water being an item of great scarcity in the area. In 1987–88, Seva Mandir built a substantial water reservoir in Shyampura village. The villagers had been promised this structure by the district magistrate in 1985, but nothing happened. The successful completion of the dam created goodwill for, and confidence in, Seva Mandir among the people. It also greatly enhanced the prestige and power of the village group of Shyampura and their leaders who had lobbied for this project for a long time.

The watershed of this reservoir was highly degraded on one side. Because it belonged to the forest department, it was not possible for people to treat the land, though they realised the need to do so to prevent siltation of the reservoir. While officially the land could not be developed by people, individual farmers with the informal consent of the department were able to use the lands for their private benefit. The most active members of the Shyampura village group were those who undertook the maximum encroachments in the watershed of the reservoir. This effectively undermined the ability of the group to put collective pressure on the forest department to treat the lands, since their leaders stood to lose their encroachments. These kinds of internal contradictions were symptomatic of the social structure of the area. No common purpose existed as a rallying point for public action; instead, factional issues based on lineage, caste and hamlet affiliations dominated the political life of the people. The social base for a vision of developing the area as a whole did not exist.

The physical landscape reflects this fractured and enfeebled social context. Vast tracts of land are bereft of green cover, very few irrigation facilities exist, though the potential for this is not lacking. People cultivate one crop a year, based on the erratic monsoon rains, and as landholdings are small, people frequently have to migrate to meet their bare subsistence needs.

In 1991 there was change in forest policy by the state: local communities were given the right to protect forest land and in return to share in the benefits generated from the land. This policy, known as 'joint forest management' (JFM) gave the Shyampura community a chance to develop the watershed with the permission of the forest department. A contract was agreed to improve 50 ha of the watershed. The leaders of the group who stood to lose access to their encroached lands in the watershed were persuaded to agree to this venture with the promise that Seva Mandir would build them a lift-irrigation system downstream to compensate them for the loss of their encroached lands. In fact, their de facto ownership rights were not being taken away under the agreement; they were simply being asked to put back the land to its proper land use, (i.e., eschew grazing their animals and cultivating crops on the slopes). The decision to convert forest land into a joint property of the village was initially not appreciated by all the villagers, as it meant the option of privatisation was foreclosed. In fact, people from the neighbouring village immediately began to make fresh encroachments when they heard about the JFM contract being signed. Through protracted efforts on the part of Seva Mandir and the Shyampura group to resolve conflicts and doubts amongst the potential stakeholders, the project made headway. The prestige gained by Seva Mandir and the local group in building the dam played an important role in getting the people to agree to this project.

The success of this venture attracted the attention of other government departments in search of success for their land-development programmes. In 1993–94, 100ha of land adjacent to the JFM site was taken up for development under the national watershed programme. This was to reinforce the idea among the people that a great deal could be accomplished through cooperation and collective discipline. In turn, the leaders of these initiatives realised that for meaningful development, they needed to be more inclusive in their leadership style and share benefits in a non-partisan way with neighbouring villages. Factional rivalries were set aside, and leadership roles were shared to broaden the base for public action and collective management of the resource base.

These changes in land and social relations increased the number of people wanting to cooperate and take active interest in bringing about development. Seva Mandir helped consolidate these trends by assisting the group to set up institutions like the village fund to bring people together on a permanent and substantive basis.

Seva Mandir insists that those who directly benefit from development work should pay a small contribution to a village fund, to which all the villagers have equal claim and management right. In building the dam and subsequently developing the JFM sites over eight years, the villagers' contributions had become substantial. The common ownership of these funds was to create an off-take for all the villagers, even those who felt left out by the programmes. Institutions like the village fund provided a basis for people to come together and deliberate on their common and collective interests. Because the funds were properly managed and there were tangible benefits from treating the watershed, people's interest in participating in these initiatives increased. From a membership of only 60 per cent of the households initially, the membership of the forest protection committee went up to 90 per cent of all the households in the village. This reinforced the authority of the leaders and pressured them to be fair and transparent in their dealings. The fact that the quantum of development works had increased in the area as a result of the previous works being well done, made it easier for the leaders to satisfy a broader constituency of people. This also helped the leaders become more inclusive and more confident in working towards a broader vision of development of the area.

These developments set the stage for a political transformation in the area, similar to that in Nayakheda. Prior to the village council election of 1995, the BJP approached Nathu Lal, one of the leaders of Shyampura group to become their nominee for the post of the village council head. Nathu had stood twice for the post of village head in the past, and had lost. Knowing that Nathu had standing in the area because of all the work that he had helped catalyse in the area, the BJP saw him as a winning candidate. Nathu agreed to be their nominee. While confident of obtaining votes from rural people, he was not confident of the votes of the urban people in the consistency. Nathu won the election based largely on his reputation for engendering broad-based cooperation as a means of bringing about development in the area. Now that

Nathu holds elected office and commands authority, his rural supporters will expect him to facilitate the development of common property resources, things that they have experienced positively. They also expect him to continue to be honest and transparent, and use his authority to ensure government functionaries are more accountable to the people.

As part of the power structure and as part of the BJP, there will be pressures on him to conform to their expectations of people in authority. What will be interesting to see is whether the politics of cooperation is reinforced as a result of Nathu having gained public office, or whether he will be marginalised or co-opted by the power structure, and thereby also lose his base and support with the people. From Nathu's point of view also, he would be looking to see how much vitality there is in respect to people coming together and to articulating demands of broad-based interest.

There is evidence of growing interest in cooperation on the part of people and disenchantment with the patronage mode of seeking individual benefits. This trend seems to also invite a reciprocal interest on the part of leaders like Nathu to reinforce cohesion and community-based approaches to development.

In April of 1995, after the *panchayat* elections, people of four villages in this area came together to declare some 700 ha of forest land sacred. They did this to protect these lands from being encroached and over-exploited.

The commitment of more powerful community members promoting solidarity was made tangible, when after the elections, Nathu and some 27 members of his clan agreed to make an annual contribution to the village fund from the additional earnings they were going to get from the lift-irrigation scheme downstream of the water reservoir. The commitment to build a lift-irrigation scheme had caused resentment among people of a neighbouring hamlet, because they felt left out. This gesture to contribute to the fund is an attempt to make amends and cement ties of solidarity. These events at a micro level, while small in scale, suggest that it is possible to challenge the politics of control, and that ingredients of doing so can be identified and made use of on a broader scale.

The experiences of Nayakheda and Shyampura suggest that NGOs have role to play in empowering people. NGOs working in development as a means of engendering social cohesion can go a long way in enabling people to gain political authority. While development and democracy have not served the interests of the poor on their own, they do provide space where power can be contested. Institutions like Seva Mandir have a role to play in changing the circumstances of the poor, particularly as the poor themselves can become the custodians of their own self-interest, with a little support. The challenge before NGOs is to overcome their internal contradictions and keep pace with people at the grassroots who are able to show the way to empowerment, provided the others in society are willing to contribute.

EXTRACT 3.5
LESSONS FROM VIKSAT EXPERIENCE[9]

M. DINESH KUMAR,[10] *SRINIVAS MUDRAKARTHA AND DHIRAJ L. BHALANI*

The watershed approach to natural resource development and management is multi-disciplinary. The concept envisions development of the microclimate, which will ultimately lead to a symbiotic relationship of life with the environment. The Guidelines issued in 1994 on watershed development by the Ministry of Rural Development essentially constitute a broad framework for operationalising the watershed concept.

The Watershed Development Programme: Paradigm Shift

The approach envisaged under the Common Guidelines, differs from rural development programmes which have been conceptualised and implemented by the government of India in the following ways. First, it recognises people's capabilities and emphasises their role in the development and management of the natural resource in their locality, (though such initiatives were made earlier by the government in the case of forestry sector through the Forest Policy of 1988 and the Joint Forest Management guidelines of 1990 by the Ministry of Environment and Forests). Second, the programme tries to institutionalise community-based approaches to developing and managing local natural resources which emphasise the creation of community institutions at the local level.

Miles to Go From Here...

The Common Guidelines provide a broad framework, but cannot be a blueprint for implementing the programme across a country of such

---

[9] Source: Dinesh Kumar et al. (1998).

[10] VIKSAT, Vikram Sarabhai Centre for Development Institute, Nehru Foundation for Development, Thaltej Tekra, Ahmedabad.

vast geographical spread and varying physical, social and cultural environments. The effectiveness of the programme will require a great deal of innovations and modifications at the local level to suit specific conditions. Therefore, the speed and the effectiveness with which the programme could be implemented depend largely on the extent to which the guidelines permit innovation in project formulation and implementation.

Apart from these, there are issues that go beyond the project-implementation phase, including the sustainability of the natural resource base and the degree of equity in accessing the resource by different stakeholder groups.

To address these issues, changes will be needed in the existing legal policy and administrative arrangements with regard to access rights to forests and water. The issue of the programme sustainability also needs to be addressed, as it has strong implications for the sustainability of the resource base. The sustainability of the resource-management programme will depend largely on the effectiveness of the resource-management institutions that are promoted. For institutions to be effective, they need to have adequate representation of the stakeholders' interests, technical capability to tackle physical resource problems at the local level, organisational capabilities (including financial management), and mechanisms to resolve conflicts.

This lies very much in the degree of decentralisation and local capacity building which the programme is supposed to promote. However, in a programme which emphasises physical and financial targets, these are difficult to achieve, as participation and capacity building evolve slowly and cannot be time-bound. These issues are discussed in the following section.

Sustainability and Equity Issues

Groundwater Watershed programmes focus mainly on augmenting the existing resource base through soil and water conservation, water-resource development, water-harvesting, and recharge measures. Such plans aim to increase the availability of surface and groundwater and as soil moisture, either by capturing runoff in surface storage-structures, or by recharging aquifers using recharge systems. It often leads to increased exploitation of the augmented water resource by farmers for irrigated agriculture. In many arid and semi-arid regions where watershed development and management programmes are most often taken up, the net cultivated and irrigated area is much less than the total cultivatable area, so that increased availability of water results in farmers expanding their irrigated area. There are many institutional and socio-economic factors which facilitate uncontrolled exploitation of groundwater resources, such as lack of well defined property rights, institutional financing for well development, rural electrification, easy availability of pumps, changes in agricultural practices (from rainfed to irrigated agriculture) and heavy mechanisation of agriculture.

Further, individual decisions to shift to water-conservation measures and thereby control pumping are not likely to create any overall positive impact on the groundwater regime. Aquifers are often large, with many appropriators enjoying access at any given time. Any water saving due to individual initiatives may only result in extra pumping by neighbouring well owners.

Forestry In many areas where watershed-development programmes are taken up, forests constitute a major proportion of the watershed area, and are mostly in the hilly upper catchments. These are areas where streams originate, but at the same time suffer from the most serious resource degradation problem (soil erosion). Most of the treatments that are critical to stabilising the degradation problems (such as groundwater depletion and soil erosion) need to be carried out in the upper catchment first.

According to the Forest Conservation Act of 1980, any physical activities such as excavation, removal of stones and construction of structures which cause submergence of forest land are illegal. This reduces the ability of agencies to implement watershed micro-plans in the forest areas, as such activities are subject to approval by the Forest Department. This approval is often hard to obtain, and takes a substantial amount of time. This reduces the effectiveness of treatments carried out in other parts of the watershed as well. The manifestations are continued soil erosion, causing silting of the new ponds and reservoirs, and increased runoff, resulting in reduced natural recharge to groundwater. In one VIKSAT project village (Kubada in Kheralu Taluka of Mehsana district in Gujarat), three check-dams were proposed by the village Tree Growers Cooperative Society in the forest area. The forest area had much earlier been allotted to the tree-growers' cooperative by the Forest Department for protection and soil-and-water conservation activities. Despite this, it still took almost a year for the department to grant permission for the construction.

In some cases, the entire watershed falls in inhabited forest areas. In such situations, the implementation of the entire watershed micro-plan is to be taken up by the Forest Department. However, the Forest Department develops its own forest micro-plans; these become a priority for officials who are driven to meet financial and physical targets. The result is that the watershed plans are not implemented.

Equity in access to groundwater and surface water Watershed-development activities, such as the construction of water-harvesting and recharge structures, improve the recharge to groundwater. However, only those farmers whose wells are located in the influence area of the structures benefit, despite contributions from the whole community. One way to address this problem of inequitable distribution of benefits is to make the beneficiary farmers (who constitute the user groups) pay for the additional benefits they receive. Given the complex geo-hydrological characteristics existing in many areas (especially hard-rock areas), it is practically impossible to demarcate the influence areas of recharge structures, making it difficult to identify the farmer beneficiaries. The institutional mechanisms available under the watershed guidelines are inadequate to address the issue of access equity in groundwater for the landless, as they do not have any rights to groundwater in the watershed area.

Access to forest resources Access-equity issues are more prevalent in the forestry sector. With the 'joint forest management' (JFM) resolution, 16 states in India are implementing JFM programmes. Village-level institutions and Forest Departments in many of these states are beginning pilot experiments, with or without support from NGOs. In some areas, NGOs are promoting village-level institutions: forest-protection committees in West Bengal and Orissa, tree-growers cooperatives in Gujarat, and forest *panchayats* in Uttar Pradesh.

Increasingly, watershed programmes are being taken up by a variety of organisations, including NGOs and local government agencies such as district rural development agencies and village *panchayats* across the country. Many of their project areas are already covered under the JFM programme. The result is the presence of multiple institutions engaged in managing the same village common property.

Under the JFM programme, the tree-growers cooperatives or the forest-protection committees usually represent only a section of the village community entitled to benefits, which include non-timber forest produce and a share of the final harvest. These benefits are very tangible, unlike the case of water, where benefits are less quantifiable. Given the fact that watershed-development programmes contribute to most of the improvements in common property resources, the local watershed association also can stake claim to the resources, leading to potential conflicts in future.

Sustainability of Resource-Management Institutions

Process vs target approach   The target approach focuses on financial and physical targets rather than processes. Project implementing agencies are always under pressure to achieve the physical and financial targets, as further funds are subject to these targets being met. The total cost of carrying out watershed development activities, including social preparation, comes to Rs 2,000,000 for an average watershed of size 500 ha, of which Rs 1,600,000 is to be spent on physical activities such as watershed treatments and construction of facilities. This is an enormous activity by itself, even if one excludes human-resource inputs, coordination, and the time required for the social engineering activities such as awareness camps, training programmes, educational tours and participatory rural appraisal. This leads to project implementation agencies' giving very little attention to the various processes which need to be facilitated within the villages and those which take place while implementing the project. The result is that the implementation agencies tend to do more and learn less about the processes which are critical to real participation. In effect, the communities continue to see the programmes as driven by external agencies, and thus there is a lack of sense of ownership of the programme and the assets created therein.

Facilitating vs implementing   Many organisations involved in watershed development programmes are oriented towards the conventional approach of implementing rather than facilitating. The lack of emphasis on local capacity-building results in the local institutions developing the dependency syndrome. It is not uncommon to find local institutions such as watershed associations, watershed committees, user groups and self-help groups existing only in name. Few efforts are made by the project implementation agencies to build the capabilities of these local institutions on the technical and organisational aspects of watershed development—in spite of the fact that funds are made available for this purpose. Most activities are implemented directly by the implementation agencies in a drive to complete the tasks faster.

However, building on local institutions is essential if they are to increase the participation of local communities in programme implementation and post-implementation management, and ensure the long-term sustainability of the programme. The availability of training institutions with adequate geographic spread is also questionable. The result is that project implementation agencies end up spending very little time in capacity-building and enterprise-development programmes. This reduces the opportunities for local institutions to learn, and build their confidence and capacities. They thus become defunct after the implementing agency withdraws.

Issues in Scaling up

The kind of impact likely from watershed development programmes under the Guidelines on the natural resource regime and the socio-economic conditions of rural areas depends heavily on the effectiveness and the scale at which the programmes are implemented. Scaling-up of programmes is heavily dependent on the norms and criteria for selecting the project implementation agencies, funding and financial criteria, institutional capabilities of the implementation agencies, and the strategies and processes of implementation. An attempt is made to take stock of the current situation with regard to these in the following paragraphs.

Selection of watershed project implementation agencies According to the Guidelines issued by the Ministry of Rural Development, an agency can become a project implementing agency if it falls under any of the following categories: (a) NGOs, (b) corporate bodies, (c) government departments, (d) cooperatives and registered charitable trusts; and (e) universities and academic or research institutions. While a watershed development programme essentially promotes participatory approaches to managing natural resources, it is not reflected in the selection criteria for project implementation agencies. In the process, influential private organisations which may be driven by monetary benefits rather than social commitment, use the opportunity to become implementation agencies. This prevents genuine organisations which have established credibility in natural resources and rural development from getting involved.

Funding According to the Guidelines, the amount of funds available for implementation is only Rs 4000 per hectare of watershed for programmes sponsored by district rural development agencies. This is irrespective of physical conditions and socio-economic factors, which vary widely across regions. The nature and extent of treatment required for ravine land in arid and semi-arid climates will be very different from that in a hilly vegetated terrain in a humid and semi-humid climate. This prevents many agencies from coming forward to take up watershed programmes in their areas of interest, or in those areas which require special attention.

Scale of implementation The programme drives the project implementation agency to take up a minimum of 5,000 ha, due to the fact that a 'watershed development team' is provided only for a 5,000 ha unit. This is quite difficult for many grass-root organisations to handle, because the amount of finance involved (around Rs 20,000,000 for a watershed area of 5,000 ha) is very large in comparison to their total turnover. Thus their sensitivity to any failure in the programme implementation is potentially high, and they do not come forward to take up programmes of large magnitude. However, the criterion for a minimum area is often relaxed, and the major influencing factor is the rapport the project implementation agency has with the DRDA.

Addressing Sustainability and Equity Issues

Local management institutions   Groundwater is one of the critical resources to be managed in a watershed. Experiences suggest that top-down legal or regulatory approaches to control or regulate groundwater development are most likely to be ineffective in India, as development is taking place entirely in the hands of private well-owners. Involvement of local communities in these management efforts could help to address these problems.

Local communities are more aware of resource-management issues and the management needs than the agencies concerned. There needs to be some social agreements within the user groups regarding resource use, and the presence of community organisations is a pre-requisite to framing the necessary rules and regulations and to ensure strict adherence of every member of the user community.

The activities on village common property, such as afforestation, forest protection and management, grass-cutting and wasteland development, which are an integral part of the watershed-development activities, create avenues for individuals to join the collective action.

The role of community organisations will be to: (a) evolve groundwater-management solutions appropriate for the locality; (b) frame rules and regulations to help affect the management decisions; and (c) monitor 'use' to ensure that individual users adhere to these rules.

Defining a local management regime   Local community organisations are formed and operate at the village and watershed levels. However, aquifer boundaries frequently do not follow the village administrative boundaries. Where many villages tap the same aquifer, the decision of a village community to protect and manage their groundwater resource may not be successful unless neighbouring communities cooperate.

The first and the most important aspect of designing any resource-management institution is identifying the resource boundaries. In the case of groundwater, there are two different ways by which the resource boundaries could be demarcated. The first is the boundary through which groundwater resources are replenished. The second is the boundary through which they are used or exploited.

The direct approaches to effectively managing available groundwater supplies in a locality can be broadly classified into 'supply augmentation' and 'end-use conservation'. For any supply-based approaches to be effective, the approach has to be watershed-based, as it is the watershed boundaries that define the flow of surface water-resources that augment groundwater supplies. This is one of the factors that induce negative externalities for local groundwater-management efforts. In order to effectively regulate groundwater use, it is essential to regulate pumping at all points across the aquifer, as the uses outside the local management regime can strongly influence the resource condition within it.

Institutional structures for local management   The types of externalities which can affect the success of local groundwater-management efforts form the basis for the design of groundwater management institution for any area. They are also important in identifying the critical parameters that need to be taken into account while developing management plans that can internalise these externalities. A three-tier institutional structure is suggested here.

Watershed Association   The 'watershed association' created at the village level will be responsible for carrying out the physical activities concerned with the management of groundwater in the area. The role of a village-level institution will be as follows.

- Evolving groundwater-management solutions appropriate to the locality. This will include identification of possible physical interventions, such as building recharge systems and plantation or afforestation activities, and identifying potential users of end-use conservation schemes.
- Identifying water-use priorities of local communities.
- Framing rules and regulations necessary to help affect the management decisions.
- Monitoring the resource use to ensure that individual users adhere to these rules.
- Implementing management decisions, including various physical activities to be carried out at the village level and resource allocation according to the use priorities.

Watershed Committee   As some of the physical activities necessary to augment groundwater supplies are to be carried out at the watershed level, the activities being taken up in different villages within the same watershed need to be coordinated. The 'watershed committee', formed at the watershed level is responsible for this. It should have representatives of watershed associations from all villages falling in the watershed.

The case of people's institutions in JFM programmes has demonstrated the role of federations in scaling-up of JFM. These federations serve as a forum for discussing and solving the larger issues facing the implementation of forest-management plans, and bring more villages into the joint management efforts; they also help resolve inter- and intra-village conflicts which emerge during the process.

The specific role of such an institution is:

- *Setting up watershed associations*   It should be responsibility of the watershed committee to ensure that village-level institutions exist in all the villages falling in the watershed.
- *Coordination of village-level physical activities*   Since physical intervention activities are carried out on the watershed basis, they have to be implemented in all the villages concerned (wherever the physical situation permits) simultaneously. Effective coordination is required to ensure that the activities are taken up at the same time.
- *Resolving conflicts between villages*   Conflicts are common in natural resource use and management. In such situations, the watershed committee can intervene.

In the case of a small watershed falling completely within village administrative boundaries, there will be no need to create a separate watershed committee, as the village-level institution will be able to tackle all the issues related to implementation of the management plan.

Management institutions at aquifer or basin level   The mandate of the aquifer management committee should be to facilitate scaling up (i.e., bringing more villages under the local management regime). While the management decisions for a particular locality are taken by the village-level institution, some management decisions will need to be taken at the aquifer level. Such management decisions will include:

- permissible levels of pumping to avoid stress on the aquifer;
- the amount of water that could be captured from the basin to augment groundwater supplies using recharge systems;
- the amount of water that could be withdrawn from the aquifer, assumed on the basis of the recharge estimates;
- identification and demarcation of watersheds for implementation of local management solutions;
- identification of concentrated points of high-priority demands, such as urban demand, heavy industrial demand, etc.;

- suggestion of suitable cropping patterns for the region on the basis of the climate and soils, emphasising the increase of water-use efficiency;
- suggesting efficient irrigation-water management practices for the region;
- suggesting efficient use practices (end-use conservation, recycling and re-use) in other sectors.

Evolving management strategies for large water-resource basins will require expertise in hydrology, geology and geo-hydrology, information about the current level of groundwater exploitation, and the social and economic factors affecting resource use in the region.

Therefore, unlike the water associations and water committees, which have representation only of people in the villages concerned, this aquifer- or basin-level committee should have representation from other stakeholders. These would include the major users of water from the basin: farmers and other village communities, industry, corporations, municipalities and the local village or town *panchayats.* The aquifer committee should also have representation from other stakeholders such as the state water-resource departments, water-management specialists, and social scientists. It should also have representatives of the watershed committees and the project implementation agencies working in the basin.

In situations where the basins cut across many districts, they can be split into sub-basins, each one falling in one district, and committees can be formed at the sub-basin level. Such committees can provide technical inputs to the watershed advisory committees in each district regarding priority areas for fund allocation. Alternatively, the watershed advisory committee could be reconstituted to include the stakeholders mentioned above.

Integrating JFM with Watershed Activities

In areas where forests fall within watershed areas and where there is scope for carrying out treatment activities in the forest areas, watershed associations should be legally recognised as carrying out forest-protection and management activities. This would enable them take up treatment activities in the forest areas and avoid conflicts due to the presence of multiple institutions managing the same common property. The policy implication of this suggestion is that the areas identified for implementation of watershed-development programme which have forests, should also be earmarked for JFM activities. Further, watershed associations which already exist or are being formed require legal recognition from the Forest Department as the organisation responsible for protection and management of these forest areas. If the JFM committees already exist before the watershed development programme is taken up, they should considered as the village-level institution for implementation of watershed-development activities. This will not only increase the effectiveness of the programme, but also facilitate scaling up.

Building Institutional Capabilities for Watershed Programmes

For watershed programmes to be sustainable, local institutions need to be strong and effective. Capacity-building of local institutions for local management efforts will be of prime importance for achieving the stability of the institutions and the entire programme. Though the Guidelines envisage an institutional hierarchy—local village level, watershed and district-level agencies—in its present form it provides very little opportunity for promoting local management capabilities, both technical and institutional. Such capabilities also require building at different levels of the institutional hierarchy. Training and educational programmes are central to such local capacity-building.

Training and Education

The grass-roots organisation should have sufficient knowledge and skills to deal with the organisational and technical issues, in addition to relevant managerial skills. Therefore, the training meant for grass-roots organisations should deal with: formation and structure of village institutions, user groups and water committees; their roles and responsibilities; and account-keeping and financial management.

There should also be technical training on the range of physical aspects of watershed development and management (soil and water conservation, water harvesting, afforestation, water-supply systems and animal husbandry) with a view to build institutions that can make watershed management programmes sustainable. Professionals with a sound social perspective are needed for imparting technical training, so the training team should have sociologists, community organisers and civil, water-resources specialists or agricultural engineers experienced in community-development programmes.

Existing Institutional Capabilities

The approach and syllabus followed by each institution involved in training for watershed development is different. The thrust and depth of the themes handled also varies. Common, minimum criteria need to be set for syllabi across all training institutions. This will also make the identification and periodic evaluation of the training institution easier. However, scope for variations within the broad framework of watershed approaches needs to be encouraged, since this will bring about innovations.

The institutions involved in training should also be invited to participate in the monitoring and review of progress in watershed development. This review team will help identify the scope for skills enhancement in relation to specific project implementation agencies, and make necessary modifications in the content and the methodologies of the training.

Criteria for Identifying Training Institutions and Training Modules

The capacities to be built among key actors such as user groups, watershed committees, project implementation agencies and the local government agencies like district rural development agencies, are different, and so are their training needs. In view of this, the institutional capability requirements of the proposed training institutions and the training contents will vary with respect to the target groups. They are briefly discussed here:

Institution for training government personnel Government personnel may need to have orientation on aspects such as the concept of watershed development and management, watershed guidelines, technical and social topics (such as community organising techniques), the legal framework (Indian Forest Act, Indian Forest Conservation Act, Groundwater Model Bill/Legislation), institutional systems (village institutions, watershed committees, and other institutional arrangements at higher level), and policy aspects (national water policy, forest policy, JFM resolution at the state level, etc.).

This would not only help them recognise and appreciate field-level issues, but also help them make realistic evaluation of the ongoing programmes. They will also require special training on the monitoring and evaluation of watershed-development programmes. The training institution should have experts on land management, legal and policy aspects of natural resource development, and social scientists.

Training institutions for project implementation agencies For effective implementation and sustainability of a watershed-development programme, participation of user groups in the programme is essential. Hence, the project implementation agencies should have a sound understanding of the participatory issues in resource management, and skills in community organising and participatory planning, as well as the engineering skills necessary to deal with water-resource development, land management etc.

There is a need for training institutions to train project implementation agencies on aspects such as participatory planning exercises, the creation of user-group organisations, training community organisations, water-resource development, forestry, livestock management, and land management.

NGOs with sufficient experience in dealing with participatory issues in the field and which are proficient in development communication are considered appropriate for this training task.

Addressing Equity and Efficiency Issues

In any watershed-management programme, it is very likely that only a section of the community will obtain benefits in terms of improved water levels in the wells, increase in soil moisture and land fertility. In a local initiative for managing groundwater resources, the impact of recharge activities is limited to a small area surrounding the recharge system, and only those farmers whose wells fall within this area benefit.

It is also very likely that an increase in available supplies will lead to increase in use. Because many depletion problems occur in the arid and semi-arid regions where the irrigated area is much less than the cropped area, any effort to increase the groundwater supplies could lead to farmers bringing more land under irrigation. Other uses, such as industrial and municipal use, can stake a claim over a major share of the additional water supply. This can undermine the efforts of the local management institutions. It is evident that unless the communities can establish rights over the resource they protect, keep demands for water in check, and introduce efficient water-use practices, then sustainable solutions to the emerging problems are not likely to be found.

There are three types of issues that a local groundwater-management initiative should address: efficiency, equity and sustainability. The absence of well defined property rights in groundwater leaves no incentive for the users to use the water efficiently, and in any case, these rights are limited to only those who own land. The institutional vacuum has also resulted in the inequity in access to the resource. Such issues have to be built into the management goals of any common-pool resource. For this it is important that property rights are clearly defined.

The establishment of tradable rights for groundwater has been suggested by many as a solution to the growing issues of access equity and efficiency. Such rights could be vested either with the state or with the aquifer-management committees, who could then sell the rights to legally registered water committees and associations.

Members could then buy the rights to use groundwater from the water associations (including both landholders and the landless). The landholders who do not own wells (groundwater-extraction mechanisms) should also become members. Every member of the cooperative will have a fixed entitlement on the basis of family size, and this can be made free of cost or nominally charged. The additional water used by the member for irrigation, or any other use, could be charged by the water-users association or the cooperative at a rate much higher than the rates for fixed entitlements. This will create incentives to invest in efficient water-use practices. For example, industries or municipalities might be willing to provide financial assistance to farmers to invest in efficient irrigation technologies, and the additional water saved could in turn be sold by the farmers to the other industries. The rationale behind this idea is that agriculture continues to account for the majority of total water use in any basin, and a small percentage saving in water use will result in a large increase in effective availability of water for other uses.

Further, developing water markets (in areas where they are non-existent) would help the well-owners to sell the water saved from their usual entitlement. The market could also provide an opportunity for a landowner who does not own wells to use his 'entitlement', and for landless people to sell their 'entitlement' to the cooperative or to neighbours. Further, there is enough evidence from the field to suggest that extensive and well developed water markets help address issues of access equity and efficiency in water use.

Suggestions for Scaling up

Given the magnitude of the work to be done in watershed development, and the institutional capabilities currently available in both training institutions and project implementation agencies, it is hard to believe that the scope of the programme could be expanded in terms of magnitude and quality. Facilitating scaling up would call for changes in the Guidelines with regard to selection of project implementation agencies, scale of funding and implementation. Some of these changes follow.

- The minimum area for implementation of watershed activities should be reduced so suit the organisational capabilities of the project implementation agencies. The recent changes in the Guidelines to scale down the minimum watershed to 100 ha is a welcome step in this direction. This is likely to encourage more small organisations with strong grass-roots presence to get involved in the programme.
- The level of funding should be based on specific conditions, i.e., climate and condition of the natural resources, rather than the prevailing norms under the Guidelines.

Laying down criteria for identifying watershed-training institutions, thematic areas and training syllabus, building institutional capabilities for training, and building or setting up new training institutions in areas where they are non-existent, would also be critical to spreading the watershed programme to new geographical areas.

The conventional approach to promoting community organisations or people's institutions lays too much emphasis on the role of external agencies, and the strength of people's institutions is largely ignored. It is argued that strong, effective people's institutions can play a critical role in promoting participation by exchange of experiences and information through training and exposure visits.

VIKSAT has experimented with the concept of people-to-people process in scaling up JFM activities in Gujarat. The institutional avenues through which the concept is being practised are: (a) a federation of village-level people's institutions working in Bhiloda and a neighbouring area of Sabarkantha district in North Gujarat, named the Lok Van Kalyan Parishad; and (b) a state-level federation of people's institutions and other federations working on JFM and other forestry-related activities, named SAKSHAM. The experiments with the Parishad and SAKSHAM proved successful in terms of scaling up the community-based efforts in JFM. VIKSAT is drawing upon these experiences in the forestry sector for its participatory groundwater-management programme, which it initiated in Kheralu *taluka* of Mehsana district in North Gujarat. These concepts can be applied beneficially to a watershed-development programme.

Concluding Remarks

For watershed development under the Guidelines to be sustainable in the long-run, programme emphasis must shift from the achievement of physical and financial targets to capacity building of local institutions and the promotion of decentralisation. For this, a thorough review of the programme needs to be made in terms of norms and procedures, processes and implementation strategies, and achievements and impacts. Existing institutional capabilities for training and capacity building need to be strengthened before further expansion of the programme is taken up. Apart from this, the orientation of people from various organisations involved in the programme—from the government agencies to the project implementation agencies—regarding concepts, philosophy and strategies in watershed development is essential for successful implementation of the programme.

4   Strengthening the Participation of Women in Watershed Management

VASUDHA LOKUR-PANGARE[1] AND JOHN FARRINGTON[2]

This chapter follows the same pattern as earlier chapters. First, it sets out the broad issues. This is then followed by a consideration of provisions relating to women contained in the 1994 Guidelines, an assessment of how adequately these have been implemented in practice, and suggestions for improved strategies and practices in relation to women. This is followed by two Extracts, describing how these issues have been dealt with in two watershed projects: the Rayalaseema Watershed Development Programme in Andhra Pradesh and the Indo-German Watershed Development Programme in Maharashtra. The chapter ends with the recommendations from a workshop on women in watershed development, held in New Delhi in October 1996 (Extract 4.3).

THE ISSUES

The importance of increasing women's participation in watershed development has been recognised, and efforts are being made in this direction. However, there is still a need to sensitise policy-makers and staff of project implementing agencies to the core issues in ensuring benefits to women from watershed-development projects.

Activities currently undertaken for women in watershed development projects do not empower them to be equal partners with men. Women are currently treated as 'disadvantaged', and so are regarded as needing welfare handouts. In reality, they are integral members of the commu-

[1] Oikos, Flat No. 4 Saikrupa, 34/4 Prabhat Road, Pune 4, India
[2] Overseas Development Institute, London, UK

nity and rely on the natural resource base no less than do men. They therefore need to be involved equally in decision-making. The real reason that women are 'disadvantaged' is because their contribution to the rural economy is not recognised. Consequently, they do not receive their rightful compensation in terms of wages, or in terms of ownership of productive assets, and benefits accruing from them.

A major component of watershed development is to improve agriculture and increase land productivity. Agricultural development programmes have always targeted men rather than women, since women are rarely viewed as 'farmers'. Therefore, in watershed development too, it is male farmers who first come forward to participate in the programme. Women, however, often perform more tasks and spend more hours than men in agricultural production.

This becomes all the more important since more men than women are shifting to non-farm livelihoods, leaving agricultural tasks to women. However, in the absence of the men, women are not able to take any decisions related to the land, since the land titles do not belong to them. It is the (male) landowner who is nominated to the decision-making body for watershed development projects, although the woman may be actually farming the land. Agarwal (1994) argues that allowing women to hold land titles would motivate them to increase output and adopt better farming practices, besides increasing their access to credit, inputs and technology. Access to arable land is mainly through inheritance, which varies by region and religion. Although laws today give more rights to women, significant inequalities remain, more so because of the disinheritance that takes place in practice. Some of the important reasons leading to disinheritance are male reluctance to endow daughters with land, women's forgoing of their shares in parental property in favour of their brothers, and obstruction by government officials in the implementation of laws in favour of women.

Women's needs and priorities are similarly overlooked in relation to common-pool resources. These resources provide women with livelihood options that are not always visible. Restricting access to them increases drudgery in fuel and fodder collection, and reduces the livelihood options available to women. Assessing the interface between livelihoods and the resource base can help keep in focus issues related to the economic survival of women resource-users through the planning and implementation stages of the project.

Despite this, little attempt has been made to involve women in decision-making related to common-pool resources such as *panchayat* and forest lands within watershed-project areas, or to give them control over the management of these resources. Although some thought has been given to the formation of 'user groups' for this purpose, there is no clarity as to who are members of these groups and how they are to be constituted. The closest parallel can be drawn from the experiences of the Joint Forest Management programme, where local institutions are formed to represent the interests of the different user groups of a forest area. Even here, however, inherent gender disparities can be seen.

The formal local institutions have a three-tier pyramidal structure (Sarin et al. 1996). The base consists of the general body, which periodically elects a managing committee of seven to fifteen members, out of which three or four are appointed as office bearers. Without being a general body member, one cannot be elected to the managing committee, and it is the general body membership that has a direct bearing on who can and cannot participate in the decision-making process and access the benefits available to the members. Traditionally women have been excluded from community activities, and the village *panchayat* has been a male-dominated institution. These cultural norms make it difficult for women to participate in any local institution set up for decision making, like the general body in the JFM. In addition, the household is used as the basic unit of the general body membership, and the initial JFM orders prescribed eligibility of only one representative per household as a member of the general body. This automatically excluded women, since men were looked upon as the heads of households. Similarly, in watershed development projects, the required consent for the project from a two-thirds majority in the village is usually taken from the men as representatives of their households (Lokur-Pangare, 1996), thus effectively excluding women from the beginning.

The recommended number of women (one-third) to be appointed to watershed committees has resulted in tokenism, since one or two women on male-dominated committees are unable to contribute to the decision-making process. Besides, one or two women usually do not represent the interests of all the women in the community. Women are a heterogeneous group, and women from different sections of the community have different needs.

Women are often unable to participate in community activities without the support of their families. It is the responsibility of the project implementing agency to facilitate the participation of women in community activities by setting up support systems. It is also important, therefore, for the project implementing agency to have specially trained staff.

Since watershed development has a significant technical component, it is important that women also be given technical training so that they have the option to move up in the decision-making hierarchy controlling the project implementation.

An important area that needs to be looked into is that of equity issues in wage employment in watershed development programmes. Disparities are found in wages paid to men and women, both for agricultural labour as well as on physical works undertaken by the project.

Overall, therefore, gender disparities arise from the unequal distribution of ownership and control of productive assets between men and women. If decisions related to access and sharing of resources remain exclusively with men, it is likely that women will never receive their share of benefits. It is difficult to address issues related to benefit-sharing among households, but attempts can certainly be made to improve intra-household benefit-sharing for women through community projects.

WATERSHED DEVELOPMENT GUIDELINES CONCERNING WOMEN

The NWDPRA Guidelines make no particular provisions to ensure that the particular needs of women are addressed. The 1994 Common Guidelines governing projects, programmes and schemes under the Ministry of Rural Areas and Employment, (GoI 1994) which broadly also govern the projects implemented by NGOs and funded by the Council for Advancement of People's Action and Rural Technology, stipulate that:

A resolution from the *gram panchayat* [shall be obtained] to the effect that [it] shall be willing to share the benefits from [common] assets with the weaker sections of society such as Schedule Castes, Schedule Tribes, women and other persons below the poverty line in an equitable manner (section 25).

Priority may be given to the selection of villages for watershed rehabilitation where homogeneous groups have already been set up for activities such as Development of Women and Children in Rural Areas; where social and community-based campaigns (such as for literacy, family welfare, prohibition of alcohol etc.) have been successfully organised in the recent past; where water is allocated on a priority basis, and where other facilities are provided to 'serve' the lands of marginal farmers and of women (para 25).

At the village level, the watershed committee should have 'adequate representation' (generally interpreted as 30 per cent) of women, of scheduled tribes and castes, and any other weaker section (section 37). Of the three watershed volunteers assisting the watershed secretary, at least one will be a woman (section 38).

The watershed development team, in the period prior to decisions over rehabilitation, should help to form homogeneous self-help groups focusing on specific activities (termed 'entry-point activities'), for which up to 5 per cent of the works allowance can be used. These should include women's groups (section 70).

The watershed development team should also identify and help to form user groups, i.e. those most likely to be affected by investment in rehabilitation, in order to ensure that their interests are not jeopardised by the better off. These should include women's interests (section 75).

Finally, in states where the 73rd Constitutional Amendment has been implemented, and *panchayati raj* institutions at district, block, and village levels are taking over the allocation of watershed-development funds, then the (at least nominal) influence of women on these decisions is enhanced by the provision that at least 30 per cent of places on the *gram panchayats* must be reserved for women and members of scheduled tribes and castes.

SHORTCOMINGS IN EXISTING APPROACHES

During their review of the implementation of the Common Guidelines, Turton et al. (1998: iv) noted that 'to provide the poor and women with an equitable share of benefits requires more effort and vigilance than most implementing agencies can currently provide'. The review recognised that to remedy this would be a long-term process, involving capacity building and sensitisation at several levels. Additionally, steps would have to be taken to ensure that at least one woman held a place on the watershed development team; that 30 per cent of places on the District Watershed Development Advisory Committee and the State Watershed Programme Implementation and Review Committee would be reserved for women; and that social-science skills on watershed development teams and elsewhere should be strengthened.

The review team also found that inadequate time and resources were set aside for entry-point and group-formation activities, and that the scope for links with existing women's groups (e.g., for savings and credit) was not being fully exploited. The watershed action plans reviewed in Andhra Pradesh, Madhya Pradesh and Orissa seemed to specify inadequately how the benefits from common land—of particular importance to the livelihoods of women and the poor—were to be shared.

Turton et al. recommended changes in several further areas. These included studies on practical provisions to make it easier for women officers to undertake field duties, and on how it had proven possible in some rehabilitated watersheds to share the benefits equitably with women and the poor. A stronger element of gender sensitisation would have to be introduced into capacity-building programmes at all levels, and greater attention given at the village level to assessing women's skills and training needs.

As argued at the beginning of this chapter, development projects should not regard women as disadvantaged and therefore meriting welfare 'handouts', but as resource-users whose views need to be incorporated in development plans. A number of strategies for 'mainstreaming' the participation of women in this way were discussed at the April 1998 National Workshop on Watershed Approaches for Wastelands Development (on which this book is based), and are presented in Box 4.1.

Discussions at the same workshop led to a number of recommendations for the more appropriate inclusion of women in watershed rehabilitation and development. These are summarised in Box 4.2.

A workshop in October 1996 to assess how effectively gender issues were being considered in CAPART projects generated a

---

Box 4.1   Strategies for Mainstreaming the Participation of Women in Watershed Development

- Begin with a livelihood-resource survey rather than a technical survey.
- Study access/control dynamics in resource management in the community.
- Form homogeneous groups of resource users, containing both men and women, based on the livelihood-resource survey.
- Introduce activities that motivate the formation of these groups.
- Explain project activities so that men and women are able to identify the contribution they can make.
- Ensure that the time and venue of meetings are convenient for all members of the community.
- Set up support systems in the community to enable women to participate.
- Make technical training available to men and women.
- Identify both men and women leaders as motivators.
- Sensitise project implementation agency staff to gender dynamics in the community.
- Make 50 per cent representation of women in the *gram sabha* compulsory.
- Make equal representation of men and women in the watershed committee compulsory.
- Maintain a continuous dialogue with the men to gain their acceptance towards equal participation by women in the programme.

Source: Lokur-Pangare (1998).

Box 4.2   Recommendations for Including Women in Watershed Rehabilitation and Development

- Watershed projects should be implemented in two stages. During the first stage, the project implementation agency should understand the community, conduct a livelihood-resource survey, and build women's organisations. The budget provided for entry-point activities could be used for this. In addition, an extra budget could be provided for capacity-building for agency staff.
- The second stage should consist of the implementation of project activities. The implementation should be performance- and target-oriented, with monitoring and evaluation an integral part of the project.
- The proposal submitted by the project implementation agency should indicate how women's issues will be addressed, and what would be the indicators of success for the integration of gender issues in the programme.
- The budget available for specific activities for women is only a small percentage of the total budget. Funds should be made available for strengthening women's groups.
- Livelihood options should be provided for women through appropriate income-generating activities.
- In order to create an environment for, and facilitate the participation of women in village-level committees, the representation of women should be made 50 per cent.
- Technical training should be made available to women.
- Capacity-building for project implementation agency staff, village leaders, motivators, and committee members should be emphasised.

Source: DoWD (1998).

---

number of recommendations (Lokur-Pangare 1996). These included the need for:

- a resource survey at the pre-proposal stage, which would outline how women's access to and control of resources, and the benefits they obtain, would be influenced by the project;
- consent for major decisions from a two-thirds majority of the adults in the community, of whom initially one-third (and ultimately one-half) should be women;
- recognition of women's rights over private and common resources;
- facilitating the participation of women resource-users in decision-making;
- the payment of equal wages to men and women for equal work;
- the provision of training for women to meet their needs; and
- the establishment of a monitoring system capable of identifying how these measures had performed and indicating where course corrections might be necessary.

The full recommendations are contained in Extract 4.3.

CASE STUDIES

A number of donor-supported efforts have experimented with different ways to ensure that women receive an equitable share of the benefits of watershed rehabilitation. For instance, the Indo-Swiss Participatory Watershed Development Programme, based in Bijapur, Karnataka, has paid particular attention to the creation of self-help groups. In Bijapur, a total of 16 men's and 16 women's self-help groups were formed, with an average of some 20 members each. Loans and training were given to encourage involvement in a range of activities, such as goat and sheep rearing, wool spinning, milch animals and small-scale businesses such as tailoring. These groups have saved a total of over Rs 200,000 to date, and credit recovery has exceeded 90 per cent (Devendrappa 1998). A similar strategy is used in the European Commission-supported Doon Valley Project in Uttar Pradesh (Sharma and Virgo 1998), though considerable internal distrust had to be overcome before the villagers would risk depositing savings in a central fund, and before village leaders could be persuaded to authorise loans.

Some of the projects involving BAIF (Kakade and Hegde 1998) have taken a more strategic approach to selecting 'entry-point' activities which women's self-help groups can be encouraged to undertake. They have focused on reducing the amount of time women have to allocate to routine activities (such as grinding grain or carrying water) so that they can spend more time in the watershed-planning meetings, where matters affecting their interests are decided. The group purchase and operation of a flour mill has proven feasible, but only certain facets of domestic water supply can be taken on as entry-point activities. These include rooftop water-harvesting. By contrast, the deepening of existing wells requires more substantial investment, and has to be taken on in the main phase of project implementation.

Chapter 1 described how many of the programmes and projects supported by NGOs have a strong empowerment component, and this often extends to women. The Rayalseema Watershed Development Programme (Andhra Pradesh), which is implemented by the Deccan Development Society with funds from a number of European-based NGOs, aims explicitly to strengthen women's position in society by planning and implementing a gender-sensitive programme (Rukmini Rao 1998, see also Extract 4.1). As with many others, the programme insists on strong representation of women at all levels, and promotes men's and women's self-help groups. It is unusual in the high degree of emphasis given to gender justice in initial orientation meetings for all staff, and in its emphasis on continuous group action, mutual learning and regular monitoring. Extract 4.1 details how NGO-managed watershed-rehabilitation projects in three separate areas developed strategies to identify and deal with the women's problems, which included accessing government benefits (including those for single women), creating strategic opportunities for women to assert their demands, and affirming their rights over private and common land. A priority was to influence the opinions of men, so that opposition to women's activities would be minimised.

The Indo-German Watershed Development Programme in Maharashtra locates its approach towards women within carefully structured criteria for the selection of villages and implementing NGOs. Again, it has a programme of learning and capacity building which relies heavily on exposure visits and learning-by-doing. Extract 4.2 from Marcella d'Souza's work describes how this is done.

CONCLUSIONS

In many Indian cultural traditions, women have been given a lower economic and social status than that of men. Many of the attempts currently being made to break these moulds regard women potentially as passive beneficiaries of special concessions. In reality, women are strong contributors to the economic and social well-being of rural areas—and should be regarded as such. This implies that they should be given equal representation with men on the various committees dealing with watershed development, and equal wages in construction and other work. But they should also be given the technical and social support (such as childcare) necessary to allow them to play a full role in watershed development. We suggested in the previous chapter that more time and resources should be allocated, prior to watershed planning, to strengthening the negotiating and leadership capabilities of the poor, for example through focus-group activities. The same argument applies in the present context: homogeneous and focused women's groups need to be formed and supported if they are to develop the capacity to defend their interests in more complex (and more contested) negotiations over watershed development.

In addition, if women's interests are to be adequately represented, it will be necessary for government and project officers to be sensitised to women's roles and needs, and to ways of meeting those needs. Ways will have to be found of increasing the proportion of women officers on watershed committees and elected bodies and, especially in the case of watershed development teams, of making it easier for them to undertake field duties. Monitoring systems must be established to assess how women's interests are being defended.

EXTRACT 4.1
GENDER AND PARTICIPATION IN WATERSHED MANAGEMENT[3]

V. RUKMINI RAO[4]

This Extract describes how gender issues were treated in the Rayalaseema Watershed Development Programme (RWDP), which is funded by a consortium of European NGOs. The RWDP worked with a number of NGO project implementation agencies in Andhra Pradesh.

Processes to Orient Implementing Organisations

The NGO partners were selected after initial orientation on the programme's aims and objectives. The orientation stressed the need to ensure gender justice and people's contributions. Organisations that were committed to this decided to join the programme, while many others dropped out. Potential NGO partners were informed that they would have to ensure the availability of female coordinators for the programme. Watershed coordinators live in project villages to ensure continuous interaction with the community.

Planning for the programme started with discussions on gender relations in the project area and the status of people's knowledge. The programme stressed the need for maximising employment generation for the landless, low castes, and poor women. Continuous group action, mutual learning and regular monitoring were emphasised.

The programme envisaged a step-by-step approach for project planning that involved analysing the training needs of the staff and people in the project area. The first training focused on participatory planning, worked towards identifying different livelihood groups, and discussed their needs and problems as a basis for watershed planning. The gender division of labour and the status of women in each project area were analysed. The course also focused on the landless and how to maximise

[3] Source: Rukmini Rao (1998).
[4] Deccan Development Society, A-6 Meera Apts, Basheerbagh, Hyderabad 500029, India.

benefits for them as well as for other vulnerable groups. After the initial training, each organisation went back to its respective project area and gathered information necessary to develop its first draft plan for action. In the first year, an annual action plan was worked out. With growing expertise, each group was able to develop the total watershed plan. The phased development of the action plan made it possible for the community to learn from its experience.

By contrast with existing practice, the watershed programme was not seen primarily as a technical, soil- and water-conservation plan, but as a possibility to develop people's skills and resources. This helped to maintain a focus on 'people'—both men and women.

The groups meet regularly every six months to review their experiences and share learning. Initially project coordinators, directors of voluntary organisations, the core team of technical support staff and advisory committee members came together. Subsequently, representatives of the watershed committees and user groups also met. These meetings provided an excellent opportunity to learn from each others' experience, reflect on innovative initiatives and debate participatory approaches, including monetary and labour contributions. Strategies for conflict management and resolution were also shared. Efforts were made to promote a network of groups implementing watershed programmes to encourage lateral and continuous learning.

The programme comprises six voluntary implementing organisations in the region. The three case studies below illustrate the efforts to increase gender justice. Salient features of the watersheds are provided in Table 4.1.

Krushi: Creating Gender Justice

Gerigela Vanka Watershed Area Development Project is implemented by the NGO Krushi, and is located in Madanapalle, Chittoor district. Project implementation started in 1995. The watershed area covers a total of 700 acres, including 541 acres of private land and 159 acres of common property. The six villages in the watershed are covered by two *panchayats*. Some 281 families live in the area and belong to following castes: scheduled castes, 35; scheduled tribes, 61; backward castes, 97; other castes, 88. The total population of the area is 1,153 comprising 340 women, 463 men, 297 children, and 53 elderly people. Some 41 families were landless. They belonged to following castes: scheduled castes, 3; scheduled tribes, 9; backward castes, 22; and other castes, 7. There were 23 single women living in the project area.

Table 4.1 Rayalaseema Watershed Development Programme: Details of Watershed Area

Organisation	Krushi	Jana Jaagriti	Praja Abhyuday Samastha
Project name	Gerigela Vanka Watershed Area Development Project		Gaddur Watershed Development Programme
Location (Andhra Pradesh)	Madanapalle, Chittoor district	Tanakal, Anantapur district	Ramkuppam Mandal, Chittoor district
Private property	541 acres	400 acres	450 acres
Common property	159 acres	200 acres	200 acres
No. of villages in watershed	6	3	2
Nature of village	heterogeneous	heterogeneous	heterogeneous

Participatory problem identification   People's participation was elicited from the beginning of the programme. First, a street-theatre group toured the six villages to bring awareness of environmental degradation and its impact on people. After regular visits had created an atmosphere of trust and had opened the possibility for dialogue, participatory rural appraisals were carried out and problems being faced by the people were identified. These are listed in Table 4.2.

Women experienced a lack of power in decisions related to children's education, sale of lands, cropping patterns, etc. In particular, the group identified that women did not travel to and attend public meetings or village-level meetings, or exert influence over *panchayat* decisions. This was seen as a potential block to women's participation in the watershed.

In spite of their heavy workload, women were paid low wages. Workload analysis showed that women on average worked eight hours at home and ten hours outside (total 18 hours); men on average worked three hours at home and six hours outside (total nine hours).

**Table 4.2 Problems Identified through Participatory Rural Appraisal,
Madanapalle, Chittoor (Krushi Project)**

General	Lack of housing titles
	Lack of ration cards
	Lack of *anganwadi* (Integrated Child Dev. Services) school
	Unemployment
	Low wage rates
	Forced out-migration due to lack of work
	Scarcity of drinking water
	Shortage of fuel wood
	Seasonal shortage of fodder
	Landlessness
	Unhygienic conditions in village
	Lack of sanitation
Economic problems faced by women	Women were without assets; they did not own land or houses
	Women did not have any common group programmes
	No support from local government to poor women
	Forced migration
Specific gender role-related problems	Marital conflicts
	Atrocities against women
	Low and discriminatory wage rates given to women
	High unemployment among women
	Excessive workload on women
	Lack of decision-making power
	Girls' education neglected
Health problems	Children not immunised
	Skin diseases among children
	Women suffer from gynaecological problems and anaemia
Land-related problems	Land is hilly with steep slopes
	Land is degraded due to formation of gullies
	Topsoil is being washed away due to steep slopes, exposing rocks on the ridges
	Low productivity of land due to its degraded condition
	Gerigela Venka (the stream) breaches its bunds and washes away farmers' private land
	Government programmes do not reach the real needy; government schemes are mismanaged

The education of girls was neglected because they looked after younger children or went out to work.

After the participatory appraisals, household surveys were carried out to highlight the specific problems of special categories of vulnerable persons, such as aged and single women. Issues related to the vulnerable groups were regularly discussed.

Creating male support While physical works were being planned, Krushi emphasised the need to involve women in all levels of activity. This led to a debate in the community on the role and competence of women. The debate and continuous discussion fostered an atmosphere of support among the whole community. Male support was generated because of their increasing understanding of the women's work burden. Secondly, *dalit* men began to see that processes of oppression were similar in the public and private domains. For example, caste norms excluded *dalit* men from participating as equals in mainstream village politics. They understood that their deprived economic situation contributed to their status, and realised that the politics of exclusion was not fair. Men came to agree that women had an equal right to participate in development processes. This enabled them to take the following decisions: all committees and associations would have equal representation of women; men and women would be paid equal wages; special efforts would be made to ensure work availability to vulnerable groups such as single women; women and men would participate equally in all watershed activities.

Watershed committees were formed as in Table 4.3. The village-level committees have worked exceedingly well. In particular, women in the monitoring committees laid down and enforced strict quality norms.

Developing women's leadership Local women's leadership was encouraged

Table 4.3 Details of Watershed Committees, Madanapalle, Chittoor (Krushi Project)

	Men	*Women*	*Total*
Watershed central committee	5	5	10
Village-level committee	3	3	6
Watershed volunteers	4	5	9
Monitoring committee	4	4	8

in a number of ways. Women and men participated in all training and exposure visits in equal numbers. This was a norm for the programme. If women were not ready to travel, the exposure visits were postponed. Exposure visits and training helped to give women confidence based on knowledge.

To support the development of women's leadership, separate meetings with women were conducted regularly by the woman coordinator of the watershed. These meetings discussed women's perception of their own skills and abilities, and women were encouraged to learn new skills, articulate their needs and try out new ideas. Women were also provided with detailed information about the watershed activities. As a result, women were able to exert their influence with growing confidence.

Separate organisations of women created a forum to discuss problems and solutions freely. After coming to collective decisions in separate meetings, female members in different watershed committees were able to push their agenda forward, such as demanding and receiving equal wages. They could also forcefully demand changes in earlier discriminatory practices or decisions (such as payment only to male members of families). In several instances, work groups were reorganised to ensure employment of women.

Thrift and credit groups   Women have been motivated to form thrift and credit groups. Within 18 months, 126 women had started a savings programme and in that period had saved Rs 42,515. The thrift groups in the district are, however, facing problems from the local administration. They are being asked to save only under the Development of Women and Children in Rural Areas programme (DWACRA, a government-sponsored thrift and credit programme to take up income-generation activities), and are being forced to stop other savings.

This is the main reason why not all women in the watershed have yet joined existing groups. The government-sponsored DWACRA programme does not meet subsistence needs, and does not make funds available at the discretion of groups and their needs. This local policy (in other districts of Andhra Pradesh women are free to save in their own *sangams*) is hampering the growth of savings and self-help development in the watershed area. In spite of this women, are determined to manage their own money.

The creation of collective assets, in the form of thrift groups, gave women confidence that they could become self-reliant. Instead of going to moneylenders, they could borrow from each other in times of distress, and could start new income-generation programmes from their own funds. Access to collective funds has enhanced the status of women in the community.

Women's influence in decision making Initially, women were seen as unable to carry out certain tasks, such as building stone weirs, and were thus likely to lose work. However after several discussions, the composition (male–female ratio) of work teams was changed to ensure women's employment. Women were also trained on-the-job to do the work. Other decisions that were influenced included the type of trees to be grown in the nursery, and quality standards, which women active in the monitoring team improved. While men in the team were willing to overlook substandard work, the women insisted on good-quality work to prevent future problems. Payments were made only after the problems had been rectified, if necessary. Initially, payments were made to husbands if a couple worked. Women soon insisted that they receive not only their own wages, but also that of the husband. Constant, special efforts were made to identify vulnerable women and provide them with work. As a result, women have to date worked for 7220 days, and men for 8354. The disparity in employment had been created early in the programme before women started exerting their influence. Women as a group have received wages of Rs 216,600, and men Rs 250,650. Single women as a group received Rs 72,700 in wages.

Women's cooperative society To ensure long-term benefits to women, it was felt that women should take up self-employment schemes. To begin with, 23 single women have been constituted into a Pragati Cooperative Society. The society will be further strengthened by including landless and very poor women. The society is planning a number of activities, including establishing a brick kiln and small shops, trading in locally available tamarind, and leasing land for farming and sheep breeding. The success of the society depends on the supportive climate provided by local government.

Accessing existing government programmes The watershed activities galvanised the poor in the community to come together and collectively access government funds. The women's groups were able to access and acquire ownership rights over wasteland for ten women, including four single women. With the help of Krushi, the groups accessed the benefits shown in Table 4.4.

Meeting the strategic needs of women While developing livelihoods to meet basic needs is a long-term effort, Krushi has helped organise women to meet their strategic needs. 'Strategic needs' are defined as enabling con-

Table 4.4 Government Resources Mobilised for 23 Single Women, Madanapalle, Chittoor (Krushi Project)

Benefits	Number
Ration card	10
Old-age pension	2
Widow's pensions	4
Flood relief	1
Nationality family benefit scheme	7, worth Rs 36,000
Land allocation for 10 landless women, including 4 single women	20.25 acres, worth Rs 410,000
House sites	15

ditions which assist women in seeking gender justice i.e., better living conditions and genuine choice to manage their lives (the ability and possibility of attending meetings and taking decisions is an example of meeting strategic needs).

The struggle to meet both basic and strategic needs has been strengthened through the watershed development intervention. A process of change towards establishing equal rights has been initiated. Two organisations have been formed: the Vyavasaya (agriculture) Coolie Union, and Stree Chaitanya Shakthi. Through these organisations (the former a mixed group, and the latter only for women), women's needs and demands are projected to the community and government. Men with a reputation for fair dealings were identified to support women's self-assertion. Cases of atrocities against women are taken up by the women's organisations, and justice ensured for vulnerable women. Cases handled by Stree Chaitanya Shakthi include marital disputes, rape, cheating and the projection of anti-women attitudes in media. The organisation of women to enforce their own rights has given them confidence to deal with different government departments, including the police. A process of change towards establishing equal rights has been initiated.

Role of the voluntary organisation in developing women's leadership The intervening agency has a significant role to play in moulding the

views of men in the community. Krushi saw the watershed programme as an opportunity to create gender justice. This understanding guided its activities. Initially, the men in the area were reluctant
to pay women minimum wages and to accept equal wages along with
them, because they thought that women work less than men. An
analysis of the number of hours worked by men and women and
the range of tasks carried out by women convinced the men that all
should take an equal wage. The NGO commitment was essential in
bringing about change.

Women were viewed as less skilled and able than men in many construction activities—a view often internalised by women. These attitudes
were changed by discussing the skills needed for each kind of activity. In
some cases, it became clear that men did not have the necessary skills
either. A review of training needs of men and women created an atmosphere for learning, which helped women to cross gender barriers.

The identification of women with leadership potential and their training by Krushi led to women placing demands for gender justice. Women
refused to accept unequal wages or to hand over their wages to male
relatives, and made significant contributions to discussions and decisions—so a change of attitude was inevitable.

The separate organisation of women in the community and their
struggles for government resources also changed the view of women
as subordinate. The women's groups in the area were active in con-
fronting local elites. They faced harassment, and dealt with issues as
a group. This helped them demand and receive the status of equal
partners.

The current experience also shows that women are able to assert
themselves more in smaller groups and in their own village. In large
groups, they are still hesitant to speak out. However they have made a
significant beginning to change their own situation and the attitudes of
their community.

Jana Jaagriti: Establishing Women's Rights over Common-
Property Resources

Jana Jaagriti is implementing a watershed programme in Tanakal area
of Anantapur district. The watershed has a common resource of
200 acres of revenue land. This land has been neglected for many
years, leading to its degradation. All the tree cover was lost through
illegal tree felling, forest burning, intensive grazing and excessive
fuelwood gathering.

As part of the watershed implementation, Jana Jaagriti has intervened and supported the community to improve the common-property resource. The organisation took the following initiatives:

- Discussions were held with the community on natural resource protection and management.
- Sixty women formed two user groups to protect the entire 200 acres of the revenue land.
- An interested local man, Mr Chakra Naik, took responsibility to guard the area voluntarily with the support of other villagers.
- The women's organisation took the initiative to acquire usufruct rights for the women users' group. The allocation to a user group of the usufruct rights to government-revenue land is the first of its kind in the area. It could prove to be a model to other community organisations.
- The legal sanction of usufruct rights enhanced the interest and motivation of the user-group members to protect the resource.
- Essential interventions, such as soil and water conservation on severely degraded patches, seed broadcasting, planting, etc., are being carried out to speed the regeneration of the area.
- The user group developed a separate accounting system for managing the resource. Grass was plentiful after the first year of protection. This was sold locally, and the savings after deduction of wages for women watchers were deposited in the bank.
- After one year, the vegetation has improved tremendously due to good protection of the entire area. This was made possible by the commitment of the well-organised women's user group.

While the women have improved resources on the wasteland, one issue remains. The Mandal Revenue Officer has issued tree titles for the whole area with a reservation clause 'that this *patta* [title] shall be liable to be cancelled by the government either at the end of any *Fasli* year,[5] or at any other time after three months notice. In either case, no compensation can be claimed by the *pattadars* [title holders]'.

The women are concerned that their rights can be taken away without compensation. They feel vulnerable that after years of effort, they may not receive any benefits. It is necessary to ensure that rights remain with the user and management groups as long as they do not breach their contract.

[5] A *Fasli* year is a seasonal calendar followed by the Parsee community in India. It begins in March.

Praja Abhyudaya Samstha: Establishing Women's Rights to Private-Property Resources

Praja Abhyudaya Samstha is located in Ramkuppam Mandal in Chittoor district and is implementing the Gaddur Watershed Development Programme. A large part of the land was distributed to landless families by the government, although 82 acres were under dispute because the land was not demarcated individually, and local landlords claimed part. The land was uncultivated due to the lack of resources among the poor.

Praja Abhyudaya Samstha mobilised the whole community to establish their rights collectively as well as individually. Women played an active role in asserting their rights, and legal action was also taken. In the past women have often played an active role in demanding land reforms and in the struggle to access land, but usually men have benefited by receiving the ownership rights. In this instance, constant discussion about gender issues and deprivations faced by women, helped the community to decide that women would be given ownership rights (*pattas*)—and eventually 23 women were. The men in the community agreed to this, though somewhat reluctantly.

Struggle for joint forest management The watershed area is adjacent to forest land. A JFM group was set up in the village. Traditionally, the scheduled caste and scheduled tribe communities in the village were deferential to the local landlord, who was seen as a benevolent person, and so he was elected president of the JFM committee. He also ran a chit fund in the village, in which all the poor participated. When the poor community started organising themselves, the landlord did not oppose watershed activities directly, but started a number of land disputes, and also passed an order as president of the JFM committee that no one should be allowed to enter the forest. Since the whole scheduled tribe community was dependent on the forest for its livelihood (such as the raw material for weaving bamboo baskets) this order was a jolt to the group.

The group has become aware that their dependence on the landlord has led to serious consequences. As such, they now plan to democratise their JFM committee and elect representatives who are forest users rather than elites. They are also withdrawing from the local chit-fund system, which has ruined several families due to high interest rates, and most of the women have joined thrift groups in the watershed.

Through the process of coming together to implement the watershed programme, the group has set up a Bamboo Society with 60 men and 38 women. It has also set up a community Joint Farming Society of 43 members with 102 acres.

An interesting feature here is that Praja Abhyudaya Samstha male staff voiced concern that some men in the community were feeling left out. This was because all discussions in the community provided considerable space and time to women, and ownership of newly acquired land was given to women using the 'family' ideology. Ownership by women would still give benefits to men. Though they are happy to have acquired land, the men still feel deprived, and a strategy to ensure their continuing involvement is necessary.

Conclusion

All three cases described here have followed a systematic strategy to involve farmers in the watershed development programmes. The steps followed by each project are:

- attempt to understand the resource situation with the help of participatory appraisal methods;
- identify problems and issues in the watershed;
- collect individual action plans—each farmer plans the work to be executed on his or her land;
- form user groups of people with common problems or developmental needs and aspirations;
- identify local and exogenous technical options, and finalise an appropriate solution to the problem;
- calculate the approximate cost of each activity, along with contributions or cost-sharing between the organisation and villagers;
- summarise individual action plans into an activity-wise action plan;
- execute the approved action plan;
- establish people's monitoring committees to ensure quality control and payment;
- in the second year, raise issues of food security, non-chemical approaches to pest management, and sustainable agriculture;
- strengthen people's organisations and initiatives for self-management; this includes creating financial and systems viability for sustaining new institutions.

Participatory monitoring   Success indicators were developed collectively to monitor all aspects of the watershed development process. Table 4.5 lists women-related issues to be monitored. With additional experience, more indicators will be added (these indicators are meant to measure success in terms of establishing better livelihood conditions for women). The women identified the problems they faced, and baseline data have been collected, against which to measure success indicators.

Table 4.5 Women-Related Performance Criteria Developed with Support of Rayalaseema

Problem	Indicators for measuring success
Women do not own land or assets	How many acres of land have women acquired?
Women do not have access to or control over common resources	Have women established rights over common property resources? How many women (over how many acres) have planted trees and earned usufruct rights? Through this, how many women are earning how much additional income? How many landless and single women have established rights over common-property resources? Are women equal and active members of forest protection committees?
Women's heavy workload due to shortage of drinking water, fodder and fuel wood	What is the annual increase in production of fuel, wood and fodder on common lands? How close are these available?
Women's heavy workload, high number of work hours	By how many hours is women's work reduced? Are men participating in housework?
Lack of women's skills for income-generating agri-based activity	Have women developed new skills to take up agri-based industry?
Low female wages, discriminatory rates	Have wages for women increased, and has wage discrimination been reduced or eliminated?
No control by women over earnings	Do women control their income?
Lack of women's decision-making authority over cropping pattern	Do women grow crops of their choice?
Insufficient food to meet family needs	Does the number of months when food stocks are adequate increase annually?
Income reduced due to forest degradation	Has family income increased annually due to forest development?
Lack of women's skills to market products (ropes, etc.)	Are women able to market their products?

Table 4.5 (continued)

Problem	Indicators for measuring success
Women unable to participate in public meetings	Do women actively participate in public meetings?
Women lack a place in decision-making groups	Do women participate in a wide a range of groups and take an active role in decision making?
Girls not sent to school	Are all school-age girls enrolled in and attending school?
No social security for single and elderly women	Has a minimum level of social security been created for single and elderly women?
Women lack sanitation/latrines	Have low-cost latrines been built for women?
Inconvenient kitchens full of smoke	Have smokeless chulhas been installed?
Women lack adequate understanding of health problems and issues	Are village health workers providing adequate services? Has women's knowledge of health issues improved?

EXTRACT 4.2
WATERSHED DEVELOPMENT: CREATING SPACE FOR WOMEN[6]

MARCELLA D'SOUZA[7]

Introduction

While watershed development may initially lead to an increase in women's workloads, it can also offer unique opportunities to improve their economic situation and enhance their status in society (D'Souza 1997). Specifically, watershed development has a notable impact on employment and income opportunities, food security, fodder, fuel and water availability and access to credit. Socially, impacts relate to migration rates and the status and self-confidence of

[6] Source: D'Souza (1998).

[7] Gender specialist, Watershed Organisation Trust, Indo-German Watershed Development Programme, opposite Social Centre, Market Yard Road, Ahmednagar 414 001, India.

women. The degree of positive impact varies over time (with benefits becoming evident three to four years after a programme begins) and depends on how far development plans allow for women's empowerment.

This Extract draws on experiences from watershed development projects implemented by the Indo-German Watershed Development Programme in Maharashtra (Farrington and Lobo 1997). The majority of the watersheds are characterised by the following conditions:

- They are 500 to 1,500 hectares in size and are located in drought-prone areas, with an annual rainfall ranging from 150 to 800 mm.
- Hills and wastelands have sparse vegetative cover and are mainly barren and degraded.
- Agriculture is largely rainfed, and the main crops are coarse cereals.

The projects have the following characteristics:

- They are implemented by those living within the watershed, through a village watershed committee supported by an NGO. The watershed committee is a representative body, nominated through consensus by the *gram sabha*. Rehabilitation is planned and implemented using external and local expertise.
- A ridge-to-valley approach is followed, with an emphasis on soil-and water conservation and biomass development. Grazing is controlled and tree felling is banned in project areas.
- The total time taken for project implementation, including a capacity-building phase, is approximately five to six years.

We focus here on some options for mitigating the negative impacts of watershed development, to enable women to become more self-reliant and self-confident. We address two key issues:

- Ways to capitalise on opportunities and mitigate some of the key problems arising from watershed-development activities.
- The approach: the organisational framework and mechanisms adopted by the Indo-German Watershed Project to create space for women in watershed development.

Opportunities for Women in Watershed Development

There is no denying that watershed development, at least in the initial years, does lead to an increase in women's workload. Nevertheless, women indicate their willingness to carry out this extra work, provided it leads to the fulfilment of four basic needs:

- Access to a reliable source of safe drinking water within a reasonable distance, and improvements in health and hygiene.

- Access to a steady flow of income to ensure food, fuel and financial security. The latter is especially important in times of crisis—for instance if the women are abandoned by their husbands or widowed.
- A future for their children through education.
- Participation in household decision-making (in decisions regarding utilisation of funds, upbringing of their children, farming) and in village affairs, and acceptance in and respect of society.

This Extract focuses on some possibilities for mitigating the negative impacts of watershed development on women. The first few sections provide some practical examples of options and mechanisms for capitalising on opportunities created by watershed development efforts. These are followed by an outline of the Indo-German Watershed Development Programme approach to 'creating space' for women in watershed development.

Financial Security

In rural Maharashtra, financial security comes from wages (preferably a regular source within the village) and returns on investments and inputs. *Wages* A desirable wage is one which not only meets survival and social needs, but also enables investment for further contingencies—sickness and old age—and acquisition of income-generating assets such as dairy cattle.

It is important, therefore, that any watershed-development effort should provide a wage sufficient to ensure that savings can provide some buffer for the period after the end of the project, as well as allowing investments in livestock and other livelihood or income-generating assets. Moreover, it should also allow for increased travel and participation in social, cultural, religious and other events, which widen horizons and boost self-confidence.

The local agricultural wage is generally lower than that provided to people for project-assisted work. After the watershed development project, however, agricultural wages tend to be higher (assuming favourable weather), due to an increase in the net irrigated area, greater agricultural and land productivity, and the withdrawal from the labour force of some small and marginal farmers, who return to their own farms once their productivity increases. To ensure that at least a fair wage is available, it is important that the measures adopted during the project lead to a substantial increase in land productivity. Soil- and water-conservation activities are not enough; a substantial portion of arable land should be able to produce at least two crops a year.

Returns on investments These generally come from four sources: (a) income from private farms; (b) farm-based activities; (c) non-farm activities; and (d) savings and credit activities. These are dealt with in turn below.

Income from private farms While increases in agricultural productivity might occur as a result of watershed development, on-farm gains are usually appropriated by men, and increased drudgery is borne disproportionately by women. Although this is difficult to change, it is possible to introduce improved agricultural implements and mechanisation that will reduce drudgery and save women's time. Much remains to be done in the area of improving and disseminating non-mechanised farm tools. On common land or private fallow land, grass production and cutting is generally perceived as a woman's chore. This can also provide income for women, especially when, through project intervention, intensive cultivation and management of nutritious and improved fodder species is undertaken. It is possible to introduce effective tools for cutting fodder.

Farm-based activities Bans on free grazing, pasture development through tree and grass planting, and soil- and water-conservation measures lead to an increase in fodder production on both common and private lands, and increased availability of drinking water. This can lead to an increase in the number of crossbred animals and stall-fed goat rearing. Fish farming, using water in the check-dams, is another potential source of income, and also produces nutritious food. Small livestock such as goats are usually the preserve of women, and they often retain the income from goat production. Care should be undertaken to ensure that small ruminants are penned and, as far as possible, managed collectively. This denies men the excuse of taking over the management of these livestock on grounds of alleged incompetence and the destruction by free grazing of plantations 'they' have raised. It also provides some assurance that the earnings generated will remain with the women themselves.

Non-farm livelihood activities Due to the heavy demand for forest and horticultural species during project implementation, raising nurseries can provide women with substantial income. Nurseries also provide a training ground in the dynamics of group management and functioning, by developing skills in negotiation, conflict resolution, bargaining and management, which are necessary to successfully run any micro-enterprise. Once the project is completed, the demand for trees declines (if external markets have not been obtained), although the demand for high-value horticultural species is likely to remain. It is therefore essential that nurseries should be of a composite nature. Appropriate skills and training in seed selection, nursery raising and grafting should be given to women.

With the increasing demand for organically grown crops and food products, the production of compost manure, bio-fertilisers, vermicompost and bio-pesticides (for example collecting and processing seeds of neem and other local plants) can provide income as well as inputs to improve land quality and productivity. Fortuitously, this is an area that is traditionally viewed as women's work. NGOs need to provide technology, management and marketing support from the outset of the project to ensure efficient group functioning.

Establishing income-generating activities is a more difficult proposition for remote villages. Non-farm activities are especially important during the lean period when there is less work in the fields, or when there are elderly people at home. These activities should be based on local raw materials and chosen to fill a demand for the end product. Possible options include mushroom cultivation and plate production.

Savings and credit activities   Savings and credit activities provide an important means through which women can control their own finances. Individual savings are pooled to form group capital. This is used to provide loans to meet productive and consumptive needs. It is important that groups understand that 'cash floating is cash alive'. That is, cash given in loans multiplies. Women themselves can control access to their funds if they are taught simple accounting and the maintenance of ledgers. Training can also assist women to take decisions over the prioritisation of loans, and can enable individual women to withstand pressure from men by claiming helplessness in the face of group ownership.

Food and Fuel Security

With an increase in land productivity, men frequently choose to increase the production of cash crops such as sugarcane, timber and cotton. It is important, therefore, that women are included in decisions about land use and crop planning to ensure that household food-requirements (vegetables, fruit and a variety of grains) are adequately provided. It is important that both men and women be given information about the nutritive value of various foods and their importance to health, so that the family readily sets aside a sufficient amount for home consumption. As cooking fuel is scarce, women need to be involved in choosing fuel and fodder species. Women and self-help groups can handle the distribution of interim and end products from these plantations.

Education

Women lay great store in education for their children and the acquisition of information, knowledge and skills for themselves. Middle and secondary schools and higher education centres are often located far away, limiting attendance, particularly of girls. Cultural norms and poverty require girls to do household chores and look after younger siblings. Income sources provided by the project and related developments can help reverse this situation. As watershed projects work with the community, the opportunity to promote education, especially for girls, should not be missed.

For tribal people living in remote areas, problems are particularly acute. Apathy and a lack of hope in obtaining productive employment result from poverty and isolation from society in general. In mixed villages, where tribal people and other cultural groups live together, working side-by-side on watershed work, attending watershed committee meetings, *gram sabhas*, self-help groups and *mahila mandal* (women's organisation) activities breaks down barriers and encourages tribal people to take advantage of development and send their children to school. However, in homogeneous tribal villages, special attention and efforts have to be made to promote education.

The increasing integration of urban and rural areas, market development and the widespread use of radio and television are leading to the breakdown of traditional thought patterns. Women, even in remote areas, are increasingly aware that they are being bypassed by progress and are therefore unable to enjoy the benefits of modern development; as such, they are becoming more vocal about their rights. Fortunately, women are beginning to be supported in their quest by men, who are gradually realising that their home situation is a reflection and consequence of the level of knowledge, information and skills women possess. If women are active and capably manage the home, the status of men also increases, particularly in the larger society in which they socialise or conduct commerce. A man's status in rural society is increasingly measured by the image his wife presents socially. While previously women themselves would not think of spending a night away from the family, men increasingly allow women to participate in training of two to three days outside their villages.

The experience of the Indo-German Watershed Development Programme shows that the demand for 'literacy' comes later, usually two to three years after the beginning of the project. Women's initial priority is for information, knowledge and skills related to their daily responsibilities. NGO field workers need to be sensitive to this need, and short, 'action-oriented learning' sessions should be organised accordingly.

Exposure visits, training programmes and *melawas* (social gatherings) give women opportunities to express themselves in public and improve their self confidence. As confidence increases, leadership emerges. These leaders or *mahila pravartaks* (village women promoters) need to be identified and trained to conduct women's group meetings and sessions. This will ensure continuity and functioning of women's groups after the project ends.

Water, Health and Hygiene

While watershed development can lead to an increase in groundwater levels and ensure water is available in the village for longer periods, obtaining water for household needs still consumes on average, one-and-a-half to three hours of a woman's day. Water sources (especially open wells) are often unhygienic. Women should be provided with information on the causes of water contamination, its consequences for health, and simple purification methods. Water sources (open wells, hand pumps, springs) that are susceptible to contamination should be protected by masonry aprons or structures. Wherever possible, a piped drinng-water scheme within the village should be established by the government, other projects or community contributions. The formation of village-level committees or user-group committees can be established (preferably of women) to ensure that water sources are well maintained and protected.

Women bear the burden of their family's ill health. The health and nutrition of women and girls are usually the last priority. Providing information can improve nutritional status. 'Action-oriented learning' sessions on health, hygiene, sanitation, family planning and nutrition are thus important. Keeping kitchen gardens or homestead poultry, and building latrines can help address some of these needs. Soak pits can drain away waste water and improve the hygiene of surroundings, so reducing skin and diarrhoeal infections. Improved, energy-conserving *chulhas* (earthen stoves) and biogas units can reduce time and effort spent on fuel collection (on an average, eight hours a week), as well as cut smoke levels in the kitchen (the cause of many respiratory illnesses) where women and small children usually sit.

Decision Making

Women repeatedly stress that any change in gender relations must be obtained in a manner that does not threaten the harmony of their homes or their security. To create space for women in society, sessions on gender sensitivity need to be organised for men. The approach and method adopted for awareness generation and integration should be consensual, even if at times change appears imperceptibly slow.

Some accompanying initiatives that can prove helpful in accelerating the inclusion of women in decision-making roles include:

- Strengthening women's participation in the *gram sabha*. This requires a determined effort to encourage women to share their problems actively and to seek solutions within their own self-help groups. Savings and credit operations can be a 'nursery' for the acquisition of crucial management, negotiation and bargaining skills.
- Ensuring a minimum of 33 per cent representation of women in the watershed committee. While a 50 per cent representation is preferred, this may not be immediately achievable.
- Active participation in land use and crop planning, as well as in the selection of plantation species and raising of nurseries.
- Fostering and facilitation of activities of women's groups and self-help groups.

IGWDP and the Women's Sector

When the Indo-German Watershed Development Programme was launched in 1993, women were included in the overall programme strategy, but not as a separate sector. It rapidly became clear that unless they were given special attention, their effective contribution in watershed development would not be realised. Moreover, it was recognised that, without the active participation of women in all aspects of the project, the sustainability of the watershed development was questionable. The Women's Promotion Sector was therefore introduced in late 1995. This late addition has had several disadvantages:

- Several of the projects that had begun in 1993 focused on land and water problems. Issues of concern to women had been taken up by only a few projects, mainly at the initiative of NGOs. Since land and water issues are primarily the domain of men, women played practically no role in the decision-making process. At an early stage therefore, watershed development unintentionally became a male-dominated programme. By the end of 1995, only eight out of 43 projects had undertaken some women's activities (kitchen gardens, nursery raising, women's group meetings, etc.), and only five had established savings and credit groups.

- The focus of the NGOs and villagers was on getting work done and on enhancing the productive status of the land. Introducing an intervention for women's promotion was perceived by many as an unnecessary distraction. Where it was accepted, it was viewed as a sectoral intervention, isolated from the main effort of natural resource management, and therefore unrelated to the processes of decision-making in the project.

- Not all NGOs give equal priority to women's development as they do to land, water, and income-generating activities. They do not extend equal support to women staff, resulting in a loss of enthusiasm, inefficiency and discouragement. *Mahila samaj sevika* (female social workers) face particular difficulties. Village women are free to meet only at night, and young social workers are unable to travel to villages alone: they must be accompanied by another staff member. Hence this sector is viewed as a burden by some NGOs. Staff turnover is also high (particularly if the social worker is young and unmarried), resulting in a lack of continuity.

The challenge facing the Indo-German Watershed Development Programme was therefore how to organise a meaningful and productive effort for women's integration and involvement for sustainable watershed development, in a manner that would elicit men's interest and active support.

Towards Women's Integration: A Graduated Response

The goal of intervention in the women's sector is to develop the capacity of women to enable them to actively participate and take up responsibilities for integrated and sustainable development of their watershed. The objectives are:

- To enhance financial and food security, and improve health, hygiene, nutritional and living conditions.
- To reduce drudgery and mitigate some of the effects of the additional workload.
- To improve women's input into decision-making processes in families, institutions and village life.

To achieve this, the Indo-German Watershed Development Programme has adopted several guiding principles (Box 4.3).

Box 4.3 IGWDP Guiding Principles

In order to empower women, men must be taken into confidence. Hence, the focus will not be on women *per se*, but on the family. Without the support of men, they will make little or no progress.

Strength is derived from fellowship and partnerships, which arise from group formation and organisation. Women are therefore encouraged to organise in groups. Activities, even if undertaken individually, are promoted and supported by their group.

Knowledge and understanding is the key to motivated action and efficiency. Efforts are made to help women gain information and knowledge to manage natural resources, improve their managerial skills, increase efficiency, and reduce drudgery.

Access to financial resources empowers and gives societal status. Women should increasingly have access to income sources and have control over the income earned. In this regard, the potential of women to save will be capitalised upon, particularly on a group basis. Group activities that provide livelihood opportunities will be encouraged.

Possessing skills and competencies that are valued by both the household and the village ensures an active role and a valued membership. The skills and competence of women and groups will improve so that they are able to play a contributory role in project implementation and in village and family affairs.

Owning an asset, even a common one (e.g., land), gives a sense of identity and enables alliances for mutual support and advancement. Efforts will be made to transfer land or a lease to the name of women's groups. Moreover, they will then be able to acquire various income-generating assets, which will contribute towards a sense of self-dependence and fulfilment.

Women-to-women' and 'group-to-group' extension is not only effective but also offers a learning and feedback mechanism and creates enthusiasm and synergies. Local women as facilitators and mobilisers, individually and in groups, should be encouraged and employed. They enable quick rapport building and bonding, which greatly promote group functioning and consensus building, and inspire a commonality of purpose and enthusiasm.

Work and needs unite. Watershed activities that involve everyone break down caste and social barriers. This has profound implications both for social dynamics and the quality of life in the village. Women with common needs and concerns from all social groups will be encouraged to come together irrespective of caste, creed or financial status.

Sustainability and replicability are greatly enhanced when local institutional actors, such as government and private agencies, are involved in the delivery of goods and services. Wherever possible, existing government programmes and networks will be accessed and schemes and other projects used. This will help create a sense of 'joint ownership' of the project, necessary for maintenance and continuity.

To ensure sustainability, it is important that lessons and experiences be transmitted from one generation to the next. As the future lies with children, they should be introduced to the why, how and what of environmental regeneration and conservation.

Source: IGWDP (1996).

Phase-wise Proposed Measures

Since 1993, the Indo-German Watershed Development Programme has consisted of two phases. The first consists of a capacity-building phase, where both the NGO and the village grapple with the meaning of participatory watershed development, understand its implications, and experience the initial benefits. This phase is supported by the Watershed Organisation Trust, and is assisted financially by the German Agency for Technical Cooperation (GTZ). This is followed by the full-implementation phase, when both the NGO and the village—especially the watershed committee—are deemed capable of undertaking project implementation. This phase is supported by the National Bank for Agriculture and Rural Development, assisted by the Watershed Organisation Trust and financially aided by the German Bank for Reconstruction and Development.

Capacity-Building Phase

The capacity-building phase comprises two stages. In stage one, the NGO mobilises the watershed community. Most NGOs entering the programme are small and relatively young, with little experience in large-scale implementation of projects to manage natural resources. Their experiences are usually restricted to sectoral interventions. Furthermore, even in the case of well-experienced NGOs, the initial period after entry into a village is one of uncertainty. An intervention like watershed development, which involves all the social and economic groups of the village, necessarily challenges the existing power structure, as well as existing relationships and transaction arrangements. It creates anxieties, insecurities, expectations and aspirations. In the initial period, the situation is often one of ambiguity, and the response of the village is unclear. The entire effort of the NGO is geared towards creating awareness, motivation and mobilising the village's traditional structures. Given the sensitive nature of men–women relationships, interventions with regard to women's promotion and gender integration must be non-threatening, easily achievable and quickly visible.

Both the NGO and the people have to establish their willingness, basic ability and need to implement a watershed project. One of the crucial activities in this stage is the 'exposure visit' to a successfully completed or on-going project. The NGO should encourage the participation of women in the exposure visit, as well as initiate dialogues with the men about the importance of including women in the watershed-development process.

Stage two consists of 'hands-on' experience through soil conservation and tree-planting activities in a micro-watershed. This serves the dual purpose of demonstration and training, and normally lasts about 10–18 months. At this stage, efforts need to be made to prepare the ground for the involvement of women in decision-making roles. Having obtained the support of men for women's activities during stage one, stage two should be used to strengthen and establish women's organisations and self-help groups. A female social worker should be appointed, preferably within three months of the pilot activities. Simple activities that bring quick results should be encouraged, such as kitchen gardens, soak-pits and improved *chulhas* to motivate women to work together and build their group confidence. Savings and credit activities particularly encourage women—and also men to permit their women—to participate in group activities.

During the capacity-building phase, a small fund (up to Rs 20,000 in the case of the Indo-German Watershed Development Programme) may be used for activities that will strengthen the group. If it is used for small income-generating activities, women should be encouraged to treat this as a loan and create a revolving fund of the returns. By the end of this phase, women should have at least a 33 per cent active representation on the watershed committee.

The Full-Implementation Phase

The full-implementation phase also consists of two stages. Having successfully gone through the capacity-building phase, the NGO and watershed committee now prepare a project proposal—the feasibility study—for the entire watershed. This normally takes about six months. The women's groups should have developed a sense of identity, cohesiveness and competence in areas such as managing their finances. By this time too, women's groups would also have seen the benefits accruing from small activities such as kitchen gardens and improved stoves. As a group they should have acquired a measure of mutual confidence and have experienced the possibilities and benefits offered by group action. This should be further strengthened during the feasibility study.

The aim is to ensure that women are involved wherever possible, in different aspects of project planning, especially with regard to land use. In this area, men should be encouraged actively to consider the women's point of view, resulting in joint decisions. After the women's needs have been identified and prioritised, a project proposal should be developed and incorporated in the feasibility study. This proposal should include activities to reduce the workload of women, support child-care and development, and plan for income-generating activities that will be managed exclusively by the women's group. Meanwhile, emerging local women leaders should be identified and given training as village women promoters to conduct their own group meetings and promote various issues and activities.

Implementation is the second stage. It begins with project and feasibility study approval and lasts up to 48 months. Once implementation starts in the capacity-building phase, it continues without a break (assuming favourable conditions), even though a complete project proposal will not have been prepared and formally sanctioned. This is to ensure that there is no break in mobilisation, enthusiasm and organisation.

Until now the measures and steps undertaken will have largely been organisational in nature, bringing women together and building their confidence. The primary focus of stage two is to strengthen and elaborate on the processes initiated in the capacity-building phase, and to undertake specific activities which will strengthen women's technical and managerial capacities, their financial position, and their ability to collaborate in village decision-making processes. Those women not already in self-help groups should be motivated to form groups. Men's self-help groups should be encouraged, as this promotes a better use of saved income. During this phase, the activities generally consist of training and exposure visits directly or indirectly related to watershed development. Care should be taken that activities do not create additional burdens for women. They should be sequenced to gather momentum gradually, so that when the project is over, these activities provide livelihood opportunities. Emphasis is placed on the acquisition of skills by the village women promoters, female social workers, self-help groups, etc., in planning, implementation and management.

A second objective of this stage is to ensure a reduction in the drudgery and uncertainty in women's lives. Other activities having a bearing on women should also be included (for instance, arrangements for obtaining potable water, fuel for cooking and fodder within reachable distance). Sanitation, child care, health and hygiene, as well as non-formal education sessions, can also be considered. The progressive inclusion of women who were not earlier involved in the programme is also critical. Linkages with government departments, as well as with village institutions, are actively promoted. Efforts are also needed to ensure that the dependence of women's groups on NGOs and social workers is progressively reduced. Active thought should be given to transferring these values beyond the project period, so that women themselves can manage successfully what they have begun.

The expected outcome of this phase will be a definite improvement in the financial position of women, acquisition of income-generating assets where possible, and regular and active participation in decision-making meetings. A reduction in distress migration, increased food security and increased school attendance by children can also be expected. It is important that active support from the government and political establishment be gained.

Conclusion

Watershed development, if addressed in a gender-focused and sensitive manner from the beginning, can provide a space for women to capitalise on new opportunities. It calls for an inclusive and sustained effort that brings men to recognise and accept the contribution that self-confident women can bring to society.

EXTRACT 4.3
RECOMMENDATIONS OF THE WORKSHOP ON WOMEN IN WATERSHED DEVELOPMENT[8]

VASUDHA LOKUR-PANGARE[9]

Introduction

The Guidelines for Watershed Conservation and Development Programme issued by Council for Advancement of People's Action and Rural Technology, New Delhi, (CAPART 1996), state that:
'special emphasis will be given to improve the economic and social conditions of the resource poor and the disadvantaged sections of the watershed community such as the assetless and the women...'

The Guidelines recognise the fact that women are disadvantaged, and that special efforts need to be made to improve their situation. However, this statement reinforces the fact that women as a group are not recognised as an integral part of the community. What it implies is that

---

[8] Workshop held in New Delhi, 27–29 October 1996. Adapted from Lokur-Pangare (1996).
[9] Oikos, Flat No. 4 Saikrupa, 34/4 Prabhat Road, Pune 4, India.

the community consists of men, and women are a group that requires special welfare services. Women do not have rights; they are recipients of welfare services.

In fact, community participation in the context of watershed management usually refers to the participation of only the men, and not really the community, as consisting of men and women. This results from the assumption of the household as the unit of participation, and not the individual adult as a participating member of the community. Since it is presumed that men are the heads of households, the participation of men supposedly becomes synonymous with the participation of all the members of the household.

National statistics show that one-fifth to one-third of households are headed by women. With increasing out-migration of men from the rural areas, women have to assume greater responsibilities in running their households. Women contribute significantly not only to the household, but also to the village economy. In spite of this, women's participation in watershed development is judged mostly by the number of women working as labourers on construction sites, or by their 'presence' in meetings.

Although the importance of increasing women's participation in watershed development is recognised, and efforts are being made to sensitise and train project implementation agency staff to facilitate women's participation in watershed projects, it is also important to ensure equal division of benefits to women within the household and the community. Equal division of benefits for women can be achieved only if the women participate in decision making. In fact, better and more effective participation of women in community activities may improve intra household benefit sharing as well. Table 4.6 summarises workshop participants' perceptions of existing versus possible future roles for women in watershed-development projects.

Identifying Resource Users in the Watershed Community

The planning or setting up of a watershed development project begins with the formation of a watershed committee in the village, and with the project implementing agency preparing a detailed project plan with the help of engineers and technical staff. A technical survey is conducted right in the beginning because it is on the basis of the technical survey that the funds are allotted to the implementing agency. However, the technical survey generally involves only those members of the community who own land in the watershed, or those

Table 4.6 Perceptions of the Role and Contribution of Women in Watershed Development

Stage, activity	Present role	Possible future role
1. Planning & decision making		
Formation of watershed committees	Limited representation on committees	Equal representation on committees
Preparing project proposals:		
• Survey	None	Assist in survey
• Identifying soil- and water-conservation structures	None	Share knowledge and experience
• Contributing land for selected sites	None	Assist in decision making related to contribution of land
• Preparing budgets	None	Participate in decisions related to labour and other costs
2. Implementation		
Constructing conservation structures	Provide labour	Supervise, maintain ledgers, musters, make payments
Maintaining conservation structures	Provide labour	Initiate decisions on maintenance, supervision, maintaining ledgers, etc.
Developing agriculture	Provide labour; limited decision making on family lands	Receive training inputs, contribute to community-level decisions
Forestry and tree planting	Provide labour; limited decision on selection of species; maintain nurseries	Participate equally in decision making on selection of species and areas for plantation, provide technical inputs, supervise plantation sites
Fodder and grazing lands	None	Participate equally in decisions related to development of grasslands, rotational grazing, stall feeding
Horticulture	Provide labour	Select fruit, process, market
Dairy, animal husbandry	Provide labour	Technical inputs, process milk, market
3. Management & delivery systems	None	Participate equally in decision making, provide technical inputs, share knowledge & information, ensure just distribution of resources
4. Social & welfare aspects	Have limited access to health & education	Identify community needs, ensure availability of welfare
5. Alternative energy programmes	Provide labour	Identify alternate resources for energy; plan and implement

who exercise some form of control over its resources. This control could be financial or political. As a result, the landless, especially women (who form the single largest group of the landless), are left out.

On the other hand, when attempts are being made to emphasise people's participation and community organisation as a prerequisite for success, it makes more sense to begin with a resource-use survey rather than a technical survey. A resource-use survey would help in identifying the categories of resource users in the community, who need access to resources such as grass, trees, water for domestic purposes, irrigation water and agricultural land.

Watershed development and management essentially deal with people's resources—not only those of the landowners, but also those of the landless and the poorest, who depend upon common-pool resources for their survival. When decisions are being made that will affect the livelihoods of these people, it is important that their interests are represented and taken into account. This can happen only if the people have been identified in the community as resource users.

In order to understand resource use in the watershed it is important to assess which resource is used, by whom, and for what purpose according to season. After this assessment, plans should be made to incorporate the perspectives of the various resource users who have been identified. Issues related to the economic survival of these individuals need to be addressed right from the beginning.

Gender Equations in Local Planning and Decision Making Institutions

Along with the project implementing agency, it is the village-level watershed development committee that is responsible for planning and decision making. While it is debatable whether the village committee actually makes any contribution to decision making, it is definitely true that the women rarely contribute to this process. Unless those who make decisions and plan policies study the problems faced by women, the interests of women will be almost completely left out.

It is mandatory under the various guidelines issued for watershed development, that one member of the village committee should be a woman. However, this does not necessarily mean that the woman committee member is an active participant, or even that she represents the interests of the women resource-users in the community. One workshop participant recounted the following anecdote:

A project implementing agency was once asked to introduce the woman member of the watershed committee. When the agency demonstrated its reluctance to produce the woman member, discreet inquiries were made in order to identify her. It turned out that there really was no woman member. The project implementing agency had been under pressure to nominate a woman member, and had done so without consulting the woman in question, who was not even aware of the nomination. It appeared that women in the village were not encouraged to participate in community activities, and therefore when women were asked to volunteer, not a single woman came forward. Clearly, the project implementing agency had not made adequate efforts to facilitate the participation of women in the community activity, nor had sufficient time been spent in understanding the community they planned to work with.

Even when women do volunteer, and begin to attend the meetings, how successful are they in expressing their views or influencing decisions? A few influential members or well-off farmers usually dominate the committees, and women rarely get an opportunity to raise issues or voice opinions.

Apart from social and cultural constraints to participation, economic constraints also affect the participation of women. Lack of access to credit and inability to invest in community enterprise do not empower the women to contribute to community decision-making. Besides, women hardly ever have control over land resources, and watershed development activities are mostly controlled by landowners—especially since most of these activities begin on private lands, where benefits are more perceptible to farmers.

Most rural households meet their subsistence needs from their immediate environment. And it is the women in these households who are responsible for accessing these natural resources from the environment. Women are also responsible for the health and nutrition of their families, in terms of providing safe drinking water, maintaining hygiene in the home, and providing nutrition through food. Therefore when the environment is degraded, the responsibility and the work burden of women increase. They have to spend longer hours fetching water, fuelwood and fodder to meet the needs of the household. Women resource-users have a greater interest in reviving the ecosystems and conserving the natural resources. Yet they are given no place in the planning and decision-making related to the watershed development activities.

In order to facilitate the participation of women user-groups in the decision-making process, the objectives of the project implementing agency and the plans for intervention in the watershed should be made available to them from the very beginning. This could be done through the *gram sabha*, in which 50 per cent attendance of women should be made compulsory. In addition, these plans should be discussed separately with the women in smaller groups to obtain the viewpoints of different categories of resource users.

The prerequisite for signatory consent of two-thirds of adults in the community should be carefully defined to specify who these adults are. Experience has shown that generally it is the heads of two-thirds of the households in the village who sign their consent. This leaves out the poor and the landless, particularly women. Therefore, it is important that the signatures represent the census composition of the village in terms of gender, caste, occupation, and economic classification.

In the Uttan project area in Gujarat, marked differences were reported in the proposals prepared by men and by women in the community. The proposal prepared by men emphasised the construction of various physical structures for soil- and water-conservation, and the proposal prepared by women prioritised the needs of the community. Since the emphasis in watershed development is on the creation of structures, people sometimes accept structures that are not really required, because construction work provides employment. Even in technical surveys, the differing perceptions of suitable structures have to be taken into account. It is therefore all the more important to involve women resource-users in the project-planning stage.

Although watershed development may be the aim of the project, it is extremely important to prioritise the needs of different groups within the community, and deal with them in order to develop mutual trust between the project implementing agency and the community. In the long run, this is what will determine the success of the watershed development programme and will ensure effective use of public interventions.

5 Multi-Agency Partnerships in Watershed Development

Three distinct types of agencies have historically been involved in watershed development in India: (a) service-providing NGOs; (b) international funding agencies, whether lenders (such as the World Bank) or bilateral or multilateral donors; and (c) government bodies: units of Union or State governments, operating at the central or local level.

In some cases these organisations have operated in isolation (but with some cross-learning—see Extract 5.2); in others, attempts have been made to gain potential synergies by facilitating ways in which they might work together. In a limited number of contexts, these agencies have jointly designed, implemented and taken responsibility (and, where appropriate, credit) for joint activities (Extract 5.3). 'Partnership' here is defined as a comprehensive interaction of this type. In addition, there are much more limited interactions in which, for instance, an NGO might be contracted by a public-sector agency to carry out a task which is predefined to a greater or lesser degree. Such interactions are potentially valuable in bringing the distinctive qualities of a particular type of organisation (such as an NGO) to bear, and so are considered below, but they do not constitute full partnership.

This chapter is set out in four sections:

- It reviews the arguments in favour of multi-agency partnerships and the conditions that must be in place for such partnerships to function effectively, drawing on the Indian and international literature.
- It examines the provisions made in the 1994 Common Guidelines in respect of multi-agency partnerships.
- It assesses how adequately these provisions have been implemented in practice.
- It provides a number of case studies of how multi-agency partnerships have been attempted hitherto, under what conditions, and with what degree of success.

This chapter deals only with partnerships among development administration organisations concerned with watershed development. Chapter 6 deals with the interface between these organisations and the newly decentralised political bodies under the *Panchayati Raj* Act.

The Case for Multi-Agency Partnerships

The majority of experience with multi-agency partnerships in India is with those involving government and NGOs; this forms the focus of the discussion below.

In a wide-ranging review, Carney and Farrington (1998) summarise the arguments in favour of partnerships, namely that government agencies bring technical expertise and the resources for broad coverage, whilst NGOs and membership organisations generally have particular expertise in needs assessment and in promoting and supporting joint action. There is some evidence that this distinction is being blurred: Thompson (1995), for instance, notes three major cases in which the public sector is putting into practice the skills in participation conventionally associated with NGOs. Despite this, the conclusion reached by Carney and Farrington was that the effectiveness of the whole (different types of agencies working together) could be expected to be greater than the sum of the parts (separate agencies working alone). Echoing the findings of a major review by Farrington and Bebbington (1993), they go on, however, to note the very limited evidence of successful partnership between the two sides. This suggests that a major contributory factor is the long history of sole state responsibility in, for instance, agriculture and forestry sectors, together with widespread views in government that NGOs lack important technical skills and are in many cases of doubtful financial probity. Specifically in India, one observer (Arya 1998) has argued that four characteristics of how Indian government departments conventionally conceive and execute projects and programmes make it difficult for NGOs, with their ethic of participation and empowerment, to engage with government programmes. These are: (a) the government relies heavily on ready-made, technology-driven products; (b) it relies on subsidies, implying that beneficiaries should simply accept the money and get on with implementing what the government has proposed; (c) its philosophy is one of 'we will plan for you and implement it for you'; and (d) as a consequence, dependency is created and people's own initiatives to take responsibility for their own economic and social progress are undermined.

Carney and Farrington (1998) suggest that the preconditions for wider partnerships in the future include:

•   commitment to multi-agency partnerships at the highest level, but shared among middle-ranking and junior government staff, who in practical terms, have the power to undermine such efforts if they remain unconvinced;

- greater flexibility in government procedures for co-funding with NGOs;
- incorporation by each side of some elements of the skills of the other if they are to communicate adequately about objectives, implementation and outcomes;
- a forum (or several different kinds of forums—see Alsop et al. (1999) and Farrington et al. (1998)) needs to be established to facilitate communication and collaboration, jointly monitor progress, and correct the course as necessary.

In practice, the interest among many organisations—perhaps especially in government—in identifying why previous collaborative efforts have not succeeded, and the capacity to learn and spread lessons from previous experience, remain weak.

For successful partnerships, governments and donors need to promote change in several specific areas. They need to revise the performance criteria and reward systems in the public sector to stimulate collaborative action and to provide a n□□ ew sense of mission. Procedures need to be streamlined in government for allocating funds to NGOs and membership organisations, so as to accommodate the diverse requirements of multi-agency approaches. The skills necessary for closer collaboration need to be introduced and consolidated in the public sector, including stakeholder analysis, needs assessment, management of the project cycle, negotiating capacity and conflict resolution. Finally, procedures need to be introduced at the outset for monitoring multi-agency partnerships and making course corrections.

Many NGOs have expressed the fear that partnerships may result in nothing more than a single monolithic institution with a paternalistic notion of development and of how the needs of rural people should be met. This is a valid concern, yet early evidence suggests that with sensitive, shared, management and specifically adapted 'rules and regulations', this need not be the case (Alsop et al. 1999, Mosse et al. 1998).

Provisions for Multi-Agency Partnerships in the 1994 Common Guidelines

The Common Guidelines make provision for a wide range of organisations to be engaged as 'project implementing agencies', including: NGOs, universities, agricultural research and training institutes, corporations, cooperatives, banks, public and private commercial organisations, *panchayati raj* institution and government departments. In practice, the great majority of project implementing agencies have been either government departments or NGOs. Project implementing agencies have considerable latitude in collaborating with village institutions such as *gram sabhas* and function-specific groups (self-help groups and community-based organisations) in helping to design a watershed-rehabilitation programme, so that their particular qualities can find full expression. However, the relationship between project implementing agencies and the District Rural Development Agencies (DRDAs) or *zilla parishads*, through which Ministry of Rural Areas and Employment funding for watershed development is channelled, remains a contractual one. Nor is there provision for different types of organisation to work together at the local level: in each watershed setting, one or other type of organisation constitutes the project implementing agency, and there is no provision for an implementing agency to be made up of two or more collaborating organisations.

The same is essentially true of other Guidelines such as those governing CAPART disbursements, which are modelled on the 1994 Common Guidelines, or the Guidelines for the National Watershed Development Programme for Rainfed Areas operating under the Ministry of Agriculture and Cooperation.

The Common Guidelines, Project Implementing Organisations and Collaboration

At the request of the Ministry of Rural Areas and Employment, in late 1997 the UK Department for International Development commissioned ODI to conduct an assessment of how adequately the Common Guidelines were being implemented. Since the Guidelines, strictly speaking, make no provision for partnerships, the review (Turton et al. 1998) does not report directly on these. However, it identifies a number of shortcomings in wider administrative arrangements, which could be addressed if partnership arrangements were implemented properly. Furthermore, it identifies a number of further administrative conditions that would need to be in place for partnerships to function effectively. These include:

- the need for specific criteria for the selection of directors of DRDAs, emphasising the need for them to have experience in participatory approaches to rural development;
- the need for clear criteria for the selection of both NGO and gov-

ernment project implementing agencies, and for de-selection where necessary, and to ensure that project implementation agency staff are full-time;

- the need to develop the social and community development skills of government technical staff. This would help in engaging with NGOs where partnerships are possible, but also help ensure that these skills are available if, for whatever reason, it proves impossible to work with NGOs that have such skills;
- the need to ensure that adequate financial provision is made to cover NGO overheads, that provision is made for a preliminary period of work in group-formation, and that the possibility exists for NGOs (possibly in partnership with technical agencies) to provide continuing support of a technical or institutional kind beyond the end of the implementation period;
- the need to revise the Guidelines to provide greater scope for the formation of joint government–NGO project implementing agencies.

The respective strengths and weaknesses of NGOs and government organisations as project implementing agencies were identified by Turton et al.'s review (Table 5.1).

There are several mechanisms whereby the strengths of NGO project implementing agencies might be complemented by skills normally found in government, and vice versa:

- members of a government agency and an NGO might form a team to work as a project implementation agency through all the successive stages of preparation and implementation of rehabilitation;
- NGO staff might provide initial orientation or training to government agencies acting as project implementation agencies in such areas as group formation, conflict resolution, development of leadership skills, and so on;
- the more careful composition of watershed development teams— drawing in professionals with the social organising skills of NGOs as well as those having the necessary range of technical skills—may institutionalise such support on a continuing basis over the lifetime of the project. One of the few examples where explicit recognition is made of the respective skills of NGOs and government is in the creation of watershed development teams in Mahbubnagar (Andhra Pradesh). Here, NGOs have a strong influence on the selection of individuals to fill the social mobiliser posts in the watershed development teams.

Table 5.1 Strengths and Weaknesses of Government and NGO Project Implementing Agencies

NGOs	*Government*
• Strong in social mobilisation • Conceptually stronger with participatory approaches • Closer and more equal relationship with people • Flexible and adaptive to local situations	• Strong in technical competence (but not in adaptive research) • Have official standing with the community • Clear lines of accountability
But...	*But...*
• Weak in technical competence-non-availability of technical staff in the open market • Poor quality and high turnover of technical staff due to poor salary and working conditions and temporary nature of employment	• Conceptually oriented to top-down approach • Lack flexibility • Emphasise physical and financial targets • Overloaded with numerous programmes • Lack process orientation • Watershed development team members live far away in district headquarters and towns • High rates of transfers • Watershed development team members often not full time • Unable to apply technical knowledge to local circumstances and build on indigenous practices

Source: Turton et al. (1998).

- comprehensive programmes of cross-learning might be arranged, in which project implementing agencies of one type (e.g., government) visit watersheds being rehabilitated with the support of implementing agencies of a different kind (e.g., NGOs);
- mechanisms should be introduced for monitoring the presence of particular kinds of skill at a local level, and corrective action taken where necessary;
- a society could be promoted at the state level for implementing innovative approaches to watershed development. There are precedents for such NGOs promoted by government, but de-linked from government departments, including the Lok Jumbish Parishad in Rajasthan working with the SIDA-supported programme for universal primary education to be achieved by 2007. Such an agency could undertake projects on a pilot basis, and develop new ap-

proaches and field practices for participatory watershed development. Staff seconded to such an organisation could eventually go back to their NGO or parent department and 'graft on' some of the more suitable approaches;

• at the district level, a multi-disciplinary team might be created to provide support to watershed development teams. Some experience with this approach has already been gained in Andhra Pradesh, and could be built upon (Turton et al. 1998).

Finally, one of the most rigorously structured and potentially most powerful examples of combining the strengths of NGOs and the public sector is found in the organisational structure of the Indo-German Watershed Development Programme in Maharashtra. Here, the clear strategy has been to place only NGOs as implementing agencies at the village level, given their skills in participation and social organisation. Technical backup is provided by a much larger NGO (Watershed Organisation Trust), which has a presence at several project centres, and also has the capability of drawing in technical expertise from elsewhere, including NABARD, the Department of Forests and, after rehabilitation, the state departments of agriculture, horticulture, etc. In some ways, this experience parallels the arguments made above for a strong multi-disciplinary team at the district level (see Turton et al. (1998) for information on Andhra Pradesh's experience in this respect). A detailed account of the Indo-German Watershed Development Programme approach is given in Extract 8.4.

EXTRACT 5.1
CO-OPERATION WITH NGOS FOR PEOPLE'S PARTICIPATION IN WATERSHED DEVELOPMENT PROJECTS[1]

TRILOCHAN NAYAK[2]

The Danida-funded Comprehensive Watershed Development Projects in Orissa and Madhya Pradesh are based around close co-operation between the government and NGOs. In each watershed, one NGO is given the responsibility to facilitate local initiatives that lead to institution and

[1] Source: Nayak (1998).
[2] Danida Adviser, Comprehensive Watershed Development Project, Jeypore, Koraput, Orissa, India.

capacity-building of people's organisations on a sustainable basis. This Extract outlines how proper planning arrangements have persuaded NGOs of the importance of coalition building with the government for development activities in the watersheds. It draws on the experiences of the Comprehensive Watershed Development Project in Koraput, Orissa.

Introduction

Koraput and Malkangiri districts are two of the poorest districts of Orissa, with 90 per cent of households below the official poverty line, and literacy just above 10 per cent. Poverty, ignorance and illiteracy are the root causes of backwardness. Hunger, malnutrition and under-employment are the main problems. Eighty per cent of households are landless, small and marginal farmers; they own only 35 per cent of the land. The majority (75 per cent) of households belong to scheduled tribes; 10 per cent are scheduled castes, and 15 per cent are other castes.

Dryland farming is the predominant activity in the area. Any programme for poverty alleviation must therefore aim to increase agricultural productivity and generate employment. Erosion is extensive in both districts, where the plains are almost completely denuded of trees except around villages.

The Comprehensive Watershed Development Project in Koraput and Malkangiri districts has an initial phase of seven years from 1993 to 1999. The project covers 12 watersheds, consisting of 85 villages and 160 hamlets, with a total area of 42,651 ha, involving 11,207 households with a population of 50,000. Watersheds range from 2000 to 5000 ha.

The project started its field implementation from 1994 in three sub-phases, covering four watersheds per year. The project approach is comprehensive, as the aim of the various activities is to develop the natural resource system in a sustainable manner and to increase agricultural production, without causing excessive stress on the environment. The three main components of the project are: (a) awareness building for target-group participation through NGOs; (b) improved agricultural practices promoted through training and extension; and (c) implementation of soil and water conservation measures.

Overview of the Participatory Planning Approach

The project is implemented through the Soil Conservation Department, Government of Orissa. Given their workload, it is not possible for government field officers and technical staff to work effectively to create village-level institutions. Traditionally, government staff have the tech-

nical and organisational knowledge of technology alternatives, but lack
the social science skills; whereas NGOs have high ideals of social service. For the effective implementation of socially acceptable technical
options, NGOs were engaged from the beginning in order to create
alliances with the government.

In all, twelve NGOs are responsible for awareness building, and assist the villagers in articulating their needs to government organisations.
The NGOs have established field offices at the watershed level, which
are staffed by two field organisers—one male and one female. The NGOs
have a network of 'village youth facilitators'—one male and one female
in each village—who work as link persons between the villagers and
project personnel for training, extension and demonstration activities.
At present, 24 field organisers and 210 village youth facilitators are working in the project. The NGOs working with the project aim to create
effective village-level institutions that bring people together, spurring
them into action and ensuring the protection of assets created by the
project.

Selection of NGOs

NGOs are engaged to facilitate local initiatives for institution- and capacity-building on a sustainable basis. Memoranda of understanding were
signed between the selected NGOs and project director after the approval of the District Collector.

Selection of Youth Facilitators

NGOs associated with the watersheds selected one male and one female youth facilitator for each village from among the beneficiary group.
Literacy was one of the criteria for selection, but 30 per cent of watershed villages did not have even one literate person. Hence it was decided
to select facilitators even if they were illiterate. The NGOs took the
responsibility for providing them with literacy skills.

Induction and basic training were then provided to NGO workers
and the youth facilitators. Orientation training was also organised for all
government field staff. The most difficult situations arise when NGOs
and government field staff are not aware of the existing situation of the
watershed villages and the problems faced by villagers.

The first job assigned to the NGOs was to collect socio-economic
data for each village and to engage in informal discussions with local
leaders, particularly older community members. Subsequently the NGOs
organised village meetings to explain the goals and ideas of the project.

The villagers selected four committee members in each village: a head man, one landless person, one woman and one small or marginal farmer. Training programmes were organised for the committee members to explain the content of the project and to outline the specific roles the members were to play. In both the courses for youth facilitators and those for village committee members, the (government) watershed team leader and the (NGO) field organisers acted as resource persons. The main aim was to create a cooperative atmosphere between the government field staff, NGOs and watershed residents.

After the training, the NGOs, youth facilitators, government field staff and watershed committee worked out the details of the project, its objectives and components. Village-level meetings informed the villagers of the different benefits of the project, and villagers were able to express their needs and preferences. Team leaders made detailed field surveys, while the NGOs completed the socio-economic survey. The team leaders convened watershed-level meetings, where all village committee members, field organisers and the team leader sat on a common platform to prepare the annual plan for the project for each village and each watershed. The elected *sarapanch*, who covered several villages in the watershed, chaired the watershed-level committee.

In order to enhance the status of the youth facilitators and field organisers, and to create early project impact, fruit-tree seedlings were distributed in the first year of implementation. The youth facilitators took the responsibility for supervising the distribution of these plants and observing whether people took care of them.

Care has been taken to obtain the approval of the watershed committee members before bringing the project activities into an 'annual action plan' for approval at district- and state-level committees. NGOs co-ordinated with field staff to ensure common planning and implementation based on the needs and preferences of the people, so that no activity was implemented without the people's agreement. A 'project co-ordination committee' meets every two months, where the project director, Danida adviser, team leaders, field organisers and chairman of the watershed-level committee attempt to resolve any problems arising due to improper co-ordination. Working constraints, the review of monthly progress, and work plans for the next month are discussed. If any field problems are beyond the control of team leaders and field organisers, the NGO chief, project director and Danida adviser make a combined visit to solve them.

Experience and Lessons

The governmental system is based on targets and their achievement. Top-down planning rarely meets people's needs. Targets are fixed according to the budget available. This approach does not encourage people's participation. In order to make watershed-development programmes participatory and sustainable, bottom-up planning must be encouraged from the beginning of a project. The emphasis has to be on increasing productivity while conserving the resource base. The mobilisation of community participation is a prerequisite.

The NGOs associated with the watersheds had experience in literacy, health care and some tree-planting activities. Awareness-building, target-group participation and NGO–government collaboration are new to government officials as well as the NGOs. The NGOs do not wish to lose their independence of action and their freedom to criticise. They are afraid of becoming bogged down in bureaucratic proceedings. Professional pride and administrative demand often discourage the government from asking for help from NGOs: implementing authorities were reluctant to accept NGOs at the beginning of the project, and in some cases, mutual suspicion and lack of mutual respect prevented closer co-operation. It took two years to change the thinking, traditions, practices, attitudes and outlook of all concerned.

Participatory rural appraisal exercises conducted in the villages brought people together to initiate their thinking and to gather information on what they know and want. Villagers were brought into a process of information exchange so that they became aware of the various benefits and drawbacks of different technologies, and understood how these related to their existing capacities and experiences.

In the first year of the project, certain activities were started such as land treatment on eroded land, and plantations in 'ridge' villages. However there was little awareness among people about the project or its underlying principles. Farmers did not feel any immediate need for these long-term activities, and so they were poorly accepted. There was a feeling that any activity on common land, or even on private land, would be taken over by the government. Some farmers even approached the authority to return their land. The project tried to alter these views through constant dialogue in meetings and training.

The project focuses on soil-conservation measures for increased production. Most of the activities started on government land alone. Some crop-demonstration activities were begun. High external-input supply had previously been the norm for demonstrations, but this project focused on technologies suitable for small and marginal farmers. The landless obtained some benefit as wage labourers. A number of income-generating activities were also initiated, involving 276 individuals with local skills such as blacksmithing, carpentry, rope-making and bamboo crafts. The project assisted 73 self-help groups to undertake activities such as bamboo crafts, pottery and leaf-plate making. The NGOs have been vital in identifying beneficiaries and creating self-help groups.

Tribal women in the project area are severely disadvantaged. They have no share in decision-making at any level outside their families. Very often, women take part in decisions within the household, but men dominate outside. Women play an important role in all types of agricultural work, collecting water, gathering fuel wood, forest products and grass, caring for livestock, and working as labourers. They also migrate seasonally. As far as their economic status is concerned, women play such an important role that bride-prices are paid instead of dowries.

Women do not participate in meetings unless the issues discussed directly concern them. The inclusion of 105 women youth facilitators and 12 female field organisers in the project has increased women's participation. So far, 105 women's self-help groups (*mahila mandals*), each consisting of 10 to 15 women, have been formed around activities like bamboo crafts, leaf-plate making, duck-keeping and spice-making (Table 5.2). They have also raised 69 nurseries for seedlings.

These groups have so far saved about Rs 66,000; this has helped to free women from indebtedness to local moneylenders. Though these women are illiterate, they are able to make monetary transactions with local banks and post offices. Members of the self-help groups are able to take out loans at low or zero interest during times of need. This arrangement creates a feeling among them of being important outside their home and family.

Local initiatives and leadership among women are developing gradually. Awareness of the importance of cleanliness, health and sanitation and the use of safe drinking water has improved. Women are no longer afraid of government officials or moneylenders; they are now trying to get rid of social evils and illiteracy. While the impact of the government's social developmental programmes is scarcely visible, NGOs associated with the project have initiated educational, motivational and consciousness-raising programmes among the people, working through village committees, self-help groups and youth forums.

The methods adopted by the project to motivate, educate and ultimately bring about social transformation include: (a) village meetings,

Table 5.2 Details of *Mahila Mandals* (Women's Self-Help Groups), Koraput, Orissa, December 1997

Watershed (Block)	*Mahila groups (benefited)*		*Total members (benefited)*		*Project assistance Rs*
Kanagaon (Boriguma)	16	(16)	207	(207)	35,969
Baminjori (Kundura)	19	(2)	199	(25)	16,000
Sindhiguda Manikpur (K. Guma)	6	(6)	35	(35)	23,500
Potagugarh (Malkangiri)	3	(3)	65	(25)	7,250
Kukudanala (B. Guda I)	10	(5)	72	(47)	10,400
Phubugaon-Mohantiput (Kotpad)	19	(1)	172	(5)	1,000
Niliguda (Podia)	3	(0)	23	(0)	–
Damandei (Khairput)	7	(3)	42	(14)	5,736
Kurulunadi (B. Guda II)	10	(10)	78	(78)	23,400
Temurpali (Mathili)	3	(1)	10	(10)	500
Tamsanala (Korkonda)	8	(0)	233	(0)	–
Gublernala (Kalimela)	5	(1)	50	(10)	510

(b) the involvement of village youth facilitators, (c) regular trainings, and (d) field days for the villagers.

Village youth facilitators are assigned the responsibility of ensuring that village plans are implemented and that statutory minimum wages are paid to labourers. Very often participation has been low when the community members are viewed as cheap labour, not as equal partners. Outside labour can be brought in only with the villagers' agreement.

Effective communication within the community is essential to ensure that all groups are aware of the project. Difficult situations arise when the proper transfer of information does not occur from the project to the grassroots level in the planning stage. In such situations, people do not know which activity will be done by the project, its cost, and who will be involved. Overall, community interests must take precedence over other considerations, provided that this does not lead to inappropriate technical solutions.

The need to achieve physical targets among government organisations often leads to speedy implementation at the expense of long-term success. Institutional development at the community level is necessary.

More complex interventions such as plantation and pasture activities on common land are undertaken only in the third year of the project, when inclusive participatory planning processes are well established. This contrasts with situations where government staff pursue an authoritarian approach on common land, and villagers simply become onlookers.

Demonstration patches on wasteland within watersheds encourage people to think of similar activities in their own villages and on private plots. It is clear that if maintenance requirements are too high for the local population to manage, the system will not be sustainable. Hence a range of technologies and options should be identified, from which the community can choose the most feasible and affordable.

Pasture activities and the construction of village ponds have been carried out on common land. In some cases, user groups for these activities have been formed. These groups have organised themselves into co-operatives and contributed labour to create these assets. They have been encouraged to set up revolving funds to manage the profits. This will stimulate development and overcome the risk that, after the project leaves the area, no further expansion of the system takes place. Extra funds generated can be used for other local improvements for which the community needs. These successful attempts have been made through constant dialogue with the people throughout the stages of planning, implementation and monitoring of the activities.

Planning to Improve People's Participation

Several issues are worth bearing in mind for the future:

- In order to change the attitude, outlook and thinking of field staff and NGOs, field visits are necessary to successful projects where government officials are implementing field activities and NGOs have created an atmosphere of community participation.
- There is enormous diversity in the watershed villages. For instance, land-use systems differ greatly between a village in a valley bottom and one on the slope. Planning can be attempted only at the village level, village by village.
- Detailed information needs to be gathered on households' income-generating activities in order to discover what people need and want. This job can be done only when NGOs work very closely with people, and try to bring a common group to work in a united way and impress the implementing authority to include them in the project activities.
- Project activities on common land should be brought under the

control of the village committee. The community must be involved in protecting these areas, and it has to decide how the benefits will be shared. This process is difficult, but if NGOs are guided by ideals and dedication, it is possible.

• In every village there were informal village committees before the project, but these had been slowly dying. NGOs associated with the watershed project should work to revive these organisations.

• In the beginning, people in the watershed area had no interest in the project. Easy money received through the various programmes has added to their lack of interest. Collaboration between the implementing authority and NGOs created a favourable atmosphere to modify their attitude in order to encourage the community to participate fully in project activities.

Conclusion

NGOs have played an essential role in facilitating the participation of villagers in planning, implementing and monitoring project activities. The role of NGOs is recognised by the government, even if grudgingly! At the same time, NGOs are also beginning to realise the importance of building coalitions with the government for development activities in the watersheds, rather than being confrontational. However, the project still has a long way to go.

EXTRACT 5.2
PEOPLE'S PARTICIPATION IN WATERSHED DEVELOPMENT SCHEMES IN KARNATAKA: CHANGING PERSPECTIVES[3]

KAUSHIK MUKHERJEE[4]

Kabbalanala: Experiments with Water and People

Kabbalanala is the name of a 30,000 ha watershed taken up for treatment in 1984 in the dry tracts of Bangalore district. This World Bank-assisted project has been a torch-bearer for the southern part of the country. Its innovative thrust in developing orchard horticulture on mar-

[3] Source: Mukherjee (1998).
[4] Executive Director, Karnataka Watershed Development Society, No. 250, 1st Main, Defence Colony, Indiranagar, Bangalore 560 038, India.

ginal lands is well recognised, as is its pioneering effort in the use of a dedicated multi-disciplinary team. The lack of coordination between line departments, the Achilles' heel of so many watershed projects, was not apparent in the Kabbalanala project, as the entire multi-disciplinary team worked under an exclusive project director. The project staff were freed from procedural shackles, and were encouraged to experiment.

For all its technical appropriateness and innovation, Kabbalanala would not have been a 'pilgrimage' for watershed connoisseurs had it not experimented with popular participation. Interestingly, the component of participation came into the project as a 'mid-course correction' rather than as a pre-conceived parameter. Groups were formed at Kabbalanala by bringing together farmers in a micro-watershed.[5] The main objectives of forming these groups (or *sanghas*, as they were called) were to:

* provide local input to micro-watershed planning;
* manage common-property resources developed by the project;
* act as thrift and credit groups beyond the clutches of exploitative moneylenders and the cumbersome banking system; and
* help in the continued adoption of improved techniques and draw out non-cooperative farmers from their indifference.

To keep the groups from becoming unwieldy, the membership was generally restricted to 30. Each member contributed Rs 100, while the project contributed a further Rs 300 for each member; these amounts formed the initial seed capital of the group. These *sanghas* were deliberately kept informal to free them from statutory red tape, and the project coordinators tried not to spoon-feed them. The groups were engaged in the preparation of treatment plans. The treatment plans emerged after repeated interaction between the villagers' groups and the project specialists. The most important contribution of the Kabbalanala project was the hypothesis that a less-than-perfect solution with roots in participatory methods is more sustainable than a technically perfect fix.

It is revealing to see how popular participation changed the emphasis of the project. Orchard horticulture, which had been just another project component, became a movement. Water-harvesting structures far in excess of designed numbers had to be provided. An eye-opener was the general rejection of vegetative barriers of vetiver grass. In spite of strong pressure from the World Bank and the project staff, the popular attitude to vetiver was indifferent at

[5] The idea came from MYRADA's credit groups, which have been operational in Karnataka since 1982.

best, and outright hostility was not unknown. Conversations with farmers suggested the following reasons:

- Planting of vetiver on contour (key) lines may have minimised soil loss, but it also came in the way of routine agricultural operations like manoeuvring bullocks.
- Unlike some local grasses, vetiver did not make good fodder.
- A vetiver line with gaps caused gullies to form, because water flowed fast through the gaps.
- Repeated re-planting in ill-maintained vetiver lines on farmers' fields by project staff convinced farmers that the government was duty-bound to look after these vegetative strips.

At that time everyone except the farmers was convinced that vetiver was the panacea for all kinds of erosion. There were conferences on vetiver, and a lot of studies showed that farmers coveted it highly…but the potential of self-deception through questionnaire surveys is well-known. There were those die-hard vetiver adherents who even produced syrup out of it. The truth is that never more than 30 per cent of farmers voluntarily adopted and enthusiastically preserved vetiver vegetative soil barriers. Today it is no wonder that respectable (and somewhat red-faced) scientists are having a second look at vetiver.

Now that the watershed project has withdrawn from Kabbalanala, a visit to Dombaradoddi, one of the micro-watersheds is interesting. The mango trees are tall and laden with fruit. The check-dam nearby has water. The *sangha* has had to repair it once. The seed capital of the *sanghas* has grown, though the president castigates a few defaulters. Farmer's fields do not exhibit cultivation along precise mathematical contours, but it is in general across the slope. Inter-cultivation of pulses has come to stay. The farmers have even preserved a few blemish-less lines of vetiver for the occasional specialist visitor!

Self-Help Groups: Beacons of Sustainability

Self-help groups were created by MYRADA to overcome the inadequacies caused by an unresponsive and indifferent rural banking system. The idea of using such groups to plan and preserve structures in micro-watersheds came later. The groups functioned by exerting cohesive moral pressure on their members to keep them from straying. So important was the necessity of cohesion, that initially NGOs went about forming socially homogenous groups to ensure their stability. Needless to say, the recovery of loans advanced by self-help groups is far better than the recovery in the conventional banking system. Typically, in MYRADA's Huthur watershed project, a mere Rs 6,921 is outstanding against the advance of Rs 1,438,355[6] by all the self-help groups. In almost all the watershed development projects in Karnataka, spearheaded by NGOs, the following could be observed:

- Farmers who are members of self-help groups are willing to contribute anywhere from 10 to 33 per cent of the amount required for agreed work involving soil conservation. The groups also agreed to maintain the structures out of their own resources.
- Substantial reductions in unit costs (up to 50 per cent) have been achieved for structures due to the initiative of these groups.
- The groups take up activities which have the potential of quick payback.
- Groups of women and the landless were formed, in addition to the regular groups.
- The sphere of credit activity of any group went much beyond the technicalities of watershed development. A high priority was given to the need for consumption-related credit.

NGOs gained the confidence of the rural communities by contributing to their development initially by traditional means (so called entry-point activities). When the people became receptive, group formation was attempted. Studies have shown that the long-term survival of a self-help group is heavily dependent on its initial motivation. Strong self-help groups have been shown to be the key to sustainability, and project designers were willing to bear the extra cost and time required to set them up. It became possible to expect a contribution from the beneficiaries of a watershed project even at the design stage.[7]

Another bonus was the tendency of self-help groups to minimise the regime of inequity inherent in a watershed development project. Self-help groups of landless villagers are encouraged to take up productive non-land-based activities. It was realised that the biggest challenge of watershed development is to create in it a stake for the landless and marginal farmers. While the classical technical ingredients of watershed development remained relevant, the rigid 'ridge-to-valley' was abandoned. It was realised that rural communities cannot be equally receptive or simultaneously prepared. There was also more willingness (on the part

---

[6] Source: MYRADA Huthur Project statement of accounts ending December 1995.
[7] All watershed projects now operating in Karnataka have an element of people's contribution.

of project facilitators) to accept a 'less than optimal' technical solution for soil conservation with the guarantee of greater sustainability.

The current picture that has emerged shows that the partnership of NGOs and the government has come to stay. In Karnataka there is no bilateral watershed project running without the involvement of NGOs. In the national government, programmes funded by the Ministries of Agriculture and Cooperation and of Rural Areas and Employment; in-built packages exist for NGOs. The scheme floated by the Ministry of Rural Areas and Employment even integrates locally elected bodies with the development of micro-watersheds.

Common Properties: Uncommon Management

In most watersheds in Karnataka, common-property resources hold the key to sustainability as well as suffer the most acute degradation. The conventional method of treating common lands was to afforest them or to turn them into pasture. Very little thought went into the productive capacity of the common property in relation to the population that had access to it. The result was severe depletion of biomass on these lands, making them useless to the community, which in turn became more tolerant to encroachment[8] by adjacent farmers. Though on paper, the common property belonged to the local institutions (*panchayats*), in actual fact, they were exploited by all and managed by none. There were no 'social fences' to protect the thousands of small patches of forest created as commons under various programmes. The upper reaches of many treated watersheds were denuded within less than five years.

A beginning was made in the management of common-property resources when the self-help groups gained control over them. Since they now figured in the community's participative plan, the yield of common lands was sustained consciously. The community decided the species of trees to be planted on these lands. Grazing blocks were rotated appropriately, and fines were levied for the violation of collective decisions. The pressure on the commons exerted by the landless was deflected by providing them with small businesses and income from non-land-based activities. Where the area of common land was inadequate, the self-help groups showed ingenuity by leasing the lands of absentees on mutually beneficial terms. In many watersheds of north Karnataka, the non-arable upper reaches are privately owned, and arrangements with absentee landlords are the only way to create biomass on such lands.

[8] On three separate occasions, the government enacted schemes to regularise such encroachments.

In a far-reaching decision on 12 April 1994, the government of Karnataka operationalised a scheme of Joint Forest Planning and Management. Besides common lands, the community was given control of degraded forest areas outside sanctuaries and national parks. Village forest committees were set up, and these committees channelled 25 per cent of the produce from the forest to the beneficiaries. Half of the output went to the government, and the remaining 25 per cent to the 'village forest development fund' operated by the village forest committee.

The 'P' of PIDOW

The Participative Integrated Development of Watersheds (PIDOW) programme operates in Karnataka with the collaboration of the Swiss Agency for Development and Cooperation in the semi-arid district of Gulbarga. This was one of the earliest programmes in which peoples' participation was seen as important an objective as the treatment of the watershed. The statement of objectives of the project has a familiar ring to it:

To evolve and test a replicable strategy for participative, integrated, sustainable development and rehabilitation of small watersheds in semi-arid areas with special consideration of the interest of the weaker sections of the rural communities such as small and marginal farmers, landless and women.

This would seem quite boastful, but for the fact most has been in fact been achieved in the last 12 years. The PIDOW programme, which started as a community development scheme in 1984, later blossomed into one of the finest watershed projects known. The project is a joint partnership between the Swiss and Karnataka governments and MYRADA, which put into use its experience with self-help groups.

The self-help groups were federated into apex-level 'watershed development associations' at the level of the sub-watershed. The associations play an extremely important role in macro-planning, and act as management engines where MYRADA has withdrawn. The ingredients of sustainability are clearly seen (Table 5.3).

Studies have shown that crop-yields have increased by 20–50 per cent in the watershed. The self-help groups in the project have substantially added to the common-property resource by leasing lands from absentee landlords. Interestingly, the farmers stuck to indigenous soil- and water-conservation practices, refusing to toe the experts' line. Some of these examples are stone-bunds, diversion drains and silt-harvesting structures.

Table 5.3 Self-Help Groups in MYRADA Projects in Karnataka

No. of functioning self-help groups	125
Total common fund	Rs 5,856,300
Total savings	Rs 1,532,774
Loans	Rs 11,133,176
Total number of members	2,759

Source: MYRADA (pers. comm.).

Not that these technologies were unknown to the project specialists, but acceptance of the farmers' practices (with slight refinements) paved the way for better community participation. In some cases it sowed the seeds of 'participatory technology development'. The success of PIDOW has enabled the replication of this model to four other districts of Karnataka.

EXTRACT 5.3
TOWARDS A RELATIONSHIP OF SIGNIFICANCE: A DECADE OF COLLABORATION BETWEEN GOVERNMENT AND NGOS IN RAJASTHAN[9]

VED ARYA[10]

Collaboration among the government and NGOs has been one outcome of the greater emphasis on popular participation, sustainability, and democratic processes in development activities. New roles are therefore required of the government, and new organisations outside the government play an increasingly significant role.

New Approaches

Approaches to development have undergone a dramatic change. Although the old-style, top-down delivery of services shows no signs of disappearing, new-style programmes based on bottom-up planning are here to stay. The challenge of reaching out to large numbers of the poor has compelled governments to invite NGOs, who are, it is hoped, more cost-effective and better at targeting beneficiary populations. The development bureaucracy, whose size is difficult for the exchequer to sustain,

[9] Source: Ayra (1998).
[10] Director of SRIJAN, C 152 DDA Flats, Saket, New Delhi 110017, India.

suffers from a lack of motivation to eradicate poverty. Centralised decision-making, which remains a norm in government, is proving less effective than what seems possible with users' groups, though process work in the latter is intensive and need not be low-cost. Local human resources, appropriate technology, and traditional systems of resource management and health care are being given space in designing more sustainable programme interventions.

New Roles and New Actors

The role and space for elected government in development is being redefined. The private, for-profit sector and voluntary agencies are playing roles earlier reserved for the government. Many NGOs that used to depend entirely on external funds are beginning to work with government agencies, and are discovering new roles for themselves in influencing or substituting for government. *Panchayati raj* institutions, armed with their new constitutional mandate, are carving a new space in grassroots development, particularly in programme implementation—once dominated by state governments and NGOs. Increasing institutional plurality has opened the door for new ways of role and space sharing.

Recognition of inherent complementarity has replaced the perception that the government's and NGOs' roles are essentially adversarial. There is an increasing interest among international donors—bilateral and multi-lateral—to support such relationships in the projects they sponsor. The Government of Rajasthan has, over the past few years, devised many creative ways of working with NGOs. It has drawn up strategies which, with the help of NGOs, increase outreach and enhance the effectiveness of its programmes. It has made a number of institutional changes to shape a new and more effective relationship with the NGOs. Despite these efforts, some of which have been operative for almost a decade, the two still remain 'uneasy bedfellows', and a huge potential remains untapped. Critics of collaboration continue to equate it to 'co-opting' and 'sub-contracting'.

In this Extract, we observe how NGOs and government converge on a number of development objectives that have become social and political imperatives, and divide roles on expected lines and prevailing notions of each other's capacities. While succeeding in some aspects, they still end up with problems in others. The Extract draws lessons from ten years of experience of cross-sectoral collaboration in Rajasthan (see Table 5.4 for a list of projects studied).

Table 5.4 Watershed Projects in Rajasthan Examined for Government–NGO Relationships

Sector	Project	Donors and other partners
Watershed	Pahal	SIDA, Govt of Rajasthan (GoR), local NGOs
Forestry	Joint forest management	Govt of India, local forest dept., local NGOs
Animal husbandry	Artificial insemination	GoR, BAIF
Primary education	Shiksha Karmi	SIDA, GoR, NGOs
Primary education	Lok Jumbish	SIDA, GoR, Lok Jumbish Parishad, NGOs
Minor forest-product marketing	*Tendu* leaves	GoR, ASTHA, other NGOs
Rural credit	Self-help groups	NABARD, banks, PRADAN, SAHYOG
Women's empowerment	WDP	UNICEF, GoR, NGOs
Health	Swasthyakarmi	UNFPA, GoR, NGOs
Command-area development	Saving Water Courses (IGNP)	World Bank, GoR, URMUL
Micro-irrigation	Utthan Project (Madhya Pradesh)	Govt of Madhya Pradesh, PRADAN, banks
Micro-irrigation	Karnataka	Govt of Karnataka, PRERNA, banks
Micro-irrigation	Bihar Plateau Development Project	World Bank, Govt of Bihar, PRADAN

Typology of NGOs

NGOs are, at one level, an expression of voluntarism by the citizenry. They do not work in the same legal and institutional framework as government agencies; they are not sponsored by government. But distinguishing NGOs from government is not enough, as they are not a uniform set. Their diversity needs to be recognised. It is reflected in their voluntarily chosen ideologies, modalities of catalysing change, scale of operations, and connectedness or remoteness from grassroots action. We notice the following distinct categories in Rajasthan:

- *Private philanthropy and charitable trusts*   Their basic motivation is relief and welfare. Mahavir Trust is an example.
- *Intermediary organisations*   Their main agenda could be variously to conduct research, support and train, or bring grassroots NGOs together on a common platform and common agenda. The Indian Institute of Health Management and Research, Rajasthan Voluntary Health Association and Sandhan are some examples.
- *Grassroots development support organisations*   These are involved in implementation of grassroots development projects and promoting groups. Their leadership may, or may not, be local.
- *Membership organisations*   These include local people's groups and organisations with local leadership such as those of artisans (UMBVS) or women (self-help groups), or users' groups.
- *State-sponsored or dependent NGOs*   A new breed, sometimes called 'GONGOs' (government-organised NGOs), promoted outside the rigid framework of government to gain flexibility (from accounting and financial procedures particularly), sometimes less interference from political processes, and less scrutiny. Shiksha Karmi Board, Lok Jumbish Parishad and Bharatiya Gyan Vigyan Samiti are some examples.
- *Social action groups*   These groups are motivated by governmental or structural change; they adopt mobilisation and confrontation as methods to challenge existing structures and mindsets. These are not at all interested in implementing field-level projects. Mazdoor Kisan Sangharsh Samiti is an example of this kind.

In this Extract, we are mainly concerned with NGOs as grassroots development support organisations.

Needs and Objectives of NGO–Government Collaboration

NGOs seek collaboration with government for various reasons: to gain funds, technical or managerial resources; to earn legitimacy or recognition; to adapt a programme to their area; to obtain appropriate solutions to development problems; to enhance people's participation in government programmes; to promote greater accountability and transparency; and to promote reforms in public systems.

Government agencies work with NGOs to enhance people's participation in their programmes, to cover poorly served areas and groups, to test and replicate innovative approaches, and to achieve greater cost effectiveness. Behind NGOs' interest in working with the government (or vice-versa, the government extending invitation to NGOs) lie a convergence in development objectives and practical needs—though fears of losing one's identity also operate (Table 5.5).

Government and NGOs converge on development objectives We observe that the following are the basic premises that motivate government and NGOs to collaborate. These represent the broad rationale that underlies collaborative behaviour.

- Collaboration facilitates the generation and replication of innovations and alternative approaches to development.
- Collaboration is an efficient means of improving the delivery of development programmes and services to rural communities.
- Collaboration has the potential of inducing system or institutional reforms, such as reorienting departments towards bottom-up planning and implementation.
- Collaboration is an effective means of improving people's ability to place demands on public systems and services.

It is not necessary for both government and NGOs to hold similar views on these premises. Indeed, they may also guide those, including donors, who are concerned about promoting government–NGO collaboration as a development strategy. We will now discuss these premises in some detail, using examples from Rajasthan.

The *generation and replication of innovations* to solve development problems is a common objective among government and NGOs. In the process of developing appropriate solutions to problems in a specific area, some NGOs, if not all, develop approaches that might be adopted elsewhere. For example, to address teacher absenteeism in remote villages in a backward region, one NGO experimented with recruiting and training local youths for the job. This was the precursor to the government's Shiksha Karmi programme in the entire state, which involved many NGOs as project implementation agencies. The generation and demonstration of innovative approaches is a role which the state readily agrees that NGOs can perform, and it is prepared to support them in this regard.

Field-testing and refinement of innovation requires flexibility, imagination and an accurate understanding of the local situation: traits that some NGOs possess. However, they may not have the resources or structures to work on a large scale. Hence collaboration with government can

Table 5.5 Convergence in Objectives and Practical Needs of Government and NGOs

Development objective	Role division	Type of NGO required	Relationship	Examples
Service delivery	NGO implements, government funds, often under well-defined schemes	NGO as local organisation (size and innovation capacity not necessary)	Schematic/contractual	Swasthyakarmi
		NGO upscales its own scheme	Dyadic	BAIF's artificial insemination services, PRADAN's lift-irrigation system
Innovation	Government role as funding innovation/research	NGO to think up unconventional ideas	Dyadic or institutional	Initial phase of Shiksha Karmi
Empowerment and participation	NGO as a pressure group and people's organiser, government accountable to people	Strong participation/empowerment orientation	Catalytic (facilitative, confrontational)	Tendu-leaf collectors' cooperatives, self-help groups
System/institutional reform	Role division depends on the type of change introduced: new working methods or new culture in government, or NGOs substituting it in service delivery. Both may mean adjustment by government staff, thus termed as reform	Strong participation and empowerment orientation or systemic understanding to pull through the changes suggested	Institutional-possible mix of the above three	Lok Jumbish Programme, PAHAL, PAWDI, Right to Information Campaign

greatly improve the chances of successful replication of proven approaches. There are two variants for replication: the diffusion of innovation through the government, or the NGO itself undertaking the responsibility of 'scaling up', with government financial support. The case of BAIF, an NGO experienced in the livestock sector, taking up artificial insemination in 13 districts[11] is a classic example of the second strategy. It may be worthwhile to point out here that not all NGO innovations are automatically replicable by the government system. The choice of actors, technology, local demand, and capacity to manage a larger system without losing quality are some important considerations while designing for 'scaling up.'

A second area where government and NGO objectives converge is in efforts to *improve the delivery of services*. This could be done either by filling functional gaps or by reaching remote areas unattractive for government staff. The growing acceptance of NGO participation in government programmes reflects recognition that (a) these programmes and services are not performing adequately, and (b) NGOs have skills and relative advantages that can improve the quality of many programmes. NGOs are local institutions, work closely with community, have a limited geographical area to work in, and respond flexibly and reasonably quickly to a community's demands. A better outreach and more effective targeting of benefits are expected, and at reasonable cost. NGOs' participation in government schemes is the most substantial way of collaboration. Pure examples of this type in Rajasthan include Swasthyakarmi Yojana and the Union government's recently introduced watershed programme (Turton and Farrington 1998).

A third area of convergence is *inducing system or institutional reforms*. System reform could imply structural changes as well as changes in values, attitudes and work cultures. The need for such changes arises from the desirability of improving transparency, accountability and efficiency. While system reforms in government agencies are often initiated externally by donors or by political mandate, the objectives of senior government officials may sometimes converge with those of NGOs. Where such a convergence exists, NGOs with the requisite skills and experience can productively collaborate with government in introducing and refining new approaches. To improve the efficiency of poverty-alleviation programmes such as Integrated Rural Development Programmes and Jawakar Rojgar Yojna in Alwar district, a joint implementation team

---

[11] Similarly, an NGO promoted lift-irrigation schemes in 10 districts (south Bihar) with government funds; the project was externally funded (by the World Bank).

was set up that comprised professionals from an NGO and the block-development administration. Another example is the Lok Jumbish programme, where the attempt is to mobilise the education department to achieve the goal of universal primary education in Rajasthan through promotion of a GONGO, Lok Jumbish Parishad.

Finally, collaboration is a means of addressing the *participation and empowerment* objectives in government programmes. The desirability of people's participation is generally accepted by the state, although NGOs are not always seen as legitimate intermediaries between government programmes and rural communities. NGO philosophies often carry the concept of empowerment considerably further than government is comfortable with. NGOs view their own involvement with government as a means of improving the ability of communities to work directly with government. In the conservative social milieu of Rajasthan, the government initiated a radical programme for women's empowerment, known as the Women's Development Programme.[12] Not only were many non-officials involved in shaping the programme; the NGOs were cast in a role of trainers, employing training as a strategy for empowerment. Less radical examples include negotiations between NGOs and Rajasangh[13] to help tribal cooperatives collect and sell *tendu* leaves, and to facilitate collaboration between NGOs and the National Bank for Agricultural and Rural Development to link small, informal savings and credit groups with the banks.

Practical Needs Draw Them towards Each Other

What are the 'needs' of the NGOs that make them seek collaboration with the government? The following needs are gleaned from the examination of collaborative experiences in Rajasthan:

- to garner resource support in the area of operation;
- to gain legitimacy by working with the system;
- to support an innovative government scheme;
- to expand into new areas and sectors;
- to influence the government to adopt an innovation.

Broadly speaking, these needs are a function of the direction and pace of organisational growth or leadership orientation. First, the needs of an NGO change as it grows in size and scale. In the initial stages, the need to survive is crucial. Government resources and linkages may be sought for that purpose. In the later stages, when there is relative stabil-

---

[12] Precursor to the national *Mahila Samakhya* Programme.
[13] A parastatal marketing minor forest products procured from tribal collectors.

ity of funds and a sufficient pool of experience to draw upon, the NGO may be motivated to make larger-scale impacts or inform public policy through its work.

Second, the ideology and the quality of leadership strongly influences the motivation of the agency in working with the government. Many NGOs are led by strong, dynamic personalities, who have set up these organisations to carry out a defined agenda. The personal motivations and beliefs of the leader have a strong bearing on the organisation's strategy.

Mutual fears in joining hands   What about mutual fears? What might they lose if they collaborated? An organisation's self or public image (identities), attitudes, and ideology affect this relationship. Most NGOs have developed autonomously, giving them a sense of pride and independence. On the other hand, government officials might feel they have earned the right to run the country.

NGOs may lose their independence, and government may lose its power and control over the resources its hands out to people, or over information. Government organisations may not want to be seen as inferior to NGOs in service delivery, and NGOs may not want to go to the government for funds as long as other, 'softer' sources are available. Large, established NGOs often have enough donors to give them money with fewer strings attached. Government funds bring the accounting controls, reporting requirements and the problems of follow-up for getting further funds. Decisions on whether to collaborate, and the very success of collaboration, thus depend to a large extent on meeting practical needs and coping with mutual fears, even if there is an agreement on development objectives.

Role Division and Management of the Relationship

How do the government and NGOs agree on a division of labour in collaborative programmes? What forms do such relationships take, and what are their dynamics? And once programme implementation begins, what management processes and structures are designed by stakeholders to oversee this role division and relationship? These are some questions addressed in this section.

Role division: A function of development objectives and perceived NGO capacity   The roles and space that NGOs acquire, or are assigned, depend on the programme's development objectives and the perceived capacity of NGOs to meet these (and conversely, the perceived lack of government capacity). In the previous section, we identified a set of development objectives over which the NGOs, government and external donors could agree. We now consider for each such objective, the roles that government and NGOs share.

- Innovation to resolve a development conundrum needs an NGO with a capacity to think up bold, unconventional ideas and to undertake action research to go deeper into the problem. The government's role is often limited here to funding innovation and research, but could allow the NGO to work with a tiny part of its system as well. This complexity of relationship would be determined by the scope of innovation. The Social Work and Research Centre Tilonia worked with the *Panchayati Raj* Department to introduce the Shiksha Karmi concept in a few schools where teacher absenteeism was diagnosed as a problem.

- For providing services, often the only requirement is that a local institution is available to reach the targeted population or to serve a specific function (such as training or artificial insemination) perhaps better than the government. Innovative capacity may be desirable but not necessary. 'Commitment' to serve the poor (or a targeted population) is often cited as a critical requirement. 'The NGO implements, the government funds' is the basic formula. These roles are most common.

- Empowerment and popular participation in government projects require that NGOs act as pressure groups and people's organisers, and possess understanding and skills to influence the system. NGOs need a deep commitment to this, as the process may be drawn out and the results intangible and unpredictable. The government must be accountable to people's needs and must fulfil its constitutional duty in a democracy.

- The objective of pursuing system or institutional reform in government is a complex process; indeed it is a combination of the above three objectives. Rarely can this be achieved by a single actor, let alone by a single NGO. We may need actors or NGOs with a strong participation and empowerment orientation on the one hand (like the mobilisation agencies of the Lok Jumbish Programme), and those with a systemic understanding to push through the changes in government departments on the other (e.g., the role that Lok Jumbish Parishad plays *vis-à-vis* the education department). Institutional reform could take the shape of introducing a new methodology in a department (like micro-level planning in Participatory Approach to Human and Land Resource Development (PAHAL)) or substitut-

ing public services with NGOs (like watershed-development programmes).

Form and dynamics of relationships that evolve Four major forms of relationship are found: *schematic, dyadic, catalytic/facilitative, and institutional.* There
is the fifth form—*confrontational*—when either side attempts to change
or constrain the other. This could be subsumed in the catalytic.

The nature of these linkages is decided by (a) the type and perceived
capacity of the participating NGOs and their positioning in the decision-making structure, (b) the scope and coverage of the programme or
scheme, (c) the degree of pre-determined designing of components,
target or goal orientation, and (d) the way the roles of the two sides are
conceived and divided. Consequently the relationship could be mutually
supportive or confrontational, could exhibit parity or be patently unequal, may or may not have elements of innovation and flexibility, and
could be static or allowed to evolve.

Most common is the relationship which we term as *schematic.* For
each development scheme, the government proposes standardised criteria of NGO selection, technical and cost norms, preferred approach
and mode of implementation. The scheme is often open to all NGOs,
and a large number of NGOs participate. NGOs often do not feel happy
about being treated any different from a telephone or electricity sub-
scriber. The electricity board or telephone department operates in the
general milieu of scarcity and monopoly, making the relationship an
unequal one. Thus the relationship between the government and NGOs
in the schematic relationship may be the one between *data* and *yachak*
(benefactor and beneficiary).

Dyadic (or *bilateral*) relations develop between government and an
NGO, to execute a mutually agreed project. Projects try out an innovation, as when the Command Area Development Authority asked URMUL
to try new methods of covering sand-clogged watercourses. Or the government may provide financial support to an NGO to upscale its successful project. In some sense, this could be considered a special case of
the schematic relationship, but here the NGO is in a more prominent
position. The government strikes a relationship with a single NGO, because of a certain confidence in the latter's capability. Examples include
BAIF's scaling up its artificial insemination services to improve cattle
breeds.

Catalytic roles and relationships exist where the government and NGOs
work with each other to enhance the benefits of the third stakeholder—the
disadvantaged community. The initiative may often lie with the NGO, which

raises issues pertaining to the community it seeks to serve and pressures the government to truly play its role of a welfare state or protector of the weak, ensuring equity. A radical instance of this is the Right to Information Campaign. In another instance, other NGOs worked with the various levels of government hierarchy to demand an increase in the wages of tribal *tendu*-leaf collectors in south Rajasthan, and even persuaded a government agency to give them license for and finance *tendu*-leaf marketing. The government would often find it difficult to finance this work, but external agencies support NGOs. This relationship is open-ended and could exhibit 'flip-flop' behaviour, now cordial, now adversarial. Many new frontiers are won, or at least new doors opened, following this strategy, and can result in a programme where the role of NGOs is more clearly legitimised. Joint forest management is a well-known example. Another variant of this is when an official agency undertakes reform of another official agency. The National Bank for Agricultural and Rural Development's attempt to push commercial banks and Regional Rural Banks to lend to the poor is a classical example; it takes help from NGOs to link self-help groups with banks. Lok Jumbish Parishad, a GONGO, acts as a pressure group on the education department in a bid to reach the goal of universal primary education in the state.

Institutional relationships are being attempted where the programme approach is radically different from the conventional one, and when results are unpredictable or the scope of change is at once drastic. In some 'process projects', where the attempt is to move away from the blueprint approach, NGOs are important vectors of change. Often there is a division of roles between the government and NGOs, along now predictable lines. NGOs are generally assigned process-intensive or software roles, and the government takes on physical implementation or hardware roles. Role division necessitates coordination in the field, a greater need for mutual adjustment, and unusual sensitivity to mutual needs and compulsions, and thus systems exist for periodic experience-sharing, co-learning and conflict resolution. Some cases even have a package deal for a specified role and outputs, as opposed to narrow line-item controls on salaries and overheads. Partner NGOs could also enhance their roles and carry out innovation if they have a proven competence. Last, such flexibility and learning-sensitive approaches are backed by allowing an operating structure delinked from the usual government bureaucracy. Lok Jumbish, PAHAL and the Participatory Watershed Development Initiative (PAWDI) are examples of this manner of institutional relationship.

Processes and Structures Devised to Manage the Relationship

The sharing of roles and spaces of innovation and implementation requires even more sensitive and alert management from the 'owners' of these projects. In a dyadic relationship, where a single NGO works with a government agency either to promote innovation or to provide services on a large scale, committees review periodic progress. In facilitative relationships, a mainstream institution together with an NGO (without any formal agreement, but exercising constitutional rights or 'social contract') promotes people's participation in governance, access to formal institutions such as banks, or wage increases. In such relationships, the coordination mechanisms do not take any definite shape. Negotiations could be long, or may be concluded quickly. In some cases, confrontation arises when these negotiations break down.

It is in the other two types of relationships—schematic and institutional— that coordination or management mechanisms have to be designed. In these relationships, the scale of operations is large, the process of change is complex, a number of NGOs are involved, and the relationship is devised formally to implement projects.

Management of schemes   The schemes are managed by Union ministries, state government departments or special organisations created for NGO funding such as the Council for Advancement of People's Action and Rural Technology (CAPART). NGOs submit their project proposals for approval to these agencies. Committees that include technical experts screen these proposals. Recently at the central level, NGOs have been represented, though in Rajasthan this is true only for Swasthyakarmi Yojana (a Rajasthan government scheme which hires local women as health workers to provide primary health services in remote villages). Disbursements are made in instalments to ensure better performance, and they often are based on reports of target achievement and accounts submitted by the implementing agency. Schemes are not often known to provide flexibility, easy channels of feedback, grievance redress, or cross-learning between relevant departments and NGOs. The more distant the location of the sanctioning authority (such as CAPART), the more adversely affected are the NGOs by poor communication and inflexibility.

Management of institutional relationships   Institutional relationships, where roles in programme implementation are shared between NGOs and government agencies, are a relatively new phenomenon. They represent a recognition of the fact that participation is absent in top-down, 'one size fits all' development approaches followed by government programmes. NGOs are asked to mobilise people for participation in project decision-making, to help them participate in micro-planning, or to afford disenfranchised groups or 'weaker sections' (i.e., low castes, women) opportunities in community decision-making so far monopolised by others.

By implication, management processes must also respond: they must provide adequate space for decentralised decision-making, offer flexible and diverse approaches, allow evolution and innovation instead of adhering to prescribed blueprints, and so on. Management that follows these conditions cannot flourish in the existing bureaucratic environment; it would die a premature death. A new management structure needs to be found—one that is sufficiently de-linked from government to meet the demands of the new charter.

Programmes involving this type of collaboration are set up in pursuit of some innovative idea or a highly desirable social goal. Since the early days of Shiksha Karmi and the Women's Development Programme, both of which represented radical departures from conventional approaches to education and women's empowerment as well as using NGOs as partners, there has been a tendency to create organisational structures de-linked from the government machinery.

These new entities are government-sponsored (and -controlled), but are registered as 'societies'—legally the same as NGOs—so they are sometimes referred to as government-organised NGOs, or 'GONGOs'. Their governance structure is filled with politicians and officials. Examples include the District Women's Development Agency (in the Women's Development Programme), Shiksha Karmi Board, Lok Jumbish Parishad, and PAHAL, which is now a separately registered entity.

This de-linking is guided in part by the desire to protect the projects from rigid bureaucracy and systems. The underlying assumption is that there are people in the government who, given sufficient operational space, financial powers and flexibility, will produce results not possible in a purely government setting. Once in GONGOs, they will engender innovation, and cocoon it till it is ready for replication.

Many donor agencies, too, prefer this arrangement and indeed may put their weight behind it. Besides seeding innovation, they are also motivated by the possibility of a direct link with the project (instead of going through the departmental maze) and of a more transparent flow of funds (if this could be achieved within the existing set up, would we still need de-linked structures?)

Creating de-linked organisations is also considered better for improving the quality of collaborative actions and arrangements. The government is aware that NGOs, particularly those that have adequate resources of their own, do not react favourably to delays and rigidities, and would rather not participate in a programme unless assured that their operations and autonomy will not be hampered. It may be surmised that NGOs have been called in to reinforce alternative work cultures in these new structures and organisations.

Institutional collaboration is a major opportunity for mutual exposure and cross-learning between government and NGOs. The quality of this exposure and learning varies between individuals on both sides. Some may learn, and some may not. For NGOs while such an arrangement affords a more substantial partnership with the government, it also means greater accountability for their actions and performance. Their actions are subject to periodic external review, which is a rare phenomenon in the NGO sector.

Constraints to Government–NGO Collaboration and Lessons from Experience

Why does collaboration run into difficulties, despite government and NGOs converging on objectives and dividing roles along the expected lines? Under what circumstances is the collaboration long lasting, and desirably so? On the other hand, should we not see collaboration only as a means to initiate change in government, and once that happens, the NGO role loses its significance and withdrawal is desirable? Are conflicts a temporary phenomenon and a part of the evolutionary process of mutual coming-to-terms? Or do conflicts occur only with certain kinds of NGOs? How could conflicts be anticipated and processes designed to manage them? These are some of the questions asked in this section.

This section highlights those factors and constraints (and is based on experience from Rajasthan) that hinder healthy collaboration between government and NGOs. These factors may be generic (they apply to all manner of government–NGO collaboration), or they may be unique to the specific type of arrangements. We identified the following as the major factors:

- departmental domains (technical arrogance, resource control);
- NGOs seeking autonomy and budget parity;
- mismatch between expectation and actual capacity of NGOs;
- management structure too weak to effect change;
- role of individuals, personalities and inter-personal equations;

- inadequacies in consultation with NGOs;
- lack of NGO networking;
- design and administration of schemes for NGOs (specific to the schematic type of relationship);
- role division (specific to institutional relationships).

The following is a brief description of the salient points (see Table 5.6 for a summary).

Departmental Domains

Resistance to NGOs arises when the government engages it in a task that also constitutes the core activity of a government department. Any overlap or infringement of the department's domain can create conflict with the NGO. We observed conflict in three aspects:

- administrative, when a department regulates the ownership and use of natural resources such as forests (the joint forest management case);
- technical (when professionals such as engineers and medical doctors have little or no confidence in the NGOs' capability (Swasthya-karmi, artificial insemination services, design for covering water-courses); or
- financial, when the department employees feel their legitimate or illegitimate pecuniary benefits are threatened (commonly supposed but difficult to prove, and is a bone of contention in the Right to Information Campaign, PAWDI, and agriculture extension services contracted to NGOs).

For one or all of these reasons, lower department levels may not share the perception of their superiors in granting certain space to NGOs. In the JFM programme, the forest department's role as protector of forests and regulator of its use is reinforced and NGOs' role is only suggested. Consequently at operational levels, divisional forest officers do not feel obliged to entertain them.

NGOs are generally perceived to be low on technical skills, and technical experts view their entry into such areas with scepticism. This is well illustrated in the case of URMUL's collaboration with the Command Area Development Authority (CADA), where the former undertook to demonstrate new techniques of covering watercourses and new designs of school buildings. Further, it sought to do this at a cost lower than CADA's rates, thereby suggesting unwittingly that CADA had 'commissions' built into its costs. URMUL's efforts ran into problems since the lobby of engineers in CADA felt that URMUL was encroaching on

Table 5.6 Role Sharing, Management Structures and Issues in Government–NGO Collaboration in Rajasthan

Development objectives	Role sharing among government & NGOs	Management structure	Issues	Recommendations for collaboration designers
Natural resources management				
Dev particp, integrated land-use mgmt for degraded areas (PAHAL, Dungarpur)	NGOs to form people's groups, train extension cadre, while govt officers on deputation provide tech expertise.	Govt and NGO jointly guide proj, though proj leader was junior officer; donor reviewed progress and appointed resident consultant.	High innov load, flexibility misused by govt; NGOs capacity high in implem but limited in innov and training; inadequate external inputs in process mgmt and tech innov.	• Need for stronger, more committed mgmt or leadership? • Need for clear participatory methodol and activity priorities, possibly with help of external resource inputs. • Most NGOs could be given service-delivery roles. • Need for sensitive, flexible mgmt.
Community particp to rehab degraded forests (JFM, Udaipur)	NGOs convince villagers to join prog, but Forest Dept not obliged to invite NGOs; Forest Dept employee sec & *patwari* member-sec of Forest Protection Ctte.	Entirely controlled by Forest Dept; district-level supervisory ctte to assess Forest Protection Ctte's performance.	NGO particip resisted by Forest Dept; scheme not monetarily attractive to villagers; strict control-mindset of Forest Dept.	• Unless NGOs are given a more legitimate role, collaboration is non-starter.
Stone cover for watercourses to stop clogging (Command Area Dev, W Rajasthan)	NGO as innovator in tech area, with govt funding support.	Under CADA Commissionarate; initiative treated as independent proj where grant given to NGO.	CADA opposed NGO entry: engineers found tech snags; accountants delayed payments.	• NGO should also be ready to take on a tech lobby, with help of others (as the Social Work and Research Centre took CET help to dev Shiksha Karmi prog), or by having the innov assessed by another govt tech agency.

Table 5.6 (continued)

Development objectives	Role sharing among government & NGOs	Management structure	Issues	Recommendations for collaboration designers
Natural resource management (continued)				
Lift irrig for small/marginal farmers in remote, water-abundant areas (Micro-irrig in Bihar, Madhya Pradesh & Karnataka)	Fund release, water permission and electricity connection, etc. with govt & bank gives loans; most field proj installation and mgmt with NGOs (tech design, group org, training in maintenance & irrigated ag).	District proj approval cttes and regional authority in World Bank-aided Bihar Plateau Dev Proj; DRDA and Ag Dept collaborate in Madhya Pradesh Utthan Scheme; depts or agencies (eg scheduled caste/tribes) in Karnataka.	While grant-based, NGO-supported small lift irrig successful due to NGO skills; it expanded quickly. Bank-financed schemes slow to take off due to unfriendly procedures, little attention to group schemes, and risk-averse staff. Weak higher-level coord between banks and implementing govt depts (rural dev & ag)	• If NGO wished to replicate it through the govt, an assessment by a govt agency would legitimise it further. • To scale this model up, or try some others, a feasibility analysis by competent agency is needed, backed up by policy statement by Union and state govts. • External agency funds may be needed to kick off govt-NGO collaboration in various states.
Livestock				
Livestock Improve cattle and buffalo breed by artificial insemination	NGO mainly as provider of a service that Dept of Animal Husbandry was not equipped to provide; funds provided by Dept of Rural Dev.	State-level ctte to approve contract for an area to NGO; district-level cttes to review progress, verify, and approve NGO's annual claims.	Resistance from dept tackled by NGO's non-confrontational stance, sound tech base and highly motivated staff. In tribal areas some questions about cost-efficiency & effectiveness of insemination.	• Although NGO has admirably delivered a service for almost two decades, the dept has learnt little. In its gopal yojana the NGO could usefully be called in as a partner. • Without much competition, NGO has not taken bold initiatives in Rajasthan it has elsewhere. Eg, it could promote small insemination-service entrepreneurs.

Table 5.6 (continued)

Development objectives	Role sharing among government & NGOs	Management structure	Issues	Recommendations for collaboration designers
Credit				
Improve rural poor's access to formal credit (self-help groups)	NGOs promote self-help groups like foster parents, and work with NABARD to link them with rural branches of Regional Rural Banks or commercial banks, with or without financial support from NABARD.	NABARD is nodal agency to guide collab; supports familiarisation workshops for bank staff; district staff follow up with NGOs & local branch managers; NABARD can support NGO overheads.	Prog expanding slowly as it requires intensive process work by NGOs with self-help groups; not all NGOs sufficiently enthused.	• NABARD facilitated NGOs' links with banks by legtimising their role, realistic assessment of their strengths, their early particp in planning, ensuring parity and adjusting pace to local reality. • NABARD worked with local managers, stressed mutuality with NGOs, and used formal authority. • Banks have found NGOs to be reliable, low-cost intermediaries, with latter doing process work with self-help groups. • Role of self-help group federations limited.
Health services				
Better family welfare services in inaccessible villages (Swasthyak-armi Prog)	Govt funded; implem by NGOs; training roles unclear	Well represented standing ctte for NGO selection and periodic review; overall responsibility of IEC Directorate; supervision by district	Weak mgmt structure to effect change; opposition from ranks not confident in NGOs (at best 'contractors') and obsessed with targets, no mechanism for training *swasthyakarmis*	• Human-resource dev interventions should include training of new grassroots cadres and induction of 'pro-change' govt officers. • New prog should be in cocoon, not buffeted in initial stages. • New prog could not be run like dept scheme. • Need for stronger and committed mgmt. • Develop NGO ownership in prog.

Table 5.6 (continued)

Development objectives	Role sharing among government & NGOs	Management structure	Issues	Recommendations for collaboration designers
Primary education				
Universal Primary Educ (Lok Jumbish Prog)	NGOs map community needs & mobilise opinion; Lok Jumbish Parishad nudges Educ Dept response; NGOs & govt agency given budget parity.	Lok Jumbish Parishad (a GONGO) free to operate, liaises with Educ Dept & NGOs, employs govt. Staff deputed through open recruitment.	Successful despite bureaucracy's resistance, but NGOs mostly in grassroots implem, their potential to be partners in changing the system under-utilised.	• Clear operational methodology, clear roles for implementing agencies helped. • Frequent, responsive, sensitive mgmt processes to build symbiotic relationship with field. • Flexible mgmt to respond to fresh challenges. • Strong mgmt to elicit response from govt dept.
Primary educ in remote villages, lower teacher absenteeism (Shiksha Karmi)	NGOs ensure right selection of *shiksha karmis*, and *panchayat samitis* implement.	Shiksha Karmi Board, a GONGO, manages state-wide prog; local supervision both by NGO and *panchayat samiti*.	Successful start; now Shiksha Karmi staff more like govt staff, less innov; Shiksha Karmi Board insensitive to field problems; difficult for *panchayats* and NGOs to collab; training by some NGOs.	• Has quality of the prog suffered? • If yes, could it be improved with better NGO involvement? • If NGOs need to be involved, how to manage interface between *panchayats* and NGOs?
Commodity				
Better wages for tribal *tendu*-leaf collectors, license to market leaves	NGO formed tribal collectors, persuaded govt agency (Rajsangh) to increase their wages, recognise marketing coops and give loan.	Essentially negotiation between NGOs and Rajsangh for better deal for tribal collectors (higher wages, marketing license, and loan for operations).	NGOs organised tribal collectors, whose wages jumped; but prog stuck due to lack of marketing ability; frequent leadership changes and no formal interaction processes.	• Gradual prog expansion & building NGO capacity in marketing preferable. • More formal role for NGOs & relations with govt agency in next phase. • Networking strengthened all NGOs and coops. • NGOs understand political class (*prashasban* (bureaucracy) accountable to *shashan* (politicians)).

their professional turf and trying to discredit them. Even in cases where the NGO is professionally competent, there can be resistance. BAIF, which expanded its artificial insemination services with government financial support (the Department of Rural Development), has had to face opposition in some districts from the Department of Animal Husbandry. To eliminate competition, BAIF had to leave areas where the department had subsequently developed insemination facilities. A relatively recent cause of resistance from lower cadres is their perception that NGOs are eroding employment security in the government by offering cheaper contractual services. The employees' trade unions protested when agricultural extension and Integrated Child Development Service work was offered to NGOs.

The phenomenon of encroaching on technical and administrative domains is less likely to occur when NGOs work with departments focusing on specific segments of the population, such as the rural poor, tribals, women and children.

NGOs exhibit a general inability or indifference to manage lower ranks in the government. Most NGOs prefer to enter into agreements at senior levels, while dynamics at lower levels are left to sort themselves out somehow. This neglect rarely works in favour of collaboration. There are exceptions too, such as BAIF's ability to smooth out contentious issues at district levels, and Sahyog's ability to work with district and sub-district officials and local bank managers.

Lessons The promoters of collaboration on both sides need to be aware and prepared for the potential opposition from government staff. What strategies can be used to manage this competition and reduce turf conflict in mutual relations? Experience suggests:

- *Anchor the collaboration outside the technical department, whenever possible.* BAIF has been able to sustain a long-term arrangement with the government in the field of artificial insemination in spite of active opposition from the Department of Animal Husbandry. One of the reasons has been that it gets funds from the Special Schemes Organisation and not from the department. On the contrary, URMUL sought funds from CADA while trying to seed change within it. These attempts were thwarted by the blocking of payments for work done.
- *Proven ability of the NGO in the area* permits it to deal effectively with government resistance, as well as to manage a separate geographical domain competently. BAIF and PRADAN have been able to sustain long-term relations with the government because

they have high proficiency in the field of artificial insemination and lift irrigation respectively. They can negotiate well with the government, as well as work without depending on it for technical support. While this competence does not remove all tension, it certainly removes one of the main grounds of complaint by government functionaries.

• *Avoid geographical/functional overlaps with the government department.* An important corollary of this lesson, brought out in several instances, is that, at least in the beginning, it is much easier for NGOs to move into gaps left by the government development agencies. PRADAN has been successful in mobilising government funds in South Bihar earmarked for lift irrigation schemes, because the government department was disallowed from participating in the programme.[14] Similarly, When BAIF came into Rajasthan, the Department of Animal Husbandry did not have artificial insemination services in its portfolio.

The above lessons read together should not be interpreted to mean that avoiding collaboration is the best strategy. If service delivery (not departmental reform) is the agenda of the programme, as in the case of BAIF and PRADAN, then it does not matter which department the funds come from. In such cases, it may be preferable not to seek funds from a department that has that service as its core agenda—in other words, anchor the collaboration outside. But if the NGO's agenda is to reform public policy or programmes, a closer interaction between the government and NGOs may be necessary. However our analysis of the collaboration experience suggests that even in such cases, reform may be best possible through indirect means, through demonstration of alternatives in another less hostile setting, through cross-learning by gradual exposure to alternative models. By separating geographical domains, the two systems may be brought together in creative competition, where the two learn from each other. And that organisational learning may occur better from a distance.

Sense of Autonomy and Budget Parity Sought by NGOs

Most NGOs attach a great value to their independence from the government. They see themselves as voluntary organisations. In fact their

---

[14] BHALCO, a government agency existed, but its track record was poor. Only 12 out of the 232 schemes it had installed were functioning. The World Bank, the external funding agency in the project, insisted that the government department should not be allowed to participate in the programme.

very *raison d'être* arises from a critique of the government. Affiliation with the government dilutes their separate identity in the eyes of society, and of their target community or peer groups in particular. In instances of collaboration, they guard their identity even more zealously. This is reflected in their demand for treatment at par with the government agencies, in decision making and sometimes even in facilities.

NGOs also resent excessive government interference in their internal matters. There are examples of NGOs' withdrawing from a government programme because they felt that the government procedures were an undue interference. Take, for instance, government attempts to insist upon salary and staffing pattern for NGOs prescribed in project designs. This is often a contentious issue. Most well established NGOs have a salary structure of their own, which has evolved over a period of time and is rooted in its own history and development ideology. Typically in NGOs people perform multiple tasks. NGOs are most comfortable in a system where they have consolidated provisions for salaries for performance of certain tasks. NGOs normally resent externally or funding-induced changes in their salary structure. Their logic is that they cannot have a separate salary structure for separate projects they undertake. Outside pressure for change produces acrimony and can even lead to their withdrawal from the project.

In departmental schemes, the phenomenon of depressed budgets for NGOs is even more marked. In numerous schemes there is no provision for covering staff time or even overheads that the NGO may incur. This poses unrealistic constraints on the agency expected to perform the required task.

Lessons

- NGOs must be treated at par with the government functionaries. This parity must be built into the project design.
- While allocating salaries for the NGO personnel, the best policy is to allocate a consolidated amount for performance of defined tasks. Its further break up should be left at the discretion of the NGO.

Mismatch between Expectations and Actual Capacity of NGOs

As discussed earlier, there are three kinds of capacities that could be expected from NGOs—innovation, service delivery, and empowerment and participation. A fourth one is institutional change in the government, which is rarely achieved by a single actor.

Many programmes are based on eliciting community's participation, and NGOs are expected to devise methods on the lines of micro-level planning or participatory rural appraisal. These programmes expect NGOs to deliver on 'participation'. Since control of resources is still with government agencies, the NGOs' role reduces to raising awareness or gathering people for a meeting, with little control over the decision making. Since most field NGOs are not expert in using training as an empowerment strategy, they fail miserably. In the Women's Development Programme, however, this strategy was adopted, suitable NGOs were found, and the programme was a resounding success.

What kinds of problems arise when NGOs have independent projects? Here the problem is not so much with individual NGOs but with those who masquerade as such. We see an uncontrolled growth of NGOs, since many new schemes are announced for NGOs and large sums allocated to them. Often proposals are invited from NGOs through newspaper advertisements. In a typical case, a genuine NGO would not pick up a newspaper to look for 'business'—unlike Public Works Department contractors who look for 'tenders'. Not unexpectedly, a large number of well-written and sometimes apparently identical proposals land on the desk of the issuing agency. This makes NGO screening difficult. Some funding agencies, such as the Aga Khan Foundation, have adopted word of mouth and workshops as methods of letting prospective NGOs know of schemes. In ActionAid and Ford Foundation, programme officers make personal visits to learn more about the ground capacity of the applicants.

A third variant is when NGOs are expected to provide services in a new sector. In Swasthyakarmi Yojana, rural women were to provide certain family-welfare services. The NGO would recruit women and supervise their work. But the Yojana could not provide the requisite training, and nor could the NGOs. In the Shiksha Karmi programme, where a new organisation (Sandhan) was promoted to provide training, many more NGOs could participate, and they only had to ensure the right selection rather than provide training themselves.

A fourth situation occurs when a 'process project' is designed to carry out institutional reform, and a reputed NGO is inducted into a collaborative relationship with the government. Why does it find it difficult 'to live up to its reputation?' Often it may have built its reputation primarily on good service-delivery or through protests against the government that champion people's causes—but the role required in such projects may be different.

Lessons

* NGOs playing only a 'participation' role should be prepared in using training as an empowerment strategy.

- Any programme that is planning a large-scale induction of NGOs should develop better procedures for screening NGOs, such as workshops and personal visits. It should prepare a capacity-building module for the gradual growth of fledgling NGOs, especially those engaged in a sector new for them.
- In process projects aiming at institutional change in the government, NGOs should be specifically prepared for this role.

Management Structure Too Weak or Not Committed

A new project aims for a change, and thus causes a flutter in an existing bureaucracy, especially in lower cadres. The natural resistance to NGOs' entry needs to be creatively managed—and indeed buffered from possible fatal attack. In Swasthyakarmi Yojana, the NGOs were assigned task of family welfare, and their work was to be supervised by the very people whose domain was being challenged. When the NGOs faced difficulties, the only managing body—the Standing Committee on Voluntary Agencies—was not able to save them. In the case of PAHAL, although a separate society was registered to enhance flexibility and financial powers, the project director pursued financial expenditure as an objective rather than evolving an innovative, participatory and decentralised approach to land-use management for degraded areas. On the other hand, the Shiksha Karmi Board successfully created and protected a niche for NGOs' entry. The long-standing track record of the leader, and his ability to create a broad, supporting coalition, have provided the Lok Jumbish programme a long lease of life, despite mainline bureaucracy's resentment to the flexibility given him.

Lesson
- Resistance to change in the system should be countered by strong, committed, and sustained programme leadership.

Role of Individuals, Personalities and Interpersonal Equations

There is a unanimous agreement between government and NGOs that individuals, personalities and inter personal equations can make or break relations. The difficulty is that this is perhaps the most subjective and unpredictable issue in government–NGO relations. A large number of initiatives in working together are rarely institutionalised or made formal, and hence they last as long as the individual government officer remains in post. An enormous amount of energy may be spent or wasted, if the NGO has to convince a new incumbent to fulfil commitments made by his or her predecessor.

Personal relations between the leaders of NGOs and senior government officers have their own dynamic, and in a number of cases this has led to more creative institutional partnerships. But any perceived links between NGOs and senior bureaucrats may also result in increased alienation of the junior levels in government from the NGOs.

Since transfers are routine in the government system and the number of 'pro-NGO' or 'pro-people' officers may decline, programme designers and NGOs have to come up with broader coalitions, perhaps including politicians too. In the *tendu*-leaf case, some politicians hindered attempts by tribal collectors to gain a marketing license and finance. In the Lok Jumbish programme, however, support from the Chief Minister has ensured programme longevity, despite bureaucratic resistance.
Lesson
• Build broader coalitions to support the programme, including political leaders, to make programmes 'transfer-proof'.

Inadequate Consultations

Consultations between government and NGOs are an increasing trend, but exhibit several drawbacks. They are often one-off events, often hastily convened, and containing a preponderance of high-profile NGOs, thus failing to capture the diversity of views. There is a tendency to 'tokenise', apparent in rushing through issues and discouraging discussion on substantive matters. Consultations are one-sided, in that 'the government invites, and the NGO attends'; the reverse is difficult to achieve. Consultations on controversial or contentious issues are generally avoided.

A fundamental problem is the near-complete lack of effective forums or mechanisms by which government and NGOs can interact with each other on a continuous basis. These are generally absent in line departments, both at the district and state levels. They are similarly weak or erratic at the other levels of development administration, such as the District Collector or commissioner level. Nor is there yet any state-level mechanism by which NGOs can regularly interface with the government on development issues, or on topics that affect their capacity to work with each other.

Lack of NGO Networking

An underdeveloped link in the collaboration scenario of Rajasthan is the lack of involvement of NGO networks with the government. Though networking among NGOs is increasing, there is no state-wide or regional, broad-based coalition of NGOs either for servicing the interests of the sector, or for managing the interface with the government. There is no consensus among NGOs on how to pressure the government on development issues. Exceptions are the networks of social action groups that are able to demand government attention for their causes. The government response to these networks is often of extreme caution or outright dismissal.

Management of Schemes for NGOs

There is a preponderance of small, struggling NGOs that avail of government schemes. With the lack of transparent mechanisms, such agencies, whose competence and even integrity is doubtful, have begun to feature increasingly as scheme recipients. As a result, the general credibility of the NGO sector has eroded, and there is an increased sense of frustration in serious-minded NGOs at the rampant proliferation within the sector.

Aside from the phenomenon of low provisions, there are a number of problems related to the designing and administration of schemes for NGOs. Mainly these relate to: (a) a lack of consultation with NGOs at the design stage, resulting in laying down of unrealistic goals and activities, and low levels of participation by quality organisations; (b) inadequate selection criteria and mechanisms for competent organisations and procedures for screening NGO proposals and their approval; (c) the lack of timely disbursal of funds; and (d) poor monitoring and evaluation of schemes.

Role Division

We find that the division of roles between government and NGOs does not work well over a period of time. In several instances, NGOs are given the task of organising and mobilising the community, while the responsibilities of implementation rest with the government. Such role divisions are derived from the notion of comparative strengths, and are observed in projects such as PAHAL, WDP, and more recently in PAWDI.

Problems are quick to manifest themselves in these situations. Often, physical execution and achievement of financial targets assume a more central role, whereas NGO-led village-level processes are jettisoned. There are also power connotations in this kind of role division *vis-à-vis* the community. Government functionaries continue to enjoy the power derived from their control of resources and their discretion regarding the priority and pace at which the programme is to be carried out. Delays and deviations happen, so NGOs often end up facing a crisis of credibility with the villagers.

In such institutionalised collaborations where the government and NGOs work together in different roles, we observe that over the years there is a decline in the NGOs' role and involvement in key areas. This phenomenon can be seen in the case of WDP, Shiksha Karmi and PAHAL. Experience suggests that once learning takes place within the context of the project, NGOs' participation becomes redundant or marginalised. New and more evolved roles are not found for the NGOs in these projects, whereas their initial skills and strengths get passed on to their government counterparts (the system learns!); over time, the government staff are able to manage on their own.

Role of Donors in Government–NGO Relationships

Donor agencies occupy an influential niche in the affairs of governments and NGOs. What is the present and potential role of donor agencies in this realm? What aspects of government–NGO collaboration merit the attention of donor agencies and are likely to be positively influenced by a more proactive and considered donor response? This section draws out issues and concerns that relate to donor agencies.

Donors in Rajasthan are at least as heterogeneous a group as the government and non-government agencies they support. Generally, donor agencies have specific mandates and resources that guide the intensity of their work with government, NGOs, or both. By virtue of their origin in governments and the size of their resources, the multi- or bilateral agencies (the United Nations system, SIDA, USAID, SDC, NORAD, CIDA, etc.), extend development cooperation to national and state governments. They also have a 'window' for direct assistance to NGOs; this is relatively small, and often built in as a component in awards to governments. Private donor agencies and charities (Oxfam, CARE, Action-Aid, Intercooperation, etc.) often exclusively support NGOs; a number are (northern) NGOs in their own right (and origin), and find it prudent, because of the small size of funds at their disposal, to work with local NGOs.

Undoubtedly, the increase in flow of resources to NGOs in the past decade has been a major factor in the increase of NGO presence and activity, increasingly in such domains that were once considered exclusive to government. The flow of external resources to the government has also increased in absolute terms, but questions have been posed in terms of effectiveness, reforms, cost-efficiency, sustainability and participation. The emphasis on provisions for NGOs in externally funded government projects is now marked. This is driven in part by the experience of northern NGOs back home, and by pressure from indigenous NGOs, as regards what southern NGOs can bring to bear in large-scale development interventions.

Donors may bring in their specific agenda and mandate, but there is little general consensus among them on issues of community involvement, cost-effectiveness, coverage, equity and replicability in the context of the interventions they support. Both bilateral and private donor agencies need to be concerned about the potential represented by government–NGO collaboration to fulfil these overall goals.

Differing Perceptions of NGO Roles

Various donors see the NGO role in relation to the government differently. At the risk of over-generalisation, we surmise that bilateral aid agencies tend to view NGOs' role as an intermediary and in some cases transitory one in relation to the government's links with people. Thus NGOs are involved in such functions that will help the government understand community needs more accurately, and generally help the community improve its linkages with the government programme. In some cases, NGOs may be invited to perform tasks that the government cannot do because they require a high degree of flexibility, cost efficiency and proximity to the community. Thus NGOs are involved as *instruments* of improved service delivery and outreach.

Private, non-government donors agencies tend to be much more intensely involved with NGOs, since often they work exclusively through them. NGOs are seen as *catalysts* of social and economic change, with an ability to innovate and articulate the needs of the community. Their work and intervention in an area is not seen to be dependent on the government, though there is an overall notion (often unverified by donors) that the NGOs' work is filling an existing gap in government resources or programmes. These donors are, however, less likely to be concerned about the complementarity of their NGO funding support with existing government resources in an area. Exceptions exist, but these are few. Some private donors (ActionAid) have identified *advocacy* as a valid role for NGOs to play *vis-à-vis* the government. They do not fund the government, and the non-funding links of private donors with government agencies are rather thin.

The NGO Capability Question

In either of the two roles described above (instrument and catalyst), *NGO capability* must remain a major donor concern. One trend seems to be the increased assumption of 'NGO-type' roles by the government (for example, forming user committees, working with village-based workers, engaging in participatory planning), while NGO capabilities in government-type functions such as technical support and implementation remain limited. Tokenism of community and participatory processes in large-scale government projects is common, and if anything, is growing. How can external donors ensure that the elements of participation and equity are not rendered ineffective in the government interventions they support? In the context of government projects, what is the experience of involving NGOs in these processes? What skills are required in NGOs to be able to seed these elements in a government programme?

Private donor agencies perhaps need to be more concerned about the strategic relevance of their support to NGOs. Public systems, despite their inherent flaws, are too costly to society to be ignored. At a macro level, gains can hardly be made unless the state's development apparatus overcomes administrative inefficiency, unresponsiveness, corruption and chronic inability to reach the poor. Can their support to NGOs help them to negotiate better resources from the government for the communities of their concern? Would it be worth considering the ability or willingness of an NGO to engage with public systems as a criterion for support? What kind of non-funding roles are possible for them to play in order to improve government–NGO relations in the context of their particular support?

Attention to Content

There is a need for increased attention from donor agencies to the elements of design in government–NGO collaboration. The evidence from institutional collaborations such as PAHAL, PAWDI, Shiksha Karmi as well as purely schematic, contractual arrangements in Rajasthan, suggests that conflicts between government and NGOs arise on account of unrealistic role divisions, problems of domain, salary/budget differentials, lack of conflict-resolution mechanisms, and mal-administration of funds.

6 Democratising Development? *Panchayati Raj* Institutions in Watershed Development in India

PARI BAUMANN[1]

INTRODUCTION

This chapter examines the interface between political decentralisation (in the form of *panchayati raj*) and administrative reform (in the form of decentralisation of government supported watershed development as governed by the 1994 Guidelines).

Panchayati raj is a system of democratic governance which has been integral to Indian political debate since independence, with fervent arguments made both for and against the system. Until 1993 it operated sporadically and was included in the Constitution only as a directive principle. In 1993 the Constitution was amended, and *panchayati raj* became part of the democratic system. The Constitution specifies that there should be three tiers of local government: village, block and district. The XIth Schedule, which accompanies the amendment, specifies development areas over which the *panchayati raj* institutions will be responsible. Of particular relevance to this chapter is that the XIth Schedule specifies that *gram panchayats* should be responsible for watershed development.

This chapter is therefore not about whether the *panchayati raj* institutions should take over such functions as watershed development. Rather, it is about *how*, and *how rapidly*, this should be done.

The chapter is based largely on a number of field interviews and observations made in Karnataka and Andhra Pradesh in mid-1998. These two states have adopted differing approaches to the *panchayati raj* institu-

---

[1] Overseas Development Institute, London, UK.

tions. At one extreme, the tendency in Andhra Pradesh has been first to try to strengthen the efficiency and transparency of development administration, in tandem with some strengthening of community-based organisations to identify their needs, make appropriate demands on government, and monitor the efficiency of project implementation. Such strengthening is perceived to be a necessary precondition for transparency and accountability in the functioning of *panchayati raj* institutions. By contrast, in Karnataka, many of the designated development functions have already been handed over to *panchayati raj* institutions, and some amendments to the state-level legislation mandating *panchayati raj* institutions have been made in order to strengthen their interface with development administration.

This chapter examines four particular issues in the links between the two systems: *panchayati raj* and watershed institutions.

- the philosophy and objectives of *panchayati raj* institutions and the 1994 Guidelines with respect to watershed development;
- the difference in roles and modes of operation between them and how the balance of power is established. The respective roles and comparative advantages of *panchayati raj* institutions and watershed institutions is also the focus of Extract 6.1;
- the nature of the linkages—both formal and informal—between watershed institutions and political bodies. Extract 6.2, which describes the linkages between an NGO working in watershed management and *panchayati raj* institutions, contributes to this discussion;
- the mechanisms which exist for ensuring transparency and accountability of these institutions at the district, block and village levels.

The chapter then draws a number of conclusions—which are necessarily tentative in view of the scarcity of evidence—on how the interaction between decentralised development administration and decentralised political authority can best be managed for the future. Although this chapter is focused very narrowly on the Guidelines, the implications are relevant for most natural resource management schemes and related community-based organisations. As with other chapters, it then concludes with evidence and arguments from a number of case studies presented at the April 1998 workshop.

Concept of Decentralisation in the Amendment and the Guidelines

The 73rd Amendment to the Constitution and the Watershed Guidelines are entirely different legal entities. The Guidelines, as an executive order of a Ministry, are subordinate to the 73rd Constitutional Amendment. *Panchayati raj* institutions at all levels have full statutory powers, whereas watershed institutions have no statutory powers and no authority that is independent of a specific project, scheme or programme (see Extract 6.1).

Decentralisation of development planning and implementation are central objectives of both *panchayati raj* and the Guidelines. However they are based on fundamentally different notions of decentralisation. There are two main objectives of decentralisation: one is to enable communities to meet their basic needs, and the other is the realisation of democracy and local autonomy in development planning. Whether these latter are included as an explicit purpose of the decentralisation programme, and if so, whether they are included as fundamental rights or simply as laudable goals, affects the political character of the decentralisation programme. The *panchayati raj* legislation aims to build local units of self-government that provide people with a means through which to decide democratically how to meet their basic needs. Decentralisation in the Guidelines refers to local participation in the context of a particular scheme or project. Participation here is intended to empower local people and enhance project effectiveness by ensuring that people have a stake in the project. The participatory process, however, does not influence the definition of priorities at the district, state or national level, and as a component of an externally assisted programme, it is insulated from the formal political process.

The difference in the notion of what decentralisation entails, and how to promote participation, is based on a difference in the underlying explanation for development failure. The participatory philosophy of the Guidelines supposes that the cause of development problems lies primarily in individual behaviour and attributes, rather than property rights and the social and policy orientation of the state. There is no recognition of the importance of democratic politics in deciding development priorities, with the implication that these priorities are not open to political contestation. By contrast, the logic of the *panchayati raj* system supposes that democracy and development are intertwined, and that without *panchayati raj*, the democratic system does not offer voters a true choice.

Panchayati raj and the Guidelines also differ in their conceptualisation of the community and empowerment. The community in *panchayati raj* is treated as an integral part of the wider social, economic and political system. The three-tier structure networks the *gram sabha* to the block and district levels, and ultimately provides an avenue for the representation of local needs in the national government. The community in the Guidelines is atomistic; watershed projects do not address external influences on the local community; and there is no system whereby local communities can decide on their needs and express these at higher decision-making levels.

The concept of empowerment inherent in the two systems is a reflection of this conceptualisation of the community. The Amendment reserves seats for scheduled castes, scheduled tribes and women at all three tiers of *panchayati raj* institution, in recognition that some of the causes for their marginal status are not local. The objective is to bring socially and economically weaker segments of the community into mainstream politics, and to ensure that their priorities are incorporated into development planning and implementation. The Guidelines make normative recommendations on reservations for women and scheduled castes, but do not enforce these in the various tiers of watershed institutions. Instead the tendency is to put poor and marginal people into self-help groups, whose purpose is to deal directly with their needs in isolation. As the name reveals, the underlying assumption is that poverty and disempowerment are problems with local solutions.

In the preceding paragraphs, the lines between participatory development (as envisaged in the Guidelines) and democratic development (as provided for in the Constitution), have been drawn sharply for illustrative purposes. The difference *is* tangible. However, both government and NGO respondents in the study reported here saw the boundaries between the two as more fluid. They all agreed that *panchayati raj* is an essential long-term goal. The difference in opinion arose over whether *panchayati raj* institutions are ready to take on the responsibilities of development planning. Proponents of participatory development argue that they are governed by elites and would therefore not be sensitive to the needs of the poor and more vulnerable sections of local communities. They argued that *panchayati raj* institutions were not ready, and that a transfer of responsibility would have to be preceded by progress on literacy, land reforms, and empowerment of the socially and economically disadvantaged. Supporters of *panchayati raj* argue that the state administration has failed, and that the various community-based organisations established by the government and NGOs are dominated by the elite. The *panchayat* is a microcosm of society, and should be part of the process through which local structures of inequality are changed.

Spirit and Letter of the Law in the Amendment and the Guidelines

The discussion above considers the Amendment and the Guidelines in the 'spirit' in which they were written. They are both progressive on paper, but the striking difference between the spirit of the law and practice was a recurring theme in discussions with respondents. The legislation in both systems has numerous loopholes that provide escape routes from transferring power and authority to local bodies. For example, in the case of the Guidelines, the watershed secretaries, project implementing agencies, watershed development teams and watershed committees are all approved from the hierarchy above them. All of these institutions are dependent on the hierarchy for funds, and are in the final instance accountable to the government. The tendency for the Collector to retain control over decision-making has persisted in the implementation of the Guidelines: 'Collectors continue to retain control over decision-making processes, rather than moving towards a more facilitative and supportive role, emphasising a decentralisation of power and responsibility' (Turton et al. 1998: 6).

The Amendment has been widely welcomed as landmark legislation, but the development of *panchayati raj* institutions is being hindered by their lack of functional, financial and legal autonomy—a manifestation of political and bureaucratic opposition to the decentralisation of power. For example: although the Constitution defines *panchayats* as units of self-government, most state governments have chosen to interpret self-government as 'agency for the implementation of development projects'. In most states, decentralisation has been limited to development works on the 29 subjects listed in the XIth schedule and, even in this narrow domain, the transfer of authority has been haphazard and the division of powers unclear. Most poverty-alleviation projects still flow to the District Rural Development Agency; watershed development, which is on the XIth schedule, is a case in point. Further, functional autonomy has little significance without financial autonomy, but *panchayati raj* institutions have survived mainly on grants from central and state governments. Under the Amendment, *panchayati raj* institutions are eligible to raise revenue and to a share of the state revenue. However the details of this are left to the finance commissions, and most have yet to specify their conclusions.

Several conclusions can be reached from a consideration of the philosophy and objectives of the Amendment and the Guidelines. The first is that legislation is a necessary, but not a sufficient, condition for decentralisation. Without specific measures to implement laws on decentralisation, it is likely that the current balance of power will continue to dominate. The second conclusion is that it is important to deconstruct what is meant by decentralisation, and not to confuse the roles of the administrative and the political system. Both systems have vital and very distinct roles to play, as the following sections will explore (see also Extract 6.1).

Role of *Panchayati Raj* and Watershed Institutions

The Guidelines specify that *panchayati raj* institutions can be involved in the implementation of watershed-development programmes:

The *zilla parishads*/DRDAs, as the case may be, shall be responsible for implementation of these guidelines at the district level...the *zilla parishads, panchayat samitis* and the *gram panchayats* are also entitled to take on the responsibility of implementing a cluster of watershed projects in the capacity of project implementation agencies, if they so desire.

These provisions have a special significance because the *panchayati raj* institutions are constitutionally part of a national democratic system. The ideology, mode of operation, and objectives of *panchayati raj* institutions differ from those of the district administration. The Guidelines, by using clauses such as 'as the case may be' and 'if they so desire', remain vague about responsibility, roles and coordination. The implementation of *panchayati raj* varies from state to state, within the broad parameters specified by the Constitution. In most states, relations between *panchayati raj* institutions and the district administration hang in the balance. Despite their constitutional importance, the former often lack political and administrative support, as well as funds. This is the context within which the Guidelines will be implemented.

The uncertainties of the Guidelines are not, by definition, a problem. There is a possibility that the uncertainties can be resolved at the district, block and village level to the mutual benefit of the two systems. However, there is also abundant empirical evidence of conflict between the district administration and *panchayati raj* institutions, which impairs the development of the systems, especially *panchayati raj* institutions, and dilutes the effectiveness of development programmes.

There are several specific areas in which a duplication of functions and confusion of roles might arise between *panchayati raj* and watershed institutions.

*   The Guidelines (article 39) provide for the establishment of a 'district watershed development advisory committee'. The Amendment

provides for the establishment of a 'district development committee', and the XIth Schedule lists watershed development as one of
its areas of control.

• The Guidelines state that 'the *zilla parishad* at the district level and
the *panchayat samiti* at the block level shall have the right to monitor
and review the implementation of the programme'. Given the past
experience of working relations between *panchayati raj* institutions
and the administration, these provisions are very vague.

• Watershed institutions are not legal or statutory bodies, and there is
considerable uncertainty concerning their legal rights over renewable natural resources and the contractual arrangements which should
govern the relations between them and the owners of resources
(state governments or *panchayati raj* institutions). Watershed institutions have the right to register themselves, and are encouraged to
do so in the Guidelines. Sporadic efforts have also been made to
federate these groups at the district and sub-district level. As independent organisations, these groups can federate at whatever level
they want to, but if they are supported by development organisations and donors, then they may conflict with higher-level *panchayati
raj* institutions (see also Extract 6.1). The *panchayati raj* institutions
have been created for decentralised development, so perhaps there
should be more of an explicit appreciation of their ability to provide the umbrella institution.

These clauses have contributed towards some confusion over the respective roles and responsibilities of *panchayati raj* institutions and watershed institutions. *Panchayati raj* and watershed institutions have different
objectives, different visions of the community, and a different perspective on the process of collective action. However these differences need
not be a point of conflict, as long as watershed-management policies
respect the designated roles of these two systems. For example, a central
reason given by respondents for not involving *gram panchayats* is that they
are too big for watershed management. This is confusing a technical
matter with a principle. The appropriate size for watershed institutions
is an on-going issue of debate, and is usually negotiated anew with each
project: should it be based on a micro- or macro-watershed? Should all
the households in a watershed be included, or only those belonging to a
particular village? Similarly, the appropriate size of the *gram panchayat* is
much debated: are they not too big to be representative of the needs of
the village? Are they not too small to incorporate economies of scale in
development plans?

These logistical problems are not a reason for treating these institutions as if they are interchangeable. *Panchayati raj* institutions are not an implementation mechanism for projects but units of self-government. *Gram panchayats* are meant to develop a plan for the management of all the natural resources within their boundaries. However the jurisdiction of the *gram panchayat* is usually too big to manage micro-watersheds, and with all the other issues listed in the XIth schedule, the *gram panchayat* would also not have sufficient staff or salaries for such management. There is therefore clearly a need for community-based organisations to manage watersheds in a locally sensitive manner, with a local negotiation of costs and benefits. This is the role of watershed institutions. There is no conflict if watershed institutions aim to empower local people, educate them about their rights, or provide them with economic tools for a better life. Nor is there a conflict in the roles of *panchayati raj* institutions and watershed institutions if the latter choose to set up federations at regional or national levels. The problems may arise, however, when the roles of the watershed institutions take on those of the *gram panchayat*, and when watershed institutions start planning the broader development process.

The Guidelines have three limitations in promoting equity in watershed management across the country. The first is that they do not provide an institutional mechanism with which to scale up this empowerment, or a process whereby the poor can enter mainstream institutions. The second is that watershed-management projects are increasingly being targeted at communities that have shown a willingness to cooperate. Whilst this is a sensible move for a project, it abandons many people who might stand to gain from watershed projects. Finally, most watershed projects are still land-based, and have not seriously tackled the problem of how to build up the livelihoods of the landless or land-poor. Common-property areas have also received less attention than private land, which, assuming that the link usually made between poverty and dependence on common land is correct, biases projects towards those with more private land.

Balance of Power between *Panchayati Raj* and Watershed Institutions

The balance of power between *panchayati raj* and watershed institutions is dependent on the wider policy environment and the progress made in merging *zilla parishads* with District Rural Development Agencies. Many of the respondents mentioned that development planning at the mo-

ment is in a transition phase that will have costs and benefits for the state administration, NGOs, *panchayati raj* institution representatives, and groups within local communities (see Extract 6.2). The respective role of *panchayati raj* and watershed institutions in the implementation of the Guidelines is not merely a technical issue, but a question of the balance of power between the systems. The Guidelines have to operate with already existing institutional alliances and conflicts, for example: between sectors (government, NGO), within the government (centre, state, district); and between *panchayati raj* institutions, governments and NGOs.
Administrative and political conflict over decentralisation   The biggest obstacle in the way of *panchayati raj* is a political and administrative conflict over decentralisation. It is not a single 'organised' obstacle against decentralisation, but a web of shifting alliances, the operation of which is much debated. The Amendment reveals a recognition that some power will inevitably have to be decentralised. However as, a retired Indian Administrative Service officer commented, 'the government feels as if it is holding a tiger by the tail. They know that in the long run they cannot hold a tiger, but they are scared that if they let it go it will bite them'.

The major movements to re-establish functioning *panchayati raj* institutions in the last decades have come from state governments, often as part of their drive to gain autonomy from the centre. However at the state level, members of the State Legislative Assembly are one of the biggest sources of opposition to *panchayati raj*. This is their constituency, and state legislators have a considerable amount to lose from a fully functioning *panchayati raj* system. The centralising tendencies continue at the district level and below. Within the *panchayati raj* system, the centralising tendencies work against the transfer of powers from the *zilla parishad* to the block level *panchayats* and the *gram panchayats*. Within the state administration, the tendency for centralisation within line departments, for the long line of command and upward accountability, is well-known.
Relations between panchayati raj institutions and the state administration   These structural conflicts over power and resources are manifested in differences over work patterns, incentive structures, and work cultures between *panchayati raj* institutions, NGOs and the state administration. Much work has recently been done on differences between the state administration and NGOs (see Chapter 5), as well as on how some of the more superficial differences can be resolved. The relations between the state administration and *panchayati raj* institutions are more complex, and there has so far been less room for cooperation. On paper, the *complementarity* of these two systems is obvious and an integral part of any democratic

system. However the bureaucracy has, since independence, been given such a central role that it is now unwilling to consider itself as a tool, a merely administrative arm, of elected representatives.

The conflict between *panchayati raj* institutions and state administration is also one of class. The *panchayati raj* institutions may be dominated by the local elite, but it is a *local* elite. Government officials (especially Indian Administrative Service) and NGOs, often have—whatever their differences—a common class background.

NGOs and panchayati raj institutions   What role will NGOs play if the *panchayati* system starts working, and how do NGOs feel about the *panchayati raj* system? The answer from one respondent in ActionAid is representative: 'frankly, NGOs feel threatened by *panchayati* raj institutions'. The role and scope of NGO involvement in development projects, development programmes and, now even development policy formulation, has grown enormously in the last two decades. The potential conflict of interest between NGOs and *panchayati raj* institutions revolves both around the role that they would play and the funds which they would access.

However, there is also room for collaboration. Many NGOs have over the last decade been specialising in 'capacity-building' skills, which provide an ideal basis for informing people of their rights and encouraging them to act collectively to claim them. A close consideration of the subjects in the XIth Schedule which are under the jurisdiction of *panchayati raj* institutions, and those issues in the Seventh Plan identified as being the role of NGOs, reveals that there is room for cooperation. Most of the XIth Schedule concentrates on subjects that should by developed by the *panchayati raj* institutions (such as watersheds, schools, and drinking water). The description of the role of NGOs in the Seventh Plan concentrates on facilitation: 'to supplement the government efforts...to disseminate information...to de-mystify technology'. Whilst there are certainly areas that conflict, there is also a lot of room for collaboration (see Extract 5.2).

Formal and Informal Links between *Panchayati Raj* and Watershed Institutions

There are few formal links between *panchayati raj* institutions and the state administration at the district or block level. In Karnataka, projects are routed through the *zilla parishad*, but this is simply a pathway for the funds. The projects are managed by the chief executive officer of the *zilla parishad*, and the system for planning and the final accountability is effectively the same as if the project were routed through the DRDA.

The main formal and informal links between the two systems is at the level of the *gram panchayat* and the watershed committee. Although the Guidelines specify that '*gram panchayats* are also entitled to take on the responsibility of implementing a cluster of watershed projects in the capacity of project implementation agencies, if they so desire', there are very few *gram panchayats* operating as project implementing agencies or watershed committees. NGO respondents explained that they are reluctant to work with *gram panchayats* for four reasons: (a) the *gram panchayat* is too big a unit, and its boundaries rarely coincide with those of a watershed; (b) *gram panchayats* are too heterogeneous and are dominated by elites; (c) *gram panchayats* pursue short-sighted political goals, and these usually revolve around more immediate tangible projects such as house and road construction; and (d), underpinning all of the above is the perception that the *gram panchayat* and the *sarapanch* do not represent the *gram sabha*.

Despite these problems, in both Karnataka and Andhra Pradesh the link between *panchayati raj* and watershed institutions is strongest at the village level. The watershed associations and watershed committees usually include a few (1–3) members from the *gram panchayat*, including the *sarapanch*. The rationale for this is to include *gram panchayat* members in decision-making and to benefit from their power, but not to allow them to take over. *Gram panchayat* members often become members of the watershed association, because their land lies within the project area. In such cases, the chances are that they will be larger landholders, so the benefits that they can bring to the watershed association, in terms of official support, have to be weighed against the possible disadvantages of their priorities in watershed management for smaller landholders.

The reason for including *gram panchayats*, or forming links with them, varies from project to project. The reason given by many (over half the respondents involved in implementing projects) for forming links with *gram panchayats* was functional. They were contacted because they could not be easily avoided. For example, the permission of *gram panchayats* must be sought when common land is taken up for afforestation or soil conservation work.

Of more interest are the instances when *gram panchayats* are involved for the explicit purpose of building sustainable links between *panchayati raj* and watershed institutions. The *panchayati raj* institutions are progressive in the potential support that is given to the poor (for instance, through the reservation of seats for scheduled castes, scheduled tribes and women). The NGO respondents who have taken a policy decision to work with *panchayati raj* institutions were unanimous in their opinion that simultaneous support for *panchayati raj* and watershed institutions is essential. Both sets of institutions contribute towards a process whereby disadvantaged people can negotiate instead of either remaining loyal or taking radical exit measures. One respondent described these changes as 'the elite know that if they are not careful they will kill the golden goose'.

In Karnataka there was a general perception that the experience of *panchayati raj* has had a positive effect on local understanding of politics and their rights in it. An NGO respondent in Bellary commented that:

The weaker sections are at a learning stage now, but this is the chance for the government to help them. In the next five years they will start coming up. They are learning how to mobilise for funds. The next elections will be very tough.

Building more formal links between the two systems is one way in which the capacity built through watershed institutions and other community-based organisations can be scaled up. There are instances of these linkages between community-based organisations and *panchayati raj* institutions emerging in many instances. In Andhra Pradesh, 800 women from self-help groups contested the *panchayat* elections; 400 were elected. A respondent said that such a turnout would have been impossible if community-based organisations and self-help groups had not enabled women to recognise their own capacity. At a recent Telugu Desam rally, a woman *sarapanch* from Warangal district publicly asked the Chief Minister why there were no women in his circle of advisors (*Deccan Chronicle*, 29 May 1998). In the MYRADA area, 54 women who were members of self-help groups have been elected to *panchayati raj* institutions.

The movement of people from self-help groups to *panchayati raj* institutions often happens without any external encouragement. Government representatives in Andhra Pradesh were especially conscious of the success of this process and its rapidity. The habitation committees of the Janma Bhoomi project also consist of members of community-based organisations and *gram panchayats*. This is one of the most interesting findings of the linkages between *panchayati raj* and watershed institutions, and is a process whose potential needs to be explored further.

Many organisations are already involved in assisting the poor to enter the *panchayati raj* system and to voice their demands. However most of these organisations are advocacy based, there are very few field-based NGOs amongst them. For example, ActionAid has recently released a CD-ROM on women in *panchayati raj*. UNICEF supported a telephone and television conference via satellite, in which elected women from all over Karnataka could share their problems and ask questions of a panel in Bangalore.

Much of this chapter touches on aspects of multi-agency partnerships. Box 6.1 brings together issues specifically relating to relationships among *panchayati raj*, government and non-government institutions, raised at the April 1998 National Workshop on Watershed Approaches for Wastelands Development (on which this book is based).

Mechanisms for Transparency and Accountability

One of the defining differences between *panchayati raj* and watershed institutions is the principle of accountability on which they operate. *Panchayati raj* institutions are accountable to the electorate and can be voted out. Watershed institutions are accountable to the government, which can stop funds and disband committees if procedures are not followed as specified. *Panchayati raj* institutions seek to endogenise the mainstream political process to ensure its accountability. The Guidelines seek to exogenise the political process, as this is seen to subvert accountability. The question of accountability is therefore at the heart of the operation of the political and administrative system. It is also at the heart of the question of what links exist, and should exist between the two systems.

Accountability 'is a highly abstract concept, sometimes interpreted in formalistic and legalistic terms, and sometimes used in a more concrete way to refer to the social, economic, political, etc. mechanisms through which some agents become responsive to other agents' (Moore 1995:42). The obscurity in which accountability is enshrouded prevents an examination of the mechanisms through which it could operate. This appears to be the case for both *panchayati raj* and watershed institutions. The former are enshrouded in so many amendments, provisions and ordinances that, as one respondent put it, 'the law itself has become a moving target. How can we possibly implement it?' The latter have an elaborate system of monitoring and evaluation that disguises the fact that the accountability is to the top: governments and donors.

A deconstruction of the concept of accountability is imperative for an understanding of the political and administrative systems for development projects. In Karnataka, there was a widely felt opinion that 'the system' was not accountable to local people. *Panchayati raj* institutions have become a channel for the delivery of development projects to the village, and the *gram sabha* is not sufficiently politicised to hold the *gram panchayat* accountable. *Gram panchayats* are accountable not to the *gram*

Box 6.1 Additional Implications of *Panchayati Raj* **Legislation for Multi-agency Partnerships**

- Central government funds currently flow direct to the district level and are managed by DRDAs or *zilla parishads*. But many problems and opportunities cannot be resolved here, since *zilla parishads* are widely seen as remote from village realities. Ways need to be worked out for the *panchayat samitis* and (especially) *gram panchayats* to influence how resources are allocated.

- Technical support will still be needed, especially at *gram panchayat* level. Some equivalent of the watershed development teams will be needed to work with the *panchayati raj* institutions. To achieve consistency with the *panchayati raj* legislation, all technical committees (watershed development teams, multi-disciplinary teams, watershed committees) will have to have the same caste and gender reservations as the *panchayati raj*. A broader sensitisation of recently elected *sarapanches* in their responsibilities, and in participatory approaches to development, will also be needed. There seems to be no problem with a continuing role for NGOs more generally in watershed development, as long as they recognise the *gram panchayat* as the constitutionally elected village body and, in agreement with the *gram panchayat*, they develop an exit strategy so that their services are time-bound and not open-ended.

- The Common Guidelines are currently uniform across all states, whereas political conditions differ considerably, as does implementation of the 73rd Constitutional Amendment. Some local adaptation of provisions to dovetail development support to the *panchayati raj* institutions is therefore needed.

- The *panchayati raj* system poses several challenges to people's participation in rural development. One is the division of voting along party-political lines, which often corresponds with a division along caste lines. Where this occurs, it is likely to exacerbate rather than diminish disputes within the community over natural resources management and watershed rehabilitation. Consensus-style selection of the *sarapanch*, as for instance in Ralegaon Siddhi, Maharashtra, is ideal, but relies on sensitive mediation by a non-political (and usually charismatic) individual or organisation, so is rarely achievable.

- A difficulty of a different magnitude is that the *panchayati raj* institutions generally see themselves in a vertical relationship to each other, at the expense of close relations to constituencies at each level. In reality, the *sarapanch* as head of the *gram panchayat*, is elected by the village assembly (*gram sabha*), and so should be accountable to that assembly. NGOs have a potentially powerful role in building up this relationship of responsibility between the *panchayati raj* institutions and the *gram sabhas*. Unless the *gram sabha* exercises its constitutionally mandated monitoring over the activities of the *sarapanch*, then the disbursement of development funds, including those for watershed rehabilitation, will become merely a matter of personal discretion by the *sarapanch* and his or her *panchayati raj* superiors.

sabha, but to higher hierarchies in government for the implementation of these projects. The monitoring and evaluation procedures are basically audits of money spent and structures built, rather than the local impact or benefits of the project. However most respondents did not think that the *panchayati raj* institution system was inherently less likely to be accountable than the state administration. A former Secretary at the Ministry of Agriculture in Bangalore commented, 'the irregularity with *panchayati raj* institutions is far less than with the government. The *zilla parishads* are already handling large amounts of money, so why not trust them with implementing the Guidelines?'

One of the reasons given for aborting the Karnataka *Panchayat* Act of 1987 was that *panchayati raj* institutions were corrupt. However there is much dissent on this conclusion. No one disputes the existence of corruption, but most argue that it occurs less than in the government. Further it is argued that it is the people who should ultimately judge this:

If a case is built up by using charges of corruption in order to scrap the system or diminish the importance of people's representatives, this is tantamount to throwing the baby out with the bath water. After all, in a democracy, isn't it the people who should punish their corrupt and wicked representatives as and when the next elections take place? Instead these very elections were postponed indefinitely. What kind of logic is this? (Mathews 1995:61).

Conventional systems of ensuring bureaucratic responsibility are important. Traditional bureaucratic means for monitoring and evaluation have been on the decline since the wave of populist poverty alleviation programmes started in the 1980s and 1990s. Monitoring and evaluation now are basically an audit of fund disbursement and a catalogue of structures that have been built. However *panchayati raj* institutions have the potential to demand greater accountability from the bureaucratic system. The Right to Information movement in Rajasthan, the demand to see 'utilisation certificates' and to make public funds received, are all part of a growing demand for greater accountability. 'The *panchayats* will break this centralised information system when 30 lakh elected members ask for information on a variety of matters that affect the people's lives' (Mathews 1995:50).

Building Links between *Panchayati Raj* and Watershed Institutions

This chapter has argued that the Amendment and the Guidelines embody different concepts of decentralisation, the community and collective action. In the watershed-management context, *panchayati raj* institutions have so far been evaluated for their effectiveness as project-implementation institutions, whether project implementing agencies or watershed committees. However *panchayati raj* institutions are not interchangeable with watershed institutions. The two systems are compatible if one recognises that one is a system for local self-government, and the other a system to enable the implementation of a specific project. This section will examine in some more detail the potential of building on complementary links between *panchayati raj* and watershed institutions.

The main reason for involving *panchayati raj* institutions in watershed management is that they are sustainable institutions that have the mandate to plan local development and integrate various activities. The three central concerns of current watershed programmes are how to ensure their sustainability, how to 'scale up' the projects, and how to integrate watershed management with other activities. It is widely acknowledged that watershed management is not a sufficient basis for improved local livelihoods, but needs to be linked to other activities, especially for the landless, to ensure its sustainability. The concept of 'watershed-plus' has emerged to describe this process. Watershed-plus has been used to describe broad development objectives, such as equity and empowerment, as well as related means such as credit, employment, and drinking water.

With the identification of such broad objectives, the next logical step in the discussion is the question of how to scale up the financial and human-resource capacity to implement such a programme. Many NGO respondents mentioned that they find it difficult to implement programmes under current financial allocations.

There are several arguments for involving *panchayati raj* institutions in watershed management, especially when it becomes a broad rural development programme rather than a narrow technical one. First, they are responsible for development planning for the *gram panchayat* and would be the natural apex body for linking watershed development with other objectives. Second, in many states the management of the commons and wasteland is under the control of the *gram panchayat*, and they have been given the responsibility of preparing action-plans for their development. Efforts to strengthen the capacity to develop micro-plans have already been started by state governments and NGOs. The National Institute for Rural Development in Hyderabad, at the request of the Ministry of Rural Areas and Employment, has produced a suggested scheme for the devolution of powers and functions to *gram panchayats*, and has dwelt at length on neglected areas like land reform, protection and maintenance of village commons, and water management.

Third, *panchayati raj* institutions are statutory bodies and have the powers to raise revenue and collect taxes. In practice, the ability of *gram panchayats* is usually restricted, and most State Finance Commissions have not yet specified the subjects which will be handed over to the *gram panchayats*. Commentators have argued that the devolution of revenue-raising powers to the *gram panchayat* is critical (Oomen 1995, Rajaraman et al. 1996) and that fiscal devolution should be linked to the functions which are listed in the XIth Schedule. In the case of watershed development, levies on water resources and royalties on use of common property would constitute the natural domain of local government. A *gram panchayat* empowered to raise such revenue could become an important and possibly well-resourced nodal point for integrated resource development. The suggestion in the approach paper to the Ninth Five-Year Plan, that funds be routed straight to *gram panchayats*, would add to this strength if it were implemented.

Fourth, and related to the point above, *gram panchayats* are in a strategic position to be able to oversee a cluster of watershed projects within their *panchayat* boundaries. Similarly, the *panchayat* at the block level is in a good strategic position to manage watershed projects within its block. The block is the operational headquarters of many development programmes and an ideal place for planning and integrating programmes. This comparative advantage will probably be incorporated into the watershed projects under the Long Term Action Plan in Western Orissa.

Fifth, capacity-building projects in support of *panchayati raj* institutions are growing, and watershed management should be integrated into these, and vice-versa. In all states, hundreds of thousands of newly elected representatives are being trained on the rights and responsibilities of *panchayati raj* institutions. In Maharashtra, an NGO (Yashwantrao Chauhan Pratisthan) is providing this training to some 6,000 persons per year in collaboration with the government of Maharashtra. In Orissa, several NGOs have tacitly supported *panchayati raj* institutions and are now developing all their projects in collaboration with them (see Extract 5.2). Many mainstream NGOs, such as ActionAid, have taken a policy decision to work with *panchayati raj* institutions. In Andhra Pradesh, Karnataka and Tamil Nadu, a study coordinated by the Centre for World Solidarity is focussing in particular on the relation between *panchayati raj* and watershed institutions.

Sixth, and related to the above, this capacity building reflects a slow but growing recognition that a significant section of local, and rural, civil society is demanding greater involvement in decision-making. That is, they are demanding that they be involved in a discussion of the terms of their participation. This is reflected in the Right to Information movement sustained by the Mazdoor Kisan Shakti Sangathan in Rajasthan. It is also reflected in the 'vigilance committees' that have been established in many districts and the move towards greater transparency about fund flows at the *gram panchayat*. This does not necessarily suggest that civil society is acting collectively for a common purpose: merely that people have learnt how the system works and how to voice their demands for inclusion. Watershed institutions should integrate with this movement and contribute towards a process that ensures that the weaker sections have some stake in it.

Summary

Panchayati raj and the Guidelines are both systems that aim to decentralise control over development to local communities. The former is a constitutional part of Indian democracy, and the latter is an executive order of a ministry. Apart from the fact that they both aim to decentralise, they differ in their legislative status, objectives and approach. The debates about 'the perfect fit' between physical watersheds and the social units that should manage them, miss a fundamental point. This is that the two systems were established for different purposes. The *panchayati raj* institutions are not implementing committees or agencies for projects, but units of local self-government. It is more than likely that a *gram panchayat* will not coincide with a watershed, but it does have a mandate to make a plan for natural resource management within its boundaries. There is no contradiction in establishing watershed committees within a *gram panchayat*. However, when watershed committees receive government and donor funding to expand their roles, and take on many of the functions assigned to *panchayati raj* institutions, there is a need to be careful of not undermining the respective roles of the two systems.

Much of the recent enthusiasm over 'watershed-plus' has led watershed management into territory that is in the domain of *panchayati raj* institutions. Whether or not this creates a conflict is highly dependent on local and state politics. However in all cases it is a matter of missing the 'spirit' of the legislation underlying both *panchayati raj* and the Guidelines. Further it misses out the comparative advantages of both systems. In the case of the Guidelines, these are committees especially established for watershed management with a support network of line departments, NGO expertise, and specialised supervisory teams. In the case of *panchayati raj*, these are sustainable local institutions that have the statutory power to plan natural resource management, open bank accounts, etc, and represent local needs at higher levels.

There is unexploited room for cooperative work between *panchayati raj* institutions, NGOs and watershed institutions at various levels. It will take some time before *panchayati raj* institutions are operating effectively, and many NGOs have accumulated skills in 'capacity building' which are needed by *panchayati raj* institution members. There is also room for cooperation work between *gram panchayats* and watershed committees at the grassroots.

This chapter has suggested that *panchayati raj* and the Guidelines have very different approaches to supporting local collective action. Both approaches are important, and comparing their potential for watershed management is futile. Many of the discussions about the comparative advantage of *gram panchayats* versus community-based organisations become embroiled in a comparison of the track record of these institutions. This exercise has limited utility. It is now fairly clear that community-based organisations of all kinds need sustained external support, and that most are not particularly representative of the needs of the poor. It is also evident that *gram panchayats* are dominated by the elite, and that so far they have been used to entrench elite interests. The ultimate objective is local empowerment and development, and both types of institutions have an important role to play in facilitating this. However, this involves a political decision to follow the 'spirit' of the legislation in both *panchayati raj* and the Guidelines.

EXTRACT 6.1
DEVELOPMENT OF DEGRADED LANDS: SOME POLICY AND INSTITUTIONAL ISSUES[2]

J. K. ARORA[3]

Sporadic efforts have been made to federate self-help groups or community-based organisations at the sub-district and district levels and, in a few cases, at the higher levels also. As independent institutions, these organisations are free to organise any such federations and actively promote them. But when such an effort is officially supported by a donor-

[2] Source: Arora (1998).
[3] Consultant, Department for International Development, KAWAD, No. 250, Main Defence Colony, Indiranagar, Bangalore 560 038, India.

or state-funded development project or programme, then one must examine whether such federations are likely to generate any conflicts with
the higher-level *panchayati raj* institutions. The fallout from any such conflicts is ultimately to be faced by the states and therefore, it will be desirable to examine this question to assess whether the states should be
financing such higher-level federation efforts.

The *panchayati raj* institutions have been created for effective decentralisation and for people's participation in some of the regulatory functions, and for social and economic development of the community. There
is obviously either a lack of appreciation of this role, or the *panchayati raj*
institutions have not been properly equipped so far to discharge their
role effectively. Some states may not have any village-level *panchayats*, as
one *gram panchayat* may cover a group of villages, so there may be a total
void of any institutional arrangements at the village level. There is no
doubt that most local problems can be best addressed through community participation, but then cannot one think of bringing such village-
level self-help groups or community-based organisations under the *gram
panchayat*? The Karnataka *Panchayati Raj* Act, through an amendment in
1997, provides for the *gram panchayat* to set up special-purpose committees with non-elected persons as members. This arrangement overcomes
the lack of any institutional arrangement at the village level to involve
the community in development work. The self-help groups and community-based organisations could thus possibly become committees of
the *gram panchayat*. In any case, only time will show whether these organisations would like to remain as outside the purview of the *gram
panchayats*, or would opt to become its committees. They should, however, have the freedom to make their own decision in this regard.

Panchayati raj institutions are a constitutional requirement. They are
being set up with a view to decentralising administration (including development administration), as well as to ensure that local people are not
only associated in the planning and implementation of development
projects but are actually in command of the entire development process. In other words, the *panchayati raj* institutions are to be taken as community institutions, and community participation is to be achieved
through them. However, in reality *panchayati raj* institutions are not at
present strong institutions in most states, particularly below the district
level. Particularly at the village level, there is therefore a lack of any
effective community institution that can be involved in any developmental project. This void is being filled by a variety of NGOs facilitating
the development of self-help groups and community-based organisa-

tions. Many development projects are designed with these realities in view, and considerable investment is made in capacity-building among self-help groups, community-based organisations and NGOs.

There is, therefore, a need to take a view at the national level whether projects funded by the government, or by other funding agencies under agreements with the government, should use only *panchayati raj* institutions for community participation and build their capacity, or whether a combination of NGOs, self-help groups and community-based organisations should continue to be used.

Many people argue that *panchayati raj* institutions in the state are being set up and developed in the image of the respective state governments, and all the characteristics of the government can be seen in them. They argue that *panchayati raj* institutions follow the same decision-making process, which is essentially slow and bureaucratic, and which has predominant political content; their funding and accounting are equally cumbersome, and there is little flexibility. *Panchayati raj* institutions therefore, they claim, are not the best-suited institutions for ensuring effective community participation in development. One school of thought favours the involvement of *panchayati raj* institutions only in regulatory functions and in social development in rural areas. Economic development should be achieved through a multi-pronged approach in which all possible agencies should be involved, including the state line departments, *panchayati raj* institutions, NGOs and others.

EXTRACT 6.2
PRADAN'S COLLABORATION WITH *PANCHAYATS* IN WATERSHED DEVELOPMENT IN PURULIA, WEST BENGAL[4]

PRADAN TEAM[5]

Why Collaborate with *Panchayats*?

Empowering rural communities is a core objective of PRADAN. Therefore, in carrying out projects for enhancing livelihoods PRADAN collaborates with and strengthens rural community-based organisations where they exist, and fosters such organisations where they do not. In

[4] Source: PRADAN (1998).
[5] Contact: Deep Joshi, PRADAN, 59 Community Centre, Niti Bagh, New Delhi, India.

this spirit, there is great potential to work with *panchayati raj* institutions. Specifically, PRADAN personnel can contribute by transferring knowledge and skills, and inculcating values and attitudes among village people so that they can meaningfully participate in development programmes, and eventually in all affairs of *panchayat* institutions.

Beginnings of a Collaborative Relationship

West Bengal is one of the few states where *panchayati raj* institutions have been implementing rural development programmes for some time.

PRADAN already had a team working in Purulia district, aiming to improve livelihoods based on rainfed agriculture. The Hindustan Fertiliser Corporation was also implementing a project in the region to improve rainfed agriculture. Corporation staff invited a PRADAN professional as a resource person to help them design and conduct village-level events aimed at community organisation. This is how PRADAN was introduced to Brajarajpur village of Barabazar block, chosen by the corporation for its demonstrations. This interaction led to farmers implementing the Jaldhar model of *in situ* moisture conservation developed by PRADAN, with no financial support from outside. Seeing their enthusiasm, PRADAN staff decided to work there regularly, especially as the corporation was also keen to work together.

Arnab Chakraborty of PRADAN began working regularly in Brajarajpur in April 1994. Farmers were keen to treat more land with the Jaldhar model, even if they had to borrow money to do so. PRADAN was also keen to test the idea of promoting the model through bank loans. However, the local bank was not ready to give loans, and farmers were reluctant to go to the bank.

The PRADAN team decided to extend loans at an annual interest of 12 per cent (the prevailing bank rate). As PRADAN had limited funds, farmers agreed to borrow just enough money to meet their subsistence needs for the days they would work in their own fields to implement the Jaldhar model. Otherwise, they said, they would have to go for wage labour elsewhere and could not work on their own land. Farmers repaid the loan along with interest after the harvest. Though the extent of work done this way was small, it generated a lot of interest in surrounding villages. Villagers voiced demands for wider implementation of the Jaldhar model in the *panchayat* meeting (*gram sabha*).

The PRADAN team was excited by this unexpected development. It would be a breakthrough if the model were to be included in the *panchayat*'s schemes; it would then spread far and wide. The PRADAN team had no experience with *panchayats*; it had so far only worked either directly with the community or collaborated with village clubs implementing various livelihood projects. When Chakraborty came to know about the developments at the *gram sabha*, he decided to meet discreetly with *panchayat* leaders. He met the *sabhapati* (president) of Barabazar Block *Panchayat Samiti* (BBPS) in early 1995, briefed him about PRADAN, and conveyed his availability should the *panchayat* committee need help in their development work.

The *sabhapati* invited Chakraborty to a meeting of the BBPS, and announced the decision to incorporate the Jaldhar model in the Block Plan. He also sought PRADAN's help to give necessary technical guidance, introduced Chakraborty to the block development officer, sub-assistance engineers and job workers of the block, who normally implement such work, and requested him to train the engineers and workers so that they could help farmers at the field level.

Early Interaction with Panchayats

The BBPS sanctioned Rs 600,000 for the Jaldhar model in 15 villages across 10 *gram panchayats* from funds allocated for wage-employment programmes. Chakraborty visited all the locations, conducted meetings, and narrated the evolution and potential of the model with the help of a slide projector and photographs. He organised impromptu training in the field for engineers, job workers and farmers in laying out the pits, measurement of earthworks, ensuring proper slopes, and other technical matters. He also met the *sabhapati* and block development officer regularly to apprise them about the progress of work.

The quality of work was not uniformly good in all the villages, and depended on the role played by village leaders. In only two villages was the model implemented in contiguous patches, as it should be. Here village leaders heeded Chakraborty in designing and implementing the work. In most other villages, pits were dug in isolation in a haphazard way. In some cases even the quality of pits was not satisfactory in terms of depth and side slope. Because of time constraints, the work could not be finished. Yet, this process brought Chakraborty close to the BBPS leadership.

The goodwill thus generated was also reflected in other contexts:

- The *sabhapati* of Barabazar Block invited Chakraborty to accompany him when he went to meet the head of a regional NGO resource centre.
- Since the implementation of the Jaldhar model by BBPS was hap-

hazard and additional funds were not available from BBPS, PRADAN proposed to raise funds from external sources to fill in the gaps to increase the efficacy of land treatment. The *sabhapati* readily agreed, and when PRADAN mobilised a grant from Action-Aid the project was discussed at length in the *panchayat*. Subsequently, the *sabhapati* directed the engineers and his party colleagues to extend support in all respects to implement this project. He would himself come to village meetings in ActionAid-funded villages whenever the PRADAN team faced any difficulty.

- Two *gram panchayats* jointly bore half the cost of an exposure visit of 60 farmers from ActionAid project villages to Balarampur so that they could learn how to implement the model.
- The *sabhapati* and two other key members of BBPS on their own travelled 150 km to Ranchi to see PRADAN's work there.
- The BBPS formally invited PRADAN professionals to act as resource persons when it conducted a block-level training programme on watershed development.

Role of the District Administration in Collaboration

At PRADAN's invitation, the district magistrate came to see PRADAN's work in promoting the Jaldhar model. He was accompanied by the district planning officer, the principal agricultural officer, divisional forest officers, the deputy director of sericulture, the soil conservation officer, and the project officer of the District Rural Development Agency. During his visit, the magistrate assured farmers that the DRDA could finance such land development work to the extent of 1,000 hectares every year. Based on the magistrate's assurance, PRADAN helped Manara *gram panchayat* prepare a proposal on the Jaldhar model. The *sabhapati* of Purulia-1 block (under which Manara falls) could not finance it, as this block had concluded its annual plan, but recommended the proposal to the DRDA. The DRDA did not respond. When PRADAN pursued the matter with the district magistrate, he advised them to go to the soil conservation officer.

The soil conservation officer said that the funds available were not for carrying out work through the *panchayat*. He suggested that villagers could apply directly to his office with detailed plans, on the basis of which his office would issue work orders. After the villagers had completed the work, his staff would carry out physical verification and he would release funds on the basis of their reports. Given such a tedious process, PRADAN decided against pursuing the proposal. Instead,

PRADAN helped villagers in Brajarajpur to submit to the soil conservation officer a small proposal, which was approved. Since payment of wages would be made only after the work was verified by officials, the Barabazar villagers borrowed Rs 5,000 from PRADAN, on condition that they would repay as soon as they received payment from the government. It took a long time to get repayment. Lower-level soil-conservation officers found it difficult to make time to visit the site and provide a completion certificate.

The district magistrate's visit, and subsequent interaction with district officers, generated some awareness in the administration about PRADAN and its work. The magistrate and planning officer took a personal interest in spreading the Jaldhar model. They requested different block authorities to consider it in their block plans.

Rooting Collaboration in a Long-Term Programme

During the same period, the new Guidelines for watershed development came into being, with provisions for *panchayats* and NGOs as well as government agencies to act as project implementation agencies.

PRADAN was invited by the district administration and *zilla parishad* to participate in discussions concerning the Integrated Watershed Development Programme. They asked what role PRADAN could play in the programme. Since the programme would be implemented according to both the Indian government guidelines and the state government's (yet to be formulated) guidelines, PRADAN's role could not be articulated. Eventually, the state government took the decision that only *panchayat* institutions would be project-implementing agencies, but NGOs could assist in training. The district magistrate then requested PRADAN to prepare training modules. He later told PRADAN that the district had accepted these modules, and that the state was also likely to accept them. He advised PRADAN to rent the district youth hostel as a training centre. Soon thereafter, he was transferred to another post, and the process stopped there. The next district magistrate could not give priority to this. Later, the decision was changed, and the task of training was given to the State Institute of *Panchayat* and Rural Development (SIPRD).

SIPRD again invited PRADAN to participate when it began conducting the training programmes. The district planning officer and project officer of the DRDA verbally repeated the invitation to the PRADAN team leader to send his people. PRADAN agreed, as it would at least be an opportunity for mutual learning. The assistant director of SIPRD, a young state civil-service officer, was very happy with PRADAN's involvement in the process. He later wrote to PRADAN, exploring whether PRADAN could depute two professionals to SIPRD to help it carry out training for the Integrated Watershed Development Programme. With this reference, PRADAN wrote to the joint director in the State Ministry of Rural Development, suggesting that instead of deputing staff to SIPRD, PRADAN could have an institutional collaboration. This did not move further as the incumbent was transferred.

In a parallel process, the district administration invited PRADAN to a review meeting where the *zilla parishad* was taking stock of the watershed programme and planning future actions. The meeting was attended by the *sabhadhipati*, district magistrate, district planning officer, senior development officers, the DRDA project officer, and all other district officers. PRADAN and Kalyan were the only NGOs present. There was little discussion about the role of NGOs, and at the end of the meeting, the NGOs were requested to help five blocks (*panchayat samitis*) delineate five micro-watersheds. PRADAN representatives raised the issue of institutionalising long-term collaboration in the programme. Unfortunately the officials and *panchayat* representatives got the erroneous impression that PRADAN wanted to be the project implementing agency, whereas in reality, PRADAN was concerned only that the expected roles and responsibilities of all the collaborating parties be clearly defined from the beginning to avoid confusion and consequent indifference towards the programme. PRADAN therefore wanted the district administration to define the role they expected it to play in the long run. The question is yet to be resolved.

PRADAN, however, responded positively to the request for training and completed the task on time in the five blocks.

In one block, PRADAN's experience was encouraging. All the watershed development team members were present. The block development officer himself spent time with PRADAN professionals in the field. The *sahasabhapati* (vice president) and block development officer addressed a meeting where the watershed programme was being discussed with the villagers.

After the meeting villagers demanded that PRADAN staff should remain with them throughout the programme-implementation process. Seeing the impact of PRADAN's involvement, the block development officer and *sahasabhapati* of the block inquired about PRADAN's mode of operation. They asked whether PRADAN could help them. PRADAN personnel explained the role they could play, emphasising that if the block wanted to involve PRADAN in a sustained way for a long period, the two parties could sit together to develop a memorandum of under-standing. The block development officer unfortunately was transferred before such a meeting could be organised.

In the other four blocks, the task of delineating watersheds became more of a routine assignment. Predictably, it did not help build a long-term relationship. The DRDA reimbursed all PRADAN's expenses in-curred in the delineation process, and also paid a professional fee. PRADAN decided to charge a fee to emphasise the formal and institu-tional nature of the collaboration it was seeking. This created an impres-sion within the DRDA that PRADAN was in the consulting business, when, actually, PRADAN was repeatedly seeking a partnership as a grass-roots action agency.

In July, 1996 PRADAN wrote to the Minister of *Panchayat* and Rural Development in the Government of West Bengal, apprising him of its work and seeking a meeting to discuss possibilities of working together in the arena of rural development. His office responded, advising PRADAN personnel to meet him during his next visit to Purulia. At the meeting, however, PRADAN were not able to give him a clear picture of the kind of relationship it wanted with the government. The meeting ended with some discussion on watershed development.

The next day, the Minister had a meeting with the district administra-tion to review literacy and watershed programmes. The PRADAN team also attended, but only as observers. In his address, the Minister empha-sised *in situ* moisture conservation in watershed development pro-grammes. It seems the Minister had fully grasped the core idea behind the Jaldhar model.

After the meeting, the Joint Secretary in the State Ministry of Rural Development and a member of CAPART's Standing Committee for Watershed Development, who was also with the team accompanying the Minister, visited the Jaldhar model being implemented by PRADAN and BBPS at Huchuabhapati. After the visit, the Joint Secretary said that his department would include the model in the watershed guidelines to be published shortly. In the following month, in a circular to the district administrations engaged in watershed-development programmes, he in-cluded Jaldhar along with other water-conservation measures.

PRADAN's Role in BBPS Watershed Development Programme

The BBPS began its first watershed-development planning exercise at Rupapetya village. Three PRADAN professionals joined the *sabhapati* to initiate the planning exercise.

During the first two days, the PRADAN team tried to follow the process outlined in various watershed-development training courses conducted by the state government. It consisted of a door-to-door and plot-to-plot questionnaire survey. The pace of work was very slow. Field surveys were done mostly by local volunteers, selected under the programme, who did not have adequate training. The data collected was far more than required, but hardly of the quality needed for planning. The intensity of people's involvement was also very low. On the third day, the PRADAN team proposed some changes in the process.

There was some reluctance to accept the new approach. PRADAN staff reassured the planning team that if the new approach was not found effective within a day, the old process could be restored. The PRADAN team demonstrated the technique of participatory resource mapping and resource potential analysis, using local names and terminology known to the villagers. The planning team appreciated the idea and it was meticulously followed throughout the planning exercise. The *sabhapati*, despite his busy schedule, kept visiting and encouraging people from time to time. PRADAN staff stayed in the village at night. Villagers arranged for free accommodation and food. This helped build a close relationship with the villagers, leading to a trustful and informal atmosphere.

The PRADAN team did not stop the questionnaire survey already underway. Rather, it identified problems being faced by field surveyors and modified some questions which people did not feel comfortable answering.

Instead of a door-to-door household survey, the PRADAN team formed small groups to generate data caste- community-wise, as there seemed a high degree of correlation between economic status and caste or community. In groups of similar socio-economic status, people felt more confident in sharing their concerns and opinion. Also, bigger hamlet-wise and watershed-wise meetings were held to crosscheck data generated in small group meetings. The PRADAN team was always conscious about its responsibility to elaborate and explain all that it was doing to the people, and took special care to transfer relevant skills to local volunteers and watershed committee members.

To generate land-, water- and vegetation-related data, the PRADAN team first made several transects, observations and complete resource maps. Instead of plot-to-plot field surveys, the watershed was segmented into smaller patches of land put to similar use, with common problems and a local name. Use of local categories to classify land was of immense help, and villagers could easily relate to them.

To identify problems and analyse resource potentials, the PRADAN team facilitated group meetings to generate as many alternative options as they could. The team also tossed different ideas in the meeting. One set of options was generated involving the women; another set by involving different landless communities, in separate meetings. Other sets of options were generated by involving owners of similar types of land, classified according to local categories.

The team gave special attention to resource allocation in preparing plans. The general trend was to allocate more resources to development of already existing water bodies. The more vocal people demanded funds to develop water bodies and land that would benefit them individually. The ownership of resources to be developed did not get enough attention. The PRADAN team facilitated a process through which norms were established to prioritise the options generated for the plan:

• landless people;
• women;
• bad land owned by poor people;
• better land owned by poor people;
• bad land owned by better-off people;
• better land owned by better-off people.

These norms were generated by taking the *sabhapati* into confidence. When he saw the usefulness of setting such norms, he appreciated it. In the process, some better-off farmers got frustrated, but the *sabhapati* assured them, saying, 'Let us not violate the spirit of this exercise. I will arrange separate funds to meet your demands'.

Another challenge was to prepare the final document which could be shared with the DRDA and other offices concerned. The watershed committee members requested PRADAN personnel to help organise and write the document, as it was the first of its kind in the block.

After Rupapetya watershed, PRADAN was requested by the BBPS to help them with three more watersheds. One of those was Tentlo. But the local leaders were doubtful, so PRADAN's involvement was limited. Planning in the other two watersheds is going on.

Simultaneously, PRADAN is also involved in programme implementation. In Rupapetya watershed, PRADAN staff attend meetings, help the watershed committee prioritise activities, encourage members to see good work done by other agencies, give guidance in adopting new technologies (on *in situ* moisture conservation), and sensitise them to involve women by promoting self-help groups.

PRADAN's Role in Jhalda-1 Block

When the district administration requested PRADAN to help Jhalda-1 block to delineate one micro-watershed along with other four blocks, the officials in this block *panchayat samiti* showed interest to seek PRADAN's help. But because of transfer of the then block development officer, the process was set back.

When the new block development officer joined, PRADAN received an invitation to collaborate formally in the watershed development programme. A formal agreement was signed, defining the roles and responsibilities of both parties. According to the agreement, PRADAN is expected to plan and implement one watershed project. The *panchayat samiti* will assure a smooth flow of funds through its own system. PRADAN will not handle money.

Here also, PRADAN's purpose is to demonstrate the potential of PRADAN–*panchayat* collaboration. Lessons from this experience will be documented and shared with policy-makers.

Conclusion: Factors Constraining Collaboration

The arrangement in Barabazar is more in the nature of a personal rather than an institutional relationship. In Jhalda-1, though the relationship appears to be formal, it is also very weak in the sense that the higher echelons of government do not recognise this formal relationship. A commitment to work with *panchayat* institutions is motivating PRADAN to explore possibilities and opportunities to build relationships with *panchayat* leaders. So far this has been more of a hit-and-miss rather than a planned process. Due to uncertainties about how their actions would be interpreted, PRADAN team members many a time hesitate to take a stand they think would improve the quality of the watershed-development programme. As of now PRADAN, does not have a legitimate space, recognised by the government; nor is there any explicit demand and sense of mutual accountability on either side. PRADAN's contribution is more in the nature of what it can volunteer, not what it is required to deliver—as would be the case if there was formal collaboration. A strong demand from the other side would challenge PRADAN to stretch more and to be more creative.

7 Capacity-Building among Agencies and Individuals

This chapter traces through the evolution of thinking and action in relation to capacity-building for watershed development. This can conveniently be divided into three phases:

- The 1994 Common Guidelines set out a structure for capacity-building, which was farsighted at the time.
- A review of experience by the Eswaran Committee (GoI 1997) revealed low engagement in capacity-building (both as trainers and trainees) by departments and agencies responsible to the states, and made recommendations to address this. In addition, a number of wider recommendations were also made to reinforce the prospects that women and weaker sectors should be able to assert their needs in the design and implementation of watershed development.
- Two further events were the review of the implementation of the 1994 Common Guidelines by Turton et al. (1998), and the April 1998 National Workshop on Watershed Approaches for Wastelands Development (on which this book is based). Both stressed the role that NGOs could play in helping to strengthen capabilities, the need for experiential learning to permit feedback and course corrections as necessary, and the scope for innovative field-based techniques such as cross-visits. They were also realistic enough to emphasise that no matter how effectively skills were imparted, they would be implemented only to a limited degree unless civil-service performance criteria and reward systems were appropriately adjusted.

These three phases are now discussed in turn. Extracts 7.1 and 7.2 contain relevant material presented at the national workshop.

Capacity-Building Provisions of the 1994 Guidelines

The 1994 Guidelines represented a major shift in the philosophy of rural development towards participatory, administratively decentralised approaches. The architects of the Guidelines were aware of the additional demands that this would make on (especially) local-level government staff, and accordingly made provisions for their training.

For instance, paragraph 44 of the Guidelines makes provision for the training of watershed users, the watershed secretary and volunteers in the technical aspects of *in situ* soil- and moisture-conservation techniques, the operation and maintenance of civil works, nursery and plantation techniques, and livestock and fodder management. It also covers the setting up and management of groups, conduct of meetings, maintenance of accounts and procedures for execution of civil works. In addition, training for the paid staff (such as watershed secretaries) includes record-keeping, and the administrative and accounting procedures of *panchayati raj* institutions, the DRDA and state departments.

Paragraphs 61–65 of the Guidelines cover the training of the watershed development team:

Each member is to receive a one-month training course comprising four units each of one week, including watershed-treatment technologies, participatory rural appraisal and community organisation; group behaviour and convergence of government services; project-management techniques; and administration of rural development programmes through the DRDAs, etc., including measurement and auditing procedures, inspection and audit, computerisation and report writing.

The state governments were given the responsibility for arranging these courses, commissioning state or national institutions to carry them out, and ensuring that the training approach was participatory and interactive, with the emphasis on field-based problem-solving.

For the long-term, it was envisaged that the State Institutes of Rural Development (SIRDs) would build up their own cadre of faculty members, who, supplemented by visiting agricultural scientists and staff from management institutions, would develop the capacity to run training programmes. The National Institute of Agricultural Extension Management (MANAGE) would organise programmes for the training of trainers.

Recommendations of the Eswaran Committee

In 1997, the Ministry of Rural Areas and Employment commissioned a team to review training arrangements for all watershed-development projects, programmes and schemes. The team, which was led by V. B. Eswaran, was asked to cover activities covered under the 1994 Guidelines, the NWDPRA of the Ministry of Agriculture and Cooperation, and CAPART.

The Eswaran report (GoI 1997) commented on the low uptake of the training provisions made by the Guidelines. For instance, after some initial enthusiasm, the persons nominated by States for the MANAGE course either did not attend or were not connected with watershed development (paragraph 3.40). The programme for training of trainers suffered a similar fate, and the programme for project directors, DRDA staff and district collectors was abandoned once the extent of non-attendance or the nomination of 'second- or third-level officer' substitutes became clear (paragraph 3.42). The programmes conducted by the State Institutes of Rural Development were merely 'of a general nature'.

The Eswaran report recommended a range of improvements, many of which went beyond the immediate remit of training, but all of which were relevant to the wider question of how the interests of disadvantaged sections of society (women and the poorer strata) could be represented and defended. These included:

- the increased representation of women (increased to one-third of membership in most cases) on the range of committees at different levels concerned with aspects of watershed development;
- the need for arrangements to ensure the equitable sharing of benefits from new and rehabilitated community assets (forest, grazing, water, fisheries) among the weaker sections;
- improvement in the emoluments of watershed development team members in order to ensure that appropriately qualified and experienced persons could be attracted;
- increase in the provision for cost of works by approximately 50 per cent; the provision of Rs 1000 without matching contribution to self-help groups to enable them to set up income-generating activities; and the provision of an additional preparatory period of one year to allow for group formation and community organisation;
- a tightening of financial provisions made to government departments when working as project implementation agencies, and an insistence that they strengthen the coordination of inputs by other government departments; improved financial flows from DRDAs/ *zilla parishads* to watershed committees;
- the conduct of a basic resource survey prior to a participatory rural appraisal.

Specifically with regard to training, the Eswaran report identified needs at the micro-watershed, project, block and district, and state levels.

Micro-watershed   A one-day workshop to sensitise and enlist the support of village-level government functionaries was seen to be necessary, with shorter training of a few hours in the evenings (on a fortnightly cycle) for user-groups, self-help groups, women's groups and the watershed association. Members of the watershed committee would be given training of two days at a time on aspects of watershed management, whilst watershed secretaries would receive a training course of two weeks.

Project level   Members of the project-implementing agency should receive one week's training at an appropriate institute on the watershed-development programme in general, and on technical aspects of the programme. Members of the watershed development team should be given a three-week training programme.

Block and district levels   The need to build up community organisation, technical issues and sustainability, should form the major components of training of officers at these levels. The duration and level of courses should vary according to whether the trainees are drawn from block/ *zilla parishad*, DRDAs, or line departments.

State level   An annual two-day workshop was seen as essential to generate awareness among senior officers at the state level, and to allow them and NGOs and others to exchange experiences in watershed development.

The Eswaran Committee endorsed the provisions of the Common Guidelines for a massive programme of training of trainers, again placing the major responsibility with State Institutes for Rural Development, but also stressing that others, including NGOs, should be engaged in a complementary fashion, and that all should meet acceptability criteria. Additional resources from within and beyond the watershed programme would have to be made available for the preparation of course materials at a range of institutions. Importantly, the heads of SIRDs should serve a fixed period of tenure in order to avoid excessive turnover, and new staff should be recruited to specialise in watershed management.

Conscious of the limited engagement of the state governments in training to date, the report recommend that the cost of training of trainers should be borne by the Indian government, and that this should bear 80 per cent of the cost of faculty or infrastructure at state, district or regional level. Finally, the states should prepare action plans for watershed development, incorporating provision for training components.

Monitoring of all centrally supported watershed-development programmes, projects and schemes should be conducted by a national standing committee for watershed development. A sub-committee would
monitor the implementation of the training aspects.

Review of Implementation of the 1994 Guidelines

The review of implementation of the Common Guidelines by Turton
et al. (1998) suggests that the Guidelines severely underestimated the
range and depth of training that would be required. In particular, if the
challenge of developing watersheds in an institutionally and environmentally sustainable fashion were to be met, then skills would have to
be sufficient to ensure that the interests of women and of the poor
could be adequately identified, represented and defended over time.
Even in the most favourable circumstances, this would be a daunting
task. However, the prospects of achieving it are severely diminished
because of:

- the chronic shortage of social-science perspectives and skills
  among (especially) government department staff at the local
  level;
- the lack of gender awareness in all levels of training;
- the continuing lack of expertise in participatory methods, gender,
  group formation, etc., among trainers in the training institutes identified for this work;
- the need for training in awareness and attitude change among collectors and other DRDA staff, to sensitise them to the benefits of
  and needs for participatory approaches;
- the need for a programme to assess the current skills and training
  needs of rural women;
- the lack of a forum for state-level functionaries to exchange ideas
  and discuss strategies on watershed development;
- the absence of any component of watershed development in the
  university curricula for engineering and agriculture.

Clearly, public-sector reform will have to address these issues over
time if the prospects for successful large-scale training are to be
enhanced, and careful long-term monitoring of performance standards among trainers and training institutions will be needed. Meanwhile, the two extracts that follow provide an indication of what
can be achieved through capacity-building at individual and institutional levels, given adequate motivation, skills and resources among
trainers and facilitators.

EXTRACT 7.1
LEARNING PROCESSES: THE APPROACH OF OUTREACH[1]

JIMMY MASCARENHAS[2]

In OUTREACH's experience, there is now 'spontaneous adoption' of participatory approaches by communities near our projects: requests and applications are being received from neighbouring communities to start similar activities in their villages on the same terms. Several key issues must be addressed to ensure the sustainability of participatory approaches.

Training and Human-Resource Development

Though training and human-resource development measures address the needs of watershed communities, a substantial amount of such measures are also needed among staff of the various development organisations that are involved, especially in respect of 'behavioural' training. This touches upon a range of topics such as communication and listening, sensitivity, interpersonal relations, leadership, teamwork, and so on, which empower individuals and therefore enhance the quality of the outputs of various individuals and organisations. It is particularly important that a culture of participation and sharing is developed within and between the development agencies themselves in order to enable community participation to take place.

Developing a Learning Process

Many past natural resources and other development projects have pursued an inflexible 'blueprint' approach which, among other things, has hindered experiential learning: the documenting and reflecting on experiences, discussing and analysing them, and revising and re-adapting the approach.

Experiential learning implies different agencies working together as teams, sharing their experiences, and developing a common understanding, vision and approach. Most of all, it implies a sensitivity to what client communities are saying and a response to their needs and suggestions in the context of natural resources management.

Part of the foundation for experiential learning can be laid by village-based participatory workshops (participatory rural appraisals), in which

[1] Source: Mascarenhas (1998).
[2] OUTREACH, 109 Coles Road, Fraser Town, Bangalore 560005, India.

watershed communities and staff of various agencies try to arrive at an understanding of indigenous technologies and systems of management developed and used by the community. They also try to understand how the community sees the project and how it is impacting on them. The future approach of the project is derived from this knowledge.

The exploratory exercises in these appraisals are particularly powerful: they generate information on trends (historical transects, trend diagrams) in resource use, land-based and non land-based livelihood systems, the status of resources and patterns of their use, relationships of the watershed with the main village and neighbouring villages, and seasonal patterns of activities and events. They also provide a range of socio-economic information, including wealth-ranking.

Amongst development agencies there is a similar interaction, also of a participatory nature, where staff are encouraged to interact and share their experiences about watershed development with one another. This form of experiential learning has proven itself in developing a more open and shared understanding of the project, and allows mid-course corrections or minor adjustments to be made consistently. This in itself is a major factor contributing towards sustainability.

Institutional Arrangements

If a process of participation in natural resource management projects is to be fostered, it is important to consider what types of institutions need to be involved and how these should relate to each other to provide complementarity and combine existing strengths.

Basically, there are two major types of institutions that need to link and interface with each other. The first is at the level of the community, and starts with various self-help and user groups. These need to be in some way federated at the watershed and regional levels, and also form some sort of linkage with the local *panchayati raj* institutions. A common error in natural resource management and other rural development projects is that the withdrawal and handing-over process starts towards the end of the project, rather than at the beginning. As a result, local community institutions do not develop the basic capabilities that are required for post-project management, resulting in repeated failures of projects. The development of apex community institutions that are capable of carrying the resource management process forward on their own is therefore an important precondition for sustainability.

A second set of institutions consists of all those involved in project implementation (external stakeholders), such as local government and other government departments at different levels, NGOs and funding organisations.

Each of these institutions has a role to play in natural resource management projects, as each one brings with it certain strengths and areas of expertise. Whatever the type of interaction adopted, it is important that two things be given top priority: the capacity-building of various institutions in relation to participatory natural resource management, and constant, steady attention to the interests of women, landless and other marginal groups.

Policy Framework

It is important that the lessons learnt from various natural resource management projects be distilled and fed back into the policy level. Policy-makers also need periodic exposure to the field, in order to observe and understand processes that are taking place there. This not only includes bureaucrats and senior members of funding organisations, but also elected representatives of local government and members of the political executive. The orientation of this group is an important input in natural resource management projects, and must start as part of the preparatory process itself as earlier described.

Conclusion

Sustainable natural resource management is an effort to arrest and reverse the process of depletion of natural resources. Hitherto, it has rarely been characterised by an integrated or comprehensive approach, which recognises the right and duty of communities to participate in the restoration and development of their habitats.

Rural communities have survived in these often hostile, uncertain and marginal conditions over generations, and have evolved their own strategies, technologies and management systems. These need to be inventoried, validated and included as inputs and resources in the development process.

Perhaps the two most critical elements in respect of community participation in this regard are:

- the need for a 'preparatory process' prior to project implementation, in which watershed communities are organised and the ground is prepared and for the main project; and
- the development of a community stake in the programme.

Ways need to be worked out to make certain that these take place. A policy and institutional framework that support this process are a must.

EXTRACT 7.2
TRAINING FOR NGOS: THE APPROACH OF THE AGRICULTURE, MAN AND ECOLOGY PROJECT[3]

EDITH VAN WALSUM, MANS LANTING AND J. JANGAL[4]

Objectives

The Agriculture, Man and Ecology Project (AME) has the *long-term objective* of promoting sustainable land use—the present use of agricultural and non-agricultural land should not render this resource less productive or less enjoyable for future generations. We believe that all stakeholders in land use should participate in the effort to increase its sustainability, and get their fair share of what the land has to offer. Thus negotiations between the stakeholders need to be given a structure, and issues should be discussed with a holistic perspective i.e., should deal with economic development, social justice, gender equity, protection of nature and culture,[5] as well as agricultural and industrial development. This may appear to some like a romantic ideal, but we think it is a bare necessity: without effective collective action there can be no sustainable land use.

Our *practical aim* is to assist NGOs in strengthening their capacities to implement sustainable agriculture and watershed-management programmes. The focus therein is on narrowing the gaps in the soil-nutrient balance, water balance and energy balance, whilst promoting bio-diversity and ecological processes, as well as economic and social development. We endeavour to achieve these aims and objectives through an approach that incorporates a mix of participatory methodologies: participatory technology development, participatory rural appraisal, and concerted stakeholder action (Box 7.1).

Different Starting-Points for Different Types of Organisations

AME deals with a variety of NGOs. We distinguish here between five types of organisations,[6] as we have observed that each type requires a

---

[3] Source: Van Walsum et al. (1998).

[4] Agriculture, Man and Ecology Project.

[5] The *panchayat* is mandated with many of these functions and it is supposed to handle the watershed-maintenance funds released under the DRDA programme. However, in some circumstances it has a composition in which not all stakeholders are properly represented.

[6] In practice, organisations can be a mixture of the five 'types'. They can also develop over time from one type into another.

Box 7.1   Stakeholders and Participatory Technology Development

Stakeholders are all those who affect, or are affected by, the policies, decisions and actions pertaining to land use and its sustainability. They can be individual men, women and children; different categories of farmers, communities, social groups or institutions; policy-makers, planners and administrators in government; research institutions; commercial input suppliers; banks and moneylenders. Participatory technology development is essentially a process of purposeful and creative interaction between rural people and outside facilitators. Through this interaction, the partners try to increase their understanding of the main traits of the local farming systems, to define problems and opportunities, and to experiment with a selection of 'best-bet' options for improvement. The options are based on ideas and experiences derived from both indigenous knowledge and formal science. This process of technology development is geared not only towards finding solutions to current problems, but also towards developing sustainable agricultural practices that conserve and enhance the natural resource base so that they can still be used by future generations. Most important of all, participatory technology development should strengthen the capacity of farmers and rural communities to analyse ongoing processes and develop relevant, feasible, and useful innovations (van Veldhuizen et al. 1997).

---

different training approach (Table 7.1).

While some organisations work in relative isolation, we have also found many others that participate in networks. Such networks can focus on a single issue, e.g., promotion of the interest of *dalits*, or on multiple issues, where the network is an active partner in discussions with the district authorities on development issues. In the first case, all NGOs participating in the network have the same goal and focus in their own work. In the latter instance, network members tend to have a wide range of individual organisational objectives, and consequently address various issues within their respective organisational mandate.

Many NGOs have apprehensions about collaborating with either the commercial sector or the government.[7] As a result, they often isolate themselves from these sectors. This in turn reduces their access to resources—be it knowledge, money or physical inputs—essential for development. Smaller NGOs tend to display this behaviour more strongly than the larger and well-established ones.

---

[7] The following constraints are faced by NGOs in working with the government: lack of understanding about the roles played by NGOs; bureaucratic approach and delays in processing applications from NGOs; inability of lower officials to understand NGO philosophy; mutual distrust among government and NGOs; attempts to co-opt NGOs rather than collaborating with them; apprehension among government officials that the increase of NGO activity would progressively reduce the role and importance of government in society (Narasimha Reddy and Rajasekhar, 1997).

Table 7.1 Types of NGOs Implementing Watershed Programmes

Organisation type[a]	Main focus	Target group	Activities/approach	Implications of taking up watershed programme
Social action groups	Empowerment of oppressed groups (e.g. dalit' struggle for land and political power)	Oppressed social groups	Awareness raising; supporting formation of unions & other support organisations; advocacy and lobbying	Radical shift in working style and target-group orientation required
Community development organisations	Creation of social infrastructure in the community; social & economic activities	Different categories of community: women, men, youth, children (sometimes specific sections of community)	Sangam group formation; savings & credit self-help groups; women & children programmes; literacy; primary health care; agroforestry; agriculture; use of participatory appraisal methods	Moderate shift
Community dev & watershed-mgmt orgs	Watershed management for sustainable livelihood of community	Same as above.	Same as above. Plus, dev of watershed-mgmt institutions and & physical implementation of treatment plans; extensive use of participatory appraisal	Often started as community dev orgs, then incorp watershed approach. Integr of community groups & watershed institutions
Ecological agriculture organisations	Eliminate use of fertilisers and pesticides; restore soil health; revive indige-nous knowledge	(Individual) farmers	Promotion and testing of eco-friendly technologies; documentation of in-digenous practices; advocacy & lobbying	Important shift in working style and target-group orientation required
Watershed organisations[b]	Watershed management	Different categories of community(ies) in watershed	Development of watershed institutions & physical implementation of treatment plan; use of participatory appraisal	Some started in response to opportunity provided by Govt of India under new Guidelines

[a] Organisations can be broadly divided into these five categories. In most cases the majority of characteristics of a certain category will apply to an organisation, but not necessarily all.

[b] This type of NGO was a small minority. So far we have not trained such organisations, so will not discuss them further in this paper.

Key Features of AME's Training Approach

The general direction in which we try to steer the training process is towards the creation of negotiation platforms in which land-use stakeholders are properly represented. The route to reach that objective starts at a different point and leads through a different landscape for each organisation. Thus for AME the support given to each stakeholder is specific: a different starting point, and covering a mix of social and technical issues.

. The common elements in our training are the following:

- Training is a process towards the creation of negotiation platforms for sustainable land-use, in which different stakeholders are represented. This process takes at least four years.
- We aim for a long-term association with NGOs which allows us to go from simple to complex interventions, as and when the interest increases and skills of the staff and farmers improve.
- Each organisation's training process is a unique combination of elements, depending on its background and experience.
- Training is participatory and experiential: the participants' own experience is the starting point for both practical and theoretical learning.
- Social and technical matters are dealt with in an integrated way.
- Intensive, field-based training is given to the field staff and farmers, whereas chief functionaries are involved in short, strategic workshops, planning and evaluation sessions.
- Season-long practical training is given, in tandem with events in the field: frequent needs-based training inputs, classroom sessions combined with fieldwork for both NGO field staff and farmers.
- We aim at an equal men-women ratio in training programmes, but the minimum should be 30 per cent women. To enable women to participate, flexibility regarding training timings and venue is a must. Women must be consulted about these aspects.
- Participation of men and women participants is closely monitored during the season. Drop-outs should be prevented to the extent possible; reasons for drop-out are recorded, and if possible attended to.
- Training a network has a better impact than training individual organisations, especially when the latter are small.
- We aim at building up a network training team that can handle the training needs of member organisations in the long term. This will ensure sustained capacity-building and a lateral spread of efforts within the district.

At present we work with about 12 NGOs and five networks. Table 7.2 gives an overview of training activities undertaken by AME, and their progressive levels of complexity.

Different Organisations Moving towards Integrated Watershed Management

We will now discuss different types of NGOs and what it means for them to take up watershed management. For each type again, we will discuss the approach followed by AME in supporting the organisation. When training organisations, we go through a series of (at most) eight 'steps' (Table 7.3). As we explained earlier, the particular route with each organisation is different. With a few organisations we have reached Step 7, whereas in other cases we have not moved beyond Step 2. We do make loops also. Sometimes we go back from Step 7 to Step 3.

Table 7.2 Training Activities of AME and Levels of Complexity

Training activities		*Complexity*
• Groundnut production techniques • Paddy production techniques • Cotton production techniques	1	Focus on technical aspects of single entry point crop
• Organic vegetable production and marketing • Technical issues in watershed management • Social organisation in a watershed	2	Technical plus socio-economic aspects of production/land-use system
• Biomass production and composting for enhancing soil organic matter and feeding livestock in a developed watershed, where men's and women's credit and savings self-help groups are established	3	Broader approach to land-use system
• Groundnut production, social organisation, credit and savings self-help groups, input and output marketing, feedback platform to research institutions, national programmes and input suppliers (including banks)	4	Integrated approach to land-use system and 'stakeholders system'.

Social-Action Groups

Social-action groups (e.g., *dalit*-based NGOs) have a style of work, management and target-group organisation which differs in various ways from agricultural and development work. Their target group is often organised along the lines of a labour union and comprises only a particular section of the community. For a long time, the focus of these organisations has been on 'the struggle for land' rather than on 'how to use the land'. A practical but significant difference in their style of work:

Table 7.3 Training Routes with Different Types of NGOs

Steps in training process	*Type of organisation*			
	Social action	*Community development*	*Community dev & watershed mgmt*	*Ecological agriculture*
1. Changing perspective	♦♦	♦	–	♦♦
2. Capacity building in watershed mgmt & sustainable ag	♦♦♦	♦♦♦	♦♦ (focus on ag)	♦♦
3. Develop social organising capability	♦♦	♦	–	♦♦♦
4. Diversification of farming system	♦♦	♦♦	♦♦	♦
5. Formation of learning platforms	♦♦	♦♦	♦♦	♦♦
6. Scaling up	♦	♦	♦♦	♦♦
7. Strengthening social orgs for market dev	♦	♦	–	–
8. Formation of negotiation platforms	–	–	–	–

♦♦♦   considerable importance given to this step in the training process
♦♦   importance given
♦   less importance given
–   not (yet) taken up

social-action groups do much of their work during office hours and in the evening, whereas most farm work is done in the early morning.

Step 1: Changing perspective   During initial discussions with the organisation we make our objectives explicit: when aiming at a land users' negotiation platform, all sections of the community need to participate. So an NGO should have access to all sections of the community. Social-action groups therefore need to shed a strong reluctance to work with other sections of the community. As it entails a fundamental shift in their core values, not all such groups are willing to make this switch. This applies also to their social organisation. For their work they need the union type of organisation. For watershed development this type of organisation is not suitable.

In the past three years, we have developed a fruitful partnership with a few organisations which have taken up the challenge of changing their approach. This is a gradual process. We have attempted to find a compromise in which sub-unions have been formed at the village level. These village-level unions handle most of the tasks that are usually done by watershed committees. This is now a workable alternative, as the *dalits* live in distinct parts of the watershed.

Step 2: Capacity-building in watershed management and sustainable agriculture   The main support we give is capacity-building to deal with watershed and agriculture development. We also provide support in social organisation, but this is more difficult since the mode of organising social-action groups is considerably different from what we feel is necessary for watershed and agricultural development.

We had agreed with one organisation and the farmers that the main cash crop of the *dalits*, groundnuts, would be a good entry point for agricultural interventions. This is also a good way of maintaining relationships with the community during the period in which no physical watershed infrastructure can be built. Participatory technology development was taken up for testing various techniques to increase the productivity of groundnut. The technology tested is low-cost, aiming to enhance the sustainability of production. Chemical inputs are—to the extent possible—replaced by non-chemical alternatives.

Step 3: Social organisation development   Though yields and income increased considerably, a major problem persisted. Farmers had to borrow money at an interest rate of 10 per cent per month from moneylenders who are also the groundnut traders and determine the prices they are willing to offer. We now assist the NGO in exploring other ways of marketing and mobilising finances for the inputs required: savings groups linked to banks, revolving funds, and seed production and storage in the village. Much of the initiative is taken by the NGO, and we act only as sparring partners to explore the ideas and give comments based on wider development experience.

Step 4: Diversification of the farming system: Towards increased sustainability   One NGO is due to start a programme for biomass production by reducing the area under groundnuts. This is acceptable to the farmers, as the groundnut technology package tested by them has given on average a 30 per cent income increase. Thus the basis has been created for diversifying the farming system.

Step 5: Formation of learning platforms   We promote an organised interaction with farmers on these issues, and encourage the sharing of ideas at a wider, district-level platform comprising a number of other organisations with different backgrounds. Through structured and regular interaction (once in three months) with other NGOs and farmers at the district level, a wider sharing of experiences occurs which enhances the learning process.

Step 6: Scaling up the efforts   Most social-action groups form part of larger networks, which have considerable constituencies. Once experiments conducted with farmers on a small scale have been successful, the organisations are keen to share experiences in their network, and hence the basis is laid for scaling up. Limited staff capacity and shortage of funds then turn out to be the constraints. AME provides assistance to networks in preparing proposals for funding the scaling up of successful activities. However, we do *not* involve ourselves in the actual writing of proposals and in negotiations with donor agencies. This is the responsibility of the network. Some networks have been successful in securing funds and are now in the process of scaling up.

Community-Development-Oriented Organisations

Many NGOs in our area belong to this category. Some of them have a variety of activities, others concentrate on one or two: savings and credit (self-help groups) programmes with women and men, non-farm income generation activities, literacy programmes, community health activities, etc. These organisations usually work in quite a number of villages located in different watersheds.

When such organisations embark on watershed programmes, sometimes a drastic restructuring of their work is required: staff have to be transferred, and new ways of community development have to be organised in the watersheds. They can, at best, make limited use of the social organisation structures built up for their previous programmes, because these were formed for a different purpose. Only one of our partner organisations that entered into watershed management chose to do so in an area where they had no previous programmes.

These organisations need training in watershed management and sustainable agriculture. Their strength lies in social organisation. Though a shift in their approach to organising groups is called for, this is often not as radical as in the case of social-action groups. The intensity of Steps 1 and 3 of the support process depends on the existing experience of the NGO in organising communities. Steps 2, 4 and 5 of the support process are similar to that for social-action groups.

Step 6 Scaling up takes place in various ways. First, some of the technologies promoted have spread fast, directly among farmers. Second, NGOs have scaled up experimental efforts within their area of operation, in some cases quite successfully. Third, by sharing experiences within their networks, foundations have been laid for further scaling up (see Box 7.2 for examples).

Organisations Combining Community Development and Watershed Development

These are mostly organisations that launched watershed management programmes a number of years ago. In an earlier phase, their focus was on community development or social action; a watershed approach was gradually blended into, and partly replaced, their earlier programmes. Some of these organisations are large and well-established, and have a good rapport with government institutions. Their experience has served as a source of inspiration in the formulation of the 1994 Guidelines for Watershed Management. Their social and technical competencies are fairly well developed, but these two competencies are not well integrated in all cases.

Though their watershed programmes are well established, the agricultural component is often relatively underdeveloped. From a sustainability point of view (of treated watersheds as well as the livelihoods of its inhabitants), it would be desirable to work further on issues of sustainable agriculture.

When such organisations approach AME, it is often with the specific request for support in strengthening the agricultural component. We join hands with the NGO and the farmers' groups to start a participatory technology-development process (Step 2). Established social organisations in developed watersheds thus function as the

---

Box 7.2   Examples of Scaling up

Through farmers   One NGO started training farmers in two villages in the use of biofertilisers in 1994; it was tried out successfully on 100 acres. In 1997 biofertilisers were used in 20 villages, covering an estimated 5000 acres. Farmers had made collective arrangements with assistance of the NGOs for purchase and delivery of the biofertilisers.

Through NGOs   The effectiveness of a groundnut-technology package proposed by AME was assessed by field staff of a large NGO and the farmers' groups participating in the participatory technology development experiments. The NGO decided that in the coming year it would introduce the same package into a large UNDP-funded programme in which it is involved.

Through networks   A comprehensive training package has been developed which consists of eight training modules on sustainable agriculture in a watershed. The aims are to:

- strengthen the NGOs' implementation capacities to handle technical, social and institutional challenges of watershed management;
- give the NGOs confidence and strengthen their ability to secure the funds to implement such programmes.

Prior to the training, a workshop was organised where the network members analysed their strengths and limitations. Internal linkages between the NGOs were analysed, and a SWOT (strengths–weaknesses–opportunities–threats) analysis was done with the key functionaries and their staff. The training itself is presently under way and consists of the following elements (modules):

- integrated watershed development;
- community organisation and gender issues in a watershed;
- water cycle;
- nutrient cycle;
- energy cycle;
- integrated pest management;
- planning a watershed-development project.

---

anchoring point for participatory experimentation addressing problems identified by farmers. The components introduced by AME are confined to agricultural production technologies, and the specific approach employed is participatory technology development. This approach is easily incorporated into the participatory appraisal approach already applied by the NGOs. Since these organisations are already geared towards land-based programmes, the systems are well in place; thus with a relatively small effort from our side, interesting new components to strengthen the watershed programmes can be introduced. Moreover, these NGOs have the potential to effectively scale up successful efforts (Step 6). Training the NGO staff and community members on the participatory technology development approach and other technical aspects of sustainable agriculture are AME's contribution; the NGO itself takes care of scaling up. Participation in wider platforms for experience sharing becomes very effective.

Organisations Focusing on Ecological Agriculture

The primary concern of this category of organisation is to promote a healthy agricultural alternative that is in harmony with nature, and to eliminate the use of pesticides and fertilisers. They prefer to rely on traditional seed varieties and indigenous knowledge to the extent possible. The tendency is to work with interested individual farmers rather than with groups or communities, so the focus remains on individual farms rather than on the watershed. Social organisation may be attempted to varying degrees, but is given relatively less importance. We have encountered this category of organisations mainly in Tamil Nadu. Most of them are small NGOs that are members of fairly large networks. The strategy of our support for these organisations is as follows:

Step 1 As in the case of social-action groups, some of these organisations may find it difficult to shift their approach, as it hits their core values. They have a strong, nature-focused ideology and find it difficult to make the shift to a broader development perspective.

Step 2 Step 2 implies another shift of focus from individual farms to the watershed level, from promotion of eco-friendly techniques to agro-eco-systems analysis and development. Confidence building is important here, since small NGOs, in particular, often display reluctance to take up water-shed management as they feel lack of competence and the means for doing so. The challenge is to break out of the vicious circle of limited competence and limited access to funds. It is on these counts that smaller NGOs with the potential to take up watershed-management programmes, have as yet to translate this potential into action. They find it difficult to access government funds for implementing watershed programmes.

Step 3 Step 3 refers to the process that pays attention to the social-organisation aspects of sustainable agriculture and watershed management: a new area for most of these organisations.

Once the first three steps are completed, the next steps become relatively easy. Since many of the NGOs are constituents of well-developed networks, the potential for Steps 5 and 6 taking place is definitely strong.

However, before reaching the stage of building broader platforms, some important obstacles in 'mindsets' have to be tackled. Attitudes towards government and other NGOs not on the same wavelength, tend sometimes to be rather cool. We have realised, however, that

---

Box 7.3   Actors' Meeting

AME conducted a two-day workshop with farmers, NGOs, researchers and Department of Agriculture staff to discuss problems in agriculture. Many participants commented that this was the first time they ever had met in such a forum, and that it was very refreshing. Even small but important points did not go unnoticed. One NGO worker said he was very surprised to hear from a department official that he had started work at 4 a.m. that morning because he did not want to miss the workshop. NGOs were also surprised to discover that the same official had so much practical knowledge about biological pest-control methods.

---

the simple act of bringing people from various institutions together to work on a concrete issue jointly, is a simple but effective first step in increasing mutual understanding (Box 7.3). Much more can be done in this direction.

New Directions

Step 7   Step 7 involves strengthening of social organisations for market development. For instance, with a group of organisations involved in sustainable groundnut production, we are now trying to improve the forward and backward linkages with markets and agricultural input suppliers (Box 7.4).

Step 8   Step 8 involves the formation of negotiation platforms between the various stakeholders in the watershed. Nowhere have we yet reached this stage. This requires time. At present, negotiations centre around the placement of structures for watershed development and (for a part of the community) on ways of obtaining better prices for their agricultural products. Negotiations about common property resources such as land, forest, and grazing areas do take place at times. However, there are other pertinent issues about which little or no negotiation takes place—for instance the usage, development and maintenance of groundwater resources and tanks, the proportional contributions towards maintenance of the upper reaches of the watershed, and employment opportunities in the watershed area.

These issues need to be discussed thoroughly, so that fair agreements can be arrived at by the different interest groups. This is what the spirit of equity and sustainability is all about.

Concluding Remarks

The essential role of NGOs in watershed management as an interface between government and the people is increasingly accorded recognition. However, in order to allow them to play this role effectively, a proper

---

Box 7.4   Efforts to Improve Forward and Backward Linkages

Linkages are established with suppliers of biofertilisers, rock phosphates and bio-control agents, to facilitate farmers' access. Farmers have organised themselves to store their groundnut seeds together, thereby becoming independent of seed suppliers. In three organisations, farmers are now being guided in the production of quality groundnut seed. A market survey is being conducted to determine groundnut products that fetch a good price, and the location of appropriate markets.

---

understanding is required regarding what NGOs stand for, what they can and cannot do, and what their needs for capacity building are. AME tries to address these needs by following a tailor-made and step-wise approach to training. This may seem cumbersome and expensive to the outsider; however, after applying this approach for four years, our tentative conclusion is that it is worth the effort.

Figure 7.1 summarises our approach.

We begin with concrete and simple entry points, and from there

Figure 7.1.   Conceptualisation of AME's Approach to Capacity-Building

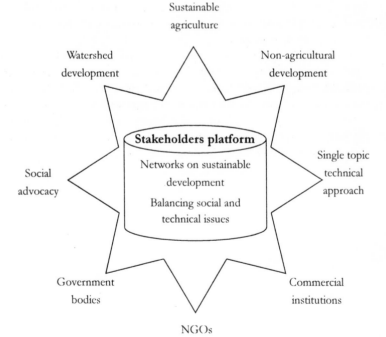

we gradually move towards more complex interventions. In an area, we often start with one NGO or a homogeneous group of NGOs, and gradually develop activities which necessitate the involvement of a wider platform of organisations. Along the way, cooperation with government bodies and the commercial sector is promoted to create the necessary forward and backward linkages. With social-action-oriented organisations, we focus on developing their technical capacities. We strengthen the social dimension of NGOs that have a technical orientation. In the initial stages, sustainable crop production is emphasised, using a specific crop or crops as entry points. Gradually, the approach is broadened to address a variety of issues in sustainable watershed development. We work eventually towards the establishment of negotiation platforms between various land-use actors: farmers, *panchayats*, NGOs, government departments, input suppliers, etc.

Given the fact that different people and institutions operate with very different perceptions and interests, the establishment of negotiation platforms is a difficult and time-consuming process. We are only at the beginning of this process. We do however, see an increasing recognition among the many actors involved that the survival of people and ecosystems in dryland areas calls for a comprehensive collective action.

We conclude that AME's approach does make a modest but relevant contribution towards the scaling-up of participatory watershed approaches, because it addresses two essential conditions: first, the formation of a critical mass of human resource potential in the NGO sector in the districts, and second the establishment of functional negotiation platforms for sustainable land use. There are still many challenges ahead, but our experience so far is encouraging.

8 Wider Scale and Stronger Momentum?

THE PROBLEM

A major study of watershed programmes by Kerr et al. (1998) came *inter alia* to the conclusions that:[1]

- projects with a more participatory approach performed better than others;
- different technical approaches are favoured in different areas, though some (bunds crossing fields and purely vegetative barriers) are not maintained because they are almost universally found to be inappropriate;
- soil-conservation works on rainfed plots are much better maintained where farmers themselves have made a financial contribution towards their cost;
- women and the poor receive some benefit from employment created during rehabilitation, but otherwise their interests are widely neglected;
- careful selection of villages with favourable characteristics for watershed development is an important ingredient for success;
- participatory approaches offer the best prospects of success, partly because on a small scale they attract some special treatment and some of the best NGOs. Both of these advantages may be difficult to sustain as they attempt to expand, but may in part be compensated by innovative government–NGO collaboration.

This chapter is concerned with two further questions: how the benefits of watershed development can be sustained beyond the period of public-sector support (i.e., the 'project period'), and what arrangements are needed to replicate sustainable approaches on a wide scale. In this chapter, we draw on a range of evidence to identify how three of the key ingredients for success can be developed and sustained: (a) participation and developing a stake in the development process, including

---

[1] A fuller version of the findings is given in Extract 1.1.

users' financial contribution to conservation and maintenance; (b) the formation of and support for local institutions to ensure that benefit flows are equitable and sustained beyond the project period; and (c) the pressures towards increased accountability in service provision. This introductory section concludes with a forward-looking perspective of the major challenges for watershed development in the coming decade. The six Extracts deal with various examples of efforts to sustain watershed development efforts.

Participation and Developing a 'Stake'

In well-functioning markets, neo-liberal economics suggests that private funds should be used to invest in soil- and water-conservation activities, if the benefits they generate can be captured privately. Anil Shah (1998) refers to the extent of farmers' willingness to contribute towards the costs of works as a 'litmus test' of their level of interest and commitment, noting the dictum by Meinzen-Dick et al. (1995) that to avoid insisting on payment forgoes an opportunity to build participation. Public funds should be used where benefits cannot be captured in this way, or where there are considerable externalities of costs or benefits which cannot be internalised. In reality, markets function very imperfectly. For instance, it is almost impossible to obtain bank credit for soil- and water-conservation measures, even on private land; for this reason alone, the level of private investment in conservation may be lower, and the pace of rehabilitation slower than would be socially optimal.[2]

In recognition of these difficulties, projects, programmes and schemes under the Ministries of Agriculture and Cooperation, and of Rural Areas and Employment, allow the use of government funds for the rehabilitation of both private and public lands. The 1994 Guidelines do, however, specify that those benefiting from works on private lands should make a contribution of 10 per cent[3] of the total cost, against 5 per cent to be paid in respect of investment in works designed to benefit the community. In practice, it has proven difficult to collect either of these charges in full, and at village level the ways in which charges are set and recovered are at times less than transparent. However, the review by Turton et al. (1998) urged that stronger efforts be made by project implementing agencies in this regard, and that a graduated system be introduced in respect of private land, in which a fixed rate of subsidy would be provided for a specified area on each farm, and thereafter farmers

[2] For a discussion of methodologies which address externalities, see Chapter 2.
[3] 5 per cent for poorer sections of a community.

would have to pay more on a sliding scale if further areas were to be rehabilitated.

Other projects and programmes are considerably stricter on beneficiary contributions. These arrangements are summarised in Table 8.1.

The Indo-German Watershed Development Programme insists on a contribution by villages of 16 per cent of the cost of unskilled labour needed for rehabilitation. This can be paid in kind, in the form of joint voluntary labour (*shramadaan*), and landless and poor single-parent households are exempt from contributing. Of this 16 per cent contribution, half is deposited in a maintenance fund to be managed by the village watershed committee (Farrington and Lobo 1997, Extract 8.4).

The Indo-British Western India Rainfed Farming Project provides a subsidy of nominally 50 per cent, but which in fact works out somewhat higher once the value of materials provided free of charge is taken into account (Smith et al. 1998, Extract 8.1).

Numerous other arrangements exist, ranging from the insistence by the NGO MYRADA, at one extreme, that all works on private lands should be fully financed by the individuals concerned, to projects under the National Watershed Development Programme for Rainfed Areas and the World Bank, in which effectively no charge is made.

In response to the question, 'Will people take loans for treatment measures on private lands in a micro-watershed?' the answer is unequivocally yes. Evidence of this is contained in the three case studies presented by Fernandez (1998) in respect of the MYRADA experience (see Box 8.1), and in the report by Mascarenhas (1998) on the experiences of OUTREACH (Extract 7.1). However, it must be noted that the loans taken were not from the banking system, but from self-help savings-and-credit schemes within the watershed being developed. In one case (MYRADA) these originated in substantial grants from the NGO concerned, which then formed the capital which could be converted by the self-help groups into a rotating loan fund. Other innovative forms of financial support to project beneficiaries are found in, for instance, the Danida-supported projects in Tamil Nadu and Orissa (Seth and Damgaard-Larsen 1998; see also Extract 3.2).

In Tamil Nadu, if a farmers' association opens an account in a bank or post office and builds up savings over a minimum of three months, then the project will give matching funds of up to Rs 3000 to meet the costs of operating an office and running meetings. A further sum of Rs 5000 'seed money' may also be made available for lending to members at agreed rates of interest, for the purchase of implements to hire out to

---

Box 8.1 The MYRADA Experience: Will People Take Loans for Treatment Measures on Private Lands in a Micro-watershed?

There are 71 farmers in the Keredoddi Watershed Association. Of these, 19 belong to four self-help groups in adjacent villages, which have been functioning since 1989–90. All, however, also have lands in Keredoddi micro-watershed. Though they have now become members of the Keredoddi micro-watershed association, they continue to hold membership in their respective self-help groups.

The land in Keredoddi have less than 3 per cent slopes. The initiative to treat the micro-watershed and form a watershed development association was taken by the 19 farmers who are members of the four self-help groups.

As this micro-watershed programme started after similar activities in the adjacent watershed, where the 19 farmers also have land, it was not difficult for them to accept and persuade others that all investment on private lands should be on the basis of loans from the watershed development association. The visible, positive impact of treatment in a neighbouring micro-watershed, which used a 30 per cent contribution from the people and based on a 70 per cent MYRADA grant, gave these farmers confidence to take loans to treat their private lands.

MYRADA provided grants to the watershed development association, which converted them into 100 per cent loans for treatment of private lands. The association charged no interest on these loans. The association set up several sub-committees similar to those in the other micro-watersheds. Several training programmes and meetings were also conducted.

Of the 71 farmers, 48 took loans from the watershed development association for treatment of their lands in the first round. Work on their fields started in 1996 and continued through 1997. The overdue loans are not substantial, except in a few cases. During discussions with the farmers, they assured the watershed development association that overdue loans would be cleared as soon as the maize held in stock was sold.

---

members, and for the establishment of nurseries. The project also provides them with assistance in obtaining seasonal credit from the National Bank for Agriculture and Rural Development for inputs such as seed and agrochemicals.

In Orissa, support is provided to self-help groups concerned with household-based production systems (such as poultry or basket-making) once they have demonstrated an ability to save money regularly for three months. The project assistance is limited to Rs 3000 per family, and this is paid in instalments at a pace commensurate with their growing financial-management capability.

Forming and Supporting Local Institutions

As emphasised in Chapter 3, considerable time is needed for group formation prior to the village-level discussion of what rehabilitation measures should be introduced. These efforts include identify-

Table 8.1 Cost-Sharing Arrangements in Watershed Projects

Project	Source of funds	Extent and nature of cost sharing	Individual benefits	Effort made
SDC, Bidar	Bilateral	Farmers contribute 15-20% of treatment costs in their fields. They also collectively contribute to treatments along the drainage line.	High	High
Danida, Dharwad and Bijapur	Bilateral	Farmers started contributing recently. They pay by cash part of costs (50%) of plant material in horticulture & forestry components. They contribute labour for other activities on private fields. No contrib for drainage-line treatment.	Significant benefits from horticulture and forestry on farm. Drainage-line treatment has resulted in significant irrigation benefits.	Medium
Danida, Koraput	Bilateral	Farmers were asked to contribute only recently. Contribution is only as labour (10%)	High	Medium
CISF, Ajmer	Bilateral	10% of wages withheld	Probably high	Low
SDC, Pratapgarh	Bilateral	Contribs through both cash & labour (25%)	Marginal	Medium
SIDA, Dungerpur	Bilateral	Contributions collected by withholding part of wages (10%)	Benefits from some of the project activities	Low
NWDPRA, Madhugiri	Government	None	Many structures are in private fields or benefit small groups of farmers	None

Table 8.1 (continued)

Project	Source of funds	Extent and nature of cost sharing	Individual benefits	Effort made
NWDPRA, Keonjher	Government	None	Horticultural plantations are beneficial. Check-dams along the drainage line benefit those with fields in the line.	None
MoRAE/EAS, Keonjher	Government	None	Significant; farmers are willing to contribute.	None
NWDB, Kalahandi	Government	None	Significant if village plantation is maintained well.	Low
NWDPRA, Kalahandi	Government	None	Little apparent demand for fodder produced in common pastures. Low benefits likely.	None
NWDPRA, Ajmer	Government	Contribution collected by withholding 10% of wages. Farmers willing to contribute cash to build water-harvesting structures.	High	Medium
MoRAE/EAS, Pratapgarh	Government	Contribution collected by withholding 10% of wages	Marginal	Low
DPAP, Dungerpur	Government	Contribution collected by withholding 10% of wages. Farmers are willing to pay more.	High	Low

Table 8.1 (continued)

Project	Source of funds	Extent and nature of cost sharing	Individual benefits	Effort made
NWDB, Udhaipur	Government	Contribution collected by withholding 10% of wages. Farmers said that they could not contribute as they were very poor.	High	Low
World Bank, Khorda	Multilateral	None	Marginal	None
World Bank, Bilwara	Multilateral	Contribution collected by withholding 10% of wages.	Marginal	Low
World Bank, Udhaipur	Multilateral	Contribution collected by withholding 10% of wages. Farmers also indicated they are willing to pay more.	High from treatment on private fields	Low
MYRADA, Kollegal	NGO	None on community works. Farmers pay entire cost of treatment on their fields. 30% of costs borne by farmers initially. The rest, for which they receive loans, is paid in 5 instalments.	Benefits from bunds in fields with 10-15% slope are high	High
Parivartan, Kalahandi	NGO	Farmers have contributed labour, about 5% of project costs.	Significant benefit form plantation and irrigation when completed.	Medium

Source: Kolavalli (1998b).

ing existing (fairly homogenous) groups of various kinds, helping in the formation of new ones, and strengthening them in the skills which will be needed in whole-village negotiations (leadership, problem diagnosis, assertiveness, conflict resolution, and so on). A major recommendations from Turton et al.'s (1998) review of the 1994 Guidelines was that the financial provisions should be modified to allow an additional year of such preparatory work before the village assemblies would be invited to participate in specifying what rehabilitation should be undertaken.

Kolavalli (1998b) and Adolph and Turton (1998) argue that resource-user groups and self-help groups should serve as the 'building blocks' of community decision-taking and action. The creation of watershed-user groups without this foundation and without adequate preparation invariably means that they function merely as an extended arm of the project implementing agency, as is the case, they argue, with most government implementing agencies. Kakade and Hegde (1998), whilst concerned primarily with how to form and strengthen groups of disadvantaged people, stress the need to negotiate constructively also with the better off concerning how their needs can be met if they are not to undermine pro-poor initiatives.

Several lessons have emerged regarding the preconditions for successful functioning of the watershed committee (which, in turn, impacts on its capacity to relate successfully to the watershed-user group and to specific self-help groups).

Villagers will relate more confidently to the watershed committee if it is encouraged to function with transparency in its decision-making and management of funds. In particular, care needs to be taken to display at a prominent point the amount of funds at the committee's disposal, and to do so in ways—possibly pictorially—which allow monitoring by non-literate villagers.

Watershed committees may be sustained for the longer term (i.e., beyond the end of the project period) by encouraging them to join neighbouring committees in a federation. This, in turn, may lead to economies of scale in input supply, processing and marketing of outputs, and so on. Profits from these enterprises would then be distributed back to the membership.

One element of sustaining watershed committees relates to the new activities that the committee secretaries and volunteers might be encouraged to undertake. They are likely to have been engaged on the

strength of skills relevant to the rehabilitation process. There will therefore be a need to support them in building new skills over the subsequent period.

Government project implementing agencies typically withdraw at the
end of the project period, and there seems to be little that can be done
to retain them.

To defend the interests of groups of disadvantaged groups in the
period following rehabilitation requires vigilance, advice and possibly
arbitration, and so the continued presence of an independent body carrying some weight is important. Some NGOs have a more permanent
presence in or near the project areas and can be expected to remain
there for the longer term. This, combined with their concern for social
organisation in ways supportive of the livelihoods of the poor, offers
the prospect that they may be persuaded to maintain an involvement
with the rehabilitated watershed. This may be promoted by making available specific watershed-related funds, or by ensuring that any new watersheds in which they become engaged are not far from the completed
ones. In all events, to retain existing NGOs and to engage the interest of
new ones in providing follow-on support requires some strategic thinking.

The selection of NGOs willing and able to work as a project
implementing agency in the first place is of crucial importance (as is
de-selection in cases of non-compliance) and the 1994 Guidelines
remain inadequately specific in this area. As a minimum, selection
criteria should include past experience in participatory development,
familiarity with the Ministry of Rural Areas and Employment's watershed programme, and the availability of professional staff. To
stratify NGOs according to their capacity would help in deciding
the type and number of micro-watersheds to allocate to them, and
the type of further capacity building they may require.

The system operated by CAPART allows NGOs some six months
to build their capacity after selection. During the same period, working as a project implementing agency, the NGO would recruit watershed-development team members, arrange for training as necessary, and establish contact with villages selected for rehabilitation,
explaining the watershed-rehabilitation scheme and their own roles
and responsibilities. If satisfied with the performance of the NGO
in this context, the DRDA might allocate it some 2–3 micro-watersheds for rehabilitation. Once they have gained some years of experience in implementing micro-watershed rehabilitation, such NGOs

might be allocated from the beginning a further 10–12 micro-watersheds. Larger, well-established NGOs with substantial experience in watershed rehabilitation and participatory rural development, with qualified professional staff able to supervise and support watershed development teams operating in the same or nearby areas would initially be allocated some 20-50 micro-watersheds.

The Indo-German Watershed Development Programme, based in Maharashtra, has devised a detailed and comprehensive set of criteria for selecting NGOs and villages for treatment, and a coherent scheme for scaling up and for post-rehabilitation support. This relies heavily on the existence of a central 'service' NGO, the Watershed Organisation Trust, staffed by professionals and financed by the programme as a whole (Extract 8.4). This concept of supporting participation through NGOs at the local level, complemented by a more centrally-based team which, in turn, supports the NGOs in technical matters, is similar to the multidisciplinary team concept in Andhra Pradesh (see Extract 3.1). Were it not for the dearth of suitable NGOs, it might provide a model for wider implementation.[4]

Also of note is the model pioneered by MYRADA, in which village-level groups, with some support from the implementing agency, use the funds they have generated to contract-in individuals with the requisite experience. These are typically retired university or government department staff. It remains to be seen whether this approach can be scaled up to a wider area.

For the majority of the projects, programmes and schemes governed by the principal central government guidelines (i.e., the National Watershed Development Programme for Rainfed Areas under the Ministry of Agriculture and Cooperation, and the 1994 Guidelines under the Ministry of Rural Areas and Employment), there remain major lacunae in both the organisational/institutional and technical components of follow up.

An example is the issue of improved availability of stored water (surface or subsurface), which reduces the risks of rainfed farming (so promoting higher levels of inputs), extends the growing season, and provides an option for cultivation of an additional crop. In the majority of cases, this will require new crop varieties and possibly other new inputs. Ideally, the state-government line departments (agriculture, horticulture, animal production) should be engaged suf-

---

[4] Note, however, that the IGWDP approach includes the establishment of new NGOs from community-based organisations in successful watersheds (Extract 8.4).

ficiently with the processes of watershed development, and with the locations where it is taking place, to provide farmers with a number of new technology options. In reality, this rarely appears to be the case in projects governed by the 1994 Guidelines— not least because the state-level authorities have little engagement in the processes of selecting areas for rehabilitation, selecting project implementing agencies, monitoring or evaluating the progress of rehabilitation, or in the design of rehabilitation itself (Turton et al., 1998). One of the few links with state authorities currently designed into the 1994 Guidelines is the State Watershed Programme Implementation and Review Committee. However, Turton et al. found that only one of these was operational in the three states visited.

Increasing Accountability for Service Provision

Growing awareness within India of the public sector's inefficiency as a provider of services has led to experimentation with alternative models. The Common Guidelines represent a modest departure from the conventional pattern, and this section suggests what areas of further investigation are required if accountability is to be improved.

In the conventional public-sector approach to service (Figure 8.1), the enabling agency (usually a ministry) provides both the mandate and the funds to one of its departments to provide specified services. The views of users, of their associations or of organisations such as NGOs working with them, may be sought and taken into account in identifying these services, but the extent to which this happens tends to be limited. The government is thus both the enabler and provider of services, often with unclear specification of required outputs and a conflation of objectives between departments, or between departments and the ministry (Extract 5.3). Performance monitoring tends to be weak in these circumstances, and service providers tend to be accountable only upwards—i.e., to the parent ministry providing the funds. NGOs may act as 'go-betweens' between users and service-providers in an effort to strengthen the users' voice in the design and delivery of services

A number of principles have driven the introduction of new approaches to service delivery into the training curricula for officers of the Indian Administrative Service. These principles comprise two major elements. One is (albeit in very moderate form) the neo-liberal view that the state should withdraw from activities which can be undertaken by the private sector. It should instead concentrate

Figure 8.1   Linear Model of Institutional Roles in Service Provision

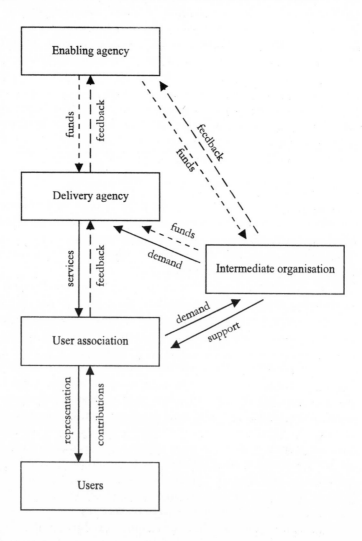

Note: Enabling and delivery functions may be conducted by the same or by separate
agencies. This is a highly simplified representation. For instance, there are likely to be
direct links between users and service-delivery agencies, and *panchayati raj* institutions
may be located between enabling agencies and user associations.

on facilitating and regulating these activities, and on providing services where market failure is widespread or where such services relate to 'public goods'—i.e., those relating to environmental quality, health and safety and so on, from which streams of benefits cannot easily be privatised. The second view is that resource users must be empowered to have a voice in the types of service provided. There should be a clear separation between the agency responsible for setting out policy and related guidelines, and those responsible for delivering services to meet users' needs within those guidelines. Finally, there should be a plurality of service-delivery agencies so users are offered an element of choice.

The main functions of the enabling agency therefore are to: (a) set out the 'rules of the game'; (b) facilitate efficient performance by service-delivery agencies through training and other capacity-building measures; (c) establish monitoring as necessary; and (d) facilitate the development of trust, partnerships (and therefore of social capital) between users and providers of services.

This non-linear ('hub') framework for service delivery is depicted in simplified form in Figure 8.2. Again, NGOs may act to support users, or may themselves act as service providers, as may private commercial agencies. The key distinctions between this and the linear model are that, in this case, it is explicitly recognised that users will make demands on service deliverers; where possible, users will have a choice among service providers; and the service providers will be accountable to both users and enabling agencies.

The delivery of 'services' for watershed rehabilitation under the Common Guidelines clearly approaches this hub model in some respects. The central government has set up a framework in the form of the Guidelines, with funding decentralised to the district level; watershed-users' associations contribute to the planning of rehabilitation works and authorise the expenditure of funds; and NGOs provide support to strengthen user groups.

However, in other respects, much progress still remains to be made. The feedback mechanisms between users and enabling agencies are weak. There is rarely a choice among suitable service-delivery agencies. The enabling agency's monitoring of the overall system is restricted to questions of whether the funds provided have been spent appropriately, and not of whether any derived impact has been achieved on the ground, or whether it has been sustained over time.

Figure 8.2   Basic 'Hub' Model of Institutional Roles in Service Provision

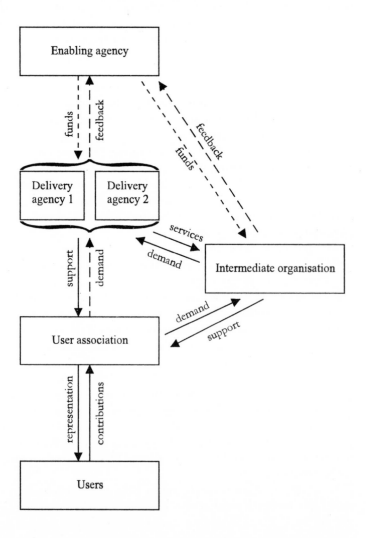

Note: This is a highly simplified representation. For instance, there are likely to be direct links between users and service delivery agencies, and *panchayati raj* institutions may be located between enabling agencies and user associations.

MOVING FORWARD: RECOMMENDATIONS FOR A NEW GENERATION OF WATERSHEDS

The experiences brought together in this book suggest a growing confidence in the contribution that watershed development can make towards the sustainable enhancement of rural livelihoods. This is particularly the case for the new Guidelines, with their provisions for participatory, equitable, gender-sensitive and decentralised approaches to watershed development. There are, however, also a number of challenges and implementation difficulties that will need to be addressed in the coming decade if the objectives of sustainable and equitable watershed development are to be fully realised. This section summarises the recommendations emerging from the April 1998 Workshop on Watershed Approaches for Wastelands Development, on which this book is based.

General Recommendations

National standing committee   There is a need for greater co-ordination at the central level through the establishment of a 'national standing committee' with a broad mandate to review evidence on the performance of watershed programmes and projects and to provide advice on the size, composition and location of future funding for watershed development. It is also recommended that a committee be established on training and capacity building.

Coordination   There is a need for greater co-ordination among ministries to harmonise the various guidelines and dispersal of funds.

Reallocation of resources   Resources at the command of the proposed Watershed Development Programme should be re-allocated to allow the following:

- The addition of one year to the current 4-year period to allow capacity-building and more participatory preparation of watershed plans prior to implementation.
- A human -resource development programme at national, state, district and local levels. This would include, for instance, training of trainers, curriculum development, attitudinal and behavioural change, and the development of appropriate teaching materials and methods.
- A monitoring and evaluation system which engages national, state, district and local-level bodies. It would be sensitive to quantitative, qualitative and 'process' change.

- Pilot experiments with different ways of channelling watershed development funds, including via the banks such as NABARD.

Poverty and Gender

- The selection of project locations should be focused on areas that are agro-climatically and socio-economically disadvantaged.
- A pre-implementation preparatory phase should be introduced to allow groups of women and of the poor to be organised and strengthened. Sufficient provision in the budget should be made for this.
- Project design should specifically incorporate the needs of women and the poor; monitoring indicators should closely reflect project performance in respect of these equity aspects.
- Watershed development activities should be taken up specifically with those communities which are ready and able (as reflected in their emerging demand, willingness to contribute, and willingness to implement and manage projects).
- The status of the commons needs to be clearly defined prior to development of a rehabilitation plan, and rights of usufruct where necessary should be renegotiated in favour of women and the poor. Where commons are no longer available, provision should be made for the lease of private fallows for the landless and for marginal farming families.
- Cross-subsidy within a watershed project by increasing the contributions of the better-off should be considered.
- Greater emphasis and investment are needed to develop and restore the upper reaches of watersheds and the commons.
- Staff need to be trained and sensitised to aspects of poverty and gender, and the possibilities offered by networking and sharing of best practices should be exploited.
- More gender-sensitive approaches will require a larger budget and time than that currently allowed in the Guidelines for entry-point activities.
- Livelihood options for women need to be introduced through appropriate income-generating activities, with appropriate additional provisions of training, credit and project funding.
- The representation of women on watershed committees should be increased to 50 per cent. Care needs to be taken against tokenism, and the emphasis needs to be on effective participation and the creation of an environment conducive to participation.

Improving Coordination among Different Agencies in Watershed Development

There is a high degree of compartmentalisation of norms and procedures in relation to, for instance, costs, selection of projects, beneficiary contributions and reporting. In current watershed projects, programmes and schemes, there is a need for:

- a 'single window' approach at the local level;
- a single nodal authority for all schemes, etc., at the state level;
- a single nodal authority at the national level.

Relations with the *Panchayati Raj* Institutions

- Action in favour of caste and gender groups ('affirmative action') needs to be introduced more fully in the Common Guidelines and made consistent with the provisions of the reformed *Panchayati Raj* Act.
- NGOs and donors should work in support of *panchayati raj* institutions in capacity-building and other roles. They should recognise the *panchayati raj* institutions as democratically accountable actors in the implementation process, and develop strategies so that they can 'exit' and leave *panchayati raj* institutions with a constructive role thereafter.
- Watershed guidelines and the *panchayati raj* process are still evolving. Due care is needed to ensure that new or revised provisions in the former are consistent with the constitutional status and practical support needs of the latter.

Those watershed Guidelines relevant to participation and to the *panchayati raj* institutions need to be made more flexible so as to be consistent with the political circumstances of the different states.

Capacity Building: Watershed Level

- Project implementation agencies should follow a bottom-up, demand-based, step-by-step approach.
- Project implementation agencies should use progressive farmers or villagers as resource persons, covering the costs of their time and any incidentals, in order to develop a sustainable local training capacity.
- Exposure visits to other watersheds and successful projects are desirable and should be organised as necessary.
- Specialised needs-based packages may be developed for watershed

association presidents, watershed committee chairpersons, secretaries, volunteers and members.

Capacity Building: District Level

- DRDAs/*zilla parishads* should develop and use progressive project implementation agencies as exposure centres.
- DRDAs/*zilla parishads* should run orientation programmes for the *panchayati raj* institutions to enlist their cooperation.
- DRDAs/*zilla parishads* should act as clearing houses for information, support and coordination for training centres, resource persons, materials and methods within the district.

Capacity Building: State Level

- State governments should play a lead role in coordinating the efforts of state training institutes and NGOs in identification of training needs at all levels, upgrading and equipping training facilities, developing faculty skills, and ensuring synergy and optimum capacity utilisation.
- State training institutes should collaborate with DRDAs/district institutes to run programmes for project implementation agency, watershed development team members and line departments within the districts.
- Each state training institute should develop its own field-level experience by taking up a watershed project as a project implementation agency.
- State governments and universities should include agriculture, and particularly watershed management, in school and college curricula.
- State governments/DRDAs should follow the example of CAPART in recruiting young management professionals from the Institute of Rural Management, Anand (IRMA), or the National Institute of Agricultural Extension Management (MANAGE) to support project implementation agencies.

Capacity Building: National Level

- The Government of India should consider amending the Common Guidelines to incorporate more comprehensive watershed-based development, popularly described as the 'watershed plus' approach.
- The government should amend the Common Guidelines to pro-

vide for a discrete stage of capacity-building for the selected project implementation agency in project-preparation techniques.

- The government should consider setting up a participatory mechanism for a thorough review of the Common Guidelines to incorporate the experience of the last three years.
- The government should quickly implement the recommendations of the Eswaran Committee, particularly relating to watershed training and strengthening identified state training institutes.
- The government may consider bringing out more detailed guidelines or manuals for technical, operational and training of trainers.
- The government and donors should collaborate in enhancing the awareness generation and media management capacities of senior officials and supporting organisations for dissemination of the watershed management concept as the kernel of future rural livelihood strategy.

Monitoring and Evaluation

- The current emphasis on monitoring of financial flows should be supplemented by increased emphasis on the monitoring and evaluation of outputs and impacts in biophysical and socio-economic terms, and in terms of the adequacy of the 'participatory process'. This should give particular attention not only to the level of benefits, but also to their distribution.
- Particular attention should be given to ensuring that flows of monitoring information from village, to district, to state, and to national levels are adequate.
- There is a growing body of positive experience with participatory self-monitoring at the village level. Methods of promoting and facilitating this should be included in training curricula, and project implementation agencies should be required to introduce it in all villages.
- Adequate baseline data (biophysical, socio-economic, 'process') need to be collected prior to rehabilitation in order to permit accurate assessment of change.
- Caution needs to be exercised so that the performance indicators selected are not too sophisticated. The emphasis should be on few but accurate indicators requiring low levels of skill, time and other resources. Where appropriate, these can be supplemented by higher technology approaches such as remote sensing.

Sustaining Momentum beyond the Project Period: Subsidies, Savings and Investment

- Project implementation agencies should begin establishing contact with outside agencies (especially line departments) in the second year of project implementation.
- Project implementation agency attention should not focus solely on women and the weaker sectors: the needs of the middle and higher income groups must also receive some attention if they are not to undermine pro-poor initiatives.
- Self-help groups should be promoted as a means of long-term sustainability, with particular attention to the scope offered by properly managed savings and credit groups.
- For the longer term, watershed committees should not only manage the funds for watershed maintenance, but should also undertake productivity enhancement through supplying inputs, marketing, and developing linkages with external expert agencies.
- Guidelines need to be established for the selection and de-selection of project implementation agencies.
- Some continuing support and assistance by the project implementation agency or (one or more members of the) watershed development team may be desirable for 1–2 years after the 4 years currently allowed for completion of rehabilitation.
- A distinction should be made within watershed areas between public goods (broadly: community forest, check-dams, irrigation tanks, etc.) and private goods (private wells, activities conducted on private land, etc.). A high element of subsidy should be retained for rehabilitating public goods, but the Guidelines should be changed to specify a higher level of beneficiary contribution on private lands. Furthermore, on private lands, a graduated scale should be followed (the so-called 'slab system') whereby subsidies are reduced as private land area increases, and an overall limit is placed on the level of subsidy provided to any one farmer.
- Mechanisms should be sought to facilitate the provision of bank credit for conservation activities on private lands. Increased efforts should also be made to stimulate conservation and agricultural production improvements through improved technology in order to take full advantage of the new soil and water conditions.

EXTRACT 8.1
THE USE OF SUBSIDIES FOR SOIL AND WATER
CONSERVATION: A CASE STUDY FROM WESTERN
INDIA[5]

PAUL SMITH,[6] A. PARRY AND R. K. MISHRA

Introduction

The KRIBHCO Indo-British Rainfed Farming Project (KRIBP) is a bi-lateral development project which was designed to develop a participa-tory approach to rural development in degraded areas of India (Jones et al. 1996). It is funded jointly by the UK Department for International Development and by the Government of India. It is executed by KRIBHCO, a national fertiliser co-operative, in which 51 per cent of the shares are held by the government and 49 per cent by member co-operatives. The KRIBHCO project started in 1992 and has focused its attention on adjoining parts of Panchmahals district (Gujarat), Banswara (Rajasthan) and Jhabua (Madhya Pradesh). The area is populated mainly by members of the scheduled tribes, the Bhils and Bhilala. Villages are usually relatively socially homogeneous, although they sometimes include sizeable proportions of scheduled castes. The area is characterised by undulating land, deforestation, poor soils and low levels of agricultural production.

In the project area, agricultural production alone is normally inad-equate to support families throughout the year. Thus, an important fea-ture of life is the annual migration to urban areas between November and March each year, and the remittances earned during this period form a critical component of villagers livelihoods. Farmers—sometimes whole families—travel to cities up to 200 or 300 miles away in order to find labouring work. The migrants generally return for the festival of *holi* in March, some travelling back to the cities after *holi*.

KRIBP set out to give particular weight to the needs of the poor and of women, and aimed to test ways in which their needs and priorities could be taken into account. The justification for this bias on women was the rarely acknowledged, but considerable, contribution of women to agricultural productivity, household decision-making and the local

[5] Source: Smith (1998).
[6] Centre for Arid Zone Studies, University of Wales, College Road, Bangor LL57 2NR, UK.

economy in general. Men, almost exclusively, are recognised as occupying the roles of decision-makers and holders of knowledge. Women have largely been valued for their labour rather than their knowledge or opinions, and even women do not acknowledge their own wide knowledge and skills (Mosse 1994).

The project began work in five villages in 1992, selected on the basis of a lack of resources such as paved roads, schools and medical facilities and on the level of social homogeneity. As the project proceeded, new villages were added, primarily in response to requests from villages which had heard about the project's work. Programme activities cover a range of farming systems, crop trials and community seed-multiplication, agroforestry and wasteland development, horticulture, soil and water conservation, minor irrigation, livestock development, and credit management for input supply.

The project emphasises the use of savings-and-credit groups as the basis for planning natural resource and economic development in the villages. The groups are based at the *falia* (hamlet) level, and normally consist of 15 to 25 households of related families or with close social ties. Households are given an initial loan from the project of Rs 500 to Rs 1000 to provide crop inputs. Repayments are made by individuals into the group funds (partly because there are institutional constraints which prevent loans from being repaid to the project). Group funds are used to finance agricultural inputs, capital items (such as water pumps for irrigation) and also to meet social needs (such as financing weddings). To date, although these groups have been used as a focus for the implementation of conservation work, there is little evidence that group funds have been used for to maintain the conservation measures (Mosse et al. 1995b). In addition to establishing an alternative credit source and being a focal point for the implementation of natural resource management activities, the groups have helped to build organisational and conflict resolution skills. By 1998, there were 232 groups in about 70 villages, each with an average membership of 18 households. In 1997, average funds held by each group were Rs 650 per household, generated mostly from project programmes. Conservation work had been carried out on about 4,250 hectares in 53 villages, at a cost to the project of Rs 4000 per hectare.

The project employs pairs (ideally one male and one female) of community organisers to work in groups or clusters of three or four villages. The community organisers usually live in nearby towns. Village and group meetings are held regularly to carry out community problem-analysis and issue-focused participatory rural appraisals on various topics, and to discuss which simple interventions can be made by the project. In the project's early stages, the emphasis has been on confidence-building interventions that do not require complex group action—such as experimentation with new crop varieties or the purchase of small water pumps. Later, at the request of the communities, major interventions by the project may include soil and water conservation, tree planting, well construction and small-scale irrigation.

At the outset, there was a general consensus among project staff and advisors that although some form of subsidy would have to be offered for conservation work, it was desirable for farmers to make a considerable contribution themselves. It was decided that the project would pay 50 per cent of labour costs. The main justifications for offering subsidies were: the need to compensate farmers for not migrating so they could undertake conservation work; the heavy indebtedness of many farmers, which seemed to make loans for conservation work impractical at that time; and intergenerational equity arguments.

The Use of Subsidies for Soil and Water Conservation

Several authors have noted the low investment in soil and water conservation in areas where there is high seasonal migration (Kerr and Sanghi 1992, Reardon et al. 1992; Reij 1991). This has led many to advocate the use of subsidies if they are well thought out, properly administered and implemented with care and sensitivity (Sanders 1988). Stocking and Abel (1992) emphasise the need to make adequate allowance for the opportunity cost of farm labour used on conservation schemes. Sheng and Meiman (1988) advocate the use of incentives including subsidies, as farmers in degraded areas often have few resources to invest in conservation except labour. De Graff (1996) discusses the role of legislation and moral persuasion in addition to economic incentives in the implementation of watershed development projects. He concludes that subsidies may be justified when the benefits from soil conservation and watershed development do not only accrue to the farmers concerned, but also to those downstream through the reduction of flooding and siltation or to future generations of farmers.

Other observers have reported that the use of subsidies has been disappointing or even counter-productive. Kerr et al. (1996) point out that subsidised watershed development has been used for employment generation, to convince farmers to try new methods, to compensate for externalities such as reducing downstream sedimentation, and to coerce ignorant farmers to do what the project management know is best. Sanders (1988) highlights the tendency for farmers to expect subsidies from the government or other sources for carrying out conservation works, often refusing to carry out necessary maintenance unless they are paid to do so. Pretty (1995) mentioned their effects on stifling local initiative and encouraging a subsidy dependency culture. Kerr et al. (op. cit.) summarise the drawbacks of subsidies: that they cannot be extended indefinitely (thus failing to fulfil project goals of reproducibility); they are wasteful if there are feasible alternatives; they are difficult to remove at the end of the project; and there may be undesirable side effects. Side effects may include neighbouring villages postponing self-financed conservation work until the project arrives in their village, or postponing maintenance in the hope that future projects will pay for it. In such cases, subsidies may act as a disincentive. Subsidies may also discourage farmers from thinking for themselves and developing other, perhaps cheaper, solutions and so would constitute the opposite of development (see also Bunch 1982).

Few authors mention the inequity of subsidy programmes and the difficulty of taking into account the opportunity cost of subsidies. Subsidies divert resources away from other uses—if works are financed by loans rather than subsidies, the money (or labour in the case of subsidies which are less than 100 per cent of labour costs) may be better utilised elsewhere.

Although they would prefer to do away with subsidies, Kerr et al. (op. cit.) acknowledge that this will not often be possible. The best that can be done is to ameliorate their negative effects and reduce the level of subsidies below the 100 per cent commonly offered on government schemes. One suggestion Kerr et al. make is to match labour contributions, whereby farmers build half the bund themselves and the project employs labour to construct the other half. They suggest that subsidies are only justifiable when there has been a market failure, that is, when social costs and returns do not equal private costs and returns. This situation may occur when the discount rate (both notional and sub-conscious) which farmers apply to the cost of not conserving soil and water is greater than the notional discount rate that would be used by the government or society as a whole. In the case of watershed development, this may be true if the considerations of downstream farmers or later generations are to be taken into account. Another market failure (not discussed by Kerr et al.) occurs when farmers do not have access to credit at commercial rates of interest. In the KRIBP area for instance, farmers typically have to pay interest rates of up to 150 per cent per annum on loans from moneylenders.

Mosse et al. (1995a), commenting on the KRIBP, reported that even 50 per cent subsidies had distorted the villagers' view of soil and water conservation—some groups reported a need for such conservation work, when they really viewed it as an income-generating activity. However, it appears that although the desire for income in the form of subsidies from conservation activities is great, most farmers in project villages believe that they do provide genuine economic and environmental benefits. Therefore it seems therefore that some form of subsidies are essential to support farmers investment in conservation, the challenge lies in determining the appropriate balance between individual and group contributions and outside assistance.

Design of Subsidies

For whatever reason (the attraction of subsidised work or the perception of a real need for conservation that they had previously felt unable to implement), farmers have consistently requested that the project assist them in conservation work, especially bunding on private land.

Choice of conservation methods There was considerable initial debate among the project advisors as to whether the project should encourage vegetative or physical conservation methods. Although vegetative techniques are cheaper, they are relatively untried in the KRIBP area.

Insufficient soil moisture is a major reason for low crop productivity, so water conservation is a higher priority for farmers than soil conservation. Given the nature of the soils, some form of physical barrier was considered necessary by both farmers and technical advisers, since bunds allow water more time to infiltrate into the soil and encourage an increase in the soil depth near the bunds. In addition, field and *nalah* (gully) bunds were widely used in the area before the project started. Part of the more fertile lowland areas was terraced without outside assistance—but in the less fertile upland areas, various government-financed schemes have been implemented, invariably paying 100 per cent subsidies. The project therefore tried to develop new ways of implementing such schemes, building on existing technology.

There was a preference at the outset for contour bunds, but it was quickly realised that *nalah* bunds were the most popular, followed by earth or stone field bunds. In some cases, farmers developed an innovative method of using bunds to divert water from the hillside into the *nalahs*—accepting a lower maize crop in favour of the more-valued rice crop grown in the *nalahs*. Another farmer innovation has been to plant a strip, several metres wide, of rice behind contour and field bunds to maximise the area of rice production. This has the effect of increasing the cost-benefit ratio of the work, by increasing the social and economic benefits.

In addition to physical conservation methods, vegetative methods such as planting fodder grasses on terrace bunds, green manuring and mulching have been actively encouraged. Green manuring and mulching were once used by farmers in some villages, and the idea of planting of grass on terrace bunds arose naturally after group discussions on bund maintenance, the opportunity cost of the land displaced by the bund, and the shortage of fodder. The project has also helped farmers to plant small plots of trees and to establish Joint Forest Management Schemes. Unfortunately, vegetative techniques (except the latter) have met with limited success, largely due to poor soils and low rainfall (leading to poor establishment rates and growth), uncontrolled grazing at critical times of the year—and perhaps the absence of subsidies!

Financing the opportunity cost of migration   Given the cost of conservation work and the farmers' need for supplementary income (usually obtained from seasonal work), subsidies were considered essential while the conservation work was being undertaken. Loans were not thought to be viable, since the farmers were already heavily in debt to moneylenders. *Halma* is a local practice of mutual help, used for various agricultural tasks such as land clearing or planting; its use in conservation work was considered. Payment is in the form of food, liquor and *bidis* (cigars made from green tobacco and rolled in the leaf of a local tree). However, discussions indicated that less than ten days each year were used for *halma* activities, and organising conservation work on this basis was not possible. Although subsidies came to be viewed as the most practical option, the project never thought of the conservation component as having income generation as its purpose.

Intergenerational equity   Soil erosion rates in the project area are generally between 10 and 30 tonnes/ha/year (equivalent to a soil depth of 0.5 to 3 mm/year) (Smith 1997). This is equivalent to an erosion rate of 3 to 20 years/cm, or 300 to 2000 years/m. Many soils are shallower than one metre, so if erosion remains unchecked, yields in parts of the project area will diminish to minimal levels within 50 to 150 years. Already there are large areas of totally degraded land—particularly in upland areas owned by the Forest Department and in steeper village areas. Previously productive, these areas are now used as pasture. This clearly raises the issue of intergenerational equity; continued use of rapidly degrading land without conserving soil and water will reduce the potential income of future generations. Responsibility for future generations must be shared between their ancestors and the state (or the state's agents, perhaps NGOs); this is a further justification for the project using subsidies.

Several authors have discussed the large difference between the (social) discount rate as used by society at large or by international donors, and the (private) discount rate used by individuals. It is a relative luxury for farmers to consider the severely depleted production potential of future generations, even though most farmers are aware of the problem. Because of their more immediate needs, farmers tend to use quite high discount rates when (sub-consciously) calculating the opportunity cost of investment in soil and water conservation. In contrast, society will need to apply low, even zero, discount rates if intergenerational equity is to be maintained. Despite the high private discount rates, there is strong evidence that the physical measures being used in the project area can result in increased productivity over a period of a few years (Smith 1997). There is, of course, a question about the best use of money available for subsidies. For example, the subsidies might be better spent on less degraded or less steep land where the cost of treatment is lower, or on some other development activity in the project area or elsewhere.

Programme Implementation

If the community identifies soil and water conservation as a priority, an issue-focused participatory rural appraisal is undertaken. During this, participatory soil maps of the village are drawn, and the maps are used to discuss watershed boundaries, identify the most seriously eroded areas and discuss the range of techniques that might be used. Unlike many other projects where participation equates to labour contribution, farmers are involved extensively in the design and management of the work, such as deciding on the type and siting of conservation structures. There is no requirement for farmers or villagers to participate in, or implement conservation on their land, but they can still benefit from participation in the programme on other farmers' land. However, most choose to have some form of conservation on their land and to participate in the scheme.

Many subsidised programmes have been criticised for making farmers dependent on outside expertise. KRIBP has placed great emphasis on developing local skills related to watershed management. The *falia* (hamlet) groups are asked to identify trainee volunteer workers or *jankars* (knowledgeable persons), who are trained by the project to assist in the implementation of conservation activities. The *jankars* (both male and female) are given formal training for several days and regular on-the-job training. Despite the social constraints upon women in the Bhil community, many female *jankars* have been encouraged to develop innovative conservation methods, making a considerable contribution towards raising the status of women in the villages and breaking down barriers against women in decision-making roles.

The group also decides how payments for conservation work are apportioned between the group saving-and-credit fund and individual savings. Typically, 3 per cent of the project payments to the group go towards group savings, and 5 per cent towards individual savings. In addition, 3 per cent of the payments go the *jankars*.

Subsidies were set at 50 per cent of the nominal cost of labour for work done, based on the state minimum wage. In practice, the subsidy has been greater than 50 per cent, since the project has borne the cost of seeds and tree seedlings, transport and the purchase of some materials, such as wire for gabion structures. Subsidised activities include the construction of stone and earth field bunds, contour bunds, interception drains, staggered contour trenches, *nalah* bunds, and some gully-control measures such as stone check-dams. The work that each group member does is recorded by the *jankar*, and checks are made on a random basis by the community organiser or by one of the project agricultural engineers. Payments are made every two or three weeks, and deductions for the payment of the *jankar* and group savings are made at source.

In practice, the work is done in small family groups, often by a husband and wife, and these small groups usually agree to share the earnings. All participants are allocated individual savings ledger accounts in the group funds, and a fixed percentage of their earnings is paid into the account.

Participant contributions   Participants contribute in the form of labour. The average amount of time spent by each household on conservation and other watershed management-related activities is 75 days: 48 in year one, 15 in year two and 11 in year three (Smith 1997). Maintenance and improvements are estimated to account for four or five days per year. Approximately 15–20 per cent of participant contributions are used for communal-land activities such as planting trees and rehabilitating pastures.

In contrast to some government schemes in the area which offer a 100 per cent subsidy, KRIBP chose a subsidy of 50 per cent because it was thought that farmers should, and would, contribute part of the cost. It was anticipated that there would be a short-term gain in crop production in addition to the long-term benefits of reducing soil erosion rates. Participants are paid 50 per cent of the state minimum wage according to a 'schedule of rates' (a government-prepared table listing the expected amounts of earth that can be moved a day under different conditions). The subsidies are paid to participants with no limit to the number from each household who can participate. The project initially used different rates in each state according to the published schedules, but this became unworkable due to the considerable differences between states, so an average rate was introduced.

Another complication has been that the wages farmers pay to one another for casual work in the village is normally lower than the state minimum. Hence, the nominal 50 per cent subsidy is, closer to 60 to 80 per cent of local wage rates. Moreover, the schedule of rates is rather generous, so actual earnings are probably similar to the local wage rate or the net earnings (remittances) that would have been gained had the farmer migrated.

Participants who normally migrate have to decide whether the money they would earn in the town outweighs the value of the subsidy and the other advantages of staying at home: the chance to increase livestock production, grow a second-season crop, and obtain the short- and long-term benefits from watershed treatment. Since the uptake of conservation work has been high and there has been considerably less migration, we can only assume that the comparison is favourable. It remains to be seen whether increased agricultural productivity as a result of conservation and other project interventions leads to lower migration after the project ends.

Finally, it is important to remember that when group members decide whether to work on conservation, they are not concerned primarily with the good of the whole group, and altruism is not likely to figure very highly. A group will be successful only if it is perceived that all the members benefit, even if not equally. The subsidised programme also means that everyone in the household, including women, can work and receive an income directly, whereas migrants are often male.

Impact and Maintenance of Conservation Structures

Impact-assessment studies and informal group-interviews have supported the view that physical methods have increased agricultural production. The increases have resulted from:

- increased cultivated area as a result of fallow land coming into more frequent cultivation;
- increased area as a result of reclaimed gully and *nalah* areas;
- increased yield (mainly in the *nalah* areas);
- ability to change from maize to rice in ponded areas behind bunds;
- ability to grow improved varieties of maize and rice;
- higher water table in the *nalah* areas (increases up to 1 m);
- less seed and organic material washed away by surface runoff.

An added advantage mentioned by farmers is the improvement in the value of their land—an important consideration in light of the establishment of bank accounts.

Effect of subsidies on priming savings-and-credit groups   Payments from subsidies have strengthened groups and have reduced the levels of indebtedness to moneylenders. The project has become unpopular with moneylenders, and there is some nervousness among villagers that the moneylenders will no longer be there once the project is over, especially if the savings-and-credit groups begin to fail. One disadvantage of the present arrangement has been that groups acquire considerable funds before they have any experience in managing savings-and-credits groups. Another potential difficulty is that the rules for disbanding groups have not been adequately worked out—it is not clear whether if the group was disbanded, members would get an equal share or an amount proportionate to the amount paid in. On reflection, it would have been better if all funds had been associated with individuals, as it is unclear to groups and the project how individual contributions into the group fund relate to the level of credit that is available to them.

Maintenance of physical work and subsidies   Experience in other areas suggests that farmers are often reluctant to maintain subsidised works. In KRIBP, this has not been the case. Farmers have been quite conscientious in maintaining bunds and other conservation structures, perhaps because of the high degree of consultation between the project and farmers when considering the design and siting of the structures. Furthermore, the impact of poor maintenance on the effectiveness of their own and their neighbours' structures has often been discussed during group meetings, and this has exerted moral pressure on farmers.

The project area is also somewhat unusual in that the amount of share-cropping or renting of land is minimal. In most cases, farmers have title deeds to their land, so uncertain tenure is rarely a reason for poor maintenance. Farmers are willing to maintain structures if they believe the maintenance costs are less than the benefits, and if they do not think someone else will come and do it for them.

Evaluation of the use of subsidies De Graff (1996) used several conditions to evaluate the use of subsidies in watershed projects in various countries. These form the first column of Table 8.2, and are used as the basis for evaluating the KRIBP.

Wider Issues

The project has found it difficult to approve a reduction in subsidies lest activist groups accuse it of exploiting farmers. Villagers in some areas have complained that KRIBP rates are lower than those on government-financed schemes (which are usually based on 100 per cent of the state minimum wage). This difficulty stems from a perception that the farmers are quasi-employees of the implementing agent. The concept that the payments are grants rather than wages has not always been appreciated. If the idea that group members and *jankars* are employed by the project is to be removed, new ideas and ways of implementing the project are needed. The ability of groups to maintain their own financial records needs to be improved, so that group appointees can receive money from the project on behalf of the group and distribute it appropriately to the members.

Equity There is considerable variation in the size of landholding in the project villages—the average ranges from about 0.5 ha to 2.0 ha—with the result that medium and better-off farmers receive relatively more help from the project. If the subsidised payments are lower than local wage rates (and poorer farmers only do the work because there is no other work available), then larger farmers are subsidised by the poorer farmers who do more of the work. The few landless labourers in the project area lose out even more, as they do not benefit from having work done on their land. Because of this, one might expect them to be less keen to work on the project. Indeed some of the poorer farmers have complained that they contribute more than others into the group fund because they tend to do more conservation work. Furthermore, the landless receive no other benefit than the subsidised payments for the work. The present arrangements for subsidising conservation clearly discriminate against some of the poorest members of the society. To complicate matters further, beneficiaries have not always been people

Table 8.2   Evaluation of KRIBP Project [a]

Condition	Remarks	Score
Moral persuasion would not suffice	Probably not, but very little has been attempted	+
Target group would otherwise incur financial loss	Evidence is that most farmers would benefit over 3 or 4 years	+
Incentives should reach the target group, be used for the designed purpose and exclude non-target groups and other purposes	Most subsidies have been used for the purpose. However a small number of people from other villages have gate-crashed on the incentive scheme.	+
Incentives should have minimal counterproductive side-effects and should not bring about financial loss to other actors	No known negative effects. Some worries that the savings-and-credit groups seeded with subsidy money will antagonise moneylenders.	+
Value of the incentives should not exceed the net social gains (to other actors and society at large)	Very difficult to assess, but taking into account future generations and using a zero discount rate, it is unlikely that the value of incentives will exceed the gains.	+
Other actors should consider the incentives as a fair compensation for the financial loss otherwise incurred	Poorer farmers complain that they subsidise better-off farmers	−
Administration of the incentives should be flexible enough to cope with changing socio-economic or environmental conditions	Institutional constraints have made flexibility difficult	−
Incentives should leave land users flexibility to reach intended purpose in own way	To some extent, though the choice could be improved	−
Incentives should be administered relatively easily and be simplest or cheapest way to reconcile conflicts of interest	Administration of the subsidies has been very expensive for the project in time and money	−
Incentives should be temporary and withdrawn after 5-10 years without creating dependency or counterproductive effects	Yes, but subsidies may make famers reluctant to do conservation. However due to project they no longer expect 100% subsidies	+

[a] According to conditions given in de Graff (1966).

from the group. The project has found it difficult to exclude non-group members from joining in the work, and these people gain neither from the benefits of conservation on their land, nor from being able to make use of group funds.

Wider socio-economic aspects It has been argued that subsidies create dependency and discourage farmers from undertaking conservation measures on their own. This may be partly true, but is probably an oversimplification. Other factors that prevent individual initiatives are the breakdown of traditional leadership patterns and, as the population rises and plot sizes shrink, farmers have to migrate to supplement their income, so lack time for conservation.

Discussions with farmers indicate that they view project subsidies opportunistically. Once the project is over, many may revert to annual migration—though hopefully on a reduced scale. Another concern is that a temporary reduction of migration may loosen ties between migrants and employers in the cities.

Effect of subsidies on demonstration and adoption To some extent, the project has felt a pressure to perceive the disbursement of funds and the payment of subsidies as a measure of success. In this regard, it is no different than many other conservation programmes. Although a holistic approach to watershed management was advocated at the outset, most of the project time has gone into organising the physical aspects of conservation. As a result, the demonstration and extension of lower-cost methods have suffered. Techniques that have received low priority include: green manuring, implements to reduce labour needs for weeding and to promote soil formation, tree planting, rehabilitation of rangelands, planting grass on bunds and grass strips on steeper land, and planting trees on uncultivable land.

Looking to the Future

The ideal situation is one where farmers finance improvements to their land themselves because they perceive the benefits of doing so. Realistically, some way of financing improvements in land management will have to be found, especially among resource-poor farmers in the most severely degraded areas. Whilst loans need to be given more careful consideration, a subsidy culture has grown up in rural areas. In the short term, perhaps the best that may be hoped for is to reduce subsidy levels and to implement them in ways that reduce any negative impacts. KRIBP experience suggests that more equitable ways of subsidising work need to be found, or alternative incentives should be offered. Project implementing agencies need to exercise greater flexibility in their arrangements than has often been the case.

Small groups remain the best vehicles for planning watershed work and making payments. Subsidising payments for daily work is not equitable, and needs to be replaced with a fairer way of paying for land improvement—perhaps based on households or farm parameters. Subsidies will need either to be progressive (benefiting the poorer farmers more than the better-off farmers) or at least neutral (benefiting all social groups equally).

Variable subsidy rates One way of reducing inequity might be to use variable subsidy rates on a household basis, perhaps according to socio-economic class, the number in a family, or the size of holding. Class is assessed as a matter of routine in KRIBP by wealth-ranking exercises. However, offering subsidies on the basis of class may be unpopular if people are averse to being branded as poor (though this has not been the experience of the project so far). A further difficulty with this approach is that wealth-ranking may be less accurate, as there will be an incentive to be classified in a lower class. The most serious objection is that there is currently no accurate, consistent method of assessing wealth classes across villages.

Subsidies could be paid on the basis of the holding size, so that larger farms qualify for lower percentage subsidies than smaller farms. A further refinement would be to take into account the land class and offer a higher subsidy for the worst land—but this may be too complicated to work in practice.

Fixed subsidy rates An alternative would be to allocate a fixed land-improvement grant to each household or individual, irrespective of farm size or class. This would benefit poorer farmers relatively more than the better-off. Landless labourers could also be offered the same grant, if they came up with a suitable proposal, perhaps to improve a portion of communal (waste) land over which they were given some rights by the group or village officials. A disadvantage of offering subsidies to households would be that single households might be tempted to claim it was more than one in order to increase its subsidies. Another difficulty is that some poor farmers have large areas of poor land, so would be disadvantaged by such a scheme. There would also be a risk that no conservation measures would be undertaken on some land, for example on land belonging to better-off farmers who were unwilling to take out a loan. Such a scenario would mean that a strict watershed approach would not be feasible.

However, following a strict approach has always been difficult where emphasis is placed on farmer participation and where the watersheds rarely coincide with village administrative boundaries. The Forest Department does not allow conservation activities on its land by villagers (for fear of villagers subsequently claiming ownership), despite this land invariably occupying the upper part of the catchment. Offering subsidies on a per-capita basis may present difficulties because of the need to decide when to include absentee household members.

No perfectly equitable system of subsidies is possible, though it appears that a fixed grant per household would be the most equitable of the options outlined above. A refinement may be to offer a fixed grant per household and to supplement this with an additional payment for each adult family member resident in the village during the monsoon season. In addition to household grants, a grant based on land area paid to the group or the village in order to accommodate work done on communal land would also be required.

The allocation of funds on a per-household basis would still require that other group members do work on some farms. Farmers themselves would pay workers after receiving their grant (probably about Rs 1500 per household). The grant would be paid in several instalments once project staff had verified the work. To a large extent, farmers, in consultation with the group and subject to approval by the implementing agency, should be left to decide how the money is to be used (e.g., tree planting, field bunds, contour trenches, *nalah* bunds). Such an approach would be an interesting way of checking which conservation measures farmers thought were the best.

Reduction of subsidy levels The idea of weaning beneficiaries off subsidies as the project progresses is often discussed. This may work by gradually reducing the level of subsidies paid each year. The problem would be that if a watershed approach were adopted, those at the top of the watershed would get the largest subsidy. Jealousies between neighbouring villages entering the project at different times are also likely to arise, so this option is not a favoured one.

Loans Several authors (e.g., Kerr and Sanghi 1992) have proposed using credit for conservation activities that are profitable to farmers, limiting subsidies to unprofitable activities. Impact-assessment studies by KRIBP show that the cost of the labour inputs into conservation measures will often be paid back in increased yields in 2–3 years, especially in *nalah* areas. Offering loans is therefore one option of financing these measures. Farmers would need to be convinced before taking the loan that there is a short-term payback. Now that KRIBP has been established, this may work, as farmers have seen the benefits. On the other hand, many will want to know why subsidies have been stopped.

Loans have been offered by the project for items such as small pumps for irrigation. Recovery has been good, and the repayments have been made into group funds, so there is a precedent for using loans for farm improvement. Ashok (1997) makes some innovative suggestions as to how loans from banks and from the savings-and-credit groups can be given greater impetus in KRIBP. These include evolving simple accounting systems, the recovery of loans in kind, the use of indigenous self-help groups called *notra* or *chandla* (which pool resources for weddings), and the provision of training to develop more participatory structures rather than relying on the development of individual leadership.

One approach would be to offer loans to supplement a fixed land-improvement grant awarded on a household basis. The balance of the requirement for the (usually) richer, larger farms could be made up with loans from the project. Loans would not be confined to the richer farmers so long as there was an undertaking to spend the money on conservation, and farmers were convinced that conservation measures would produce a benefit more than the cost of the loan. Unfortunately, many farmers are already heavily in debt to moneylenders. Recovering a large number of loans would require a lot of administration, and projects would also need to plan for this. Although projects could hardly insist on comparable interest rates, the rate would have to include inflation and perhaps two per cent for administration.

The Reserve Bank of India and the National Bank for Agricultural and Rural Development (NABARD) have issued clear policy guidelines to all banks to encourage them to lend to self-help groups. A positive recent development has been that there are now seven groups that have access to formal credit through commercial banks under the NABARD scheme. The use of such loans for watershed improvement by local groups needs to be encouraged on an experimental basis, and monitored closely.

Title deeds in exchange for conservation work A novel approach that may work for farmers who have encroached onto Forest Department land would be to offer title deeds before the end of the customary

10 years, and to waive the annual 'fee' for illegal cultivation if the farmers undertook conservation work on this land. The cost of labour to the farmer would be considerably less than having to pay the annual fee. New national legislation would be required to allow this. A further limitation is that it is the poorer farmers who encroach onto—the often unproductive—Forest Department land. It also amounts to coercing the farmer to undertake conservation work, possibly against their better judgement. The obstacles of having such a policy agreed by, the Forest Department are likely to be virtually insurmountable.

Conclusion

To ensure that improvements to watershed management are sustainable and economically viable, subsidies for conservation work should be reduced. Any subsidy that is offered should be based on a detailed assessment of the local cost of labour and remittances from migrants, rather than the state minimum wage. If subsidies are used, they should not be paid to those undertaking the work directly, but to households on completion and verification of agreed work. There needs to be more flexibility on the part of the project managers to experiment with different forms of subsidies.

Savings-and-credit groups based on *falias* or *tolas* (hamlets) and consisting of 15 to 20 households play an important role in implementing conservation and other watershed-management activities. They provide a forum for planning activities, discussing conflicts of interest, and training. They can also be used to reduce the administrative burden on project staff when paying subsides. However, there needs to be greater emphasis on training in basic bookkeeping. Groups need to decide for themselves the modalities of any scheme to save part of the earnings from conservation work. Possible inequuities and other problems associated with placing a percentage of the earnings into a group fund, not owned by any individual, should be pointed out.

In planning improvements to the productivity and management of communal land, it may be that the village is the most efficient unit. While the preparation of village work-plans with an appropriate emphasis on integrated land-use planning is to be encouraged, such plans should also take into account possible sources of finance. It would encourage villagers to plan, in a more realistic and participatory way, if project grants were based on a notional cost per unit area.

EXTRACT 8.2
THE ACID TEST: WILL BENEFICIARIES
CONTRIBUTE?[7]

ANIL SHAH[8]

Contribution Resented

Local communities—i.e., project users and beneficiaries—are often reluctant contributors to a development activity. For decades they have benefited from such schemes for free. Even now, many schemes are implemented without any contribution required from them. This may jeopardise local people's rights to demand quality in project implementation, or their due share in the benefits. They have many previous experiences of promised benefits not materialising, whereas contributions are expected up front. The challenge for the development agency is to convince beneficiaries that the cost of their contribution will be far outweighed by the benefits, and that the agency will fulfil its part of the obligation by making resources available to implement the scheme.

However, most development agencies do not appreciate the need to insist on people's contributions. They have implemented various development schemes without people's contributions, and quite a few have succeeded in extending the benefits to the people. Even if they were convinced of the benefit of the people 'owning' a development scheme, many (particularly field functionaries) would consider the time and resources needed to convince people to contribute as not being worth the delay in implementation. There is a need to convince development agencies that people's contributions are not only desirable but also achievable without too many difficulties.

It was for this purpose that we conducted a survey to find out from several development agencies engaged in participatory development of natural resources how they viewed people's contributions, how they convinced the local community about its importance, and how they collected it. The following agencies were contacted: Aga Khan Rural Support Programme, Kundla Talu Vikaska Gram Mandal, Vikas Mandal, Lokbharti, and the Development Support

[7] Source: Shah, Anil (1998).

[8] Development Support Centre, 2 Prakurti Apartment, opp. Red Rose Restaurant, H.L. Commerce College Road, Navaranpura, Ahmedabad, India.

Centre. The experience of these development agencies is analysed and presented here.

Convincing People

Most free schemes are provided by government agencies. Discussions with local communities about the quality of such works brings out that even if individual officers have good intentions, they have to rely upon contractors or local field staff who are indifferent to issues of quality. The sufferers are the local people. When they make a contribution, they acquire the right to demand quality. When a development agency uses participatory approaches, it shows respect for people's knowledge and incorporates their suggestions in the work. People's confidence in the agency is enhanced enormously, strengthening their willingness to contribute towards the cost. In one case, soil conservation and irrigation officials jointly discussed a proposal to rehabilitate an old canal serving Thalota village and hand it over to local farmers' organisations. The farmers were free to suggest modifications to ensure the smooth running of the canal. Each aspect was discussed jointly, and the proposal was placed before the co-ordination committee and was largely approved. It was then easy to collect 20 per cent contributions, against the 10 per cent cost of rehabilitation which had been stipulated. The system is now managed by farmers' organisations and is working to the satisfaction of both farmers and officers.

Participatory appraisal can highlight cases in any proposed development intervention where benefits clearly exceed costs. For instance in a participatory planning exercise conducted by the Development Support Centre in Jaljivdi village, calculations showed that villagers' contributions of Rs 200,000 per year over four years would increase their incomes by Rs 400,000 per year, much beyond the project's four years of life. The community approved the development plan, and committed itself to contributing more than was stipulated in the watershed scheme. A similar situation occurred in a participatory irrigation-management scheme in Jaska village: farmers in the canal's command area were considering taking over the canal management. The appraisal exercise revealed that their contribution of Rs 40,000 to renovate the canal would raise production and hence incomes by Rs 1,200,000 in the first year, and would continue year after year. The development agency could convincingly argue that there was no other business where the investment would generate more income in the very first year.

Such discussions and exercises might prepare the ground, and in some cases may be convincing enough for people to take responsibility for participatory development. However if there are doubts and misgivings, exposure visits to successful development schemes can be persuasive. Any development scheme expecting participation and contributions from people should have provisions for such visits. Audio-visual aids, particularly videos of successful projects, can strengthen the motivation of groups to participate and, if required, make a contribution towards development schemes.

The very process of encouraging the local community to participate and contribute brings benefits to the development agency's staff, since they have to find out the potential costs and benefits of the scheme and discuss them with people. This was never needed for free schemes. This process requires the agency staff to know not only the objectives, terms and conditions of their own scheme, but also the people's problems and how the scheme is going to deal with them. One dictum of development could be: 'do not try to convince people by explaining the intention of a development scheme; begin by understanding people's problems.' People are interested in their problems and solutions, which may require them to make some contribution to the cost; they are certainly not interested in contributing to achieving the targets of various development schemes, which are brought to them by numerous development agencies.

A second dictum could be: 'attract people not by the lure of incentives but by the benefits of development'. Doing this enhances the understanding and capability of agency staff. The process of consensus-building should help build new relationships between the local community and the agency's staff that will prove useful during the implementation and management phases. Thus in the process of influencing the local community in favour of participatory approach, the development agency itself will be influenced—indeed be transformed.

Methods of Collecting Contributions

Once the amount of contribution to be collected by the user group or community is worked out, it may be better to leave it to them to decide how the contribution will be collected and by whom. People are used to collecting contributions for various social or religious activities, such as erecting a temple or organising religious festivals. They should be able to apply their experience to collecting contributions for development schemes.

In many cases the amount to be collected is distributed among beneficiary farmers according to how much of their landholding is planned to fall within the proposed development. This is the most favoured manner of collecting contributions under participatory irrigation management.

For a check-dam for recharging wells, the group of possible beneficiaries sometimes decides how much each farmer's share will be, according to the distance of his or her well from the dam. A participatory appraisal exercise showing the proposed dam on a village map and the wells likely to benefit from groundwater recharge, proves useful in vividly bringing out the difference in benefits for different farmers and wells. For instance, imagine Rs 15,000 of contributions must be raised, and there are 11 wells. If the group is given 15 grains, each representing Rs 1000, to be distributed by placing them on the 11 wells according to the likely benefit of recharge, they are able to estimate the contribution within a few minutes to everyone's satisfaction.

Development schemes usually provide flexibility in collecting contributions by way of cash or kind (material, transport service or labour). Some development agencies have found that to be sure that the contribution is actually made, they insist upon cash contribution, at least for part of it. For instance, the Aga Khan Rural Support Programme, Lokbharti and the Development Support Centre insist upon a good part of the expected contribution in cash. Lokhbarti insists upon an initial 10 per cent in cash, and a further 10 per cent during implementation, which may be in kind.

Contribution in kind takes various forms: supplying water for construction, supervising work; breaking and collecting stones for checkdams; supplying tractors to transport stones, surveying the market to determine the best price and quality of material to be bought; providing refreshments to workers; maintaining accounts and presenting them to the development agency, etc. Not all such manifestations of participation are reckoned as contributions.

In a few villages in Savarkundla (Vank, NO Aaro and Dhajdi Para), more prosperous farmers responded to a call for contributions to a project benefiting the entire community by offering extra amounts to make up for those who could not afford their whole share.

Dialogues and videos at large meetings may generate initial interest in the proposed scheme. A committee is then usually constituted to plan and monitor progress. The committee takes responsibility for participation of members in exposure visits and in participatory appraisal exercises when the location of development projects is decided and user groups formed.

Kundla Talu Vikaska Gram Mandal has developed an approach where an enterprising leader takes responsibility for collecting contributions from users and carrying out development work with their participation. If the user group is large, responsibility for collection may be distributed to sub-groups. This is done, for example, in case of participatory irrigation management, when the leaders of the outlet groups take responsibility for collecting contributions.

There are many variations in the manner of deciding and collecting contributions. These should be encouraged and supported, provided they are equitable and not intended to circumvent the agreed contribution. For instance, differences between the 'schedule of rates' and actual cost should not be generally reckoned as contributions.

Conclusion

People and agencies should develop awareness that participatory approaches are going to be increasingly integral to development programmes. Contributions will become a necessary condition to ensure that people's participation is genuine. It can also pave the way for beneficiaries to make a larger contribution to the cost, reducing the financial burden on development agencies. The principle of 'users must pay' can over a period be extended to the principle 'payment of cost should depend upon the extent of benefit'. This has already been done by several development agencies in the voluntary sector, which expect 50 per cent contribution when the scheme benefits individual farmers (such as shaping of their private land), even though government watershed schemes expect only a 10 per cent contribution.

The crux of the matter is that development agencies should appreciate the purpose of participatory approaches and see contributions as an integral part of them. This would help them to work amicably with local people to develop the modalities of development projects, and to achieve a better fit between the people's agenda and that of the development agency. The contribution requirement will not then be seen as a hurdle by either the community or the agency, but rather as a means of reaching higher levels of collaboration between the community and agency, as well as among groups within the community.

EXTRACT 8.3
SEARCHING FOR SUSTAINABILITY IN WATERSHED
DEVELOPMENT[9]

SHASHI KOLAVALLI[10]

Cost-Sharing

This Extract examines the extent to which the beneficiaries contribute
to costs and the impact of cost-sharing on the management of projects.

Cost-sharing is a matter of policy, and there are distinct differences
in its extent and nature in different states. In Rajasthan, cost-sharing has
been institutionalised, though there is a concern that farmers may not
have the capacity to contribute. In all the projects, farmers' share, nearly
10 per cent of the costs, is withheld from the wages paid for work on
watershed activities. The commitment to make farmers share the costs
is less clear in Orissa and Karnataka. In recent years, Karnataka, under
pressure from external donors, has collected contributions from farmers. As in other aspects of participation, projects implemented by NGOs
and supported by external donors have a better record of collecting
farmers' contributions.

At one extreme in cost-sharing is the MYRADA project in Kollegal,
in which farmers bear the entire costs of work in private fields; one-
third is paid directly, and the remainder is paid via an interest-free loan
from the watershed committee which, in turn, receives a loan from
MYRADA equivalent to the cost of work on private lands. In recent
years, MYRADA has reduced the amount loaned to the committee, so
that a revolving fund has had to be created and the incentive to recover
from those borrowing in the early stages of the project is increased.

There are other projects in which farmers contribute cash for activities which benefit them individually or in groups. In projects run by
SDC in Bidar and by Danida in Dharwad, farmers contribute 30 per
cent of the cost of fruit trees. In the Dharwad project, much of the
cost-sharing has taken place in horticulture and forestry components.
Cost-sharing tends to be more in activities benefiting individuals. Groups
of farmers contribute to the construction of structures along the drainage line in the Bidar project. The watershed committee does not seem to
face difficulties in identifying individuals who will benefit from different

[9] Source: Kolavalli (1998b).
[10] PO Box 429A, Basavanagudi, Banglore 560004, India.

structures and in making them contribute. Similarly in the Keonjher Employment Assurance Scheme project, the watershed committee had identified groups of individuals to take responsibility for maintaining various structures.

As cost-sharing is a matter of policy, it also varies across projects funded from different sources. Cost-sharing is related to both the states where the programmes are, and the source of funds. Bilaterally supported programmes place considerable emphasis on cost recovery. The amount collected is a function of how much the farmers are willing to pay and the effort made by programmes to collect contributions. Comparisons are somewhat difficult because in some projects such as that of the SDC in Bidar, farmers may contribute cash, while in Rajasthan the contribution is deducted from wages paid. Though the per cent of costs shared may be the same, cash contributions are more difficult to achieve and are better indicators of willingness to pay than are wages withheld.

The level of contributions made by farmers in different projects is influenced by the willingness to share and the efforts made by the programmes to make them pay. Willingness and the ability to pay vary considerably. The major factor influencing the willingness to pay is the expected immediate benefit. In Rajasthan, for example, farmers are willing to contribute in cash for large structures to harvest water. They are not willing to contribute anything for vegetative hedges. For pastures, they do not mind contributions being deducted from their wages (Srinivas 1997b). Across the states, the benefits are influenced by agro-ecological conditions. Organising contributions is obviously more feasible where the benefits to individuals are immediate and substantial, as in watersheds where slopes are shallow, rainfall adequate, and the benefits from bunds high. It would be unreasonable to expect similar contributions in other areas.

Regardless of the potential benefits, farmers are reluctant to contribute if they expect that enforcement will be weak. In the SDC-funded Pratapgarh project, for example, the NGO insisted on farmer contributions, but once the farmers came to know that the project was being implemented by the government, they became reluctant to contribute. The farmers expected that the work would be done regardless of their contributions, as it was a government project. The policies of the projects regarding farmer contributions may be the major determinant of the level of contributions collected.

There is little interest among government staff in making farmers contribute because it stands in the way of rapid implementation. It is perceived as an additional procedural requirement. As project staff often tend to be more interested than farmers in implementing activities, they go out of their way to show that farmers have contributed where it is a requirement. This is not too difficult in some projects. In the Karnataka Danida project for example, a farmer owning one hectare of land has to contribute only about Rs 26 for vegetative barriers and about Rs 160 for contour bunds in his or her fields. In the first case, a farmer is supposed to provide at least one labourer, 'at least a boy to separate the grass slips'. In the second case, the farmer would be persuaded to 'provide a tractor to transport boulders required to build the outlets'. In this project, many of the vegetative barriers had been ploughed under unless they were on the field bunds. It is hard to imagine why farmers would have contributed to something that they do not wish to retain.

Farmer contributions may just be book adjustments in many projects. In Rajasthan, where farmers' shares are withheld from wages, the contributor may not be bearing the costs. As the wages paid by the projects are often higher than market wages, those who work may not even be aware that they are contributing by working for watershed projects.

Such book adjustments by the implementing agencies are feasible where the estimated construction costs are higher than the actual costs. In one externally funded project, there was a proposal to build village ponds. The state department immediately suggested that a large number of them should be built. When the donor insisted that they should be built only where farmers contribute, the department was willing to show any level of contribution from the villagers because it was feasible to build the tanks at less than one-half of the estimated costs.

NGOs and some externally funded projects (MYRADA in Kollegal; Danida in Karnataka and SDC in Bidar and Pratapgarh), make more sincere efforts to collect contributions. They use entry-point activities to develop a culture of cost-sharing by financially supporting activities for which the communities can raise some funds. The activity might be building a platform for village meetings, or deepening the village tank or well. Having contributed to activities beneficial to them, villagers get used to the idea of sharing costs. In the SDC-funded Bidar project, the implementing organisation is given only 90 per cent of the costs of the work done, so it is forced to collect the balance from farmers. The value of farmer contributions in that project was estimated to be nearly Rs 1,000,000. In the SDC-funded Pratapgarh project, the NGO insists that farmers should contribute 25–50 per cent of the costs.

In many projects, the contributions go back to community funds which are expected to be used for maintenance of common structures. The total contribution collected in the Danida-funded Dharwad project was nearly Rs 2,000,000. Nearly 100 villages had contributed from Rs 5 to 50,000. These contributions have been given to watershed committees in proportion to the membership.

Impact of Cost-Sharing

Sharing of costs by farmers can have powerful effects on the delivery and outcomes of some activities. The consequence of charging farmers for the supply of seedlings in the Dharwad project is an example. When the seedlings were free, farmers took as many as they could, even beyond their capacity to care for them. The quality of seedlings was also poor, as they were obtained from government nurseries. Since the introduction of cash contributions, farmers take only as many as they need and are able to care for. They are particular about what they are given; they demand certain varieties. The project involves a group of farmers in organising supplies from private nurseries. The outcome of this is that better-quality seedlings are procured at higher prices, farmers share a part of the costs, and they take better care of the seedlings.

Cost-sharing implies significant changes for the work of implementing organisations. The processes need to be transparent. Farmers become aware of the expenses incurred on various projects, with potential pressures on the staff to keep the expenses reasonable. If the opposition to introducing cost-sharing is any indication, it is having some effect on implementing organisations. There is as much opposition from the bureaucracy to making farmers contribute as there is from farmers.

In Karnataka, the Department of Agriculture opposed Danida's attempts to introduce contributions. The change was approved by the state-level steering committee. The development commissioner was convinced of the need to introduce user contributions; the department was opposed to it. The Secretary of Agriculture even wrote a letter to the Union ministry and to the Danish Embassy, wondering why farmers were being asked to contribute for watershed development while everything else was being given to them for free. Subsequent to the agricultural secretary's letter, the Danish advisor demonstrated that farmers were willing to contribute. The departmental staff were concerned that 'their integrity would be questioned' if they demanded contributions from the farmers. A retired Director of Agriculture respected by the bureaucracy, who conducted staff training for the project, was able to convince the staff to give cost-sharing a chance to succeed.

While the belief that the state should provide certain services free to citizens may be a significant factor in opposition to introduction of cost-sharing, it is clear that other factors also contribute to this stand. Making farmers contribute requires considerable changes in the way government staff work. The work cannot be done independently of farmers, once they have been persuaded to share costs. In many cases, the implementing agencies may have to persuade farmers to contribute to activities that the farmers do not perceive to be beneficial to them. This is an additional bother for those accustomed to handing out things for free. Additionally, making farmers contribute may entail having to involve them in planning and implementation, and may result in calls for greater transparency.

Without careful effort to involve farmers, recovering contributions routinely, as done in Rajasthan, may have a regressive impact. Unless everyone in the community works on the project, the poorest in the community—the wage earners—contribute on behalf of those who do not have to work for wages.

EXTRACT 8.4
SCALING UP PARTICIPATORY WATERSHED DEVELOPMENT: THE INDO-GERMAN WATERSHED DEVELOPMENT PROGRAMME[11]

JOHN FARRINGTON[12] AND CRISPINO LOBO[13]

For several years prior to the full start-up of the Indo-German Watershed Development Programme, its architects were driven by one principal concern: that participatory watershed development should be replicable over wide areas. This stimulated the close engagement of stakeholders at international, national, district and local levels, and the creation of confluences of interest (and corresponding checks and balances) within and across these levels. It has also generated a technically sound, but participatory, watershed-planning methodology, a coherent transition from capacity-building to full-scale implementation within watersheds, and a practical framework for field-level collaboration among

[11] Source: Farrington and Lobo (1997).

[12] Overseas Development Institute, Portland House, London SW1E 5DP, UK.

[13] Manager, Indo-German Watershed Development Programme, opposite Social Centre, Market Yard Road, Ahmednagar 414 001, India.

NGOs, community-based organisations and government departments. The programme currently covers 92,000 ha of private and other land in 20 districts in Maharashtra, involving 50 NGOs working in 74 watersheds. It is set to expand within Maharashtra as new NGOs register themselves, some growing from village groups in successful watersheds and to other states through a system of franchising.

Origins of IGWDP's Approach

Many of the concepts underlying the IGWDP were developed in the late 1980s at the Social Centre founded in 1968 by a Jesuit priest, Hermann Bacher, in Ahmednagar, Maharashtra. In 1988, the Social Centre began its first watershed work in Pimpalgaon Wagha, a village of 840 ha and some 880 people. Preparations for the IGWDP's first phase also began in 1989, and the successful rehabilitation of this watershed by 1994 (Lobo and Kochendörfer-Lucius 1995) generated many of the local-level ingredients that the IGWDP began to incorporate. These included:

- social mobilisation in the village and support from an external agency in setting up a village watershed committee, which then became the executing agency for the project;
- the stimulation of confidence and ownership' among villagers through their participation in the design and implementation of watershed improvements;
- an inflow of external funds, especially in the form of wages, to stimulate the involvement of those whose livelihoods depend on common-pool resources;
- links with government departments from the outset to provide technical guidance, especially in Forest Department land where many common-pool resources (e.g., fodder and trees) are located;
- training via the agricultural universities;
- bank credit for agricultural, livestock and non-agricultural activities;
- limits on the period of involvement of external support agencies such as the Social Centre;
- a strategy to allow each partner (village watershed committee, government departments, agricultural universities) autonomy in their sphere of competence, while ensuring joint responsibility for successful project management;
- a strategy to manage social tensions which allowed the legitimate interests of dominant groups to be met only if those of the weaker groups were also met.

The principal economic gains by 1994 at Pimpalgaon Wagha included: a doubling of crop production; a ten-fold increase in milk production; year-round availability of drinking water; the creation of employment opportunities for landless labour over nine months of the year; diversification of the village economy into artisanal and other activities. Social gains included: active involvement of backward classes in the village watershed committee and in village events; confidence among the villagers to approach banks, etc., directly; registration of the watershed committee as a public trust for the maintenance of physical structures; the accumulation of the committee's own development fund; and the growth of purpose-oriented groups among village women.

One significant factor is that, as a result of experience in Pimpalgaon Wagha, motivation and organisation of a village now takes around six months instead of the 12–18 months formerly required. The success of work in Pimpalgaon Wagha and two other villages was also instrumental in obtaining support from the government of Maharashtra in the form of a Cabinet Resolution extending political, administrative and technical support to NGOs and community-based organisations involved in watershed development under the IGWDP. The Maharashtra government's agreement to implement Joint Forest Management arrangements on a watershed basis with NGOs and community-based organisations can also be traced in part to the success in these three villages.

Vision and Scope

A recent paper from the IGWDP sets out a basic precondition for successful scaling up:

Upscaling individual success stories to a large scale programme calls for a perspective of macro-management which at the same time has to be rooted in and be responsive to the micro-level. Unless there is a continuous and enabling cooperation between the key sectors and actors, such a process would be bound to get unstuck, thus seriously jeopardising sustainability as well as replicability (Lobo 1996: 5).

A tenet of the IGWDP is that scaling up cannot take place without a long-term vision of what constitutes permanent improvement in the conditions of the intended beneficiaries, the rural poor.

Improvements in the efficiency, equity, stability and sustainability of production from renewable natural resources form only one part of IGWDP's vision. In many respects a more important part is the sustainable strengthening of the capacity of local people to draw on the organs of civil society to meet their diverse needs, including those related to the management of watersheds. Furthermore, access to and the management of land and water resources involve essentially political questions, both within villages, and between local people and various levels of the administration. For both of these reasons, progress towards this vision cannot be made by reliance on local-level resources alone. Government provides not only services related to the management of renewable natural resources, but also much of the fabric necessary for the functioning of civil society (in the form of legal and administrative systems). Local organisations have to engage with government in order to draw on this fabric and these services in ways that meet their needs.

The IGWDP argues that progress towards this vision needs to be evolutionary: it requires the careful development of good relations on many sides simultaneously, the building on success wherever it occurs, and acceptance of frequent setbacks. Box 8.2 illustrates the types of

---

Box 8.2   Need for an Evolving Relationship between Village Organisations and Civil Society Organs

During a field visit to village X, two issues came to light which underline the need for village institutions to evolve.

One is that party politics potentially undermine village unity. This was clearly illustrated in recent local elections, when one party, in order to gain the votes of those who depend on herding than on agriculture, promised that it would override the village's ban on uncontrolled grazing which had been introduced as a condition of joining the IGWDP. Those who had already benefited substantially from the improved regulation of water flows and higher water tables under the project (i.e., predominantly those concerned with agriculture) were strongly opposed to this, and so the seeds of polarisation were sown. In the event, the ban on grazing was upheld, though only after considerable dispute.

The second concerns the capacity of village institutions to enforce agreements. This came to light in the same village, whose regulatory institutions (village watershed committee and forest protection committee) have had time to mature. Even so, they were placed under strain when farmer A, a senior member of the watershed committee, was found to be grazing livestock on common land. It was agreed that, as a relatively wealthy farmer, he should be fined Rs 500. He agreed to pay, but only after the harvest several months later. This was agreed. However, in the meantime, another farmer (B) in the village had been found committing the same offence, but on a smaller scale, and a fine of Rs 100 was imposed. Farmer A, a member of the watershed committee, insisted on making an example of B by bringing in the authorities, and extracted a confession from B. Farmer A was seeking to achieve two aims: first, to undermine the solidarity of village institutions such as the watershed committee (as a wealthy farmer, he felt that he would have much to gain by opting out of agreements on shared rights and responsibilities), and second, to distract attention from the fine which he had incurred in the hope that it might be dropped.

difficulty faced. Box 8.3 and 8.4 present examples of the successes achieved in improving technical and administrative procedures.

In these respects, the IGWDP shares many of the elements of 'people-centred development' philosophies characteristic of NGOs. But it differs from the philosophy of NGOs in five important respects:

- it sees a smaller role than do many NGOs for autonomous local development depending purely on the resources of community-based organisations or service-providing NGOs;
- conversely, it sees a need for government organisations at several levels to be intimately engaged in the processes of change;
- it emphasises the importance of introducing appropriate technical skills from outside: indigenous knowledge and practices are important, but have to be supplemented by modern techniques and management practices for substantive impact;
- whilst it recognises the strengths of NGOs in social mobilisation, it also recognises their weaknesses in technical matters. Preconditions for participation by NGOs in the programme include a willingness to accept certain types of training and to work with government organisations (see Box 8.5);
- it does not allow the prospects of scaling up to be undermined by some notion of an 'ideal' community-based organisation which can only be achieved through intensive, long-term focus on a narrow geographical area such as one or two villages.

Box 8.3   Supporting Innovation in the Public Sector

The divisional forest officer in one of the IGWDP districts had for a number of years been experimenting with different soil- and water-conservation measures on Department of Forestry land, primarily to enhance the survival rate of trees planted. He had eventually found that continuous contour terraces, combined with refilling of the terraces using soil gathered from above, met survival and soil-conservation objectives better than the staggered terraces which formed the Forestry Department's standard practice. However, his efforts to introduce these were met with initial scepticism from the department. When the IGWDP began to work with this officer in the Ahmednagar district (to which he had moved), it decided to try the methods he had been advocating. The programme feels that its decision has been vindicated: after two years the survival rates under the continuous terraces average over 90 per cent, much higher than survival rates under conventional practice, despite the poor rainfall during the period.

The programme's commitment to working with the public sector facilitated experimentation with new techniques within the Forestry Department, while at the same time allowing information on their potential to be disseminated through the mass media.

Box 8.4   Forging Agreement among Government Organisations

The programme has obtained the agreement of NABARD that the staff vetting the submissions and proposals from villages and NGOs for the full scale implementation phase should be drawn from a defined cadre and not from the pool of NABARD technical staff. This enhances the prospects of constructive interaction between NABARD, the Watershed Organisation Trust, the programme co-ordinator and the line departments involved at the field level (Agriculture, Soil and Water Conservation, and Forestry).

The benefits of this approach were highlighted in a meeting observed by the authors in November 1996, in which staff from all four organisations discussed the norms and procedures to be applied in the forestry aspects of full-implementation phase proposals from 16 villages. The district forestry officer, who hosted the meeting, explained that the continuous contour terraces that he intended to use in the villages involved some departure from standard Forestry Department practice, but could be achieved within the cost norms agreed between the department and the programme. Following agreement over the technical details of the terracing approach to be used, the discussion turned to the ways in which the intended joint forest management agreement with the village and supporting NGO was likely to influence costing levels. Agreement was quickly reached that certain standard Department of Forestry provisions could be removed, since these were now the responsibility of the forest protection committee.

The most complex issue was the lack of synchronisation between Forestry Department procedures and those of the programme funders. The former required interventions in any one site to be phased over four years. The latter required all disbursements to be completed before the end of the current programme, i.e. in four years' time. But to start all Forestry Department work in the current year so as to meet the deadline would be logistically infeasible, not least because the department would have to time its work outside the agricultural seasons in order to meet its obligation to use village labour. After some discussion, a complex but feasible formula of fund draw-downs and reporting on completed work was agreed to allow obligations to be met within the specified time frame.

Synergies among Individual Programme Components

An underlying concept of the programme has been the stimulation of confluences of interests among different stakeholders, and the search for corresponding checks and balances. This is done at international, national, state, district and local levels.

At the international level, the programme receives funds from two distinct organisations under the German Ministry of Economic Cooperation. One is the German Development Bank (*Kreditanstalt für Wiederaufbau*), which provides funds to the Indian National Bank for Agricultural and Rural Development (NABARD) at a national level. This is then responsible for disbursing funds to local-level agencies (see below) for the programme's four-year full-scale implementation phase according to agreed norms. This phase is preceded by a 12–18 month

Box 8.5 IGWDP Selection Criteria for Watersheds, Villages and NGOs

Technical criteria for the selection of watersheds
- Dry and drought-prone villages having assured irrigation on no more than 20 per cent of net cultivated area.
- Villages with notable erosion, land-degradation, resource-depletion or water-scarcity problems.
- Villages in the upper part of drainage systems.
- Watershed size around 1000 ha (and not less than 500ha), with an average rainfall of around 1000mm/yr.
- Village boundaries correspond as closely as possible with those of the watershed.
- Cropping systems do not include long-duration crops with high water requirements, such as sugarcane.

Socio-economic criteria for selection of watersheds
- Villages poorer than average, with a high proportion (by Maharashtra standards) of scheduled tribes and scheduled castes.
- No wide disparities in the size of land holding.
- Villages have shown a concern for resource conservation, and have a known history of coming together for common causes.

Villages must commit themselves to:
- Ban the felling of trees.
- Ban free grazing, and undertake 'social fencing' to protect vegetation.
- Reduce any excess livestock population and maintain it within the carrying capacity of the watershed.
- Ban water-intensive crops, or as a minimum, keep them to existing levels.
- Make an equitable contribution of 16 per cent of the unskilled labour costs of the project by *shramadaan* (joint, voluntary labour) or other means (landless and poor, single-parent households are exempt).
- Start a maintenance fund for watershed development.
- Take steps to achieve and maintain a sustainable production system.
- Constitute a village watershed committee and have it registered during the implementation phase. This will be mandated to ensure maintenance of the assets created by the project.
- Ban deep tubewells.

Criteria for the selection of NGOs to support village organisations
- Reputation and history; extent to which they have achieved rapport with people's and government organisations; perspectives on watershed development; technical and managerial capability.
- Length of time active in the area.
- Demonstrated willingness (in the event of weak familiarity with watershed management) to undertake exposure visits elsewhere; to send village youth and others on specific training programmes; to prepare and implement a demonstration project of at least 100 ha.
- Willingness (unless already experienced) to go through a capacity-building programme and meet the qualifying criteria before undertaking full implementation.

capacity-building phase funded through the Watershed Organisation Trust (see below) by the German Agency for Technical Cooperation (GTZ).

At the national level, the principal stakeholders are the Ministry of Finance (via NABARD) and the Ministry of Agriculture. The Ministry of Finance is ultimately responsible for the disbursement of funds, but the Ministry of Agriculture is keen to see development of watersheds on the ground, and is not without influence. There are several advantages of channelling the funds through NABARD:

- NABARD brings an interest by central government in the performance of the programme.
- NABARD has an interest in raising the repayment rates it has achieved historically in rainfed farming areas, and so can be expected to commit itself to the success of the programme.
- Individual NGOs and village watershed committees can receive foreign funds channelled through NABARD without having to go through the complexities of obtaining foreign exchange registration.
- Several dozen NABARD staff have technical qualifications in subjects broadly related to agriculture and natural resource management. They feel comfortable discussing technical issues with officials of e.g., the forestry or agriculture departments, and, in turn, command the respect of the technical staff in these departments.
- Procedures developed with and through NABARD for the disbursal of foreign funds in this way will lend themselves to any subsequent disbursal of Indian government funds.

At the state level, the principal stakeholders are the Departments of Agriculture, Soil and Water Conservation and Forestry. Ministers overseeing these departments successfully promoted a Cabinet Resolution in 1992 in support of the programme. This has been a key move in facilitating supportive action by line department staff. At the local level, during the capacity-building phase, the village assembly (*gram sabha*) nominates a village watershed committee. In matters relating to Forest Department lands, this committee works together with the village forest-protection committee (see below).

During the capacity-building phase, funds are channelled via the Watershed Organisation Trust into the NGO's bank account, and the NGO is then responsible for contracting a diploma-level civil engineer to help draft the watershed development plan, together with the villagers themselves, based on net area planning techniques (Box 8.6). The engineer is provided with training in participatory net-based planning by Trust staff. Towards the end of this phase, the village watershed committee considers the draft proposal and submits it to NABARD. If it is approved, funds for the full implementation phase are channelled into a bank account operated jointly by the NGO and the watershed committee.

The Watershed Organisation Trust provides on-going support during the full implementation phase, and NABARD and the programme coordinator are responsible for monitoring and supervision. Management costs go direct to the NGO, whereas project funds go to the joint watershed committee–NGO account. The expectation is that the role of NGOs will diminish over time, while that of local-level membership organisations becomes stronger. Once the rehabilitation works are complete, half of the 16 per cent contribution made by the village to the cost of unskilled labour is returned to the watershed committee to form the core of a maintenance fund.

As a coordinating and technical service organisation, the Watershed Organisation Trust also provides technical and managerial training sup-

---

Box 8.6 'Net Area' Land-Use Planning

The initial planning approach used by the IGWDP was based on 'gross area planning', which applied cost norms provided by NABARD for specific types of intervention and land types. A major shortcoming of this approach was that it relied on contour maps, which are inadequate to capture such features as the extent to which individual fields have been levelled. However, for the individual farmer, this is a crucial determinant of what measures are necessary and acceptable. Further, *panchayat* maps showing individual land holdings and features such as streams are often inconsistent with both contour maps and with ground reality.

In the 'net area' approach, developed by the Watershed Organisation Trust in consultation with NABARD, the Social Centre and NGOs, contour maps are not used. Instead, the approach relies heavily on consultation with farmers in their own fields. The type and location of interventions agreed with farmers are marked both on the ground (with lime) and on landholding maps. Fields (and, often, areas within fields) are assessed for slope, soil depth, soil texture, and erosion status. Fields are then classified into one of eight categories by reference to a standard chart. Computers at each of the six IGWDP regional centres allow the data gathered to be multiplied by standard costs and so converted into overall costings. The village watershed committee and NGOs are given the proposal as a whole, including maps, and a local-language copy of the principal spreadsheet, so that they can discuss it prior to submission. The 'net planning' approach requires a combination of technical skills. Proposals are unlikely to be financed unless technically sound, and based on the skills, knowledge and opinions of farmers themselves. Using funds allocated to it, the supporting NGO in each watershed is required to hire a civil engineer to prepare full proposals. These are given training by the Watershed Organisation Trust in the net planning approach.

port, and puts the NGOs and community-based organisations in contact with the line departments of the state government. Through its regional resource centres, the Watershed Organisation Trust also monitors progress with, for instance, the physical work on small portions of the watershed, conducted as 'hands-on' capacity-building during the capacity-building phase. During this phase, villagers and the supporting NGO are provided with training in technical skills corresponding with the individual components of watershed development, namely soil and land management; water management; crop management; afforestation; pasture and fodder development; livestock management; rural energy management; other farm and non-farm activities; and community development.

These include, for instance, skills in surveying, staking, and nursery raising. Villagers and NGOs are also trained in skills in interpersonal relations, social mobilisation and the management of village-based organisations. Much of the training is given in the practical context of rehabilitation of a part (typically around 10 per cent) of the watershed. Funds supplied by NABARD to the Watershed Organisation Trust provide for a 'disposition fund', which acts as a bridging fund so that in those watersheds where the full-implementation phase has been approved, work can go ahead without waiting for NABARD to complete the formal procedures.

Funds provided in both phases of the programme are provided as a grant. They can be used for: promotion and training, including cross-visits to other projects; project preparation, and hiring technical specialists where necessary; project implementation measures, such as afforestation, pasture development, dryland horticulture and soil- and water-conservation structures; personnel, equipment and transport, as well as other overheads of the NGOs involved; a limited contribution to a fund for maintaining the measures introduced. To take full advantage of the soil- and water-conservation measures to be introduced, farmers are expected to obtain loans or invest their own funds in downstream improvements in, for instance, dairy production, horticulture, wells, and new crop varieties.

Roles of Other Organisations and Individuals

Programme coordinator   The programme coordinator is responsible for communication on matters of policy with and among different agencies: the NGOs, NABARD, the Watershed Organisation Trust and government organisations. The coordinator also responds to emerging problems among the NGOs and watershed committees. Along with NABARD and the Trust, the coordinator is involved in selecting new NGOs and watershed projects, in helping NGOs and villagers improve their skills, and in project monitoring. The coordinator is also a member of the project sanctioning committee, and acts as the common link between the capacity-building and full-implementation stages.

Project sanctioning committee The project sanctioning committee has the mandate to develop standard criteria for selecting NGOs and projects to be included in the programme. It also considers NGO applications and project proposals. The committee is headed by NABARD, and in addition comprises four representatives of NGOs, the programme coordinator, three representatives of the state government, a representative of the national Ministry of Agriculture, and special invitees where appropriate.

Watershed Organisation Trust The Watershed Organisation Trust is a support organisation for NGOs and community-based organisations established in December 1993. It is also the institutional base of the programme coordinator. The Trust plays a central role in the programme's philosophy of creating self-sustaining local organisations: it provides NGOs and village organisations with support and training in awareness creation, social mobilisation, and the planning, implementation and monitoring of watershed development projects. It has 29 staff covering the disciplines of social mobilisation, women's issues, agronomy, civil engineering and computer applications. Its training approaches are tailored to specific settings, using a combination of structured workshops and less structured techniques such as village meetings and exposure visits. The Trust also provides funds (currently to a ceiling of Rs 500,000 per watershed, including administrative costs) for the development of a small part of each village watershed (generally 100–150 ha) on a 'learning by doing' basis during the capacity-building phase. The Trust has a specialised library containing 2,500 items which are used by its head office and six regional offices, as well as NGOs, research students and individuals interested in watershed management. Its proposed future activities include: the exploration of farm-based and other income-generating opportunities to take advantage of the additional resources created by watershed development; and the provision of extension advice on environmentally sustainable and economically viable dryland farming systems.

Procedures for Involving Stakeholders and Preparing Watershed-Development Plans

Decision-taking and action at the village level involve a combination of traditional authorities and new agencies. The *gram sabha*—the gathering of all those within a village boundary who have voting rights—has traditionally taken decisions on matters of importance facing the village. In many areas, it has recently been subject to party-political pressures. Nevertheless, its role is to consider, and where appropriate approve, the watershed development plan, and nominate a village watershed committee. The programme guidelines urge that the village watershed committee consist of representatives of all social groups and hamlets or other geographical subdivisions in the village, and at least 30 per cent of its members should be women.

Local-level planning is participatory, involving all registered owners of land in each watershed in the development of detailed action plans. In this way, local knowledge is brought in. However, technical teams from the Watershed Organisation Trust and the participating NGOs conduct the detailed surveys and land-use planning together with the watershed committee. In this way, the intention is to draw local knowledge and preferences into a technically sound plan.

Box 8.5 summarises the criteria used in the selection of watersheds and of participating villages and NGOs. Technical issues in the design and implementation of watershed programmes include:

- the need to cover the full area from ridge to valley, including private land and that under the Revenue and Forest Departments; any inclination by villagers to treat the lower slopes first must be resisted;
- priority to be given to soil conservation and biomass development first, and then to water-harvesting measures. Pressure often comes from farmers wishing to enhance their irrigation resources by constructing check-dams on streams. As well as being expensive, these are potentially inequitable. The overriding priority is to enhance percolation over the whole micro-watershed so that it acts as a large underground reservoir. In this way, positive distributional impact may be achieved insofar as underground flows can reach the mid-slopes some two months ahead of the lower slopes, thereby providing additional water to the (generally) lower income farmers located higher up the slope;
- the Maharashtra Department of Forests has to be involved in the planning of physical measures on land it owns, under the provisions of the government's scheme for 'forest management through

involvement of rural people' (1992)—part of the national family of Joint Forest Management agreements. Grants are available under the IGWDP for such work, and for work on any additional areas that the Department of Forestry is requested by the people to manage. Under the Maharashtra government's scheme, the setting up of a 'forest protection committee' is essential;

• the programme's innovative use of 'net area planning': in practice, this is a substantive attempt to demystify land-use planning and make the plans produced accessible to NGOs and villages. It is based not on contour maps and fixed norms regarding the type and frequency of watershed-development intervention, but on detailed assessment of the characteristics of individually numbered plots and the identification, jointly with farmers, of appropriate interventions (Box 8.6).

Envisaged Expansion Pathways

The expansion path is twofold. First, 'nodes' of approximately 1000 ha of watershed are used as a central demonstration which neighbouring villages come to see, and as a potential training area once new villages form a village watershed committee. Some village watershed committees have already begun to register themselves as NGOs, and so obtain the benefit of the funding support available for NGOs whilst at the same time serving as a vehicle for a type of farmer-to-farmer extension.

Second, the intention is that the essential features of the 'Maharashtra model' be replicated as it spreads to other states. These include: a cabinet resolution and various departmental orders analogous to those passed in Maharashtra; the role of NABARD in disbursing funds for agreed proposals; the role of NGOs in supporting community-based organisations, and of the Watershed Organisation Trust in supporting both, the commitments made by villagers, and the fusion of local knowledge and technical norms in the 'net area' planning approach. Officials from other states (e.g., Gujarat, Andhra Pradesh) have come to observe the approach and are expected to take a 'franchise' on it, allowing it to remain the intellectual property of the IGWDP.

Organisations and Issues at Village Level

Participating villages are required to establish both a village watershed committee and, wherever applicable, a forest protection committee. Land owned by the Department of Forestry falls within the watershed, and so it might appear that there should logically be only one committee. However, Joint Forest Management agreements under the Maharashtra government specify that the Department of Forestry has to be represented by two officers on all committees concerned with the management of resources on department land. Since it would be inappropriate for department officers to be represented on the village watershed committee, a forest protection committee has to be established. A further factor is that Joint Forest Management agreements under which forest protection committees are to be established, require that these be tripartite between the Department of Forestry, the villagers, and the supporting NGO. By contrast, NGOs are not required to be represented on the village watershed committee beyond the initial period.

According to a Maharashtra government resolution of 16 March 1992, NGOs may support the forest protection committee in implementing the government scheme, but will not be eligible for any benefits. The forest protection committee will be responsible for:

- afforestation of denuded areas of Department of Forestry land;
- protection and maintenance of the forests;
- appointing an executive committee to prepare details of the scheme and its implementation, but all policy matters have to be finalised in the full forest protection committee;
- managing access to the benefits of the forest in ways compatible with Maharashtra government norms (these currently provide for 50 per cent of the eventual harvest of timber, access to harvested timber at concessional rates, plus free access to specified non-timber forest products in year 10 onwards of the life of the plantation).

The resolution sees support from the village *panchayat* as essential, and, with the encouragement of the divisional forest officer, the *panchayat* should arrange elections to the forest protection committee and to its executive committee.

The executive committee is responsible for determining policy for the protection of forests, prohibiting encroachment, helping the Department of Forestry to bring action against transgressors, and helping the department to arrange distribution of produce according to set norms. The department can dissolve the forest protection committee (with very limited right of appeal) if it feels it is doing its job inadequately.

Negotiations between the programme and the department over the implementation of JFM proved to be an arduous process: starting with the Maharashtra government resolution of 16 March 1992, correspondence with the programme continued to July 1996 before broadly satisfactory arrangements were agreed.

Conclusions

Micro-watershed rehabilitation in semi-arid India not only reverses environmental degradation; largely through improved re-charge of groundwater, it permits a quantum shift in sustainable agricultural productivity in the lower slopes of watersheds. Justifiably, it has attracted major funding from government and donors. Yet approaches to watershed planning and implementation which are both participatory and easily replicable have remained elusive: most exhibit one or other of these characteristics, but not both. The experience reported here is still in its early stages, and will need to be adapted to certain variations in baseline conditions, such as the continuing prevalence of pastoral livestock in some drier areas. Also, it is more structured and directive than some NGOs (especially the larger, well-established ones) would wish. Nevertheless, it represents a significant step in the search for participatory but rapidly replicable approaches to micro-watershed rehabilitation.

EXTRACT 8.5
SCALING UP PARTICIPATORY APPROACHES:
EVIDENCE FROM A MAJOR FIELD SURVEY[14]

SHASHI KOLAVALLI[15]

Social Organisation

The extent of efforts devoted to and the approach taken to social organisation varied substantially across the projects. The efforts going into social organisation were substantially higher in bilaterally supported and NGO-implemented projects. Bilaterally supported projects employed NGOs particularly for organising the farmers. NGOs also devoted substantial efforts to organising farmers in projects they implement. The cost of social organisation in some of the bilaterally supported projects in which the NGOs are employed for social organisation ranged from Rs 500 to Rs 1000 per hectare.

In the projects implemented by the government, including those funded by multilateral sources, no special resources were devoted to social organisation. Social organisation was the responsibility of department staff. Social organisation in these projects involved identification

---

[14] This paper reports on aspects of the survey discussed by Kerr et al. (Extract 1.1)
[15] PO Box 429A, Basavanagudi, Banglore 560004, India.

of *mitra kisans* and *gopals* in NWDPRA projects, and the establishment of watershed level committees in all the projects.

The outcome of social organisation was weak in projects implemented by the government, outcomes being judged on the basis of capability to manage community assets. The effectiveness of these committees is their ability to devise rules and enforce them while keeping the level of conflict low (Kolavalli 1998a). The committees were not effective in six of the nine government-supported projects, and in two of the three projects supported by multilateral sources. One of the reasons for this could be the relatively unattractive returns from pasture development in Rajasthan. In five of the bilateral projects, and two of those implemented by NGOs, the committees seemed to be more effective. The effectiveness tended to be higher where they were managing activities that offered individual benefits.

Approaches

The approach to social organisation taken in the sample projects falls into three broad categories: building-block, direct, and leadership-oriented (Table 8.3). The 'building-block' approach recognises the difficulty in working with the community as a whole and the potential for ignoring the weaker sections in attempting to organise at the community level. Initially, they work with a few individuals to initiate self-help groups. Individuals in such groups work with others who are socio-economically similar to them or with whom they can identify. In small groups, the individuals learn that they can help themselves by working together. More importantly, they learn to work together, to develop rules of working together, and to enforce those rules to sustain group activities. This understanding of how groups work, helps them in working together at the community level, where rule enforcement may be more difficult. Making a landlord pay a fine for having grazed his animals in the com-

Table 8.3 Characteristics of Various Approaches to Social Organisation

Approach	Resource requirement	Probability of achieving sustainability	Need for leadership
Building-block	High	High	Low
Direct	Medium	Low	Medium
Leadership-oriented	Low	High	High

mon pasture is more difficult than making a neighbour pay a fine for defaulting on a payment to the group. The confidence of having managed something similar, and also possibly greater awareness of their own rights, makes those experienced in working in small groups more successful in working at the community level. This approach to social organisation, which may take from 6 to 18 months, is adopted by NGOs in projects they implement, and in projects funded by bilateral sources.

The 'direct' approach focuses on building on existing institutions such as village *panchayats* or youth clubs. Some agents may be employed to work with the community. Examples of such agents are 'link couples' in the Danida projects, and *mitra kisans* in NWDPRA. A committee is selected (or elected) by a gathering of all villagers. In projects where greater attention is given to having adequate representation for different factions, the selection or election may be delayed until the organisers feel that various factions will participate in the process. In some government projects, selections may take place in the first meeting held in the village.

Both approaches contrast with the means by which social organisation has taken place in the Ralegaon Sidhi watershed in Maharashtra. The approach adopted here is individual-based. It is 'leadership-oriented', in that the moral authority of the leader has played an important role in community organisation. The building-block approach does not require leaders who can exercise moral authority over the community. On the other hand, it can help in developing new leadership and challenging existing power relations.

In reality, the approaches used are not as clear-cut as they are stated here. A combination of approaches is used, depending on the circumstances. The *leadership-oriented* approach is not replicable, as it is constrained by the availability of leaders who can exercise moral authority in their communities and are willing to undertake such tasks. The resource requirements for this approach are low, as the leaders and the members of the community absorb the organisation costs. The *building-block* approach requires considerable resources. External agents need to interact with the communities and groups within communities for extended periods. One agent may be able to work with two or three committees at the most. The probability of achieving the desired results are high. Most importantly, this approach does not depend on existing leadership. The *direct* approach is not as demanding of resources and leadership, but it also has low probability of leading to sustainable results. Again, it depends on the type of prevailing leadership. The direct approach can be very successful in the presence of good leaders.

Required Level of Organisation

While social organisation is generally recognised as a prerequisite for sustainable development, there is less agreement as to how much is needed. The NGOs may seek empowerment of communities as their objective. Government staff, on the other hand, may feel that a committee of people, either elected or selected by the *gram sabha*, is adequate. A simple illustration should clarify what community effort entails.

The communities may be presumed to comprise of socio-economically disparate factions. The interests of various factions may conflict. For example, nomads in a particular village may wish to have grazing access to all the village lands, including common property, throughout the year, while larger farmers who produce their own fodder may be more willing to restrict open grazing. Differences in interests may arise from differences in occupation, landholding and the type and location of holdings. People may also have differential power in influencing what happens in their communities because of socio-economic disparities.

The level of social organisation to be achieved could be pegged in terms of the capability of the community to undertake various tasks. Relatively easy are activities that a group of individuals within the community may undertake unilaterally. These activities may benefit the rest of the community, but do not require their participation. Examples are the initiation of a cooperative marketing society and the installation of a street light.

More difficult activities are those which require the participation of all the members of a community. Again, here the level of difficulty depends on the proposed activity. Activities that potentially benefit all are easier: examples are temple renovation and the building of a village assembly-place. The major difficulty faced by those who undertake such activities is making everyone contribute.

Still more difficult are endeavours that impose costs, possibly differential, on everyone. An example is the decision to develop the village pasture by preventing open grazing. The people who bear the costs of such action are those who depend on common pasture for grazing their animals. They could be the poorest who do not produce fodder on their own fields. Obtaining consensus on such an activity takes greater effort. Generally the more people that need to be involved and the greater the conflicts in interest, the more difficult the collective effort will be.

Even more difficult are situations in which group activities may involve evicting those who have encroached on common lands, or getting members to agree to give the landless in the village the rights to irrigation from a new system. Some of these actions may challenge the prevailing power relations. The level of capability required would be far higher than in the earlier cases.

Many watershed projects begin with the most difficult activities. Pasture development, for example, could be a contentious issue in the village if some of the common lands have been encroached on. It is unreasonable to expect communities to achieve the level of capability observed in some of the more successful watershed projects. What may be achieved could be a 'functional' level of social organisation (Farrington and Thiele 1998). The basic requirements of such a community organisation could be: opportunities for various factions to influence community decisions; ability to maintain common activities chosen by them; and nascent capability of being able to function as a community.

Programme Design

An essential aspect of participation is being able to influence the direction of whatever one is participating in. Farmers are rarely consulted in implementing watershed programmes (Vaidhyanathan 1991:14). Participation often is interpreted to mean getting the consent of farmers to something that has already been determined. Underlying this approach is the assumption that they may not know what is best for them, or that they may choose only activities which benefit them immediately and leave out treatments which bring environmental benefits in the longer run.

In nearly all the projects in this survey (except the two managed by the NGOs), there was considerable gap between what farmers wanted and what was done in the project. Most programmes emphasised the development of common lands and treatments upstream to reduce soil movement. Farmers, on the other hand, want to conserve and harvest water. They do not expect significant benefits from *in situ* moisture conservation in lands upstream. They prefer to harvest water in the drainage line so that it can be used directly for irrigation or to replenish groundwater. They are more interested in water conservation than soil conservation, although water conservation does lead to soil conservation. They prefer to strengthen their field bunds to retain topsoil within the fields, rather than build contour bunds which use up land.

There are costs of not consulting with the communities. The first is the waste of resources on certain technologies that are implemented unilaterally. Contour bunds and vegetative hedges are a prime example. They are included among treatments under all conditions, and farmers consistently plough them under unless they are on the existing field boundaries. Similarly, common lands that are developed are not maintained. Another cost is that by not consulting farmers we may be losing benefits from traditional low-cost practices. Farmers do have traditional practices for soil and water conservation (Kerr et al. 1996). It may be more important to adopt technologies acceptable to farmers than to select them on technical performance alone (Adolph and Turton 1998).

Giving communities the opportunity to design a watershed programme does not undermine its objectives. Farmers' preferences are not totally inconsistent with programme objectives. They understand and appreciate a number of issues central to watershed development. They value *in situ* moisture conservation, but may differ on how it should be achieved. They recognise the movement of soil and the damage caused by soil losses, but disagree as to how it should be prevented. They prefer to hold the soil within their fields, while scientists may recommend that soil movement should be prevented even within fields. They may not approve of contour bunds because of reasons such as loss of a land, but they approve of large field bunds. They appreciate the benefits from drainage-line treatments. They are increasingly recognising the potential for tree cultivation and orchards under dry conditions. Farmers on the whole prefer treatments which increase productivity immediately (Fernandez 1993). A package of treatments can be made more acceptable by sequencing it to give some immediate benefits.

The prospects of participating in project planning may significantly influence participation in community activities. Social organisation may be easier if people expect to be consulted. If they exercise 'control' over a project, they are likely to develop a sense of ownership for it. Though this is a critical aspect of participation and has considerable bearing on social organisation and people's willingness to contribute to costs, it tends to be the most neglected aspect of watershed development. However, a critical requirement for giving communities the opportunity to plan activities is a level of social organisation that enables various factions within the community to influence community decisions.

Scaling up

Examining the reasons for variation in the level of participation in different programmes helps us in identifying factors that determine the level of effort that goes into social organisation (Table 8.4). All the programmes in the country emphasise participation in some way or the other. Yet the actual levels of participation vary considerably. It is most

Table 8.4 Factors Associated with Level of Effort Going into Social Organisation

Project type	Level of effort	Reasons
NWDPRA, World Bank	Low	• Inadequate allocation of resources • Insufficient pressures on the staff
SDC, Danida, NGO, IGWDP	High	• Resources commitment to social organisation • Involvement of NGOs committed to participatory approaches • Close monitoring in a small number of projects • Investments in training in participatory methodologies • Pressures from donors
Min of Rural Areas & Employ-ment	Medium	• Some resources available for social organisation • Institutional structure demanded requires some effort • NGOs committed to participation may be involved

evident in the effort that has gone into social organisation and institutional capacity-building. The differences are clear when the programmes are grouped by the sources of their funds.

Most efforts to organise farmers were made in programmes supported by bilateral sources such as Danida and SDC, and in the two projects implemented by NGOs. All of them devoted resources exclusively to social organisation. Social organisation was done by NGOs committed to and experienced in participatory approaches. There were strong pressures from the donors, as the projects were closely monitored by staff who have demonstrated their commitment to participatory approaches.

The least effort to organise farmers is made in projects implemented by the government, including those supported by multilateral donors. Resources are not devoted exclusively for social organisation. The staff organising farmers may have limited experience (and, more importantly, limited interest) in working with farmers. There are inadequate pressures from donors or superior officers to increase participation. Nationwide implementation of these projects makes monitoring costly.

In summary, the features distinguishing programmes which are participatory from those which are not include:

- the extent of resources devoted specifically for social organisation;
- the level of commitment to participation;
- the extent of monitoring; and
- pressures from the donors or superiors.

Information problem   Ensuring that staff down the line achieve participation is particularly difficult because of the nature of participation. It cannot be easily seen or measured. This creates an 'agency problem'. Those who want participation to take place cannot get adequate information to determine whether it has in fact taken place. Participation is not just an outcome; it is also a process. Though the outcome and process may be described in detail, the information costs of determining whether it has occurred are high. Only the potential participants and those organising them have full information on the outcomes. For participation to occur, either those organising it must want to achieve true participation, or those who are being organised should want to participate and also have the opportunity to influence the efforts of those organising them. This means that, in the absence of close monitoring to determine whether participatory methodologies are being adopted by the project staff, participation will take place only if the staff want it, or if local people can force them to make the process participatory.

Perhaps, neither of these conditions is adequately met in nation-wide programmes such as NWDPRA and those of the Ministry of Rural Areas and Employment. The new guidelines of the ministry specify in fair detail the kind of institutional arrangements that are required. They indicate the kind of committees that that are to be established and decision-making processes to be followed. What the guidelines specify are intermediate outcomes or what we may call 'structure' to support participation. The quality of these intermediate outcomes cannot be ascertained. The requirement that committees be established with proportional representation is an example. It does not really ensure that all factions are represented as intended. A self-help group can be registered within a day, or a staff member can work to establish one over six months. Unscrupulous persons can meet the 'requirements of participation' without making the process participatory. How to make staff committed to participatory approaches is the major challenge in scaling up.

Successful programmes overcome these problems by hiring appropriate staff and introducing processes that offer strong incentives. Projects are closely monitored. As there are few organisations or staff committed to participation, and monitoring is costly, the focus must shift to making the bureaucracy more sensitive to participation and increasing the role of beneficiaries in implementing and monitoring projects.

Transforming the bureaucracy It is clear that strategies which depend on NGOs which are committed to participatory approaches cannot easily be scaled up. There are only a limited number of them. Employing NGOs to work with the bureaucracy in organising farmers can only be a short-term measure designed to improve the capability of the bureaucracy to undertake social organisation. The bureaucracy needs to be sympathetic to farmer participation for it even to work with the NGOs. But the bureaucracy is not capable of achieving the objectives of recent policies on participation, as staff have not changed their perceptions of themselves from that of 'experts' to 'service providers'; such a change is necessary for them to be able to do bottom-up planning (Fernandez 1993: 23, GoI and Danida 1996: 50). More importantly, they are not interested in participation, but feel threatened by it (Fernandez 1993: 68). Ultimately, the bureaucracy itself will have to be geared up to develop watersheds though participatory approaches if scaling up is to become a reality. The lack of incentives to work with communities seems to be a more binding constraint than the lack of capability.

The challenge is how to build the internal capacity of bureaucracy to work with participatory approaches without fundamental changes (Thompson 1995: 1522). Training alone may not be able to make bureaucratic organisations into learning-oriented, people-centred organisations. Changes in policy alone will not result in attitude changes. The manner in which NWDPRA and the Ministry of Rural Areas and Employment projects are implemented, despite their guidelines, is a clear indication that policy changes are not adequate to influence approaches. What is needed is a 'learning process that promotes and develops new methodologies and changes the prevailing attitudes, behaviour, skills and norms and procedures within the bureaucracy' (Thompson 1995: 1523). People have to discover for themselves that participation is beneficial. Providing learning opportunities will require fundamental changes in the bureaucracy. One of the key aspects of this change should be in how work is measured, because the targets that the bureaucracy works with do not relate much to participation (Thompson 1995: 1529).

Need for learning Participation is about people being able to influence the direction and outcome of activities affecting them. There cannot be participatory approaches without room for learning. Making learning feasible for participants may require the adoption of a long-term strategy, a sequencing of activities such that consequences of actions taken earlier become the basis for future action and further learning. Learning is required at all levels. Communities need to learn, and so do organisations implementing projects. Strangely, there is usually no room for participation even in organisations that are to employ participatory approaches and promote participation.

Participatory approaches cannot be effective until there are changes in attitudes—changes which are best brought about through learning. The kind of learning required is 'double loop' in which participants evaluate not only the existing processes but step outside them to ask whether the existing way is the right way to do things (Liebenstein and Maital 1994: 257). Learning entails a continuous process of discovery, in which people can examine why they are not able to do what they want to do, identify ways of improving their work by questioning the fundamental approaches to it, and adopt more promising methods.

The bureaucracies do not provide such flexibility in working. The tendency is to increase controls in order to improve effectiveness leading to what Argyris and Schon (1978: 159) refer to as a 'stockpiling' of increasingly ineffective unilateral controls. These controls may even reduce effectiveness. Lower-level staff developing watersheds—even at the state level—are not expected to think. Guidelines are prepared at the centre as to how precisely the programmes are to be implemented. These are prepared often on the recommendation of outside experts, thus outsourcing thinking. It is remarkable the extent to which guidelines drawn up in Delhi or Jaipur can limit the implementers and farmers from making sensible decisions.

Changing the thinking is the most critical aspect of bringing about change in working. Organisations of the future have to abandon planning, organising and controlling, for vision, values and mental models (Senge and Sterman 1992: 354). The emphasis will have to shift from increasing controls alone to achieving results through making people want to achieve the desired results. Values and vision change slowly, but they require consistent effort. There is need for decentralised systems, in which the person at the end can be trusted to do the right thing.

Features of a scaled-up system   An institutional structure that provides incentives to use participatory methods at all levels, combined with ways to improve capability wherever required, will enable decentralised watershed development. The incentives could be internal (coming from attitudinal changes), or external (driven by organisational pressures). Attitudinal changes are facilitated by providing learning opportunities.

Behavioural Assumptions

The elements of an improved institutional structure can be developed on the basis of assumptions about the behaviour of the various parties involved. Some of these assumptions relate to their beliefs.

Farmers The following assumptions apply to farmers:

- Farmers are likely to work together with others only if the collective effort is likely to bring them significant benefits in relation to costs, including those of interaction.
- Farmers are likely to be more enthusiastic about working together to develop common properties that are likely to give them individual benefits than other properties that produce collective goods. For example, they may be more willing to work together to maintain a check-dam which recharges their wells than a village plantation, the benefits from which go to the village funds.
- Farmers prefer strategies that bring them immediate returns. They may prefer water-harvesting structures that increase irrigation to contour bunds on their fields.
- There is need to 'encourage' farmers to choose measures that are environmentally beneficial.
- Farmers can be persuaded to adopt less beneficial measures, providing they are accompanied by measures that give immediate productivity benefits.
- Sharing of costs is a reflection of farmers having recognised the value of a treatment.
- The overall contribution from farmers is likely to be higher if farmers have chosen the package of treatments.

Department staff The following assumptions apply to department staff:

- Staff will resist involving farmers in planning and implementation because it undermines their position and reduces their control.
- The majority do not believe that communities have knowledge useful in improving the management of land and water resources.
- Most feel that farmer participation means 'educating' them to get their consent to what is proposed, and also to get them to maintain the assets created.
- Staff believe that organising farmers' participation is the responsibility of NGOs. It is their duty to obtain consent to plans prepared for farmers. Implementation can be independent of this activity.

NGOs Several assumptions apply to NGOs:

- They believe that institutional development is a long-term process, and it is not complete until there is empowerment.

- Watershed-development programmes should take care of the prevailing inequities in rural communities.
- NGOs believe that the outputs of their work cannot be quantified and should not be subject to any time frame.

Improved Institutional Environment

An improved institutional structure needs to address farmer concerns regarding collective work, their willingness to contribute to various activities, and the bureaucracy's reluctance to work with farmers (for status reasons and because of its beliefs regarding the role farmers can play in watershed rehabilitation).

The essential features of an institutional structure that offers the bureaucracy incentives to work with farmers, improve its capability to work with farmers and takes advantage of the communities' willingness to pay for investments in land and water management may include:

- commitment of resources to social organisation and recognition for work with communities;
- training grants to private and public organisations;
- social organisation as a precondition of support to watershed activities;
- transparent processes and dissemination of information;
- demand for commitment from the communities to contribute;
- substantial freedom for communities to decide what they can do;
- implementation under the control of the community;
- review and evaluation which involve beneficiaries and is facilitated by external agents; and
- availability of further funds made subject to successful implementation of prior stages.

It is necessary to recognise that social organisation cannot be rushed. If it is to be done by the staff of government departments, it is necessary to provide them the resources, and also corresponding changes need to be made in how their work is assessed. Adequate resources need to be made available, particularly for travel. Making grants for social organisation available to both government staff and NGOs will alleviate the resource constraints of the government staff.

To improve its capability for working with communities, the government needs to be able to buy-in training from project funds. Established NGOs with considerable experience in using participating methodologies and working with communities, who may be otherwise reluctant to work with the government, can be given grants to offer training to staff from government and non-government organisations. Similarly, NGOs or communities should be able to buy technical expertise from government staff or private companies.

Collective development of the plan jointly with social organisations or communities should be a pre-condition for making funds available for watershed development. But how do we ensure that the plans that come up for funding have been prepared through people's participation? It is here that transparent processes are likely to be helpful. Information on the availability of funds, the purpose for which they are being made available, and ways communities can access that information, should be made widely available. In the long run, it is the communities that have to exercise this control. The NGO or private organisation which is given the responsibility of offering training should also have the responsibility of disseminating information on the project, so that the general population is better aware of what is transpiring in its own communities.

The overall plans prepared by the communities, along with their commitment to contribute, can be the basis for further funding. Willingness to contribute could be one indicator of social organisation having taken place. But using willingness alone could bias project financing towards better-off areas and to treatments that bring more immediate benefits.

Evaluation and reviews are to be conducted by those implementing the projects and the members of the community, with the assistance of an external agent. Such processes would yield two benefits. Those who have been involved get an opportunity to examine what they did, and with the help of the communities identify ways of doing better. The communities have an opportunity to confirm whether the projects have been implemented the way they should, and what the impacts have been.

There is no need for outside experts to conduct evaluations. The benefits of watershed rehabilitation are evident to everyone. Evaluations could focus on what works were done, whether they were done as they should have been, whether the whole community was involved in deciding what was to be done, and what the benefits have been, including increase in irrigation, yields, availability of fodder and so on. These evaluations can be facilitated by outsiders, who can ensure adequate participation of the community and also document the results.

Under an improved institutional environment, the overall package would have components focusing on capability and incentive concerns. Department staff are expected to become service providers. They will have opportunities to improve their ability to work with communities. They 'sell' their technical expertise by taking on projects to organise communities and to help them develop plans. Communities, on the other hand, would have opportunities to obtain funds for watershed-related activities that they value. As emphasis will be placed on their contributions, watersheds with higher potential for development are likely to receive priority. A larger role would be given to members of communities in evaluating programmes, by giving them access to information and other processes that make government staff and community organisations more accountable to members of the communities

Making funds available to district and state administration only if the projects are implemented with community participation is likely to be beneficial. Fiscal measures may counter the bureaucracy's aversion to transparency and to working with people. However, this is contingent on district and state administrations depending on the resources of watershed programmes. Reforms in administering watershed programmes cannot be independent of overall efforts to reform the bureaucracy.

Institutional experiments are needed within the bureaucracy. Pilot projects often focus only on the technology, and the only institutional concession that the bureaucracy makes is 'coordination' of various departments to implement them. There is need for institutional experimentation to give interested staff flexibility. The experience from these pilot projects can be the basis for broader bureaucratic reforms.

EXTRACT 8.6
DEVELOPING VILLAGE FUNDS TO SUSTAIN WATERSHED MANAGEMENT IN THE DOON VALLEY PROJECT, UTTAR PRADESH[16]

S. V. SHARMA[17] *AND K. J. VIRGO*[18]

The Doon Valley Integrated Watershed Management Project provides an example in which a major Government of Uttar Pradesh organisation has adopted the participatory methodology. With joint funding from the European Union, the project has been implementing a watershed management programme in the Doon Valley over a nine-year period, since 1993. The prime objectives are to involve the communities, especially women, fully in the management of their environment, and to

---

[16] Source: Sharma and Virgo (1998).

[17] Deputy Project Director, Watershed Management Directorate, Dehradun, India.

[18] WS Atkins International, Girton, Cambridge CB3 0VA, UK.

improve their quality of life. The emphasis is on sustainable, long-term maintenance of the assets created, and the improvements made in the use of common-property resources.

Project Area

The Doon Valley occupies 1850 square km, bounded by the Lesser Himalaya outer ridge to the northeast and the Shiwalik Hills to the southwest. The area includes four development blocks in Dehradun district.

The human population is ethnically diverse and has shown a significant increase over recent years. Land use is dominated by forest and cultivated areas (Dangroup 1990).

Subsistence farming, based on cereal production, dairy cattle and exploitation of forest biomass, predominates in the hills; some small-scale cash cropping is practised on the lower slopes, and off-season vegetables are produced in some more accessible hill villages. Some 75 per cent of holdings are smaller than 1 ha. Cash incomes from farming are low, and most rural communities depend on outside subsidies and remittances from migrant family members. Villages in the hills are widely dispersed, often with several separate caste-based hamlets, and are poorly accessible.

The project objectives envisaged a participatory approach and an emphasis on sustainability. Project activities comprise social forestry, agriculture, livestock, horticulture, minor irrigation and energy conservation, with 10 per cent of the budget reserved for cross-cutting community participation activities. Further details are given by Thapliyal et al. (1994) and Datta and Virgo (in press 1998).

General Principles

To concentrate activities and improve their impact, 42 micro-watersheds, and the individual villages within them, were prioritised on physiographic and socio-economic parameters. The top-priority villages within each micro-watershed were selected for treatment.

Project interventions were undertaken on a three-year rolling programme in each village, in order of priority. Project staff and villagers prepared village micro-plans using participatory appraisal-based techniques. Interaction with village women was strengthened by recruiting female 'motivators' onto the project team and training village women as para-professionals.

The activities emanating from these micro-plans are implemented with the villagers over the three-year period, with the aim that they themselves should be able to maintain them in subsequent years. The project is currently active in some 200 villages, 76 of which are currently at the micro-planning stage.

A fundamental part of the strategy has been to overcome the prevalent dependency syndrome, under which villagers have become conditioned to expecting subsidised inputs from government programmes, and to inculcate a sense of local ownership and self-reliance. The basic process of participatory planning and implementation has encouraged this. Important subsidiary factors for sustainability have been recognised as:

* local institutional development (group formation and training);
* reciprocal contributions by beneficiaries (in cash, kind or labour);
* encouraging formation and use of village-level funds to sustain the assets created and to enable villagers to generate income.

This Extract focuses principally on the formation of groups and village-level funds, especially in terms of the use of funds for sustaining development. The overall methods are summarised below. This is followed by an account of experiences in Nahar village, which serves as a case study. The pre-conditions for success are analysed and future policies for scaling up are then discussed.

Group Formation and Funds

During the planning process, special focus is given by project staff to motivating the communities and villagers are motivated to organise themselves and to form their own association, such as '*gaon* [village] resource-management associations' and subsidiary user groups or self-help groups. These associations and groups are then involved with the subsequent implementation of project activities identified during micro-planning. Special focus is given by the project women motivators to motivating the village women.

Each household of the village, with one male and one female representative, is a member of the *gaon* association. The association has an eleven-member executive body and four office-bearers (president, secretary, vice-president, treasurer), of whom 50 per cent are female and a proportion is reserved for scheduled caste members. The association has its own revolving fund, to which contributions are made by beneficiaries of project activities. For example the recipient of a biogas plant, costing about Rs 14,000, contributes Rs 2000 (about 15 per cent) to the fund. The level of contribution varies between villages, and concessions are often made to accommodate poorer groups. The associations manage the revolving funds and accounts; funds are held in a bank account, for which two or three of the office-bearers are joint signatories. The funds were expected to provide the villagers with the resources necessary for sustainable development and future management of common property resources after the end of the project.

Initially, the management of the revolving fund was a sensitive issue. The villagers were not ready to deposit their contributions because they did not believe that their money would be safe in the joint account: they feared that the office-bearers could misuse the money. Similarly, many project staff had their own doubts about the proper use of the funds, and feared that they themselves could be held responsible for this. Continuous meetings and discussions between villagers and staff were needed to convince both sides before joint accounts could be opened. By contrast, there was greater trust within the self-help groups, whose members confidently and regularly deposited agreed amounts into their common-fund bank accounts. The self-help groups were established for special common-interest activities, related mainly to income-generation, and thus tended to be more cohesive and homogeneous than groups covering community-wide activities.

In the early stages of the project it was envisaged that the revolving funds would be used only for the purposes of maintaining or managing common-property resources, and that their use would commence only after the project withdrew at the end of three years. The rationale was that the three years would be needed to develop understanding between the villagers, so as to ensure proper use of the funds. However, as the full costs of maintenance of physical assets would not arise until after the project withdrew, it was decided that it would be preferable to encourage the villagers to start using the funds while the project was still active in the village. This would provide opportunities for project staff to guide villagers in case of problems, and to help to ensure proper fund use; this in turn would engender the villagers' confidence in using the funds for the whole community and thus encourage regular contributions by project beneficiaries. The most practical approach was therefore to start loaning during the implementation period, to demonstrate to villagers the potential benefits of using the funds for general development activities.

This idea was floated amongst the villagers but their response was very discouraging. The association members and some other villagers still had misapprehensions: once the loan was granted to a person, what would be the guarantee that he or she would return it? Villagers were

motivated and encouraged to think over the possibilities and to formulate their own rules and regulations for loaning.

Eventually the idea of loaning caught the imagination of most of the
associations: they started thinking seriously about the modes of payment and repayment, rules and regulations for selecting borrowers, rates
of interest, etc. Several associations have now started loaning, and repayments have been received, with interest. Others have shown willingness to start the process.

Case Study: Nahar Village

The story of Nahar village is of particular interest. The total population
of 250 people includes 45 households; nearly half are under 6 years of
age, and literacy levels among women are low compared to men.
Landholdings are small, with some 85 per cent of households having
less than 1.2 ha.

Mixed farming is the main source of livelihood for the villagers. The
project motivated the villagers to increase their productivity by providing mini-kits of improved seeds and balanced fertilisers (for which recipients contribute to the revolving fund). For fuel wood and most fodder, villagers are dependent on forest areas, which are at a distance of 1–
3 km. The project aimed to reduce pressure on these forests by introducing biogas plants, encouraging stall-feeding of livestock, fodder-tree
planting and improving utilisation and conservation of agricultural by-
products.

Gaon Association and Revolving-Fund Formation

Project micro-planning activities commenced in 1995/96, two years after the adjacent village of Koti. Consequently, the villagers already knew
all about the project, including its methodology and objectives.

During the initial stages, some influential persons in the village tried
to manipulate the plans in their favour. They started dictating terms to
the *gaon* association office-bearers, resulting in reluctance by the poorer
members to contribute to the revolving fund. For nearly six months, no
monthly meeting of the *gaon* association was held. The villagers were
still not fully aware of the process, nor of the inputs being provided by
the project. Consequently, project staff thought it proper to intervene,
and a number of discussions were instigated.

At the behest of project staff, the *gaon* association office-bearers were
encouraged to fix a date for a monthly meeting and to call the meetings
regularly. Initially they showed no interest and were reluctant to call the

meeting. With further continuous motivation, and even pressure by project staff, the first meeting was called. This was attended by a large number of villagers, as well as by project staff. Matters were discussed at length, and the staff tried to convince the villagers of the potential benefits of the revolving fund. They persuaded them that monthly meetings could be effective in removing doubts about the use and misuse of the funds. During the meeting itself, the date and time of the next month's meeting was decided and announced.

The first four monthly meetings were attended regularly by project staff, who tried to persuade the villagers of the expected benefits of the revolving funds for the sustainable development of the village. Meanwhile, the association office-bearers started pressurising defaulters to deposit their contributions into the funds. At one meeting it was unanimously decided that if, by a certain date, the defaulters did not deposit their contribution, they would have to pay interest at 15 per cent per month on the balance outstanding, and that they would be excluded from any benefits of the project. This ultimatum worked well: recovery was 100 per cent, and subsequent deposits have been made regularly.

After the change in the attitude of the villagers and the association committee members, the project staff encouraged them to initiate loaning, as a means for sustaining and building-up the fund, but the village men were not interested. Meantime, however, members of a women's self-help group (formed through motivation by project staff) were each contributing Rs 10 per month into their own fund. With their accumulated capital of Rs 810, they had already started loaning to their members; interest was being received and loan repayments were taking place. This acted as a catalyst for the other villagers and the *gaon* association office bearers.

Some members of this women's group wanted to start mushroom cultivation. Training was arranged by the project, but to start production they needed Rs 10,000. They approached the project for help. After hectic discussions, it was decided that the self-help group members themselves would arrange for a Rs 5000 loan, and the rest would be borrowed from the *gaon* association revolving fund, for which the project would, initially, act as guarantor. Once these women were convinced, the entire group started putting pressure on the *gaon* association at every meeting. The project staff also sought to convince the association committee and members to provide the loan.

Finally, at an open meeting, the *gaon* association agreed to grant a loan to the women's group at an interest rate of 2 per cent per month. The women's group immediately and efficiently started mushroom production. Loan repayments were made regularly, with interest, out of income generated from selling mushrooms: there was no defaulting. Influenced by this successful repayment record, the *gaon* association members themselves decided to grant three additional loans to different-persons, and developed their own rules for lending (Box 8.7).

Fund accumulation and loaning experience   Over a period of 12 months from agreement on the first loan, a total of 31 loans have been made from the Nahar revolving fund, totalling Rs 54,000. The average size of loan was Rs 1742, with the purchase of buffalo and investment in income-generating activities as the principal purposes of loans. Of particular interest is the Rs 10,000 borrowed by the whole community to purchase chairs for renting out to other villages for marriage parties and social occasions, which has generated a new stream of income for the village. Contributions by project beneficiaries were the main source of revolving funds.

The women's self-help group loans were smaller, averaging Rs 1143, and more diverse. Although livestock purchases remain important, loans were also used for medical treatment, house repairs, marriages and loan repayments. Membership fees constituted the primary source of self-help group funds.

Several lessons can be learned from the use of revolving funds and self-help group funds to date:

Purposes of loans   Although the loans may not, at first sight, appear to be serving the primary objectives of watershed management, the focus on buffalo purchases indicates a trend towards stall-fed animals and tapping the lucrative fresh-milk market. This should reduce grazing pressure on the forest. Many of the villagers have sold their goats, considered to be the most serious agents of forest and environmental destruction, and purchased buffaloes through loans. Moreover, the loaning has generated income through milk sales, mushroom production, knitted sweaters and other enterprises (such as leasing community chairs). This should lead to a more sustainable internal cash economy, meeting the subsidiary objective of improv-

---

Box 8.7   Revolving Fund Rules Set by Nahar Villagers

- Till further decisions are taken, only Rs 10,000 will be used at a one time for loaning.
- 2 per cent per month interest will be charged for loans.
- A member asking for a loan will have to produce two persons as guarantors.
- Loans will be decided at the open monthly meeting of the *gaon* association.

ing the quality of life and reducing the economic pressure for out-
migration.

Project credibility   The success of the funds has increased the credibility
of the project in the eyes of the villagers, who are now more keen to
tackle the immediate watershed-management activities

Repayment record   To date there have been no loan defaulters in Nahar.
Peer-pressure has been effective in ensuring interest and loan repayments. This is in marked contrast to high levels of default on previous
bank loans to the villagers.

Spread of individual loans   There has been a wide spread of loans across
group members. In the women's self-help group 13 of the 27 members
have benefited from loans. The 31 loans from the revolving fund were
allocated to 29 different borrowers, reflecting a wide spread of lending,
in which 26 (58 per cent) of the 45 village families have benefited.

Confidence-building   Some of the inherent mistrust amongst villagers has
been dispelled, as illustrated by the eventual acceptance of the principles of regular saving and loaning, and by the absence of defaulters.

People in Nahar, and in other villages, are now looking to their revolving fund to meet their investment needs rather than expecting subsidies from the project. When the Nahar villagers became dissatisfied
with the performance of their 'improved' buffalo bull (provided by the
project), they sold it and purchased a new one out of *gaon* association
funds, rather than seeking a subsidised replacement from the project.
This trend towards self-help is developing in other villages.

Preconditions for Success

The participatory approach was new to the state-government staff of
the project. Although enthusiastic, they were often doubtful of their
chances of success. Initial training was an essential precondition to overcoming this hesitation: the project provided training in participatory
appraisal-based planning and implementation processes, and arranged
exposure visits to other participatory projects in India and Nepal. Re-
orientation of the villagers is equally important: exposure visits were
arranged for villagers to observe activities in other villages. Village-to-
village exchanges of news of the project significantly increased the re-
ceptivity of villages and facilitated the initial entry by project staff into
second-year and subsequent villages.

Participatory approaches require time, patience and personal commitment, not money. Unfortunately, government systems remain geared
towards meeting financial spending targets: external pressures to spend

budgets can jeopardise the participatory process (Shepherd 1995). Personnel involved in the participatory appraisal processes need to have adequate time for regular interaction and institution-building at the grassroot, village level.

Compared with other villages in Seetla Rao micro-watershed, Nahar villagers possessed a greater degree of inherent entrepreneurship, which favoured the ultimately successful use of their funds. The neighbouring village of Dhalani has yet to start using its revolving funds, even three-and-a-half years after establishment of their *gaon* association.

A prerequisite for success in Nahar was to identify income-generating activities that would catalyse local entrepreneurship. If villagers see direct benefits for themselves, they will support the village organisation and its funds. For this reason, it was important to allow villagers to use their accumulated funds for their own purposes, but at the same time to try to inculcate a sense of moral responsibility for maintaining assets created by the project. Dictating how funds will be used would have destroyed the sense of local ownership.

The Nahar case study clearly demonstrates the catalytic effect of the self-help group, motivated by a desire to obtain a loan for income-generating activities, in persuading the *gaon* association to commence loaning. Subsequently, the Nahar *gaon* association itself has served as an example and stimulus to other groups from adjacent, as well as more remote, villages.

Several other factors which influenced the success of institutional development and fund use in Nahar, and which will have implications for other villages.

A three-year period is often inadequate to develop sufficiently robust institutions, but at the same time there needs to be a defined cut-off date, so that villagers can gear themselves towards self-reliance. Keeping these points in mind, the project adopted a policy of ceasing implementation activities after three years. Thereafter advisory links are maintained with the villagers, especially by the motivators, to provide a post-project 'safety net'. This provides moral support to the nascent village organisations and encourages linkages with other outside agencies.

Villagers require guidance on the options for developing procedures, rules and regulations for using and managing funds, to minimise risks of future pitfalls. However, within these guidelines, *gaon* associations and self-help groups should be allowed to develop their own particular rules and regulations that suit their own conditions. In one village, the *gaon* association set a 4 per cent per month interest rate on loans: to an outsider this appears high, but the villagers see it as low compared with the monthly rate of 10 per cent currently charged by moneylenders.

The considerable mistrust that exists within village communities, especially in financial dealings, must be recognised. This has to be overcome and transparency established before revolving funds can work effectively. Relatively large sums of money have been accumulated in the Nahar revolving fund. Practical training is now required for the office-bearers in bookkeeping, accounting and management, so that they are seen to be able to manage the funds efficiently and transparently, and thereby retain the trust of the association members.

The membership of self-help groups should be limited to manageable numbers. Large groups will inevitably become less cohesive and demand greater management skills. In Nahar the women's self-help group initially comprised 27 members. Once the success of this group became apparent, others sought to join, but the existing members insisted that they should first deposit in the common fund the equivalent of all monthly contributions since the start of the self-help group. This will preclude the poorer members of the community from joining. Consideration is now being given to either encouraging a new group for women from the remaining households, or encouraging the original group to divide into smaller and more manageable interest-groups.

Preconditions for Scaling up

The Doon Valley Project is externally funded, with a finite time scale. Although being implemented by a government agency, the project ultimately has to withdraw from villages. This has stimulated consideration of means for scaling-up the village organisations formed by the project, to ensure sustainability, and for extending the Doon Valley watershed management processes to non-project villages in future.

Scaling up Village Organisations

Through workshops and discussions with villagers, the villagers are now realising that the project has to withdraw and that they will have to fend for themselves in future. A policy currently being evolved is to encourage clustering of villages in 'clusters' of resource-management associations. Establishing clusters can be expected to enhance the mutual support between the *gaon* resource-management associations, facilitate formal links with *panchayati raj* institutions, and engender greater confidence among villagers in seeking outside inputs, after project withdrawal, through line agencies or NGOs.

It will be important to allow such clusters to develop rationally and organically. They should comprise villages that have common interests or socio-economic affinities, rather than be imposed to suit 'artificial', physical watershed boundaries. However, one benefit of their formation would be to focus attention on the inter-dependence of villages on common resources within a micro-watershed. It can be expected that some villages may initially opt out for their own reasons. Moreover, it will be important that the cluster is not perceived as a threat by elected representatives.

As with *gaon* associations, the emphasis of the clusters should be production-orientated. It is expected that *gaon* associations would contribute to a cluster revolving fund, which would support wider entrepreneurial initiatives. These larger bodies would have greater capability and bargaining power in seeking market outlets, sources of training and support from other agencies (such as the Forest Department's Joint Forest Management programme to ensure continuing benefit from their plantations). Similarly, they would have the resources to employ villagers as para-professionals to improve the agricultural production base, support income-generation activities and seek market outlets for cluster produce. Consequently, cluster office-bearers will need training in management, accounting and marketing skills.

Nahar has natural affinities with the adjacent villages of Kotra, Koti and Dhalani. Between them, they have considerable resources in their revolving funds. Negotiations are currently proceeding with the villagers to encourage them to combine as a cluster, which would give them greater institutional strength and favour an integrated approach to the management of natural resources in the upper Seetla Rao micro-watershed. However, until the villagers of Dhalani overcome their internal mistrust and start using their considerable funds, they are unlikely to be responsive to requests for contributions to a cluster fund.

Scaling up the Process

Proposals have been prepared for extending the Doon Valley process to other watersheds in the Uttarakhand Hills (Berry et al. 1997): these are currently under consideration by the state and central governments. These proposals include an integrated, holistic watershed-management approach, combined with establishment of village organisations and revolving funds to promote local income-generation and to finance maintenance of assets created.

A crucial question, however, is the means for implementing such an

extensive programme, which will call for a wide range of multi-disci-
pline skills. The Watershed Management Directorate has the capacity to
coordinate activities and to provide training in participatory processes
and micro-planning in pilot micro-watersheds, but currently does not
have the capacity or mandate to cover implementation in all Hill districts. Logically, line agencies should be drawn in to implement the programme: as existing agencies, their involvement would provide a greater
degree of sustainability. However, pre-requisites for this would be:

- extensive re-orientation training programmes in participatory methods, for the line agency staff; and
- introduction of strong institutional mechanisms to ensure an integrated, area-based approach to watershed management, rather than
  a sectoral approach.

Annex 1
Main features of the New Guidelines[1]

In 1994, the Ministry of Rural Areas and Employment issued new 'Guidelines for Watershed Development' (GoI 1994) in respect of the schemes, projects and programmes within its mandate. Development organisations have put a great deal of effort into understanding and implementing these Guidelines (Turton et al. 1998). At the same time, large variations occur among states and among districts within the same state in interpreting and applying the Guidelines. In view of India's size and the diversity of development planning and implementation over the last 4–5 decades, such variations are perhaps inevitable. At the same time, some features of the Guidelines are basic, and district or state authorities should go beyond them without the approval of the central government. Others are flexible, and can be adapted to meet local requirements. An attempt is made below to identify those features that are considered basic. They are grouped in four categories: administrative, financial, institutional, planning and technical. References are given to the relevant paragraphs in the Guidelines.

ADMINISTRATIVE ARRANGEMENTS

1. District rural development agencies (DRDAs) and *zilla parishads* have overall responsibility for programme planning and implementation in the district (para 29).
2. The DRDA (or *zilla parishad*) appoints a 'watershed-development advisory committee' with multi-source membership of officials and non-officials. This committee advises the DRDA on the selection of project implementing agencies, watershed-development team

[1] This Annex draws on notes prepared by Anil Shah as part of the review by Turton et al. (1998).

members, watershed-development planning, training, community organising, etc. (para 30).

3. The DRDA appoints project implementing agencies, which are responsible for appointment of the watershed development teams, recommending villages for watershed programmes, planning, implementing and reviewing of watershed programmes through village-level organisations, and maintenance of accounts of funds to be spent by the implementing agency and through watershed committees (para 31).

4. A watershed development team has a minimum of 4 members representing relevant disciplines such as agriculture, engineering, life sciences, animal husbandry and social work. The team shall work exclusively and full-time for the watershed programme. The team is to be located close to project villages (para 35).

5. In each village, the watershed association shall be registered under the Societies Registration Act. The association will appoint the watershed committee, which will consist of representatives of user groups, self-help groups, *gram panchayat* and watershed development team (paras 36, 37, 80 and 81).

6. Each watershed committee shall have a secretary, who will be a paid employee of the watershed association and will be responsible for maintaining records and accounts of the watershed programme (para 38).

FINANCIAL PROVISIONS

7. The funds will flow directly from the national and state governments to the DRDA or *zilla parishad*. Depending upon the region, Rs 3000–5000 of funds are allotted per hectare. The average and most common provision is Rs 4000/ha. Each micro-watershed will consist of about 500ha; at the rate of Rs 4000/ha, this means about Rs 200,000 will be available. This should be spent over four years in the following manner:

   - Entry-point activities, 5 per cent;
   - Community organisation, 5 per cent;
   - Training programme, 5 per cent;
   - Administration of project implementing agency and watershed association, 10 per cent;
   - Watershed works, 75 per cent.

   The DRDA or *zilla parishad* will make 25 per cent of the funds available to the implementing agency. It will make the remaining 75 per cent available directly to the watershed committee on the advice of the implementing agency, depending upon the capability of the watershed committee and the progress of implementation (paras 41, 49 and 51).

8. People's participation is to be assured through voluntary donations and contribution in terms of labour, raw materials, cash, etc., for developmental activities as well as for operation and maintenance. The minimum norms prescribed are:
   - 5 per cent for community works;
   - 10 per cent for work on private property. This will be 5 per cent in case of scheduled castes or tribes and persons identified as below the poverty line (para 25).

9. *Maintenance fund*   Against such contributions from the community, an equal amount in value will be withdrawn from the watershed works budget and deposited in a separate fund for the future operations and maintenance of community assets (but not for private property). The users shall operate this fund themselves (paras 25 and 84).

PLANNING PROCESS

10. Participation of the village community and groups is central to the watershed programme. The Guidelines therefore lay down a detailed process to be followed for ensuring participatory planning.
    - *Participatory rural appraisals*   The watershed development team has to conduct various participatory rural appraisal exercises to identify potential programmes and the concerned user groups (para 66).
    - *Basic surveys*   Collection of various details through surveys (engineering, socio-economic) by the watershed development team and volunteers (para 69).

11. This process will lead to the development of a watershed plan and will contain the details of various activities, a list of user groups, fund requirements and users' contributions. The watershed-development plan will be approved by the watershed association, and then submitted to the DRDA through the project implementing agency (para 86).

12. This project plan will be prepared by the watershed development team in consultation with the watershed committee, according to the schedule of rates approved by the DRDA (para 46).

13. Implementation starts after the plan is approved by the DRDA. There is no mention of formal technical approval (para 29).

TECHNICAL PARAMETERS

14. The watershed approach gives significant benefits through various treatments intended to arrest soil erosion, restore soil fertility, and recharge groundwater by harvesting rainwater. According to the Guidelines, the planning unit has to cover all lands, irrespective of ownership, including forest, revenue, *panchayat* and private lands (para 42).

15. Since the watershed development programme plans for development of all resources within the watershed, including land, water, vegetation, animals and human resources, in an integrated manner, an organisational structure at the village level is conceived, which has to be developed in a participatory way. The project implementing agency has overall responsibility for the programme and for institutional arrangements at the village level. The agency which will employ a multi-disciplinary team to implement the watershed programme in an integrated manner.

16. Each micro-watershed will be about 500 ha (para 13). If a village is larger, it can be allotted an additional area, to be brought under the programme after the watershed association has shown its capacity for promoting people's institutions, and for planning and implementing a watershed programme covering (particularly) the public lands.

17. Each project implementing agency is expected to handle 10 micro-watersheds, totalling 5000–6200 ha (para 26).

18. Through a participatory process, the user groups and watershed committee, with the support of volunteers, will prepare a watershed development plan, which will have appropriate programme activities depending upon the agro-climatic situation of the watershed. Para 42 indicates the variety of activities that can be taken up under watershed programmes.

19. Works and activities should be low-cost, simple, easily operated and maintained (para 42). The watershed development plan should be based on local technical knowledge and solutions related to specific problems, supported by expert knowledge of the watershed team, district officers and research organisations. Around 80 per cent of works and activities should be based on local knowledge (para 20).

Annex 2
Review of Implementation of the 1994 Guidelines for Watershed Development[1]

SUMMARY OF FINDINGS

1. The Guidelines (GoI 1994) have been widely welcomed, especially by NGOs, but also by forward-looking public-sector officers. They are being adapted to local contexts and, for many areas, offer unique prospects of enhancing livelihoods in an environmentally sustainable fashion. Funds are currently available to achieve this over a wide area.

2. Current difficulties are rooted more in a dichotomy between implementation capacity and the high volume of financial resources made available under national development imperatives than in any shortcomings of the Guidelines themselves.

3. Watershed rehabilitation is an important part of rural development, but not a panacea. In particular, to provide the poor and women with an equitable share of benefits requires more effort and vigilance than most implementing agencies can currently provide.

4. A number of other implementation difficulties need to be addressed before the potential of watershed development can be fully realised:
   - Wide variability in biophysical and socio-economic conditions means that the Guidelines have to be locally adapted by implementing agencies. Few currently have the capacity to do so, and some operational procedures do not facilitate adaptation.
   - There is little evidence of cross-learning among the wealth of different approaches being developed to implement the Guidelines.

[1] This Annex draws on Turton et al. (1998)

- Watershed development is not yet being planned strategically in the context of other rural development initiatives, support through line departments, and human resource development.
- Monitoring and evaluation procedures are currently geared to administrative requirements, and offer little information to support course corrections.
- Little progress is likely to be made in strategic planning and in monitoring unless relevant departments of the state and Union governments work more closely together.

5. Donors should in future work closely with the Union and state governments in implementation of the Guidelines, and avoid creating parallel delivery systems. Donor support would be particularly valuable in: capacity building, especially in participatory approaches; cross-learning methods; monitoring and evaluation, especially 'process' approaches; and strategic planning.

RECOMMENDATIONS

General

1. The review recommended that stronger links be established between the central government, state and district levels, particularly with a view to better strategic planning and management of such aspects as:
    - training, selection and secondment of staff, and cross-learning among districts and states;
    - strategic linkage of watershed development with wider rural development initiatives;
    - monitoring and evaluation;
    - strategic selection of watershed development sites in relation to agro-ecological and socio-economic characteristics; and
    - monitoring of local adaptation of the Guidelines to ensure that they are constructive.

2. The Guidelines should be modified in order to distinguish clearly those aspects which must remain uniform across all areas from others which may be adapted to local conditions.

3. The resources available under each of the four initiatives under the Ministry of Rural Areas and Employment (Integrated Watershed Development Programme, Drought Prone Areas Programme, Desert Development Programme, Employment Assurance Scheme)

should be pooled at the district level into a single programme. Reporting and monitoring procedures should be standardised across all initiatives at all levels.

Implementation Arrangements

4. The review recommended that specific criteria be devised and implemented for the selection of directors of DRDAs, with particular emphasis on experience in participatory approaches to rural development.

5. The Multi-Disciplinary Team approach (developed in Andhra Pradesh) should be modified to specify a minimum tenure by team members of three years, and to reserve one position for a social scientist. It further recommends that other states examine the Multi-Disciplinary Team model as a means of strengthening technical support to project implementing agencies and watershed development teams, and links with the line departments.

6. Clear criteria should be developed and implemented for the selection of both government and non-government organisations applying to become project implementing agencies, and where necessary, for their subsequent de-selection.

7. Procedures should be introduced to ensure that project implementing agency staff are full-time.

8. All watershed development teams should contain one female member.

9. Given the difficulties in recruiting social scientists, investment should be made in strengthening the social and community development skills of technical staff.

10. In large villages, the additional area for watershed development may be allotted after the watershed association and committee have demonstrated their capacity to implement the scheme.

11. The 30 per cent quota for women on the watershed committee should be extended to cover the District Watershed Development Advisory Committee and State Watershed Programme Implementation and Review Committee. Furthermore, the watershed development team and multi-disciplinary teams should contain at least one female member.

12. The watershed project should develop better links with existing institutions in the village. There is particular scope for better links with women's credit and saving groups.

13. Renewed efforts are needed at Union and state government levels

to reach agreement with the Ministry of Environment and Forests and with the Department of Forestry to implement joint forest management in watershed project areas.

14. All watershed-development action plans should contain a clear statement on how benefits accruing from common land are to be shared.

15. The project duration should be increased from four to five years to allow for a longer capacity-building phase and provision for a handing-over phase. No additional expenditure on works is envisaged. Overhead costs of project implementing agencies and watershed development teams will need to be increased accordingly.

16. During the second half of the project, the watershed association and committee should produce an action plan detailing how investments will be maintained. This should include details of procedures and responsibilities for managing the funds after the project ends. This must include measures to ensure transparency and clear accountability.

17. As the first of these new-generation projects draws to a close (in two years time), a small number of NGOs should be selected and assigned responsibility to provide support to them. Each NGO would be responsible for a specific area. Their responsibilities may include provision of technical and institutional support on an as-needed basis, and providing continuous training to watershed secretaries and volunteers. Provisions for meeting the cost of these 'support teams' will need to be made.

18. Despite difficulties, continued efforts should be made to collect villagers' contributions to watershed development. The funds thus created should be supplemented by matching contributions from government, and used for wider economic or social activities.

19. Contributions for work on private land should be calculated according to a 'slab system'. In such as system, all farmers are entitled to a fixed-rate subsidy for works undertaken on land up to a specified limit, and pay a higher rate for work carried out on any additional land they own. This system should be flexible for areas with particularly serious degradation problems.

20. Greater scope needs to be provided in the Guidelines to encourage the formation of joint government–NGO implementing agencies. The modalities governing their operation will need serious thought at state and district levels.

21. State directives should be issued by the Department of Rural Development and the Department of Forestry, clarifying the position

with regard to the development of forest lands in watersheds. This should direct that whenever forest land forms part of a micro-watershed, it should be given appropriate treatment.

22. Any project implementing agency, whether government or NGO, should have action plans for forest land approved by an authorised forest officer and carry these out through a user group, which may be designated as a forest protection committee to meet the requirement of the joint forest management scheme.

23. In every watershed, a notice or board detailing financial outlays and progress of physical works should be displayed in a prominent place. Thought should also be given to the use of pictorial symbols to enable information to be shared by the illiterate.

24. An effective system of monitoring and evaluation[2] should be put in place, and the necessary training and financial provisions should be made.

Funding Arrangements

25. The sums provided under the Guidelines for the works component should remain unchanged.

26. The sum provided for administrative overheads should be calculated separately and de-linked from the rate-per-hectare formula. It should be calculated above all to ensure that project implementing agencies can operate effectively, and released to the agency on an annual basis.

27. DRDAs should compile and synthesise existing information on workloads, operating costs and financial arrangements of NGO project implementing agencies. This will enable the central government to set a more realistic figure for administrative overheads.

28. A clear statement of policy should be made at the state level on the funding arrangements for government project implementing agencies.

29. Research institutes should support the programme through the design of training curricula for project implementing agencies, watershed associations and committees, and DRDAs.

Land Improvement

30. In view of the enormous ecological and social diversity of the watersheds of the dryland areas, there should be a more site-specific approach to investments in land improvement.

---

[2] For an outline of such a system, see Annex 9 in Turton et al. (1998).

31. To take advantage of the large investments in land improvement, agricultural productivity must be greatly increased. Strong support from the line departments—horticulture, agriculture, livestock, irrigation, forestry—is needed. Support is particularly important in irrigation management, horticulture, livestock and marketing.

32. In villages with steep or highly erodible land, there should be a mechanism for sharing costs of soil and water conservation. Otherwise landowners themselves should be responsible for the work.

33. Efforts to plant trees or grass on common land should be undertaken cautiously, on a site-specific basis, given that the natural regeneration of trees and grass is rapid once areas are protected.

Further Studies

34. A short study should be commissioned to investigate practical provisions which can make it easier for women to undertake field duties.

35. Studies should be conducted in watersheds where benefits have been successfully shared with the weaker sections and with women, in order to identify the conditions for success and make proposals for their replication.

36. Studies on the economic and financial benefits of the programme over a wide diversity of ecological conditions should be undertaken to supplement currently meagre information.

37. There is a need to carry out studies of projects which have successfully motivated farmers to increase their contributions documenting the processes involved.

Human-Resource Development

38. Training at all levels should contain components on gender awareness and on the role of social scientists.

39. The Eswaran Committee Report on 'Training for Watershed Development' (GoI 1997) should be adopted. This report further recommends that high priority be given to such critical areas as:
    - developing expertise in the training institutes and giving them adequate support;
    - providing training in awareness and attitude change for Collectors to sensitise them to the benefits and needs of participatory approaches;
    - offering training for women, a hitherto neglected area, and the need for a programme to assess their skills and needs;

- organising workshops for state-level functionaries on watershed development at regular intervals to exchange ideas and discuss future strategies;
- introducing watershed development into the university curriculum for engineering and agriculture.

'Old Projects'

40. A clear policy statement is needed be issued from the central government regarding the future of projects undertaken prior to the 1994 Guidelines, given the considerable investment made in them.
41. A parallel fund should be established, to be used for capacity building and institutional development in areas covered under the old guidelines.
42. DRDAs should conduct a survey of the status of old-guidelines projects, taking into account both the nature and extent of resource productivity and the institutional arrangements in place for managing the resource. Based on the findings, and using the funds provided as above, project implementing agencies should be selected to develop local capacity to manage the resource.

Glossary

AGY	Adarsh Gaon Yojana
AME	Agriculture, Man and Ecology Project
anganwadi	Integrated Child Development Services
ASCI	Administrative Staff College of India
B/C	benefit–cost ratio
BAIF	Bharatiya Agro-Industries Foundation
bajra	pearl millet
BBPS	Barabazar Block *Panchayat Samiti*
bhusa	wheat straw
bidi	local cigar
bigha	land measure unit that varies in size from place to place. 1 standard *bigha* = 1000m²
BJP	Bharatiya Janata Party
CADA	Command Area Development Authority
CAPART	Council for Advancement of People's Action and Rural Technology
CET	Centre for Environment and Technology
chua	water-hole
chulha	earthen stove
CIDA	Canadian International Development Agency
CSWCRTI	Central Soil and Water Conservation Research and Training Institute
dalit	low-caste person, formerly known as Harijan or Untouchable.
DANWADEP	Danida Watershed Development Programme
data	benefactor
DDP	Desert Development Programme
DFID	Department for International Development, UK
DoWD	Department of Wastelands Development
DPAP	Drought Prone Areas Programme
DRDA	District Rural Development Agency
DWACRA	Development of Women and Children in Rural Areas
DWDAC	District Watershed Development Advisory Committee
EAS	Employment Assurance Scheme
falia	hamlet
gaon	village
GoI	Government of India
GONGO	government-organised non-government organisation

gopal	cow keeper/milk producer
gopal yojana	cow improvement scheme
GoR	Government of Rajasthan
gram panchayat	elected village assembly
gram sabha	village assembly
GTZ	German Agency for Technical Cooperation
halma	mutual help practice
Holi	spring festival
HYV	high-yielding variety
ICAR	Indian Council of Agriculture Research
IGWDP	Indo-German Watershed Development Programme, Maharashtra
IJAE	Indian Journal of Agricultural Economics
IRMA	Institute of Rural Management, Anand
IRR	internal rate of return
IWDP	Integrated Watershed Development Programme
jankar	expert
JFM	joint forest management
jowar	sorghum
kharif	south-west monsoon (rainy) season (July-October)
kinnow	type of citrus fruit
KRIBHCO	Krishak Bharati Cooperative Ltd.
KRIBP	KRIBHCO Rainfed Indo-British Project
mahila kisan	woman farmer
mahila mandal	women's self-help group
mahila pravartak	village women promoter
mahila samaj sevika	female social worker
MANAGE	National Institute of Agricultural Extension Management
melawa	social gathering
mitra kisan	'friendly farmer', farmer adviser
MoRAE	Ministry of Rural Areas and Employment
MYRADA	Mysore Relief and Development Agency
NABARD	National Bank for Agriculture and Rural Development
nalah	gully
NGO	non-government organisation
NORAD	Norwegian Agency for Development Cooperation
NPK	nitrogen, phosphorus, potassium (plant nutrients)
NWDB	National Watershed Development Board
NWDPRA	National Watershed Development Programme for Rainfed Areas
ODA	Overseas Development Administration (now DFID)
ODI	Overseas Development Institute, UK
PAHAL	Participatory Approach to Human and Land Resource Development
panchayat	village administrative body
panchayat samiti	committee of village *panchayats* for a block of villages

panchayati raj	rule through *panchayats*, i.e., decentralised rule at village level
patta	ownership right, title (to land, etc.)
pattadars	title holders
patwari	village land-record keeper
PAWDI	Participatory Watershed Development Initiative
PIA	project implementing agency
PIDOW	Participative Integrated Development of Watersheds project
PRADAN	Professional Assistance for Development Action (an NGO)
pragati	cooperative society
rabi	winter season
Rs	rupees (Rs 40 = US1 approx.)
RWDP	Rayalaseema Watershed Development Programme
sabhadhipati	vice president (of a meeting)
sabhapati	president or chairperson chosen for a meeting
sahasabhapati	a cooperative group with common interests
sangam	group
sangha	group
sarapanch	chairperson of village *panchayat*; head of *gram panchayat*
SDC	Swiss Agency for Development and Cooperation
shramadaan	voluntary labour
SIDA	Swedish International Development Cooperation Agency
SIPRD	State Institute of *Panchayat* and Rural Development
SIRD	State Institute of Rural Development
swasthyakarmis	health workers
SWOT	strengths–weaknesses–opportunities–threats (organisational analysis method)
SWPIRC	State Watershed Programme Implementation and Review Committee
taluka	sub-district
tola	hamlet
UNDP	United Nations Development Programme
UNFPA	United Nations Fund for Population Activities
UNICEF	United Nations Children's Fund
UNIDO	United Nations Industrial Development Organisation
USAID	United States Agency for International Development
VDC	village development committee
VIKSAT	Vikram Sarabhai Centre for Development Institute
WDP	Women's Development Programme
WDT	watershed development team
yachak	beneficiary
zilla parishad	district-level local government

Bibliography

Adolph, B. and Turton, C. (1998) 'Community Self Help Groups and Watersheds'. Partnerships and Policies Programme series, Overseas Development Institute, London.

AFC (1988) 'Evaluation Study of Soil Conservation in the River Valley Projects of Matatila, Nizamsagar,and Ukai'. Agricultural Finance Corporation, Ministry of Agriculture, Govt. of India.

Agarwal, B. (1994) *A Field of One's Own: Gender and Land Rights in South Asia.* London: Cambridge University Press.

Agarwal, C. and Saigal, S. (1996) *Joint Forest Management in India: A Brief Review.* New Dehli: Society for Promotion of Wastelands Development.

Alsop, R., Gilbert, E., Farrington, J. and Khandelwal, R. (1999) *Coalitions of Interest: Partnerships for Processes of Agricultural Change.* Sage, New Delhi and London.

Argyris, C. and Schon, D. A. (1978) *Organizational Learning: A Theory of Action Perspective.* Addison-Wesley, Reading, MA.

Arnold, J. E. M. (1997) 'Managing Forests as Common Property'. Unpublished report prepared for the Overseas Development Institute, London.

Arora, J. K. (1998) 'Development of Degraded Lands: Some Policy Issues'. Paper prepared for National Workshop for Watershed Approaches to Wastelands Development, New Delhi, 27–29 April 1998.

ASCI (1990) 'Crop Production Programme and Pastures and Fodder Development Programme for Maheshwaram Watershed'. Administrative Staff College of India, Hyderabad.

Ashok, M. S. (1997) 'Reflections on Savings, Credit and Grassroots Institutions: Report of a visit to KRIBP (West), 3–15 February 1997'. Catalyst Management Services, India.

Ayra, V. (1998) 'Collaboration for Innovation in Participatory Natural Resources Management: The PAHAL Project in Dungarpur District'. Srijan, New Delhi.

Babu, R., Dhyani, B. L., Agarwal, M. C. and Samra, J. S. (1997) 'Economic Evaluation of Watershed Management Projects: Concepts, Methodologies and Case Studies', *CSWCRTI Bulletin* T-33/D-23. Dehradun.

Baumann, P. (1998) 'Panchayati Raj and Watershed Management in India: Constraints and Opportunities', *ODI Working Paper* 114. Overseas Development Institute, London.

Berry, A. et al., (1997) 'Eco-restoration and Development of UP Hills through Integrated Watershed Management'. Watershed Management Directorate, Govt of Uttar Pradesh, Dehradun.

Bunch, Roland. (1982) *Two ears of corn.* World Neighbors, Oklahoma City.

CAPART (1996) 'Guidelines for Watershed Conservation and Development Programme'. Council of Advancement of People's Action and Rural Technology, New Delhi.

Carney, D. (ed.) (1998) *Sustainable Rural Livelihoods: What Contribution Can We Make?*. Department for International Development, London.

Carney, D. and Farrington, J. (1998) *Natural Resources Management and Institutional Change.* Routledge, London.

Chopra, K. (1998) 'Watershed Management Programmes: An Evaluation of Alternative Institutional and Technical Options'. Paper prepared for National Workshop for Watershed Approaches to Wastelands Development, New Delhi, 27–29 April 1998.

Chopra, K. and Subba Rao, D. V. (1996) 'Economic Evaluation of Soil and Water Conservation Programmes in Watersheds'. Institute of Economic Growth, Delhi.

Chopra, Kanchan, Kadekodi, G. and Murty, M. N. (1990) *Participatory Development, People and Common Property Resources.* Sage, New Delhi.

Coase, R (October 1960) 'The Problem of Social Cost'. *Journal of Law and Economics.*

D'Souza, Marcella (1998) 'Watershed development: Creating Space for Women', *Agricultural Research and Extension Network Paper* 88b. Overseas Development Institute, London.

——— (1997) 'Gender and Watershed Development.' *Agricultural Research and Extension Network Newsletter* 36, July 1997. Overseas Development Institute, London.

Dangroup (1990) *Doon Valley Integrated Watershed Management Project.* European Commission, DGI, Brussels.

Datta, S. K. and Virgo, K. J. (in press 1998) 'Towards Sustainable Watershed Development through People's Participation: Lessons from the Lesser Himalayas of Uttar Pradesh, India'. *Mountain Research and Development.*

de Graff, J. (1996) 'The Price of Soil Erosion: An Economic Evaluation of

Soil Conservation and Watershed Development'. *Tropical Resource Management Papers.* Wageningen Agricultural University, Wageningen.

Deshpande, R. S. and Rajshekharan, N. (1997) 'Impact of Watershed Development Programmes: Experiences and Issues. *Arthivignana* 39(3): 374–90.

Devendrappa, K. (1998) 'Indo-Swiss Participative Watershed Development Programme, Bijapur'. Paper prepared for National Workshop for Watershed Approaches to Wastelands Development, New Delhi, 27–29 April 1998.

Dinesh Kumar, M., Mudrakartha, S. and Bhalani, D. L. (1998) 'Sustainability, Equity, and Scaling Up: Addressing Second Generation Issues in Watershed Development and Management'. Paper prepared for National Workshop for Watershed Approaches to Wastelands Development, New Delhi, 27–29 April 1998.

DoWD (1998) Proceedings of the National Workshop on Watershed Approaches to Wastelands Development, April 1998. Dept of Wastelands Development, New Delhi.

Farrington, J. (1998) 'The Role of Stakeholders in Rural Transformation, Agricultural Research and International Cooperation'. Paper presented at the European Forum on International Agricultural Research, Wageningen, 7–8 April 1999.

Farrington, J. and Bebbington, A. J. with Lewis, D. and Wellard, K. (1993) *Reluctant Partners? Non-Governmental Organisations, the State and Sustainable Agricultural Development.* Routledge, London.

Farrington, J. and Boyd, C. (1997) 'Scaling up the Participatory Management of Common Pool Resources'. *Development Policy Review* 15(4): 371–391.

Farrington, J. and Lobo, C. 'Scaling up Participatory Watershed Development in India: Lessons from the Indo-German Watershed Development Programme'. *Natural Resource Perspectives* 17 Feb 1997. Overseas Development Institute, London

Farrington, J. and Thiele, G. (1998) 'Scaling up Participatory Approaches to Technology Generation and Dissemination among Low-Income Farmers'. In Lutz, E., Binswanger, H., Hazell, P. and McCalla, A. (eds) *Encouraging Innovation, Increasing Productivity and Conserving the Resource Base.* World Bank, Washington, DC.

Farrington, J., Gilbert, E. H. and Khandelwal, R. (1998) 'Process Monitoring in Indian Agriculture: Implications of a Rajasthan Case Study', Chapter 8 in Mosse, D., Farrington, J. and Rew, A. (eds) *Development as Process.* Routledge, London.

Fernandez, A. P. (1993) 'The MYRADA Experience: The Interventions of a Voluntary Agency in the Emergence and Growth of Peoples' Organisations for Sustained and Equitable Management of Microwatersheds'. Unpublished paper, MYRADA, India.

Fernandez, A. P. (1998) 'Will People Take Loans for Treatment Measures on Private Lands in a Micro Watershed?' Paper prepared for National Workshop for Watershed Approaches to Wastelands Development, New Delhi, 27–29 April 1998.

Freire, P. (1972) *Pedagogy of the Oppressed*. Penguin, Harmondsworth.

GoI (1994) 'Guidelines for Watershed Development'. Department of Wastelands Development, Ministry of Rural Areas and Employment, Government of India, New Delhi.

GoI (1997) 'Report of the Committee on Training for Watershed Development' (Eswaran Committee Report). Ministry of Rural Areas and Employment, New Delhi.

Government of India and Danida (1996) 'Review-cum-Appraisal Report, Karnataka Watershed Development Project, Karnataka.' Ministry of Foreign Affairs and Danida, New Delhi.

Gregerson, H. M., Brooks, K., Dixon, J. and Hamilton, L. (1987) 'Guidelines for Economic Appraisal of Watershed Management Projects'. *FAO Conservation Guide* 16, Rome.

Hardin, G. (1968) 'The Tragedy of the Commons', *Science* 162:1243–8.

Hazare, A., Pangare, G. and Lokur-Pangare, V. (1996) *Adarsh Gaon Yojana Government Participation in a People's Programme (Ideal Village Programme of the Government of Maharashta)*. Hind Swaraj Trust, Pune.

Hazra, C. R. (1998) 'Development of Degraded Village Common Lands and Arable Lands on Watershed Basis through Participatory Approach at Kharaiya Nala Watershed (Jhansi)'. Paper prepared for National Workshop for Watershed Approaches to Wastelands Development, New Delhi, 27–29 April 1998.

Hobley, M. and Shah, K. (1996) 'What Makes a Local Organisation Robust? Evidence from India and Nepal'. *National Resource Perspectives* 11. Overseas Development Institute, London.

Hueting, R. (1991) 'The Use of the Discount Rate in a Cost–Benefit Analysis for Different Uses of a Humid Tropical Forest Area.' *Ecological Economics* 3:4–57.

IGWDP (1996) 'Guidelines on Participation in Indo-German Watershed Development Programme'. National Bank for Agriculture and Rural Development, Mumbai.

Jain, T. C. (1995) 'Watershed Management Programmes: World Bank Experience, Achievements, Constraints and Future Strategy'. In Katyal, J. C. and Farrington, J. (eds) *Research for Rainfed Farming*. ICAR, New Delhi and Overseas Development Administration, London.

Jensen, J., Seth, S., Sawney, T. and Kumar, P. (1996) 'Watershed Development: Proceedings of Danida's Internal Workshop on Watershed Development. Watershed Development Coordination Unit, Danida, New Delhi.

Jodha, N. S. (1986) 'Common Property Resources and the Rural Poor in Dry Regions of India'. *Economic and Political Weekly* 54:1169–82.

Jones, S., Khare, J. N., Mosse, D., Sodhi, P., Smith, P. and Witcombe, J. R. (1996) 'The KRIBHCO Rainfed Farming Project: An Approach to Participatory Farming Systems Development'. *Research Issues In Natural Resource Management, KRIBP Working Paper* 1. Centre for Development Studies, University of Wales, Swansea

Kakade, B. K. and Hegde, N. G. (1998) 'Sustainability Indicators in Watershed Management'. Paper prepared for National Workshop for Watershed Approaches to Wastelands Development, New Delhi, 27–29 April 1998.

Kerr, J. (1996) 'Sustainable Development of Rainfed Agriculture in India'. *EPTD Discussion Paper* 20. Environment and Production Technology Division, International Food Policy Research Institute, Washington DC.

Kerr, J., Pangare, G., Lokur-Pangare, V., George, P. J. and Kolavalli, S. (1998) 'The Role of Watershed Projects in Developing Rainfed Agriculture in India'. Study prepared for the Indian Council for Agricultural Research. World Bank, Washington DC.

Kerr, J. M. and Sanghi, N. K. (1992) 'Indigenous Soil and Water Conservation in India's Semi-Arid Tropics'. *Gatekeeper Series* 34. International Institute for Environment and Development, London.

Kerr, J., Sanghi, N. K. and Sriramappa, G. (1996) 'Subsidies in Watershed Development Projects in India: Distortions and Opportunities'. *Gatekeeper Series* 61. International Institute for Environment and Development, London.

Kolavalli, S. (1998a) 'Scaling up Participatory Approaches'. Paper prepared for National Workshop for Watershed Approaches to Wastelands Development, New Delhi, 27–29 April 1998.

———— (1998b) 'A Review of Approaches to Watershed Development in India'. Report submitted to National Centre for Agricultural Economics and Policy Research, New Delhi.

Krishna, A. (1997) 'Coordination of Line Department Activities in Micro-watershed Management and Related Agricultural Development in Andhra Pradesh'. Partnerships and Policies Programme series, Overseas Development Institute, London.

Kulkarni et al. (1989) (title unknown) Paper presented at the Golden Jubilee Conference of the Indian Society of Agricultural Economics, Mumbai.

Landell-Mills, N. (1998) 'Cost-Benefit Analysis: A Useful Tool for Evaluating Watershed Development Projects?' Paper prepared for National Workshop for Watershed Approaches to Wastelands Development, New Delhi, 27–29 April 1998.

Liebenstein, H. and Maital, S. (1994) 'The Organizational Foundations of X-Inefficiency: A Game Theoretic Interpretation of Argyris' Model of Organizational Learning'. *Journal of Economic Behaviour and Organizations* 23: 251–68.

Lobo, C. (1996) 'Indo-German Watershed Development Programme: Macromanagement for Micro-cooperation'. Paper presented at the DSE/ ATSAF Workshop: Strategies for Intersectoral Water Management in Developing Countries: Challenges and Consequences for Agriculture. 6–10 May 1996, Berlin

Lobo, C. and Kochendörfer-Lucius, G. (1995) 'The Rain Decided to Help Us: Participatory Watershed Management in the State of Maharashtra, India', *EDI Learning Resources Series.* Economic Development Institute, World Bank, Washington DC.

Lokur-Pangare, V. (1996) 'Women in Watershed Development: Concepts, Issues, Strategies for Facilitating Participation'. Paper prepared for the workshop at Gram Gourav Pratisthan, Shetkarinagar, Khalad, Purandhar, Taluka, Pune, 27–30 October 1996.

——— (1998) 'Gender Issues in Watershed Development and Management in India', *Agricultural Research and Extension Network Newsletter* 38. Overseas Development Institute, London.

Mascarenhas, J. (1998) 'Organisational and Human Resource Development Aspects of Enhancing Cooperation between People and Institutions'. Paper prepared for National Workshop for Watershed Approaches to Wastelands Development, New Delhi, 27–29 April 1998; also published as *Outreach Paper* 10. Outreach, Bangalore.

Mathews, G. (1995) *Panchayati Raj: From Legislation to Movement.* Institute of Social Sciences, New Delhi.

Mehta, A. (1998) 'The Experience of Seva Mandir in Supporting Local Action for Watershed Development'. Paper prepared for National Workshop for Watershed Approaches to Wastelands Development,

New Delhi, 27–29 April 1998.

Meinzen-Dick, Ruth, Reidinger, Richard and Manzardo, Andrew (1995) 'Participation in Irrigation'. *Participation Series* 3, Environment Department, World Bank, Washington, DC.

Moore, M. (1995) 'Promoting Good Government by Supporting Institutional Development?' *IDS Bulletin* 26(2).

Mosse, D. (1994) 'Soil and Water Conservation, Group Formation, and Savings and Credit Groups'. Visit report, KRIBP, July 1994. Centre for Development Studies, University of Wales, Swansea.

Mosse, D. and KRIBP Staff (1995a) 'Local Institutions for Natural Resources Development: Principles, and Practice in the KRIBHCO Indo-British Rainfed Farming Project'. *KRIBP Working Paper* 6, Research Issues in Natural Resource Management. Centre for Development Studies, University of Wales, Swansea. 42 pp.

Mosse, D. with the KRIBP Project Team (1995b) 'People's Knowledge in Project Planning: The Limits and Social Conditions of Participation in Planning Agricultural Development', *Agricultural Research and Extension Network Paper* 58. Overseas Development Institute, London.

Mosse, D., Farrington, J. and Rew, A. (eds) (1998) *Development as Process*. Routledge, London.

Mukherjee, K. (1998) *People's Participation in Watershed Development Schemes in Karnataka: Changing Perspectives*. Paper prepared for National Workshop for Watershed Approaches to Wastelands Development, New Delhi, 27–29 April 1998.

Narasimha Reddy, N. L. and Rajasekhar, D. (1997) *Development Programmes and NGOs: A Guide to Central Government Programmes for NGOs in India*. Bangalore Consultancy Office and Novib, The Hague.

Nawadhakar, D. S. and Shaikh, N. V. (1989) 'Effects of Land-Shaping on Resource Use Structures and Productivity of Farms in Ahmednagar District in Maharashtra. Paper presented at the Golden Jubilee Conference of the Indian Society of Agricultural Economics, Mumbai.

Nayak, T. (1998) 'Cooperation with Non-Government Organisations for People's Participation in the Watershed Development Projects'. Paper prepared for National Workshop for Watershed Approaches to Wastelands Development, New Delhi, 27–29 April 1998.

ODA (1996) 'ODA's Review of Participatory Forest Management: Synthesis of Findings'. Overseas Development Administration, London.

Oomen, M. A. (1995) 'Devolution of Resources from the State to the

Panchayati Raj Institutions: Search for a Normative Approach. *ISS Occasional Paper Series* 18. Institute of Social Studies, New Delhi.

Ostrom, E. (1990) 'Governing the Commons: The Evolution of Institutions for Collective Action'. Cambridge University Press, Cambridge.

Paul, D. K. (1997) 'Rainfed Farming System Development in India: Retrospect and Prospect'. In Katyal, J. C. and Farrington, J. (eds) *Research for Rainfed Farming*. ICAR, New Delhi and Overseas Development Administration, London.

Pearce, D., Markandya, A. and Barbier, E. B. (1989) *Blueprint for a Green Economy*. Earthscan Publications, London.

Pimbert, M. and Pretty, J. (1997) 'Diversity and Sustainability in Community Based Conservation'. Paper presented at the UNESCO IIPA Regional Workshop on Community Based Conservation, India, 9–12 February 1997.

Poffenberger, M., and McGean, B. (1998) *Villages Voices, Forest Choices. Joint Forest Management in India*. Oxford University Press, India.

PRADAN (1998) 'Collaboration between NGOs and *Panchayati Raj* Institutions: A Case Study of PRADAN's Collaboration with *Panchayats* for Watershed Development in Purulia, West Bengal'. Draft, mimeo. PRADAN, New Delhi.

Pretty, J. N. (1995) *Regenerating Agriculture*. Earthscan, London. pp. 169–72.

Rajaraman, I., Bohra, O. P. and Renganathan, V. S. (1996) 'Augmentation of Panchayat Resources', *Economic and Political Weekly* 31(18).

Raju, G. (1997) 'Joint Forest Management: The Dilemma of Empowerment'. *Working Paper* 109. Institute of Rural Management, Anand.

Rao, Subba D. V. (1993) Sustainable Agricultural Development: A Quantitative Exploration for a Semi-Arid Region in India. Unpublished Ph.D. thesis, University of Delhi.

Reardon, T., Delgado, C. L. and Matlon, P. J. (1992) 'Determinants and Effects of Income Diversification amongst Farm Households in Burkina Faso'. *Journal of Development Studies* 28(2):264–96.

Reddy, M. (1998) 'Selection Criteria and Conditions for Success in the Rural Development Trust, Anantapur'. Paper prepared for National Workshop for Watershed Approaches to Wastelands Development, New Delhi, 27–29 April 1998.

Reij, C. (1991) 'Indigenous Soil and Water Conservation in Africa'. *Gatekeeper Series* 27. International Institute for Environment and Development, London.

Rukmini Rao, V. (1998) 'Ensuring Gender Justice and People's Participation in Watershed Management'. Paper prepared for National Workshop for Watershed Approaches to Wastelands Development, New Delhi, 27–29 April 1998.

Saksena, A., Bhargava, P. N. and Jain, T. B. (1989) 'Conservation and Utilisation of Runoff in a Low Rainfall Area'. Paper presented at the Golden Jubilee Conference of the Indian Society of Agricultural Economics, Mu.. bai.

Sanders, D. W. (1988) 'Soil and Water Conservation on Steep Lands: A Summary of Workshop Discussions'. In: Moldenhauer, W. C. and Hudson, N. W. (eds) *Conservation Farming on Steep Lands*. World Association of Soil and Water Conservation, Ankeny, Iowa.

Sarin, M. et al. (1996) *Joint Forest Management: The Haryana Experience*. Centre for Environmental Education, India.

Senge, P. M. and Sterman, J. D. (1992) 'Systems Thinking and Organizational Learning: Acting Locally and Thinking Globally in the Organization of the Future'. pp. 353–70 in Kochan, Thomas A. and Useem, M. (eds) *Transforming Organizations*. Oxford University Press, New York, Oxford, Toronto and Melbourne.

Seth, S. L. and Damgaard-Larsen, S. (1998) 'Participatory Watershed Development Approach with Specific Reference to Danida's Watershed Development Programme (DANWADEP)'. Paper prepared for National Workshop for Watershed Approaches to Wastelands Development, New Delhi, 27–29 April 1998.

Shah, Amita (1997) 'Watershed Development Programmes in India: Emerging Issues for Environment-Development Perspectives'. Paper presented at the Workshop on Environment and Agriculture, Delhi School of Economics, December.

——— (1998) 'Impact of Watershed Programmes in Dryland Regions: Evidence and Policy Imperatives'. Paper prepared for National Workshop for Watershed Approaches to Wastelands Development, New Delhi, 27–29 April 1998.

Shah, Anil (1998) 'What after Four Years?' Paper prepared for National Workshop for Watershed Approaches to Wastelands Development, New Delhi, 27–29 April 1998.

Sharma, S. V. and Virgo, K. (1998) 'Developing Village Funds to Sustain Watershed Management in the Doon Valley Project, Uttar Pradesh'. Paper prepared for National Workshop for Watershed Approaches to Wastelands Development, New Delhi, 27–29 April 1998.

Sheng, T. C. and Meiman, J. R. (1988) 'Planning and Implementing Soil Conservation Projects'. In Moldenhauer, W. C. and Hudson, N. W. (eds) *Conservation Farming on Steep Lands*. World Association of Soil and

Water Conservation, Ankeny, Iowa.

Shepherd, A. (1995) 'Participatory Environmental Management: Contradiction of Process, Project and Bureaucracy in the Himalayan Foothills'. *Public Admininistration and Development* 15:465–79.

Singh, Katar (1989) 'Dryland Watershed Development and Management: A Case Study in Karnataka'. Paper presented at the Golden Jubilee Conference of the Indian Society of Agricultural Economics, Mumbai.

Singh. A. J., Joshi, A S., Singh, R. P. and Gupta, R. (1991) 'An Economic Appraisal of Kandi Watershed and Area Development Project in Punjab'. *Indian Journal of Agricultural Economics*, July–Sept.

Sinha, F. and Sinha. S. (eds) (1996) *From Indifference to Active Participation: Six Case Studies of Natural Resource Development through Social Organisation*. Economic Development Association Rural Systems, Gurgaon.

Smith, P. D. (1997) 'KRIBHCO Indo-British Rainfed Farming Project: Soil and Water Conservation Programme Impact Assessment'. Centre for Development Studies, Swansea, and Centre for Arid Zone Studies, Bangor.

Smith, P. D., Parry, A. and Mishra, R. K. (1998) 'The Use of Subsidies for Soil and Water Conservation on Degraded Areas of India: The KRIBCO Experience and Some Suggestions for Alternative Approaches'. Paper prepared for National Workshop for Watershed Approaches to Wastelands Development, New Delhi, 27–29 April 1998.

Smith, Paul (1998) The Use of Subsidies for Soil and Water Conservation: A Case Study from Western India'. *Agricultural Research and Extension Network Paper* 87. Overseas Development Institute, London.

Srinivas, V. (1997) *People's Movement for Sustainable Watershed Development: The Rajasthan Experience*. Watershed Development and Soil Conservation, Government of Rajasthan, Jaipur.

Stocking, M. and Abel, N. (1992) 'Labour Costs: A Critical Element in Soil Conservation'. pp. 77–86 in Hiemstra, W., Reijnjes, C. and van der Werf, E. (eds) *Let Farmers Judge: Experiences in Assessing the Sustainability of Agriculture*. Intermediate Technology Publications, London.

Thapliyal, K. C., Lepcha, S. T. S., Kumar, P., Chandra, B., Virgo, K. J. and Sharma, P. N. (1994) 'Participatory Watershed Management in the Lesser Himalayas: Experiences of the Doon Valley Project'. *Proceedings of the 8th International Soil Conservation Organisation Conference*, New Delhi.

Thompson, J. (1995) 'Participatory Approaches in Government Bureaucracies: Facilitating the Process of Institutional Change', *World Development* 23(9):1521–54.

Turton, C. and Farrington, J. (1998) 'Enhancing Rural Livelihoods through
 Participatory Watershed Development in India'. *Natural Resource
 Perspectives* 34. Overseas Development Institute, London.

Turton, C., Coulter, J., Shah, A. and Farrington, J. (1998) 'Participatory Watershed Development in India: Impact of the New Guidelines'.
 Report prepared for the Ministry of Rural Areas and Employment
 and the Department for International Development, India. Overseas Development Institute, London.

UNIDO (1972) 'Guidelines for Project Evaluation'. P. Dasgupta, A. Sen and
 S. Marglin. United Nations Industrial Development Organisation,
 Oxford, and IBH, New Delhi.

Vaidyanathan, A. (1991) 'Integrated Watershed Development: Some Major
 Issues'. Foundation Day Lecture, Society for Promotion of Watershed Development, New Delhi, 1 May 1991.

van Walsum, E., Lanting, M. and Jangal, J. (1998) 'From Peanuts to Platforms: AME's Approach to Training NGOs in Integrated Watershed Management'. Paper prepared for National Workshop for
 Watershed Approaches to Wastelands Development, New Delhi,
 27–29 April 1998.

Veldhuizen, L. van, Waters-Bayer, A. and de Zeeuw, H. (1997) *Developing
 Technology with Farmers: A Trainers Guide for Participatory Learning.* ETC,
 Netherlands, and Zed Books, London and New York.

Wade, R. (1988) *Village Republics: Economic conditions for collective action in South
 India.* Cambridge University Press, Cambridge.

Index

89, 105, 115, 127–8, 130, 133–4,
137, 139, 156, 158, 166, 168, 170,
176–8, 216, 224, 237, 246, 263,
276, 291, 294, 309, 313, 324
landowner, 86, 94–7, 115, 119, 137, 322
Lanting, M, 247
law, legislation, 92, 103, 108, 111, 113,
136–7, 181, 210–11, 213, 215,
221–2, 226–7, 283, 297, 310
leadership, 26, 31, 59, 66–7, 74, 79, 83,
88, 94, 98–100, 126, 131–2, 134–5,
146, 163, 170, 182, 186–7, 195,
198, 203, 231, 244, 268, 293, 296,
322–3
legislation. *See* law
legumes, 28–9
Liebenstein, H., 330
lift-irrigation, 99, 101, 184, 185
linear model of institutional roles, 272
livelihood strategy, 75, 279
livestock, 1, 2, 26, 28, 33, 35, 40, 42–4,
52, 61, 68, 77, 89, 112, 114, 142–3,
155, 170, 185, 196, 240, 251, 282,
289, 308, 310, 313, 316, 321, 335,
338, 340, 347, 355
Lobo, C., 11, 68, 70, 141, 263, 307–9
Lok Van Kalyan Parishad, 116
Lokbharti, 298, 301
Lokur-Pangare, V., 13, 120, 123–4, 153

Madanapalle, 128–31, 134
Madhugiri, 265
Madhya Pradesh, 56, 70, 122, 165, 181,
196, 281
Maharashtra, 14–18, 23, 31–2, 34–7, 56,
88, 118, 126, 141–2, 165, 222, 225,
270, 308–9, 313, 318–20, 323
Mahavir Trust, 182
Mahbubnagar, 11, 163
Maheswaram, 31, 33
mahila kisan, woman farmer, 86
mahila mandal, women's self-help group,
145, 170–1
mahila pravartak, village women
promoter, 146
mahila samaj sevika, female social worker,
148
Mahila Samakhya, 186

Maital, S., 330
maize, 264, 285, 290
Malkanagire, 85
Malkangiri, 166, 171
MANAGE. *See* National Institute of
Agricultural Extension Manage-
ment
Manara, 232
manure, 2, 26, 29, 144
markets, 13, 28, 30, 37, 51, 53, 54–56,
67, 75, 115, 139–40, 144–5, 155,
164, 181, 186, 190, 198, 204, 251–
3, 258–9, 262, 268, 273, 280, 284,
301, 305, 307, 324, 340, 344, 355
Mascarenhas, J., 11, 67, 244, 263
Mathew, 223
Mathews, G., 223
Mathili, 171
Mazdoor Kisan Sangharsh Samiti, 182
Mazdoor Kisan Shakti Sangathan, 226
McGean, B., 10
Mehsana, 104, 116
Mehta, A., 90
Meiman, J. R., 283
Meinzen-Dick, R., 262
migration, 17, 65, 74–6, 99, 130, 140,
153–4, 170, 281, 283, 286, 289,
293, 341
millet, 32
Ministry of Agriculture and Cooperation, 7, 15, 26, 71, 162, 177, 223,
240, 262, 270, 314, 317
Ministry of Environment and Forests,
7, 102, 353
Ministry of Rural Areas and Employment, MoRAE, 3, 7, 9, 13, 71–2,
121, 162, 177, 224, 240, 262, 266,
269, 270, 327, 328–9, 346, 351
Ministry of Rural Development, 15,
102, 107, 234, 235
Mishra, R. K., 281
mitra kisan, farmer adviser, 322–3
mobilisation, 4, 67, 95, 134, 137, 149,
150, 152, 164, 169, 182, 186, 188,
192, 198, 200, 205, 220, 232, 253,
308, 311, 316–17
moisture conservation. *See* conservation
moneylenders, 30, 74, 132, 170, 174,

Rukmini Rao, V., 125, 127
Rupapetya, 235, 237
Rural Development Trust, 67, 78–81
RWDP. *See* Rayalaseema Watershed
   Development Programme

Sabarkantha, 116
sabhadhipati, vice-president, 234
sabhapati, president, 231–2, 235–7
sahasabhapati, cooperative group, 234
Sahibi, 36–7, 40–1, 47
SAHYOG, 181
Saigal, S., 10
Saksena, A., 31–2
SAKSHAM, 116
Sanders, D. W., 283–4
Sandhan, 182, 202
Sanghi, N. K., 283, 295
sarapanch, *panchayat* chairperson, 85, 168,
   219–20, 222
Sarin, M., 120
Savarkundla, 301
Saving Water Courses, 181
savings, 19, 66, 69, 75, 84, 122, 125,
   132, 136, 142–4, 147–8, 151, 179,
   186, 249, 251, 253–4, 263, 280,
   288
scaling up, 4, 71, 107, 110, 112, 115–16,
   185, 189, 216, 220, 224, 252, 254–
   6, 261–345
scheduled caste, scheduled tribe 67, 72,
   89, 121–2, 128, 137, 166, 196, 212,
   219, 281, 313, 336, 348
Schon, D. A., 330
SDC. *See* Swiss Agency for Development and Cooperation
sediment, 26, 27, 39–40, 47, 61, 79, 283
Seetla Rao, 342, 344
self-help groups, 8–9, 72–4, 80, 83, 85–
   7, 106, 122, 125, 145, 147, 151–2,
   162, 170, 175–9, 181–2, 184, 190,
   197, 212, 220, 227–9, 238, 241–2,
   249, 251, 254, 263–4, 268, 280,
   296, 322, 328, 336–7, 339–43, 347
Senge, P. M., 330
Seth, S. L., 68, 81, 263
Seva Mandir, 67, 70, 90–102
Shah, Amita, 6, 34–5

Shah, Anil, 69, 262, 298
Shah, K., 2
Shaikh, N. V., 31–2
Sharma, S. V., 69, 125, 334
sheep, 21, 28, 125, 133
Sheng, T. C., 283
Shepherd, A., 342
Shiksha Karmi, 181–4, 188, 192, 195,
   198, 202–3, 206, 208
Shivlal, 96–7
shramadaan, voluntary labour, 263, 313
Shyampura, 97–101
SIDA. *See* Swedish International
   Development Cooperation
   Agency
Sikar, 35–6
Sindhiguda Manikpur, 171
Singh, K., 31–2
Singh. A. J., 31, 33–4
Sinha, F., 70
Sinha. S., 70
SIPRD. *See* State Institute of *Panchayat*
   and Rural Development
SIRD. *See* State Institute of Rural
   Development
Siwalik, 31
slab system, 280, 353
Smith, P., 263, 281, 286–8
social fencing, 68, 80, 89, 313
social organisation, 5, 15, 70–1, 165,
   251, 253, 255, 257–8, 269, 321–9,
   332–3
social relations, 73, 75, 77, 93, 100
Social Work and Research Centre
   Tilonia, 188
soil conservation. *See* conservation
Soil Conservation Department, 166
soil erosion. *See* erosion
soil fertility, 29–30, 349
soil moisture, 25, 27, 103, 114, 285. *See
   also* conservation
sorghum, *jowar*, 27, 31–3, 41, 44
soya, 27
SRIJAN, 179
Srinivas, V., 102, 304
stakeholder analysis, 54, 161
stakeholders, 12, 54, 57, 63, 83, 99, 103,
   111, 161, 187, 189, 245, 247–8,